THE

LONGER I'M

PRIME

MINISTER

PAUL WELLS

THE LONGER I'M PRIME MINISTER

STEPHEN HARPER AND CANADA, 2006–

RANDOM
HOUSE
CANADA

PUBLISHED BY RANDOM HOUSE CANADA

COPYRIGHT © 2013 PAUL WELLS

www.randomhouse.ca

Random House Canada and colophon are registered trademarks.

LIBRARY AND ARCHIVES CANADA CATALOGUING IN PUBLICATION

Wells, Paul (Paul Allen)
    The longer I'm Prime Minister : Stephen Harper and Canada, 2006– / Paul Wells.

Includes bibliographical references and index.
Issued also in electronic format.

ISBN 978-0-307-36132-5

    1. Harper, Stephen, 1959–. 2. Canada—Politics and government—2006–.
3. Conservative Party of Canada—History. 4. Prime ministers—Canada—Biography.
I. Title. II. Title: Stephen Harper and Canada, 2006–.

FC641.H37W43 2013   971.07'3   C2013-901523-X

Cover and text design by Andrew Roberts
Cover image: ZUMA Wire Service / Alamy

Printed and bound in the United States of America

10 9 8 7 6 5 4 3 2 1

For Katie and Thomas,
who taught me to do my best.

CONTENTS

"I will tell you what I will do and what I will not do. I will not serve that in which I no longer believe, whether it call itself my home, my fatherland, or my church: and I will try to express myself in some mode of life or art as freely as I can and as wholly as I can, using for my defence the only arms I allow myself to use—silence, exile and cunning."

— James Joyce, *A Portrait of the Artist as a Young Man*

THE BALLAD OF
THE OLD GREY MAYOR

If all you look at is Stephen Harper, you won't see all of the story. If all you look at is "anger" or "control freak" or "Alberta," you're left with a mystery, because how could an angry control freak from Alberta get anywhere all by himself? Look around him. Look around yourself. Look over here, just for instance, at Dave Crapper and Paul "Boomer" Throop, driving north to Mont-Laurier on a Friday night in February 2003.

Dave and Boomer began their trip in Chelsea, an affluent Quebec village fifteen minutes from Ottawa. Chelsea is where you live if you need to be able to get to Ottawa but you want peace, quiet and a fair-sized property at a decent price. A lot of Progressive Conservatives from Ottawa retreated to Chelsea after the electoral debacle of 1993, when the party collapsed into mutually hostile constituent elements—Bloc Québécois, Reform Party and a rump of PC dead-enders—and the party's once-imposing parliamentary majority was reduced to a mating pair, Jean Charest and Elsie Wayne.

That's what Dave and Boomer had done. After the huge majority of 1984, Dave had worked for Jake Epp, a square-shouldered Manitoban who served, unspectacularly, as Brian Mulroney's minister of national health and welfare. After a while Dave left Epp's office to become one of the party's pollsters. Boomer became the wagonmaster for Mulroney's tours, a logistical ace who always managed to keep the leader, the crowds, the cameras and the surly court stenos on their appointed rounds. Cocks of the walk, until it all blew up.

"After 1993, everybody left town," Crapper told me much later. "Elizabeth and I went up to Chelsea and started raising kids."Throop and his family bought the house next door. Crapper ran the Ottawa office of the Decima Research public-opinion firm for a while, then started his own company in the same line of work. He mostly kept his nose out of politics. Elizabeth Roscoe, his vivacious wife, worked for a lobbying firm. Life was quieter, and a quieter life has its charms. But. "After ten years of that, I thought, 'Maybe it's time to get re-engaged.'"

The easiest way to get back into a party's action was to get elected as a delegate for its leadership convention. Joe Clark's second coming as PC leader hadn't gone great. He'd finally given up trying, and the party would have a leadership convention in May 2003. Peter MacKay, a big, nervy son of a veteran Mulroney cabinet minister, was running for the leadership. Crapper figured he could be a MacKay delegate. Throop could vote for him. The two of them climbed into Crapper's car and he steered it toward the future.

Well, to be fair, this was true only to the extent that any car is pointed toward the future. What it felt like was winter-driving hell, and close to pointless to boot. Pontiac, the riding Crapper lived in, covered 27,000 square kilometres, half the area of Nova Scotia. The delegate selection meeting was being held in Mont-Laurier, nearly a three-hour drive from Chelsea. "I'd never been farther north than Maniwaki,"

Crapper said. "I thought it was the end of the earth. Mont-Laurier is even farther away."

When they finally got to the meeting, there were maybe six or eight people in the community hall. One couple had driven from the west end of the riding, four and a half hours. "I think there were as many delegates eligible to go as there were people in the room."

But if you have done politics for long enough in an earlier life, the reflexes come back without too much strain. "A party organizer working for MacKay shows up from the old Mulroney days, who I know. She instantly recognizes me, and I recognize her, and all of a sudden she's got somebody to work with now." When MacKay won the Tory leadership that May in Toronto, Crapper was one of his delegates.

MacKay did win the Conservative leadership, but it got a bit hairy there in the home stretch. MacKay was first on every ballot, but he showed no growth from ballot to ballot and it was frankly pretty nervous-making. So between the third and fourth ballots he signed this weird little pact with David Orchard, a Saskatchewan farmer with a droopy moustache and a stack of conspiracy theories about how free trade was the nation's bane. Paranoid nationalism has always had its subscribers, and Orchard came to the convention with 600-odd delegates who would not go anywhere or do anything except on David Orchard's say-so. MacKay couldn't be sure Orchard wouldn't take the bunch of them to Jim Prentice, the prim and manicured Calgary lawyer who was too close behind MacKay for comfort. So MacKay and Orchard signed a loony handwritten deal promising to re-examine the impact of Canada–U.S. free trade and forswearing any merger talk with the Canadian Alliance, which Orchard judged too right-wing, too pro–free trade, and way too pro-American. Sealing the pact with Orchard was all it took for MacKay to win.

Before too long it turned out he'd signed the Orchard deal with his fingers crossed behind his back, just like Eddie Haskell on *Leave It to Beaver*. It was actually free trade he'd ignore and the Canadian Alliance he'd re-examine. Before the year was out, the Progressive Conservative Party of Canada was dead as a legal entity, Stephen Harper was running to lead a new Conservative Party, and Peter MacKay wasn't doing anything but watching.

The party Dave Crapper had given his adult life to was gone. He was furious, right? "Didn't bother me. By that point the mathematics of it all was really very apparent to everyone. Everybody was looking at Chrétien leaving and Martin coming in, and we knew we'd be obliterated again if we didn't get back together." And after the Elsie Wayne years, "We knew what obliteration looked like. Whatever resistance there was at that point evaporated really fast."

And actually, even though the new party was called Conservative and the old party was called Progressive, for much of his career Crapper had worked for people who not only would have been at home in the new party but had in effect already beaten him to it. The first MP he'd ever worked for, as early as 1979, when Joe Clark became prime minister, was a Mennonite from Kitchener named John Reimer. Reimer supported Stockwell Day in the 2000 Canadian Alliance leadership race, although he found Day a bit too relaxed about abortion. Crapper's next boss, Jake Epp, was another Mennonite from the riding Vic Toews would one day represent. He joined the Alliance and supported Stock Day in 2000 as well.

So to Crapper the new party looked mostly like its old self reconstituted. Though the ingredients were now mixed in different proportions. "In the Progressive Conservative days, the progressives were on the top, typically, and the conservatives were the grouchy guys at the back. And now it was the conservatives who were on top and it was the progressives who were grouchy. Or otherwise."

For the most part, Crapper wasn't grouchy. In any case there was little time for introspection. Harper became the new party's leader. Paul Martin, the new prime minister, flinched only briefly before calling the 2004 election. The Conservatives needed a candidate in Pontiac, Crapper's riding.

"The danger of getting yourself re-engaged in a Quebec riding as a Conservative is that there's often very few of you," he said. "So when it comes to campaign time, the few of you around get leaned on. And it's sort of like, 'If you don't find somebody to run, it's going to be you.' Which is a ridiculous proposition. I'm not gonna be the candidate."

Crapper started looking around for an idea. He didn't have to look far. Perhaps the Old Grey Mayor would run again.

The Reform side of the party had already found the candidate they called the Old Grey Mayor in 2000. "She was the mayor of Chelsea and her name was, and continues to be, Judy Grant. She was sort of a kind of Elsie Wayne without the class. Hang 'em high, shoot first, ask questions later. Just a charming, wonderful diamond-in-the-rough type personality. I love her to bits. Foul-mouthed, ill-tempered and big-hearted. A great old lady."

So the Old Grey Mayor had run for the Alliance in 2000, in a Quebec riding where no Reform candidate had ever run, and she came in third with almost 15 percent of the vote. That's more than triple what Joe Clark's candidate got in Pontiac that year.

There was, in fact, some Conservative history in Pontiac, just as there was in any number of places across Canada where the Conservative gene hadn't had a chance to express itself, whether because the vote was divided among competing parties, or supporters were demoralized, or whatever. In 1984 and 1988 a fellow named Barry Moore from Maniwaki had ridden Mulroney's coattails into Ottawa. Moore lost in 1993 like everyone else, but while representing Pontiac he'd had some luck putting down Conservative roots in what was, historically, a very Liberal riding. If you took away the Ottawa River you'd see very little difference between the western portion of Pontiac riding and the Eastern Ontario ridings that routinely return Conservative MPs from the Reform wing of the party, such as Scott Reid and Pierre Poilievre. In this region, county after county is full of people who want nothing better from the federal government than a good letting alone.

So, as the 2004 election approached at a heady clip, Dave Crapper and Boomer Throop and Barry Moore took Judy Grant out for dinner and said, "Look, Judy, this is something you should give another shot at." And she let them twist her arm, and she did run again, this time as a Conservative.

She gave it a hell of a go. Crapper knocked on the door of a couple of young entrepreneurs living in Chelsea, Sean and Lisa McAdam, former Reform Party staffers who had connections to some of the founding members of the Reform Party out west. "There was a real desire on the part of the Western guys to see the party succeed in Quebec," Crapper told me. Sean and Lisa were enlisted to work the phones. Soon campaign money was coming east, and the Pontiac riding Conservative association went into the writ period with $65,000 in the bank. By the time the votes were counted, in a riding where 73 percent of the residents speak French at home, the Old Grey Mayor, whose French had always been rudimentary, walked off with 22 percent of the vote. Which was the third- or fourth-best score for the Conservative Party in all of Quebec.

Longing on a large scale, Don DeLillo wrote, is what makes history. In 2004 Judy Grant was running for Parliament for the second time, but she had a fresh wave of new company: in that year, fully 222 people ran for the Conservative Party as first-time candidates. In Cardigan riding on Prince Edward Island, Peter McQuaid, Premier Pat Binns's former chief of staff, took a run at Lawrence MacAulay. That was a doomed enterprise if ever there was one, but at least it showed some cheek. In York-Simcoe, Peter Van Loan, a former president of the Progressive Conservative Party of Canada, won easily against a Liberal who was herself running for the first time. In Saskatoon-Humboldt a mining geophysicist and rock-ribbed opponent of abortion named Brad Trost won the closest four-way race in the country, ahead of a New Democrat, a Liberal and the independent Jim Pankiw, a one-time Reformer who had a hard time keeping friends. In the pretty farm country of Durham outside Oshawa, a former executive vice-president of CTV named Bev Oda became Canada's first Japanese-Canadian Member of Parliament.

Everywhere you looked in 2004 you could find new Conservatives who were not, of course, newly conservative but who had decided now was the time to make their move. Leslie Soobrian in York West, the president of the Cricket Council of Ontario. Lida Preyma in Etobicoke Centre, an international-relations specialist from the University of Toronto. Payam Eslami, a financial advisor in Saint-Léonard–Saint-Michel. All of them had a story to tell. Each had friends egging them on, a network of supporters, a volunteer staff. Many fought off challengers at nomination meetings for the right to be a candidate. Each raised money, organized a campaign office, rallied thousands of voters on election day. Together they reflected an enormous cultural potential that had gone largely untapped during years of Liberal rule. In many cases, they were conservatives who hadn't felt at home in Mulroney's PC Party either, for all its electoral success.

Most of the new candidates didn't win in 2004. In his first election as Conservative leader, Stephen Harper won 29.63 percent of the popular vote, eight points less than the combined Alliance and Tory vote in 2000, and 99 seats. Voters weren't sure what to make of the new party and its cool, brittle leader. Harper gave serious thought to quitting politics after 2004, but eventually decided his position at the top wasn't one of the changes the party needed to make.

The changes he did make were the subject of my 2006 book, *Right Side Up: The Fall of Paul Martin and the Rise of Stephen Harper's New Conservatism*. I won't belabour them here. But for the purposes of this prologue, it's worth noting that one thing he did was to appoint Lawrence

Cannon, a former Quebec Liberal minister for communications, as his deputy chief of staff and Quebec lieutenant in 2005.

Cannon wanted to get into Parliament. He was thinking of running in Aylmer, right across the river from Ottawa. Dave Crapper gave him a visit, showed him the 2004 election returns for Pontiac, showed him the riding association's $25,000 bank balance, and pretty soon Lawrence Cannon was happy to declare himself a son of Pontiac. The Conservative breakthrough in Quebec, ten seats including Cannon's, was one of the great stories of 2006.

Along the way Crapper had done some polling for the Conservatives. Harper paired him up with Dimitri Pantazopoulos, the old Alliance pollster. One Tory and one Reformer, for balance. "From a research perspective pollsters from the Reform side of the party think in terms of values," Crapper said. For illustration's sake, he improvised a question of the general sort Harper liked to see in a poll: "'Some people think that it's important for Canada to have an independent foreign policy and getting too close to the Americans is not a good idea. Other people say that we're economically intertwined and geographically tied to the United States and so to cooperate with them is in our best interest. Which of these two views is most like your own?'" The goal of a question like this is not just to find out who's likely to support some measure that's being considered right now. It's to glean a broader sense of respondents' values, not just as a group but as a set of subgroups the party can follow, and learn to appeal to, over time.

"One of the first pieces of our research was that we wrote up a questionnaire. I said to Dimitri, it's a good questionnaire, we're ready to go, we know what we're going to get. He said, 'We're not done yet.' I said, what else do we have to do? He said, 'We have to run it by Stephen.' I'm thinking, who's Stephen?"

The Stephen whom Pantazopoulos was referring to was Harper. Crapper said, "The questionnaire goes in the fax machine to his office and the next day it comes back and there are whole questions struck out, there are new questions scrolled in pen, words substituted throughout. Stephen Harper was reviewing, editing questionnaires!"

Crapper had been on Allan Gregg's staff for almost the entire time Gregg had been Brian Mulroney's pollster. He had done polls for Pat Binns for a decade while Binns was premier of PEI. Neither of them had looked at a poll before it went into the field, let alone proofread draft lists of questions. "I couldn't believe it. Sign of things to come, obviously. I had just never seen that level of hands-on involvement in my trade before by any politician I had ever worked with. Guys are always interested in what you're doing and certainly curious about what you find out, but they're never writing the questions."

Did Harper make the questionnaire better? "Yeah, it was good value actually. I can't remember the specifics but I remember reading and saying, not bad."

———

I have taken the long way around to Stephen Harper's appearance in a book about Stephen Harper because if you stare too closely at him you miss context and tumble into caricature. The driven loner. The obsessive knot of resentments. The floating brain in a jar in the basement of 24 Sussex, surrounded by cats and the souls of crushed Liberals. Of course, he is all of those things. But he could not win elections without widespread support in the land, and he could not win again and yet again without a sense of how to guard and grow that support. Lightning does not strike three times on the same forehead. Which suggests that Harper has what every successful federal leader has needed to survive over a long stretch of time: a superior understanding of Canada.

That is the argument of this book. It sets this volume apart from others, already written and still to come, which portray Harper as little more than a vandal. I offer no blanket endorsement of the twenty-second prime minister. Much of what he has done makes me angry; much more is open to serious debate. But too many people in this country have spent too much time trying to ignore Harper, or to dismiss him, or, with varying degrees of ineptitude, to defeat him. He endures. I figure it is not too soon to try to understand him.

Most of this book is devoted to examining Harper's method and political philosophy. He is a very particular fellow: fiercely intelligent, combative, secretive, intense. Watching him work will take most of our time. But I don't ever want to get too far away from a realization that he comes from deep and broad currents in Canadian political culture. Most people who have voted Conservative at some point since 2004 have done so with real enthusiasm, and most have voted Conservative more than once. As any polarizing figure would, Harper has loud and persistent critics. But he also has admirers, and they number in the millions. Readers who still cannot bring themselves to believe he is the elected prime minister of this country not only misunderstand Stephen Harper. They also misunderstand Canada.

He has been called a dictator so often that it's easy to forget how simple it should have been, at first, to defeat him. He won in 2006 with the weakest minority in Canadian parliamentary history. All the opposition parties were situated to the Conservatives' left. The surprise was not that they sought to ally against him in 2008 but that they waited so long before they moved. And that they moved so poorly. He cannot have expected to last as long as he has.

And yet he needed to last, because most of what he wanted to do could not be done quickly. He wanted to disabuse Canadians, especially immigrants, of the expectation that they would be governed by Liberals. He wanted to implement deep changes in the practice of federalism, foreign policy and budgeting, a degree at a time as if boiling a frog; and to make those changes as hard to reverse as it would be to reconstitute the frog.

On November 7, 1984, Brian Mulroney, a newly elected forty-six-year-old with the largest governing caucus in history at his back, popped some tormentor in the House of Commons on the rhetorical snoot with words that would become famous. "We have only been in power for two months," he said, "but I can tell you this: give us twenty years—and it is coming—and you will not recognize this country."

Twenty years later, Mulroney was long gone from power. Another string of Liberal governments had reversed some of his reforms and integrated others into its familiar and highly recognizable narrative. Stephen Harper was warming up on deck. He shared all of Mulroney's ambition and almost none of his method. He would reorder the cart and the horse by making continued and repeated victory a higher priority than sweeping reform. He would not bother to butter up the parliamentary press gallery. He would assume their antipathy, even provoke it, rather than trust anyone with a notebook to save his hide. He would flatter the most ardent Conservative voters, not the fickle centre, to ensure his base's loyalty over what would necessarily be a long haul.

Harper knew what a jilted supporter looked like. It looked like him. He and millions like him had turned away from Mulroney because they had felt Mulroney turning from them. Harper would not make the same mistake. He would never leave conservatives wondering whether it was worth their time to be Conservative. And every day he stayed in office, he would make the decisions only a prime minister can make, knowing few would be noticed, almost none would be contested, and that together they would add up. "You know," he'd tell his staff, "the longer I'm prime minister . . . the longer I'm prime minister."

The first time he ran for the job he lost. The second time he barely won. Today he dominates Canadian politics as few before him have done. He fought his way into the history books. Here's one now.

ONE
FOOT IN THE DOOR

Sometimes it seems the very time zones conspire against a prime minister from Alberta. Jean Chrétien used to celebrate his election victories with a morning-after news conference in Shawinigan and be back in Ottawa before the capital's bureaucrats got back to their offices from lunch. It was one of a thousand ways the continuity of Liberal power—Central Canadian power—was reaffirmed. Or used to be.

On Tuesday morning, January 24, 2006, the day after the election that changed his life, Stephen Harper boarded his Airbus A320 campaign jet in Calgary at 10:30 a.m. It was already half past noon in Ottawa. The flight from one city to the other would take four hours.

In Ottawa, at the Conservative Party election office in a downtown office building, contracts for the campaign staff had run out at midnight on Monday. Only three staffers bothered to show up for work the next day. They found the phones ringing off the hook as world leaders—Jacques Chirac in Paris, Gerhard Schröder in Berlin—called to congratulate the new guy. Swiftly consulting the post-election plan, the bleary-eyed and hungover campaign workers discovered there was none for today. So they sheepishly asked the long-distance operators of world powers whether they could take the numbers and have the next prime minister of Canada call back whenever he showed up at the office.

So the first day of the new Conservative era was pretty much blown from the start. Nor could Harper assume the new Conservative era had many more days left in it.

The Canadian people had handed him a mandate fit for a pessimist. Out of the 308 seats in the House of Commons, the Conservative Party of Canada had won 124, to 103 for Paul Martin's Liberals, 51 for the Bloc Québécois and 29 for Jack Layton's NDP. That tally left Harper 31 seats shy of a majority. It was the smallest minority in the history of Canadian federal politics, with the smallest percentage of total seats and the largest number of seats short of a majority. Even Joe Clark had done better in 1979, winning 12 more seats than Harper in a Commons that held 26 fewer MPs. Fat lot of good that wider margin of victory had done Joe, because he lost everything nine months later.

So the Chrétien–Martin years were over, but unless a lot of things changed quickly the Liberals would be back.

In an early January vote conducted at the back of the campaign plane, the indefatigable wisenheimers of the parliamentary press gallery had dubbed Harper's A320 "Mr. Happy's Flying Circus." The name was suggested by Sun columnist Greg Weston, and it fulfilled the traditional mandate of such campaign-plane christening ceremonies, which was heavy-handed irony. Harper's a sourpuss, so let's make fun of that. The name was especially fitting on the flight to Ottawa, because the mood on the campaign plane of the man who would become the first Conservative prime minister in thirteen years was not jubilant.

"We'd been through this once before," one person who was on that A320 said later, "by which I mean a sense of slight disappointment as the election returns came in." Built in 2003 from the remains of the

Progressive Conservatives and the Canadian Alliance, the Conservative Party still had a new-car smell to it, but this was already its second federal election campaign. In 2004 Harper had managed to pull ahead of the Martin Liberals in voter intention in the last half of the campaign. Then the Liberals managed to shut Harper down with a potent barrage of negative ads in Ontario in the last weekend. But even as late as voting day, nobody was really sure how effective those ads had been. Harper's team had spent much of election day '04 trying to figure out what they'd do if they won enough seats to form a government. Harper was late delivering his concession speech because his staff had taken most of the day to work on a victory speech. This time he got to deliver his victory speech, but little about the results gave him comfort.

"We thought the Liberals would have a leadership campaign on a fairly short timeline," one of his senior advisors said later. "There was no fucking way the Liberals would let their leadership campaign go on much beyond the first week of September. Surely they wouldn't be that stupid. And then we'd be possibly back into an election campaign the following spring, if not by Christmas.

"What we were absolutely determined not to do was to make the Joe Clark mistake of sitting around governing like we had a majority, and saying that the other guys were going to let us govern forever. And therefore end up being humiliated the way Clark was humiliated. We thought we had a very, very short time before we would be back in the electoral soup."

The assumption here was that simple arithmetic would govern Harper's fate. He could divide the opposition parties among themselves, push them back on their heels, but he would always be outnumbered. On any day the other parties wanted him defeated they would take him down. His only real hope was to set a leader-like tone and get moving on fulfilling some promises so he'd have something to run on when the next battle came.

Since 2002, Harper had run for the Canadian Alliance leadership and in a by-election for his Calgary Southwest seat. Then he had run for the leadership of the united Conservative Party, then led it in national elections in 2004 and 2006. Five campaigns in four years. He was tired of running and believed he'd have to run again soon.

Harper's jet had plenty of newspapers on board, but on the flight back to Ottawa it was copies of the *Calgary Herald* that had the most currency. The *Herald* went to press later than the Toronto newspapers, so it had the most up-to-date election results. Fortunately, Ray Novak had grabbed a copy on his way to the airport. Novak was Harper's executive assistant—slim, soft-spoken, meticulous, so dedicated to looking after Harper's needs that he had eventually moved into an apartment over the garage at Stornoway, the Official Opposition leader's residence, so he could trot across the driveway and do whatever Harper needed doing each day before breakfast.

At the front of the plane, Harper and his chief of staff, Ian Brodie, shared the precious copy of the *Herald*. Brodie, thirty-eight, was a political scientist who had studied at the University of Calgary and taught at the University of Western Ontario. He had done odd jobs for Harper for a few years but had only been in charge of the leader's office since the previous summer. Brodie would hire most of the key players in a Harper Prime Minister's Office and in the offices of most ministers. He scanned the *Herald* columns looking for the names of Conservative MPs who might form a cabinet.

Harper was more interested for now in seeing whom the Liberals had managed to elect. He would stand up most days in Question Period and face opposition attacks. He wanted to know who would be doing the attacking.

Numbers alone didn't tell the whole story of Liberal discomfiture. Much of Martin's cabinet had gone down to defeat, and not just recent promotions of uncertain value such as Tony Valeri and Tony Ianno. Anne

McLellan, Martin's deputy prime minister, had finally lost her lonely Edmonton redoubt. Pierre Pettigrew and Liza Frulla had lost in Montreal. Reg Alcock in Winnipeg. "Their outlook is quite grim," Harper said. He wasn't gloating. This was no time to gloat. It was just data.

The Conservatives' own weaknesses were obvious. Ten seats in Quebec were more than the Conservatives had hoped for, more than they expected, but it was still only ten seats, and not one of them anywhere close to Montreal. The Conservatives were shut out of Toronto too, although if the truth be told, their caucus was full of MPs who knew Toronto at least as well as they knew their own ridings—former Ontario provincial ministers Jim Flaherty and Tony Clement, guys like Mike Chong, who had a long history as a student and businessman in Toronto. In Vancouver, too, the Conservatives were denied a foothold.

Sometimes two weaknesses add up to a surprise. "By the time we got off that plane," one of the passengers said, "it had been noted by several people that the one guy who would be truly wasted in opposition was Emerson." For years the very mention of David Emerson's name had made just about every political organizer in British Columbia drool. Whatever your criteria for success in Canada, Emerson had all the boxes ticked off. PhD economist from Queen's. Deputy minister in Finance for the B.C. government. Bank president. Lumber baron. Vicechairman of the Canadian Council of Chief Executives. Eyebrows like shelves of granite. No wonder Paul Martin had handed Emerson a safe Vancouver seat without the inconvenience of a nomination battle in 2004. No wonder he'd made Emerson his minister of industry.

Alone among Liberals, Emerson's assets looked equally good from Harper's side of the political fence. The hole he could plug in a Harper government was not just geographic but demographic. The Harper Conservatives were a populist party. Their MPs hadn't spent a lot of time in boardrooms. For the most part this was an asset. Their opponents were used to railing against "fat-cat Tories." Misunderstanding the

Harper Conservatives led the Liberals and NDP to guess wrong about how they'd react to a given situation.

But fat cats vote too, and it's handy to have a couple of them under your tent. "Once you merged the old PC and the old Reform-Alliance party in B.C., you didn't have a lot of ties to the B.C. business community," a former senior Harper advisor told me. "Jay Hill's a good guy, James Moore's a good guy, Chuck Strahl's a good guy. There's lots of good people. Stock." Stockwell Day. "But nobody with that connection to the B.C. business community."

It would not be possible to recruit Emerson without embarrassment. Campaigning in Vancouver Kingsway, Emerson had said nasty things about the Conservatives. He had, for instance, warned voters that Harper wanted a Canada where "the strong survive, the weak die." But that was just Emerson being a good Liberal soldier. Now Harper had won, Emerson was strong; and surely he didn't want to die. A few days after the election, at the Vancouver airport, Emerson ran into John Reynolds, the big, silver-haired former Canadian Alliance MP who had lent his name to the Conservative campaign as national co-chairman. Small talk turned into something else and soon Reynolds was on the phone to Ottawa. This guy isn't happy being stuck in opposition, Reynolds said. We should make something happen for him.

The negotiations went quickly. In fact they could barely be called negotiations. Would you like to keep coming to cabinet meetings, David? Why, yes I would. All righty then. It helped that Emerson had no clue about the outrage his precipitous floor-crossing would provoke among residents of Vancouver Kingsway who had thought they were voting for a Liberal. Blissfully unaware that actions have consequences, Emerson became Harper's minister of international trade.

The other surprise, when the new cabinet showed up at Rideau Hall to be sworn in on February 6, was the arrival of Michael Fortier. Fortier was a Montreal corporate lawyer, a glittering specimen with French cuffs on every shirt and a perfect little stubble beard like a meticulously tended Japanese garden. He was the other national co-chair, with Reynolds, of the Harper campaign. The title didn't mean much. The real campaign work was done by less well-known people. But Fortier's name had helped Harper's campaign look serious, and now he was rewarded with a seat in the Senate and a post as minister of public works and government services.

If Emerson's appointment was the product of hasty improvisation, Fortier's was the fruit of longer planning. Right up to the middle of the campaign, Harper had shown little strength in Quebec. The weakness preoccupied him: for a long time it seemed entirely possible he'd win enough seats to form a government without getting anybody elected in Quebec, or anybody good at least. So he and his staff developed a set of public gestures that any Canadian prime minister could make, no matter how weak his Quebec caucus, to show good faith. He could begin every public statement, wherever he made it, in French. He could visit the premier of Quebec in Quebec City instead of making the guy schlump it to Ottawa. (Incredibly, no prime minister in decades had made this simple concession.) And he could use his power to name cabinet ministers who weren't MPs, perhaps combining it with his power to appoint any adult property holder to the Senate.

In the end, Harper did pretty well in Quebec. Four of the ten who got elected in the province landed in cabinet. But he implemented most of his Quebec charm offensive anyway, including the part about putting Fortier into the Senate and his cabinet.

So, by the cold February day his government was sworn in, Harper had plugged two of the most gaping holes his team had discovered in their fortifications, as they pored over the election returns in the *Herald*, while soaring over the prairies in Mr. Happy's Flying Circus. He now had ministers from two of Canada's three biggest cities. True, a large number of the voters who had elected the minister from Vancouver would decide, upon learning of his defection, that they would like to see his head on a pike. And the guy from Montreal would never really get the hang of life in Parliament. What mattered was that Harper had them. His first move was to cement his victory by expanding his base and by reaching out, inelegantly, to segments of the Canadian electorate that had rejected him.

Stephen Harper would be called all kinds of names in the seven years that followed—inflexible, doctrinaire, dogmatic—and at times he would work hard to earn each of those names. But two things he did almost immediately on achieving power were to co-opt a once-powerful opponent who had worked hard to stop his rise and, after arguing—through two election campaigns—against an appointed Senate, to appoint a senator. You could call both moves a lot of names, but "inflexible" and "dogmatic" would not be among them.

The thing he needed to do above all others, he told himself during that long flight from Calgary to Ottawa, was survive. It was the prerequisite for everything else. He had plenty of examples of prime ministers who had not lasted long: Joe Clark, Paul Martin, Kim Campbell. Everybody liked them. Say Joe Clark's name at Hy's, the Ottawa steakhouse where partisan lines blur nightly in the universal solvent of red wine, and Liberals' eyes would mist up. Such a lovely guy. Every Liberal loves a Conservative loser.

As for the prime ministers who had lasted longer, they were imperfect models because they had started with advantages the electoral fates had denied Harper. Trudeau, Mulroney and Chrétien had ridden into power on mandates Harper could barely imagine. They could afford to be nice guys—although, come to think of it, they hadn't bothered. The prime ministers of Harper's adult life had started strong and petered out, or started weak and collapsed. He must find his own way.

All three of the parties Harper would face across the floor of the House of Commons were situated to his left on a left-right spectrum of political ideas. More Canadians had voted for those parties, taken together, than for his Conservatives. If you made those 308 MPs stand in a row according to their ideology from left to right, from Libby Davies all the way to Rob Anders, the 155th MP in line would be a Liberal. If it ever reached its equilibrium state, this Parliament would have a Liberal prime minister. So Harper would never let it reach equilibrium. He would shock the system regularly, to keep his opponents off balance, divided or both. He would hoard information for himself and dole it out, to the people and to Parliament, through an eyedropper. He would never let mere principle deny him any advantage his opponents had used, or might use if the tables were turned, to hold on to power. He would be nice when he could, reach out when reaching out would help, but when the chips were down he would not hesitate to demonstrate there could be no bigger son of a bitch in Canadian politics than Stephen Joseph Harper.

He would do all these things because he had a mission. His goal was to ensure that Conservatives governed as frequently and as durably in the twenty-first century as Liberals had in the twentieth. He had seen Conservative leaders implement radical change, only to be tossed out for many years by counter-reformationists who undid everything the Conservatives had done. Chrétien after Mulroney. Dalton McGuinty after Mike Harris. He would not be content with that. He wanted to change the terms of the Canadian debate, to re-legitimize the Right's ideas and de-legitimize the Left's. And he wanted to do so in such a durable manner that when he left politics he would hand more than rubble to his successor.

But first things first. He had to survive the year. To do that he had to be seen to fulfill his election promises, and to do that he had to avoid surprises. He wouldn't fulfil every promise or avoid every surprise. But he would do enough of both to hang on.

The centrepiece of the Conservative campaign platform had been the "Five Priorities," five easy-to-understand promises that were supposed to be the first things a new Conservative government would seek to deliver. They served several purposes. First, they helped depict Harper as a more purposeful, organized leader than the frazzled Paul Martin, who had inherited a Liberal corruption scandal he didn't know how to handle, and who seemed to have devoted more thought to taking Jean Chrétien's job than to what he wanted to do with it. Second, they were handy for countering the constant barrage of Liberal accusations that Harper had a hidden agenda of radical change. The Five Priorities are worth quoting in full as they appeared on the PM's website soon after the election:

> We are committed to:
> - Cleaning up government by enacting and enforcing the Federal Accountability Act;
> - Lower taxes for working Canadians; starting by reducing the GST;
> - Protecting Canadian families and communities by strengthening the justice system;
> - Supporting parents' child care choices through direct assistance and by creating more daycare spaces; and
> - Delivering the health care Canadians need, when they need it, by addressing the fiscal imbalance and establishing a patient wait times guarantee with the provinces.

Harper told reporters midway through the campaign, "The first four of the five things I've talked about are things that, quite frankly, we can do fairly quickly." And indeed, he would be able to demonstrate progress on the first four priorities by year's end. (He has still not produced anything resembling a wait-time guarantee.) But the priorities appealed to Harper not only because they were doable, but because they would change things. "They will have longer-term impacts," he told those reporters at the beginning of January. "The country will be different because of them."

That was the game. Lock in change that could not be ratcheted back even if he was defeated. Economists had mocked the GST reduction as the worst possible tax cut because it did less than income-tax cuts to stimulate productivity. But that was not the point. The point was to get money out of Ottawa, to reduce surpluses and restrict the ability of the government—any government—to introduce elaborate new social programs. And it had to be hard to reverse without substantial political cost. Same for the $100 cheque per month per child under six. A government handing out those cheques couldn't run daycares too, and a government that cancelled those cheques would have hell on its hands.

The Five Priorities had been the highlight of a platform document that added similarly terse commitments across most areas of government activity. Lots of bullets. The Conservatives arrived in Ottawa to discover their platform was a hit with senior bureaucrats. Not because the permanent government agreed with the new government's plans, but because it found them so easy to decode. From there it was short work to transform the platform into a stack of memos explaining how such things would be done, if Harper still wanted to do them.

Mostly he did. Harper had brought in Derek Burney, a former chief of staff to Brian Mulroney, to run the transition. The two men didn't know each other well. Turning to Burney constituted a frank admission on Harper's part that neither he nor most of his cabinet and staff knew government well. Burney's orders were to produce a lean, agile government operation. No time to waste.

Ministers traditionally receive "mandate letters," prepared by the PMO with help from the bureaucracy, telling them what the boss expects them to do. Mandate letters usually cover a year of plans or more. Harper's covered only six months.

"He actually went over them line by line with me, and in a very meticulous fashion," Burney said. If one of the mandate letters contradicted language in the Conservative election platform, Harper would have Burney fix the letter. "It was very different from what I was used to. Mulroney would have said, 'Well, what do these letters say, Derek?' And you'd explain them for five seconds and he'd sign them, or not."

Bruce Carson was a veteran Progressive Conservative from the Clark and Mulroney years who'd been brought into the Harper shop to provide institutional memory for a team that didn't have much. "It was a great way to move a very inexperienced group of people along," he said of the mandate letters. There was a note of urgency here as in so much of what Harper was doing, Carson observed. "The prime minister was very concerned that we were going to be defeated in months."

Harper brought the same message to his first cabinet meeting: one screw-up could wreck this government before it even got started. "I am the kingpin," he told his ministers, according to someone who was in the room. "So whatever you do around me, you have to know that I am sacrosanct."

While Harper had it in him to be charming, that was always strictly optional. Here he had to make it perfectly clear who would lose if any minister's actions made the government look bad. None of the ministers had played that role in a federal government before, except Rob Nicholson, the government House leader, who'd spent the summer of 1993 as Kim Campbell's minister of science. Harper's cabinet members were unbelievably green. And now the boss was telling them that if there was trouble he would cut them loose. As the years in power went on, Harper's threat would look mostly hollow. Firing a minister brings its own kind of trouble and it would take a lot for Harper to cross that line. But the greenhorns didn't know that yet, and they took the boss's warning to heart.

In Ottawa it used to be that when a cabinet minister was too green to know his boss was bluffing, a seasoned staffer could take the minister aside and whisper some wisdom into the ministerial ear. Unfortunately, in the Harper government, that wouldn't be possible for a while. "We were just massively fucking short on staff," one of Harper's senior staffers says. This was true to some extent in the PMO, and far more so in the dozens of ministers' offices around the Hill.

There were at least four reasons for this. First, the supply of seasoned Conservative Hill staffers was low. In a parliamentary system, long sentences in opposition are supposed to help a party prepare for government. But during the thirteen years after the electoral debacle of 1993 that system pretty much broke. There weren't enough of the dwindling corporal's guard who had stuck out the intervening years with a succession of Progressive Conservative leaders—Jean Charest, Clark, Peter MacKay—to run much of anything. Meanwhile few Reform and Alliance staffers had viewed their time in opposition as training for government because until very shortly before Harper nearly won the 2004 election, nobody thought a Reform or Alliance leader could do it.

Second, the inner circle aboard Mr. Happy's Flying Circus were hardly the only people in Canada to notice how weak Harper's parliamentary hand was. Government work meant leaving a job somewhere else, uprooting oneself and perhaps one's family for a move to Ottawa, and total immersion in a punishing workload, all for maybe eight months of power, an unwinnable confidence vote and a quick ticket back to ignominy. Conservative provincial governments in Alberta, Nova Scotia and Newfoundland, and Gordon Campbell's decidedly bluish B.C. Liberals, offered more stability.

Third, Harper was not in the business of making it easier for young professionals to give government work a quick try. The first of the Five Priorities he planned to tick off was an Accountability Act designed to reduce the influence of money on federal politics. In an election that followed months of lurid evidence before Justice John Gomery's inquiry into corruption among Liberal Party bagmen in Quebec, the promise of a cleaner politics had helped propel Harper to power.

A centrepiece of the Accountability Act was a five-year ban on lobbying the federal government for former ministers and their staff. So a potential eight-month tour of duty in a Hill office would get a former staffer banned from using the knowledge and connections he'd acquired to help guide clients through the Ottawa jungle—all the way until 2011. Later, Harper government sources would insist that passing the accountability legislation hadn't made the difference for many potential staffers. The likelihood that the entire government would fall at any moment was a bigger deterrent, they said. Still, among the few Conservative-linked professionals who did already have marketable skills and connections when Harper was elected, a fair number preferred to stay outside the government and trade on those assets rather than go inside and trigger the ban.

The fourth thing that limited the government's ability to hire staffers was that not all Conservatives were welcome.

I've been using the name of Harper's party, the Conservative Party of Canada, more or less interchangeably with the short name for the party that governed Canada at intervals from 1867 to 1993, the Progressive Conservatives. But of course in many ways they're not the same party. The Progressive Conservative Party of Canada was legally wound down at the end of 2003, along with the Canadian Alliance, to allow the creation of the new Conservative Party of Canada. And the culture of the new party is different from the old versions too. Sometimes the differences are too slight to deserve mention. On most days, former Progressive Conservatives work alongside former Reformers without even noticing that there used to be a distinction. But if that is so, it is precisely because Conservatives, tired of losing, worked to ensure that the Conservative Party would function as a heterogeneous but cohesive body. Sometimes that work has entailed a little judicious pruning. The spring of 2006 was one such time.

At some point Ian Brodie, Harper's chief of staff, noticed that a disproportionate number of the people applying for staff jobs had a history with the Progressive Conservatives. This made sense: the PCs had been a party of government; Reform was an insurgency. PCs were more likely to have spent time in NGOs, think tanks, university administrations and industry associations. They would fit right in at government offices.

Brodie decided too many of them were fitting in. He vetoed one appointment immediately. Graham Fox, the son of Mulroney's communications director, Bill Fox, had served before he was thirty as Joe Clark's chief of staff, during the late stages of Clark's doomed political comeback. Effortlessly bilingual, he spoke frequently on behalf of the Conservatives on radio and TV in both languages. Peter MacKay wanted Fox to be his chief of staff. Brodie kiboshed the appointment. And, sources say, he then put a young assistant with impeccable Reform credentials, Jenni Byrne, in charge of making sure the Reform and Alliance wings of the party were well represented in ministers' offices.

This was no total ban on Progressive Conservatives. David McLaughlin, who had served as Mulroney's final chief of staff and written a book about Kim Campbell's lousy campaign, became Jim Flaherty's chief at Finance. Blair Dickerson, another Mulroney-era survivor, would run Gary Lunn's office at Natural Resources. But Byrne stopped other Red Tory appointments and worked her Reform and Alliance connections to find people who could take their places. Byrne's loyalty to Brodie and Harper, her willingness to work hard, and the pleasure she took in delivering bad news and enforcing tough calls got noticed. If the cause of Canadian conservatism meant a few Red Tories had to get whacked, Jenni Byrne was okay with that. Her star began to rise in the PMO.

As the young government made its first steps, its approach could be summed up in a few words: clarity, purpose, control. These people were convinced they had to walk a fine line. They were haunted by the thought of slipping up. Talking without thinking had cost the Canadian Alliance years of turmoil when Stockwell Day had led it. Last-minute eruptions of inanity and extremism from Harper's candidates cost him the 2004 election. His own smart mouth had gotten him in so much trouble with several intemperate comments he'd made after returning to politics in 2002 that he'd determined to duct-tape his piehole shut unless he knew precisely what was going to come out of it. At a news conference in the first week of March in the foyer of the House of Commons, almost every answer from the new PM carried a red stamp that declared CLEARED BY CENSORS. "Let me just say the following things . . ." he'd say, and "Je peux dire seulement . . ." and "I can simply tell you . . ." and "Let me just say." He left the impression that a lot was going on but that the scribes would hear only selected bits of it.

Behind the scenes Harper was building an elaborate system to ensure that, while there was indeed a lot going on, the scribes would never see most of it. On Friday, April 28, 2006, the commissioner of information, John Reid, released a special report to Parliament describing part of the system in detail.

Reid was, or had spent much of his life as, a Liberal. He was elected as an MP in 1965 and defeated in 1984, then pursued assorted worthy causes until Jean Chrétien appointed him to the information commissioner's job in 1998. He was in the last year of his seven-year term when Harper took over. Reid had perhaps disappointed, and in the end had done his best to torment, Chrétien. He didn't give a damn which party was in power: if a government limited Canadians' right to know how they are governed it would hear from John Reid. He called Chrétien's 2002 "reform" of the access-to-information law "a bureaucrat's dream" because it had so many loopholes any official could easily cheat its stated goal of greater public access to information.

When it became clear that Harper would win the 2006 election, Reid wrote, he had permitted himself to hope that Harper would bring in a new era of government. Hadn't Harper mocked Paul Martin for bringing in a discussion paper on access to information instead of a full-fledged bill? Hadn't he warned Canadians that Martin wanted to "make the government more secretive than it already is"?

And yet, barely three months after the election that brought Harper to power, "the new government has done exactly the things for which its predecessor had been ridiculed," Reid wrote. Instead of reform, Harper launched a discussion paper. "All of the positions the government now takes in the discussion paper are contrary to the positions the Conservative Party took, and its leader espoused, during the election campaign." But, warned Reid, Harper wasn't just stalling, using the discussion paper to delay reform. He was actively rolling back the protections of the existing access act. The instrument he was using to accomplish this feat was the new Accountability Act.

What a jolly contradiction in terms. The Accountability Act was supposed to increase accountability by limiting the influence of money on politics. It would ban corporate and union donations to political parties and put a tight lid on private donations. It would put that five-year lobbying cap on former members of the government.

What did this have to do with access to information? The new bill sought to do two apparently contradictory things. It would extend the access act's purview to a bunch of Crown corporations that had been shielded from its provisions until now. These included the Canadian Broadcasting Corporation and the assorted officers of Parliament, including the information commissioner, the commissioner of official languages, and so on. On the face of it, this change looked like an extension of the access law's range, and therefore a good thing. The part about the CBC would delight conservatives, who were sure the public broad-caster was a grotesque money pit and could now seek to prove it, one access request at a time.

But while seeming to extend the obligation to release information in general, the Accountability Act with the other hand introduced multiple new classes of exemptions and exceptions to the laws of access, dra-matically reducing the government's obligation to release information in specific cases.

"What the government now proposes—if accepted—will reduce the amount of information available to the public, weaken the oversight role of the Information Commissioner and increase government's ability to cover-up wrongdoing, shield itself from embarrassment and control the flow of information to Canadians," Reid wrote in his report. "No previ-ous government, since the Access to Information Act came into force in 1983, has put forward a more retrograde and dangerous set of proposals to change the Access to Information Act."

Reid released his report on a Friday. The following Monday, Bill Graham, the patrician, lantern-jawed MP for the riding of Toronto Centre in the very heart of Toronto and the interim leader of the Liberal opposition during the nearly year-long interim the Liberals had already inexplicably chosen for the selection of their next leader, popped to his feet in the Commons to ask how Harper could dare do such a thing. "Will the Prime Minister now admit that his proposals are designed to accomplish the opposite of what he has promised?" Graham demanded.

Exercising the eternal prerogative of prime ministers everywhere, Harper rose to give a half-answer followed by a half-truth. "Mr. Speaker, for the first time in Canadian history, Crown corporations, independent officers of Parliament and foundations will be under Access to Information when the House passes the Federal Accountability Act," he said. And this was true, as far as it went.

"The information commissioner has expressed some reservations. He can take those to committee. One of his reservations is that when we open CBC to Access to Information the government has protected journalistic sources. We believe those sources should be anonymous. If the Liberal Party does not think so, the Leader of the Opposition can say so."

Graham got up and sputtered a bit. He tried his question two more times. Harper responded, twice more, with the reference to protecting journalistic sources.

Where had that reference come from? Everything Graham was quoting about retrograde and dangerous proposals was accurate. He conveyed the breadth and urgency of Reid's concern. To defend themselves, Harper and the PMO staff had chosen a paragraph well down in Reid's report. "With respect to the CBC," Reid wrote, quoting the new bill, "information is excluded 'that relates to its journalistic, creative or programming activities, other than information that relates to its general administration.'" So the CBC wouldn't have to cough up any information that it asserted would relate to its journalistic activities or its creative activities or its programming activities, and the sole authority for determining the criteria would be the CBC itself. Long experience with the access law shows that the strongest government instinct, when responding to an access request, is to find a rock to hide the information under. This was a huge new rock.

And that's just the CBC. There were nine other new exemptions and exclusions in the Accountability Act, part or all of which applied to every department of government.

Reid wrote that the exclusion for the CBC violated the principle that "exceptions to the right of access should (1) be discretionary, (2) require a demonstration that a defined injury, harm or prejudice would probably result from disclosure, and (3) be subject to a public interest override." And whose principle was that? Reid's, of course—but he noted that it had been "endorsed in the Conservative election platform" and "reflects the will of Parliament" as expressed in the original Access to Information Act.

But meanwhile we were being led further and further off the scent. The question from Graham, and indeed the question that arises when a government proposes sweeping changes to citizens' right to scrutinize its actions, was whether the changes, taken as a whole, were wise and justified. The peculiar genius of Question Period as it has evolved in Ottawa is that Harper had thirty-five seconds, computer-timed and monitored by a scowling fellow in black robes sitting at the table in the middle of the Commons, to parry Graham's question. So he sent the Liberal off on a goose chase about the CBC. Graham had thirty-five seconds to fire back. The whole charade was over before anyone watching could boil an egg. And that would be that.

Let us jump ahead, at the risk of ruining some suspense. The changes Reid warned against were passed. Three years after Reid issued his report, his successor, Robert Marleau, would say, "There's less information being released by government than ever before." Two years after that—this takes us to January 2011—two British academics, Robert Hazell and Ben Worthy, published a paper in the journal *Government Information Quarterly* analyzing the access-to-information regimes in five parliamentary democracies: Australia, New Zealand, Ireland, the United Kingdom and Canada. They found New Zealand had the strongest legal and institutional commitment to access to information. Canada came last.

There is a question of principle here. The point of laws mandating public access to government information is to protect the citizen against state fiat. If the government knows more about me than I can know about the government, my safety and freedom are subject to the whims of people who hold all the cards. This is obviously a libertarian argument, and more generally it can simply be called a conservative argument.

But it is not a Conservative argument—see what I did there with the "C"?—in the sense that a Conservative prime minister who surrendered any scrap of control was increasing this minority government's likelihood of reaching its Liberal equilibrium state. Information pried out from under the rocks of state by curious citizens and their nettlesome proxies in the press gallery is almost never good news to the incumbent government. Stephen Harper's enthusiasm for information faded as soon as he became the incumbent.

"If you think of Harper as a conservative ideologue," one of his MPs said over coffee one morning, "you run into no end of confusion and contradiction. But if you think of him as a Conservative partisan, most of what he does makes sense. He protects the team."

The instinct to protect the team was behind every aspect of Harper's constant effort to control the flow of information from election day 2006 forward. This was clear not just in the battle over Access to Information legislation but also in the government's everyday activity. Unelected officials in the bureaucracy soon faced immediate and unprecedented restrictions on their ability to speak freely in public or with journalists. Harper's press office became a centre, not for disseminating information, but for containing it.

"We had, over the course of several years, worked at several iterations of planning documents that eventually became the Message Event Proposal template," a former senior Harper advisor said. "And it went along with a staff process for planning an event a few days in advance and understanding what the hell we were all doing."

That paragraph is probably cryptic. It is worth unpacking. The idea of filling out a planning document for every single public event by any Conservative politician, or any public servant who happens to be working with Conservative politicians, crystallized a notion that is common enough in politics everywhere: if a politician does something in public, it must be to communicate a specific idea.

Aristotle taught that character is defined by habitual action. There is no such thing as a good man who happens to do unjust things, Aristotle believed, because what a man does defines him. Indeed, Aristotle's prescription for virtue was simply to keep doing the sort of thing a virtuous man does. Modern specialists in political communication are an Aristotelian species. If a politician cuts a ribbon at a widget factory, it must be because he wants the world to know he is a supporter of widgets and the good people who make them. If he goes to a spaghetti dinner, it is because he is the kind of guy who gets along with people who eat spaghetti. Politicians are welcome to do strange things at home—read a book for pleasure, think for themselves—as long as they do it in private and nobody finds out. A politician who does random things in public, in front of cameras and microphones, is not merely departing from the disciplined advancement of a political idea, he is undermining it.

The Harper Conservatives in 2004 had been lousy at designing events to advance their ideas, and all too good at saying things in front of cameras and microphones that produced headlines Harper didn't want to see. Harper would go to St. John's and hold a news conference in front of a bay window at the Hotel Newfoundland, with the astonishing St. John's Harbour behind him, and whatever Harper was saying, it wouldn't have a goddamned thing to do with the harbour, St. John's or Newfoundland. And then he'd get to his hotel room, turn on his TV and discover a long-time MP like Randy White talking about how important it was to ignore the Charter of Rights and Freedoms. This was a problem. He needed to become better at aligning his presence and surroundings with his message. And he needed to ensure that the evening news would less frequently feature people on his team saying the strangest things.

In 2005 the process of getting Conservatives to sing from a song sheet was accelerated by the arrival in Harper's office of Patrick Muttart, a handsome and brilliant young government-relations consultant. Muttart had been a Reform supporter since his high-school days, but before he joined Harper's office he had been working for Navigator, a Toronto lobbying and consulting firm. Muttart had used written forms to plan events with private-sector clients as a matter of routine, because business clients so rarely face reporters that they are not crazy enough to believe they can just wing it. Within a few months in 2005, Muttart quickly had Harper, all of his shadow-cabinet critics, and all of the party's MPs filling out these little forms before they did any public event a reporter might attend. It was a monumental pain in the backside for all concerned, but it front-loaded the hassle: by deciding in advance what they would say, wear, carry, stand in front of, and otherwise do at next Tuesday's event, they substantially reduced the likelihood of waking up Wednesday in a world of hurt. And when they won the 2006 elections, the Conservatives took the same planning methods into power.

It would be years before two Canadian Press reporters, Mike Blanchfield and Jim Bronskill, would get their hands on a bunch of old Message Event Proposals from the early days of the Harper government and publish their details. "An MEP template typically includes the following subtitles," Blanchfield and Bronskill wrote. "Event, Event type, Desired headline, Key messages, Media lines, Strategic objectives, Desired soundbite, Ideal speaking backdrop, Ideal event photograph, Tone, Attire, Rollout materials, Background, and Strategic considerations."

Of course, in power, event planning extends quite far beyond a party's elected caucus and frequently involves large numbers of unelected bureaucrats. The former senior Harper advisor said the Message Event Proposals were initially quite popular with civil servants. "First of all, there was paper, which bureaucrats love. There are forms; a huge bureaucracy runs on forms." Secondly, there was a measure of predictability. It is always handy to remember that Harper arrived after seventeen months of often-chaotic Paul Martin Liberal government. Meetings would run hours over schedule. Decisions would be reversed. Officials were constantly asked to implement plans Martin or his staff would abandon before the work was finished. "I think there was widespread concern across the permanent public service that the communications side of government had become awfully loose and awfully unpredictable."

Over time, however, it became clear that the Harperites intended their message control to be pervasive. At one point there was a minor fire at the National Research Council on Sussex Drive. Employees milling outside were astonished to see a car full of departmental communications advisors arrive before fire trucks did, to guard against the threat of unauthorized media interviews.

If there was one place where the Harper–Muttart Message Event Proposal mentality took a long, long time to sink in, however, it wasn't at the NRC, but across the street at the glowering ziggurat where the Department of Foreign Affairs housed its superbly educated and monumentally self-regarding workforce. Foreign Affairs had long considered itself the cream of the public service. The diplomatic corps. Heirs to the mantle of Lester B. Pearson, whose very name adorned the building where they worked when they weren't swanning around the globe. It was the people in the Pearson Building and their peripatetic colleagues in dozens of foreign capitals who took the longest to realize that this Message Event Proposal business applied to them, too.

Harper and his staff were relentless. "I don't think it's unreasonable, I never thought it was unreasonable—I still don't think it's unreasonable—for someone who has a 'Canada' label on their business card, in speaking about whatever they're going to get asked about, to spend at least as much time thinking about what they're going to say and how they're going to say it as they spend actually saying it," one of them said. "And so if people say, 'Well, what are you going to say?' and they say, 'Well, we're just going to see how it goes'—No. No, no, no, no. We didn't run the campaign that way, we didn't run ourselves in opposition that way, and we're not going to run the government that way. The idea that you, somebody I've never met before, [are] going to go out and 'see how it goes,' answer any question with whatever comes into your head—No. We're going to go through a process here. If somebody has 'Government of Canada' on their business card, they'd better speak for the government of Canada, and 'government of Canada' means government of Canada. Not, you know, somebody who says whatever the fuck comes into their head. You can't do that. For that matter, a minister can't. The PM didn't do that."

This was uncontroversial, for the most part, among officials at the Finance building on O'Connor Street. It was pretty much business as usual in the old Justice Building on Wellington, where people were well used to the notion that you had to watch what you said in public. But the toffs at Fort Pearson and the emissaries in the dip corps had a different reaction. "They were like, 'We can't do that.' Why? 'We work twenty-four hours a day, in three hundred locations around the world.'"

Now the former Harper advisor began to imitate for me both sides of a conversation that took place dozens of times with occasional variations, at different levels, between Foreign Affairs officials and political staff at the PMO and in ministers' offices in the first couple of years of the Harper government. Obviously any version of such a conversation from the Harper team's side of things will caricature the other, but it's worth letting our Harperite continue the theatre for a minute.

"It's going to be off the record," the toff [says the Harperite] would say. "So it won't be Government of Canada. It's just my personal view."

"Really," the PMO type [says the Harperite] would say. "What's the point of 'off the record'?"

"Well, we want to be able to give people the truth, not just some spin line."

"Well, hold on a minute. If what you're saying is the truth, are you saying that what the minister's saying hasn't been truthful?"

"No, no, no, no. I'm just providing some context."

"Okay. If it's not the government of Canada context, what the fuck are you doing providing it?"

After enough variations on that conversation, the diplomat would relent, or seek other employment, which was just as good from the government's point of view. About two years after Harper became prime minister, I was an invited guest at a conference of Canadian and visiting international public servants. I mentioned, in passing, that all Canadian ambassadors needed approval in writing before they could speak to local reporters in the countries where they were posted. The visitors' jaws dropped.

While the government was facing down the people who were used to pushing information out, it also endured—often with unmistakable enthusiasm—an escalating series of battles with the people who were used to hoovering up information. In March 2006, a delegation from the parliamentary press gallery met with several members of Harper's communications staff. Sandra Buckler, who had been Harper's communications director for a few weeks, spoke for the government. Buckler's lead interrogator was Emmanuelle Latraverse, a television reporter for Radio-Canada.

Latraverse said she'd been receiving a number of complaints from the members. First, that Harper wasn't going to the National Press Theatre, which would have featured simultaneous translation of his comments, for his news conferences.

"I heard from your members that they actually quite enjoy the foyer area," Buckler said. This was the lobby outside the Commons chamber, which appeared in the background behind Harper while he spoke. "As you probably have noticed, we're a different kind of government and we place a heavy value on communications. And we like the visuals and the ability to present the Parliament to Canadians. Which is one of the main reasons we like going in front of the House." Buckler made it clear that she wasn't super-interested in what reporters wanted: "We will retain the option on where we think we best can deliver our message."

Latraverse tried another tack. Harper had instituted a system whereby a PMO press officer, Dimitri Soudas, would keep a list of reporters who would be permitted to ask questions. The reporters didn't like this either. Stephanie Rubec, a Sun Media reporter and gallery colleague of Latraverse's, said reporters were nervous: "they know they're not going to get a question in because they know that Dimitri never gives them one."

"I don't know if that's fair," Buckler said. "I don't think that's a fair statement." She added that "some people have told us that they enjoy the fact that they get to get on a list." This would very much have been a minority opinion among Ottawa political reporters at the time, if in fact it existed.

Latraverse was not putting up with Harper's chief protector giving her rebuttals from phantom reporters. "I mean, we can debate this forever," she said. "You hear from the people who like the way you run things and we get to hear from the people who aren't happy."

"Right on," Buckler said. "Yeah."

Latraverse: "That's the nature of the debate."

Buckler: "Yes."

Right then. Onward. Previous governments, going back to Brian Mulroney's anyway, had held regular meetings of the full cabinet, after which milling reporters would catch ministers as they left the meetings and ask them questions. Now just about all of that system had fallen apart. Reporters suspected Harper had held cabinet meetings he hadn't announced. Hill security officers now patrolled the third-floor corridor in the Centre Block where reporters had spent much of their careers lying in wait, most weeks, for cabinet ministers. Nobody, including reporters and camera crews, was now permitted to loiter at any time in that corridor. What was up?

"Downstairs, in the foyer, is a wonderful opportunity to show Canadians their Parliament, you know, reconnecting them with the government," Buckler said. Except ministers hadn't been talking to reporters in the foyer either. They hadn't been talking much at all. "Then there's the safety element," Buckler said. "I mean it's crowded up on the third floor. There's a lot more media than there were, say, thirty years ago. There's a lot more media now than there was, say, ten years ago."

This was asinine. No reporter had ever plummeted to death, or even to a sprained ankle, from the scrum area outside the cabinet room. The meeting was fast becoming a dialogue of the deaf.

"I think for you guys to get access on all issues you report on, you have numerous opportunities," Buckler said.

Latraverse replied, "So you're actually arguing that all your cabinet ministers are available on a range of issues?"

"I didn't say that," Buckler said.

Word of the meeting spread quickly. A *Winnipeg Free Press* reporter called Buckler for comment. "I would argue that if they just gave us a chance," Buckler said of her gallery visitors, "they will see that we are going to continue to provide more access, more space and more depth of responsiveness than they have had for the last twelve years."

That would almost never be true. A summer of jostling between reporters and handlers ensued. The press gallery published a transcript of the Buckler meeting. Harper began popping up in the oddest places, in rooms some reporters had never seen before, as he sought to ensure that he kept reporters off balance, instead of vice versa. At one news event in May, briefly legendary, soon forgotten, Soudas came to reporters gathered in the Commons lobby to seek names to put on his list of approved questioners. Reporters from various news organizations told him they would not put their names on a list. Soudas left, then returned, saying Harper would make a statement but he would not take any questions. The reporters, now reduced to stenographers, left en masse. Harper made his statement to a near-empty room.

Two days later, on a campaign-style swing through southern Ontario,

Harper dropped in at the A-Channel station in London. The press gallery "has taken the view that they are going to be the opposition to the government," he told his interviewer. "They don't ask questions at my press conferences now. We'll just take the message out on the road. There's lots of media who do want to ask questions and hear what the government is doing."

By June he'd found one of those reporters in Kevin Libin, the editor of the *Western Standard* magazine, whose proprietor was the deeply conservative and combative lawyer and former Canadian Alliance staffer Ezra Levant. Harper told Libin that "left-wing ideologues" were "apparently running the show" among Ottawa reporters. Who were these ringleaders? "The key journalists causing the problem are from the CBC," Harper said. This was creative. Latraverse had been accompanied by a *Sun* reporter and one from the Canadian Press's French-language service during her meeting with Buckler, and when her term as gallery president ended soon afterward, her successor was from Quebec's private TVA network.

But this sort of quibbling was uninteresting to Canadians from coast to coast. Reporters were amazed to learn that when they told their readers and viewers about their treatment at Harper's hands, audiences were not more sympathetic to the gallery than to the PM. By autumn, most of the press gallery had stopped resisting Harper's rules for media relations.

Meanwhile, he told Libin: "I'm free to pick my interviews when and where I want to have them. The great irony is, the result is precisely the opposite of what those doing it claim to be seeking." The gallery executive was accusing Harper of seeking to increase control over his press appearances. But his feud with the scribes did nothing to keep Harper from getting his message out whenever he wanted. "I've got more control now," he marvelled.

TWO
REMEDIAL READING I

I wrote a whole book once about how Stephen Harper became prime minister. There is no need to repeat most of that story now. Short version: there was a guy named Paul Martin, who wanted to be the head of a Liberal dynasty, and it didn't work out. But let us step back from the heady days of 2006 for just one chapter, to sift through Harper's past and the recent history of Canadian conservatism. Perhaps we can find a few items that now look like foreshadowing.

If there is a dominant school of journalistic thought about Harper in power, at least among journalists who live between Montreal and Toronto, it is that Harper is a loner with the instincts of a vandal. He came to power by accident and brings no project more ambitious than an inexplicable urge to wreck the Liberal Party. In his book *Harperland*, Lawrence Martin recalls the old adage about winners making their own luck. This is "twaddle" when it comes to Harper, he writes. Harper came to power mostly by accident, and he came to wreak vengeance. His effect on the country is incidental to the damage he seeks to inflict on the Liberals. "The Liberal order and the Canadian order were almost one and the same," Martin writes. "To take down one was to take down the other."

In an influential article in *The Walrus* in October 2004, Marci McDonald wrote about Harper's Calgary associates, especially the political scientist Tom Flanagan. The new Conservative Party's course "may have already been set by Flanagan and a handful of like-minded ideologues from the University of Calgary's political-science department," McDonald warned.

McDonald depicted Harper's entourage as a compact, cohesive team, shadowy in motive, inspired by the U.S. neo-conservative theorist Leo Strauss, and alienated from the mainstream of Canadian political thought. Her article concentrated on Flanagan, who had already left his position as Harper's chief of staff when McDonald researched her article. "Little is known about the shadowy, sixty-year-old professor," she wrote. "In Ottawa, where he has refused interviews for the last three years, some journalists regard him as a modern-day Rasputin manipulating a leader sixteen years his junior."

In fact, Flanagan's influence with Harper was fading even as McDonald wrote those lines. He had left Ottawa and been replaced as chief of staff. His replacement would not last either. Nor would that guy's replacement. Flanagan went on to write a book about Harper, published in 2007; Harper viewed the act as a betrayal and the two men have not spoken since. And while other members of the so-called Calgary School have played walk-on roles since Harper won power, it has become clearer with time that they do not own him and that he does not depend on them.

This book seeks to explain Harper's success as something more than an accident and his appeal as something more than a trick. My argument is that Harper wins elections because millions of people want somebody like him to be prime minister. They have a broad sense of who he is and what he wants to do, and they prefer it to the alternatives. Indeed, there is tremendous affection toward this prime minister. This explains why voters who supported the Harper Conservatives a first time tend to do so again in subsequent elections.

Of course millions of other Canadians prefer one of the other parties to Harper's Conservatives. Harper has sought to change the distribution of money and power in this country in ways that put him at odds with the legacy of generations of Liberal governments. But in controversies that have pitted Harper against a very broad cross-section of the people who are used to winning political arguments in this country—big fights like the ones over the long-form census, the coalition crisis of 2008, and the budget cuts after 2011—Harper stuck to his guns because he knew at least a workable plurality of voters had his back.

As I have sought to explain Harper to often skeptical audiences in recent years, I find I keep returning to a few of his writings and the observations of people who were, at one time or another, close to him. These texts help put Harper in a broader cultural context. They help explain how he wins and why he wants to win.

———

Our first reading comes from a book that was an unlikely best-seller when it was published in 1986. When you mention Peter Brimelow's *The Patriot Game: National Dreams and Political Realities* to most people in Ottawa, you get a blank stare. But to Conservatives close to Harper it has enormous significance. "That book was actually influential in Harper's circle the way the Straussians were supposed to be," a long-time Harper aide said to me.

Harper biographer William Johnson notes that when *The Patriot Game* was published, Harper and his friend John Weissenberger approached a Calgary bookseller for a group discount and then bought ten copies for their friends. "No other book seems to have grabbed the future Prime Minister quite the same way," my colleague John Geddes wrote in

Maclean's. And not only Harper: you can draw a straight, short line from the sentiment of revulsion against politics-as-usual in the governments of Trudeau and Mulroney encapsulated in *The Patriot Game* to the founding of the Reform Party barely a year after its publication.

Peter Brimelow is a British-American journalist who has worked in London, Washington and Toronto at various points in his career. In *The Patriot Game* he presented himself as a "wandering WASP" who came to Canada to tell difficult truths. "There are important human reasons why outsiders can see, and even more to the point say, things that insiders cannot," he wrote. What had he come to reveal? "I argue that contemporary Canadian Nationalism is a fraud," Brimelow began, "designed primarily to benefit particular interest groups in Canada." The rest of *The Patriot Game* lays out the nature of the fraud and the identity of the beneficiaries.

Brimelow is a big fan of nationalism in general. His problem with Canadian Nationalism is that Canada "is not a nation." He argued that there was a large and growing division between English and French Canada. But neither was English Canada internally coherent, divided as it was into Ontario, the West, the Maritimes, the North and so on. No obvious resemblance united these English Canadas more closely than that all of them were bound up in a "greater English-speaking North American nation." The country's national borders, in other words, were essentially arbitrary.

So far, so unsurprising. At least in pessimistic moments, every Canadian sometimes wonders whether this country is an expression of anything real. But Brimelow made it more interesting when he argued that attempts to keep Quebec and the rest together were creating various pathologies, including an imbalance in the political system that benefited "elements in Central Canada" and inspired the weed-like growth of "an unusually large and powerful public class." This looming public class, he wrote, "has developed what Marxists call a 'dominant ideology' rationalizing and justifying its power, and has been quite successful in imposing it as the Canadian conventional wisdom." This ideology, devoted to denying what Brimelow saw as fundamental characteristics of the country, "can for practical purposes be identified with the federal Liberal Party, but it extends far beyond."

Canada, in Brimelow's depiction, did not so much resemble an accident as a conspiracy. In our out-of-the-way corner of the globe, a protection racket had sprung up to safeguard Canada's ungainly integrity at the expense of its prosperity and of a fair distribution of local wealth. Like any durable scam, this one devoted much of its energy to perpetuating its own success. "Systematic government intervention in the Canadian economy in the name of Nationalism and other edifying political ideals has been accompanied by equally continuous complaints about the economy's poor performance," he wrote, citing Goldwin Smith, a nineteenth-century British chronicler of the Canadian soul, to the effect that Canada was "rich by nature, poor by policy."

Indeed, nature and policy were increasingly at odds. The effort required to prop up the "public class" was growing. The population was moving west, away from the traditional Montreal–Toronto corridor of power. Between 1901 and the 1980s, the four Western provinces' combined share of Canada's population had risen from 10 percent to 27 percent, finally surpassing Quebec's. So the economic strategy of the central elites made less and less sense.

What was their strategy? "To concentrate rents from a resource-based economy in Central Canadian hands." The influx of money from the hinterland was used to prop up the manufacturing industry, "always regarded as a Good Thing in Canada." An assortment of policy tools were deployed to that end, including the maintenance of a weak dollar, even if the combined effect of those policies was to keep the West down. To Brimelow each of those tools was a "two-by-four" administered by Ottawa to Western Canada's face. One such assault was the government's 1977 decision "to allow a coalition of nationalists, environmentalists and 'native people' activists" to block the Mackenzie Valley natural gas pipeline to the United States. Brimelow could not imagine such a ragtag opposition stopping something Ottawa actually wanted, but Mackenzie Valley was another matter because its beneficiaries would have been mere Westerners. "This window of opportunity for the West has been slammed for a generation."

So Canada made sense as a country only as long as you lived at the bottom of a policy-induced money slope that kept cash and influence rolling toward Ottawa, Toronto and Montreal even as populations and opportunity were heading in the opposite direction. Perverse as it was, the system might have been made to last indefinitely if the restlessness of the Quebec partner in the Central Canadian protection racket had not presented a new internal challenge. Liberal victory had always been ensured by leaders who managed to unite French Canada and divide English Canada. If they lost Quebec they would lose everything.

The Liberals responded to the Quebec nationalist threat, wrote Brimelow, by turning, slowly at first and then with real gusto under Trudeau, against any element of Canadian cultural expression that might be deemed upsetting in Quebec. Official references to Canada's British imperial history were expunged from the decoration of government buildings, from mailboxes, from official stationery and more. A "stealthy campaign of attrition against the emblems of monarchy" was pursued. Trudeau eliminated "the technical convention that Canadian diplomats were accredited in the name of the Queen." He tried to have the word "Royal" removed from the name of the national constabulary. Brimelow was hardly unaware that Trudeau's ideas about federalism often antagonized Quebec nationalists. This was the tragedy of Trudeau, he wrote: the old man was selling Canada's history down the river to appease Quebec and it wasn't even working.

How could a country spend decades handing power to a political party devoted to denying its history and confounding its economics? Why would the population consent? Here Brimelow called on the theories of Antonio Gramsci, an Italian Marxist writer and political theorist. Not a likely authority, to be sure, but a handy one. To the obvious riddle of working-class consent in bourgeois rule, Gramsci replied by greatly expanding the Marxist notion of "hegemony." Hegemony didn't necessarily mean coerced rule by force, and indeed usually it didn't. Rather, in the words of his biographer James Joll, it meant that a political class "had succeeded in persuading the other classes of society to accept its cultural values." The ruling classes didn't literally have to keep their jackboots on the necks of the masses. Most of the time they could simply persuade the population that the way things were was the way things had to be.

I find this notion of hegemony perfectly fascinating, and essential to a proper understanding of Stephen Harper as prime minister. Gramscian hegemony describes winning as a process, not an event. The consent of the governed is not won once but every day; not through occasional confrontations but through countless acts of suasion.

Surely a mere political party, even the Liberals, can't hoodwink an entire society into acting against its interests for generations at a time? Indeed, Brimelow argued that the Liberals had not managed this feat alone. They had "developed a crucial political asset," he wrote, "in the shape of the emerging alliance of civil servants, educators and assorted media and political hangers-on" that had risen to prominence across the Western world with the rise of the welfare state.

Brimelow mentioned Irving Kristol, the intellectual father of neo-conservatism in the United States, who wrote in the 1970s about what he called the New Class. "As a group, you find them mainly in the very large and growing public sector and in the media," Kristol wrote. "They share a disinterest in personal wealth, a dislike for the free-market economy, and a conviction that society may best be improved through greater governmental participation in the country's economic life." Kristol's New Class was tentacular, reaching into the media, the educational system, science, law, social work and other professions. These were not only people who cashed a government paycheque. They were also the much larger class of people who prospered in the kind of society only an activist state could build and sustain.

Brimelow believed Canada's New Class was even more influential than America's. Ottawa was a relatively larger city than Washington, D.C. A larger share of Canada's population was in the civil service. "The Canadian civil servant is therefore that much less exposed to the rude populace, and that much more inclined to develop a corporate identity than his American counterpart—who has not been slow."

Brimelow was adamant that the Liberals had not won because they had avoided ideology. The notion of Liberals as a blandly efficient brokerage party is attractive mostly to Liberals. To Brimelow, the long line of Liberal prime ministers had followed "a consistent ideological and emotional thread. They were consistently on the left of their party and their community. This tradition has been all the more tenacious for being cherished in private, so as not to disconcert a less enlightened Canadian public."

The Liberals had never hauled the population hard over to the left, because the population would have noticed and objected. Instead, they dissimulated about their motives and counted on time to accomplish what haste could not. "The Liberals' relative caution in office was a source of constant frustration to socialist and Nationalist ideologues," Brimelow wrote. But the hard Left needn't have worried, because those in power were on their side. Brimelow pointed out Trudeau's many ties to the radical Left in Montreal and around the world. He pointed out that Ed Clark, a bureaucratic architect of the National Energy Program, had written a PhD thesis at Oxford with the title "Socialist Development and Public Investment in Tanzania, 1964–1973." (From 2000 to 2013, Clark was president of TD Bank Group. This long-term tenure might look like a challenge to Brimelow's depiction of the former bureaucrat as an anti-capitalist crusader. But the notion of a New Class includes plenty of room for the affluent and powerful. In 2010, when Clark advocated higher personal income taxes to counteract budget deficits, Harper's Conservative Party sent out a news release with the subject line, "Millionaire Ignatieff Economic Czar Calls for Higher Taxes.")

Inherent in the notion of hegemony is the expectation that observers living in a hegemonic order won't notice it even though they are surrounded by it. Brimelow believed he was immune because he came from outside. And his book found an enthusiastic audience in Western Canada because people there were outside the Liberal/New Class hegemonic bubble, too. "In the two thousand miles of Western Canada between the Ontario line and the Pacific Ocean, the Liberals won only two seats in 1980," Brimelow noted.

So why hadn't a durable alternative to the Liberals arisen in Western Canada? "The Liberal hegemony's greatest success . . . has been its successful subjugation of considerable sections of the Tory party," Brimelow wrote. The Progressive Conservatives might believe they were fighting the Liberals tooth and nail. In fact, they were buying the Liberal assumptions about almost everything. "This is, of course, the hallmark of a dominant ideology."

When Brimelow wrote his book, one of the most important recent Canadian political events had been the Progressive Conservatives' replacement of Joe Clark with Brian Mulroney. That Clark's was the deeply co-opted face of Liberal hegemony was obvious to Brimelow, and went a long way toward explaining why so many Western conservatives had built up such contempt for this Western Progressive Conservative. Brimelow noted that in their book *Contenders: The Tory Quest for Power*, about the 1983 leadership race, Patrick Martin, Allan Gregg and George Perlin have Clark saying he felt "distinctly uncomfortable" with other Westerners and felt "no rapport" with them.

Clark stayed on the ballot in the 1983 leadership convention after he knew he couldn't win, to split the votes of delegates from outside

Quebec and ensure that Brian Mulroney beat John Crosbie. "Clark," Brimelow wrote, "had sought to keep the Tory party on the left, preoccupied by the French-English question and disproportionately influenced by Quebec—a carbon copy of the Liberals in the Trudeau years, and certainly not responsive to the examples of Ronald Reagan and Margaret Thatcher."

From this perspective, Mulroney's rise was not a repudiation of Liberal hegemony but its purest expression. The enemies of Trudeau had found another Quebec-born, Quebec-obsessed son of one anglophone and one francophone parent to lead them. Mulroney didn't want to replace Trudeau's electoral coalition. He wanted to hotwire it and take it for a joyride. He was "trying to steal Trudeau's formula and govern Canada from a Quebec base in alliance with the Anglophone centre-left," according to Brimelow.

There is one more thing about *The Patriot Game* that gave it such power in those parts of Canada where people felt the Liberal consensus left them out: the timing of the book's publication. If it had been written three years earlier it would have been seen as an expression of English Canadian resentment against Trudeau. It would have looked like a partisan pamphlet. It's easy to imagine Mulroney waving copies of the book on the campaign trail, if it had been published before he ran for prime minister. But instead, it appeared after Mulroney had won a historic majority and begun to govern, and therefore to disappoint.

The book provided an intellectual framework for Conservatives to understand the disappointments of the Mulroney years, including the decision to award the CF-18 maintenance contract to Montreal instead of Winnipeg and then, later, the five-year agony of the Meech and Charlottetown constitutional negotiations. Mulroney did these things, students of Brimelow could tell themselves, because he was just another facet of Liberal hegemony. Or, as Reform MPs would say when they arrived by the dozen in Ottawa in 1993, "Liberal, Tory, same old story."

"Only through submitting to an almost unknown and quite atypical leader could the party of the majority come to power," Brimelow wrote. "The only solution Mulroney could offer to the party's problems, which were ultimately those of Canada, were personal, charismatic—and therefore temporary."

I do not want to give the impression that *The Patriot Game* became a user's manual for Harper. Nor was Brimelow's book influential because it was quirky or offered a wildly different worldview than its readers had seen before. *The Patriot Game* landed like a bomb among Alberta conservatives precisely because its arguments weren't novel and isolated but gave expression to something deep-seated, broadly based and cultural. The book functioned as myth, in the way Northrop Frye used that word: not as a tall tale, but as a highly charged revelation of a truth that was already present and felt in the culture before the myth gave it words.

Brimelow's book did not tell Harper what to do, but reading it helps us understand what Harper has done. In government, Harper would often seem to be borrowing Liberal methods to undo their legacy. Where Liberals had been patient, he would be patient. Where they frustrated socialist ideologues while playing a longer game, he would frustrate conservative ideologues so he could survive long enough to play a longer game. Liberals once won by uniting French Canada and dividing English Canada. Harper would take as much of English Canada as he could, leaving behind only the salons and National Capital Region cubicles of the New Class, and making only fitful and distracted overtures to French Canada. Where Liberals had worked to transfer wealth to the East, he would leave it in the West. Where they had eroded the Crown and the memory of a distinctly British heritage, he would build them up.

Undoing years of Liberalism would require years of Conservatism. Starting from a position of bewildering weakness—the leadership of the battered Canadian Alliance Party—Harper needed to figure out how to win and then hold power, not for a few tumultuous months but for many years. The next item on our reading list shows how he proposed to do that. The key idea was that he had to resist the temptation to make conservatism meaningless in order to make it broadly acceptable. He could not sell a stew that had no flavour. Indeed he needed to make it spicier.

In 2003 Harper spoke to a gathering of the secretive conservative group Civitas. The shroud of secrecy is not total: the group has a website that offers a little information, enough to suggest its activities are harmless. Civitas members meet once a year for a couple of days to talk politics. The organization bills itself as "A Society Where Ideas Meet," and the ideas that meet are the ones you might expect from a society whose founding directors included journalists Ted Byfield, Michael Coren, David Frum and Ezra Levant; author William Gairdner; Gwen Landolt, a leading figure of REAL Women of Canada; and political strategists Tom Long (who used to whisper in Mike Harris's ear) and Tom Flanagan (who no longer whispers in Harper's). It's pretty conservative. Visiting in 2003 to give a speech, Harper brought them what they wanted to hear.

The Canadian conservative movement had dodged a bullet, he said. When he ran for the leadership of the Canadian Alliance a year earlier, the party was so buffeted by controversy and defection that its members were no longer sure why it had been put on earth. "What Alliance members feared most was seeing our agenda slipping away. Simply put, our members worried less about having two so-called 'conservative parties' than about having no conservative party at all." Harper said his job was to get the Alliance past that crisis of confidence and establish it as the country's leading voice for conservatism.

There was a time, he said, when the Alliance's predecessor, the Reform Party, had been such a voice. From its founding in 1987 until about 1998, Reform had been "policy-driven," taking strong stands on spending restraint, low taxes, and the Meech and Charlottetown constitutional fiascos.

But then Preston Manning decided Reform had run its course and had to be replaced by a broader "united alternative" to the Liberals. Manning dragged his party through a succession of conferences and referendums to plan and ratify assorted expansions. He tried everything to lure interested renegades from the otherwise aloof Progressive Conservatives. This was the Reform / Alliance's "process phase," Harper said. He wasn't arguing that process must be avoided at all costs. If the Progressive Conservatives could be persuaded to merge with the Alliance, he would certainly be interested. But Joe Clark didn't want to play, and Harper saw no point in obsessing over hypothetical processes at the expense of real ideas.

Besides, whether it merged with the party next to it or not, any conservative party would always contain elements of a coalition. "Two distinctive elements have long been identifiable. Ted Byfield labelled these factions 'neo-con' and 'theo-con.' More commonly, they are known simply as economic conservatives and social conservatives. Properly speaking, they are called classical or enlightenment liberalism and classical or Burkean conservatism," Harper explained.

Economic conservatism values individual freedom most highly. It is the conservatism one is most likely to find in the newspaper columns, if one can find any. "It stresses private enterprise, free trade, religious toleration, limited government and the rule of law," Harper said.

But more of his speech was devoted to the second kind of conservatism: social, or Burkean, conservatism, after the British parliamentarian Edmund Burke. This branch of the family was familiar to many in his audience but deeply out of fashion in the broader Canadian commentariat. "Its primary value is social order," Harper said. "It stresses respect for customs and traditions—religious traditions above all—voluntary association, and personal self-restraint reinforced by moral and legal sanctions on behaviour."

Here Harper cited Russell Kirk, the founding editor of the influential U.S. journal *National Review*. A proudly fusty man, Kirk refused to drive an automobile or watch TV right up to his death in 1994. He converted to Catholicism at forty-four years of age. Social conservatism, Harper said, quoting Kirk, was "the preservation of the ancient moral traditions of humanity. Conservatives . . . think society is a spiritual reality, possessing an eternal life but a delicate constitution: it cannot be scrapped and recast as if it were a machine."

Especially because they viewed society as the complex and intractable product of generations of irrevocable decisions and omissions, social conservatives were often suspicious of economic conservatives, who seemed always to be looking around for a revolution to start. But through the twentieth century these two brands of conservatism had more often allied than competed, setting aside their differences in the face of a common enemy, "the rise of radical socialism in its various forms."

"Various forms" turned out to be a bit of an understatement. Domestically, Harper said, socialism looked like "public ownership, government interventionism, egalitarian redistribution and state sponsorship of secular humanist values." Abroad, it took the gloves off, appearing as "fascism, communism and socialist totalitarianism."

In opposition to that vast (but related!) assortment of enemies, Harper said, both neo- and theo-cons "favoured private property, small government and reliance on civil society rather than the state to resolve social dilemmas." For decades, those prescriptions had proved popular, ensuring conservative parties' dominance in much of the West. But now conservative parties were losing elections and even, as in Canada, falling apart. And it was all happening at what should have been a moment of triumph, coming as it did after Reagan and Thatcher.

"I believe that it is this very success that is at the heart of the current difficulties," Harper said. Reagan and Thatcher had thumped the left-wing parties so soundly for so long that those parties finally abandoned many of their old-fashioned social democratic ideas and adopted much of the conservative economic agenda. "Socialists and liberals began to stand for balanced budgeting, the superiority of markets, welfare reversal, free trade and some privatization." Even as the domestic opponent was shape-shifting, the unifying external threat all but vanished. The West won the Cold War. Soviet Communism vanished.

What conservatives must now do, Harper said, was to reimagine their opponent so they could adjust their response. "The real enemy is no longer socialism. Socialism as a true economic program and motivating faith is dead." In its place was a subtler kind of big government. Harper called it corporatism: "the use of private ownership and markets for state-directed objectives. Its tools are subsidization, public/private partnerships and state investment funds. It is often bad policy, but it is less clearly different from conventional conservative economics than any genuine socialism."

So if the enemy was not the international Left, and it wasn't leftist economics, what could it be? It was, Harper said, "the social agenda of the modern Left. Its system of moral relativism, moral neutrality and moral equivalency is beginning to dominate its intellectual debate and public-policy objectives."

The new Left social agenda could be seen most clearly in international affairs, he said. Remember that Harper was speaking less than two years after 9/11, and only a few months after the invasion of Iraq. "There is no doubt about the technical capacity of our society to fight this war," Harper said. "What is evident is the lack of desire of the modern liberals to fight, and even more, the striking hope on the Left that we actually lose."

Where previous generations of conservatives had to stop the Left from handing Western society over to the Communists, this generation had to stop it from handing the world over to Muslim fundamentalists and Saddam Hussein. The threat was clear in the response to the Iraq war "from our own federal Liberals and their cheerleaders in the media and the universities." Harper was positing a Liberal-affiliated New Class that responded to George W. Bush's moral clarity with all sorts of contradictory arguments: that Iraq had no weapons of mass destruction and that they did have such weapons and would use them if goaded; that war was "immoral, then moral but impractical, then practical but unjustified." When the World Trade Center went down, some said the West had done something to deserve this attack. When Saddam's statues came down in Baghdad, they were glum.

"Conservatives need to reassess our understanding of the modern Left. It has moved beyond old socialistic morality or even moral relativism to something much darker. It has become a moral nihilism—the rejection of any tradition or convention of morality, a post-Marxism with deep resentments, even hatreds of the norms of free and democratic western civilization.

"This descent into nihilism should not be surprising because moral relativism simply cannot be sustained as a guiding philosophy. It leads to silliness such as moral neutrality on the use of marijuana or harder drugs mixed with its random moral crusades on tobacco. It explains the lack of moral censure on personal foibles of all kinds, extenuating even criminal behaviour with moral outrage at bourgeois society, which is then tangentially blamed for deviant behaviour. On the moral standing of the person, it leads to views ranging from radical responsibility-free individualism, to tribalism in the form of group rights.

"Conservatives have focused on the inconsistency in all of this. Yet it is actually disturbingly consistent. It is a rebellion against all forms of social norm and moral tradition in every aspect of life. The logical end of this thinking is the actual banning of conservative views, which some legislators and 'rights' commissions openly contemplate."

Now Harper moved from diagnosis to prescription, from describing the new political gameboard to telling conservatives how they must move on it. "In this environment, serious conservative parties simply cannot shy away from values questions," he told his audience. "On a wide range of public-policy questions—including foreign affairs and defence, criminal justice and corrections, family and child care, and health care and social services—social values are increasingly the really big issues."

Expressing a mere fondness for fiscal belt-tightening could offer voters no salient distinction between conservatives and their opponents. Besides, how far could you cut taxes if you believed the state should do everything Paul Martin believed it should do? "There are real limits to tax-cutting if conservatives cannot dispute anything about how or why a government actually does what it does."

Rather, conservatives needed to get back in touch with their social-conservative side, to confront the liberal welfare-state threat to "our most important institutions, particularly the family."

Was he referring to abortion? To capital punishment? Hardly. Even as he proposed a major strategic realignment in Canadian conservatism, Harper kept a keen eye on the battles that could realistically be won in the near term. So the example he gave the Civitas crowd that day was the Liberal war against . . . spanking.

Of course, the Criminal Code set out "legitimate limits" on parents' use of force against their children. "Yet the most recent Liberal Throne Speech, as part of its 'children's agenda,' hinted at more government interference in the family." The Throne Speech in question, Jean Chrétien's last as prime minister, had included a sentence promising to reform the Criminal Code to increase penalties for abuse and neglect.

"We saw the capacity for this abuse of power in the events that took place in Aylmer, Ontario. Children there were seized for no reason other than the state disagreed with the religious views of their parents. No conservative can support this kind of intrusion, and conservatives have an obligation to speak forcefully against such acts.

"This same argument," Harper continued, "applies equally to a range of issues involving the family . . . such as banning child pornography, raising the age of sexual consent, providing choice in education and strengthening the institution of marriage. All of these items are key to a conservative agenda."

A renaissance in Burkean conservatism would also help in foreign affairs "because the emerging debates on foreign affairs should be fought on moral grounds," he said. The war on terrorism, "as well as the emerging debate on the goals of the United States as the sole superpower," needed "conservative insights on preserving historic values and moral insights on right and wrong." The Left ("with the exception of Tony Blair") had no answers on such questions. But conservatives should. "We understand that the great geopolitical battles against modern tyrants and threats are battles over values."

So how should conservatives go about amending their ways in a manner more consistent with social-conservative values? Carefully and subtly. "The social conservative issues we choose should not be denominational, but should unite social conservatives of different denominations and even different faiths. It also helps when social conservative concerns overlap those of people with a more libertarian orientation."

Second, the movement must be content with incremental gains, "inevitably" the only real ones. Rushing or attempting any kind of revolutionary upheaval "will certainly fail."

Finally, conservatives must understand that adjusting their message would entail short-term losses as well as gains. "We may lose some old 'conservatives,' Red Tories like the David Orchards or the Joe Clarks. This is not all bad." But there would be gains that should more than offset the losses. "Many traditional Liberal voters, especially those from key ethnic and immigrant communities, will be attracted to a party with strong traditional views of values and family."

In less than an hour, Harper had given clues about his leadership philosophy that would remain valuable for a decade. For many years it had been fashionable to proclaim oneself "fiscally conservative and socially liberal." It was the easiest way for a liberal to claim a brain or a conservative a heart. But in Harper's view, that was precisely the problem: any position that can be claimed by anyone cannot be defended. Harper preferred his positions with moats around them. He wanted Conservatives to go where Liberals could not follow. He believed what Clark and Mulroney never had: that there would be a voter constituency waiting for him when he staked out this new ground.

We can go further and state that forever after, whenever Harper infuriated the gatekeepers of the old consensus—the Liberals and their cheerleaders in the media and universities, to borrow his language— he would know he was on the right track. That conviction allowed him to view the loss of old-guard Progressive Conservative support with equanimity. He knew he could win support from unexpected quarters, including immigrants. This would permit the growth of a conservatism that would be the opposite of Mulroney's. Not personal but cultural. Not charismatic but persuasive at a deeper, more atavistic level. Not temporary, but lasting, perhaps longer even than Harper's own career.

All of this remains true even if we admit to ourselves that much of Harper's argument was hokum.

Any competent high-school debating team could have picked apart any two consecutive paragraphs of Harper's Civitas speech, starting with the bit where he said conservatives had spent the twentieth century fighting those notoriously connected impulses, "egalitarian redistribution" and "fascism." Harper was lumping together antagonists as varied as Petro-Canada, the progressive income tax, Auschwitz and the

Gulag. This put him on shaky ground to be criticizing anyone else's propensity toward moral equivalence.

Later he promised to illustrate the modern Left's "system of . . . moral relativism" and then announced that his opponents had "moved beyond . . . moral relativism to something much darker." Well, was the Left guilty of relativism or worse? And how could it be worse than the old Left—which Harper had already depicted as the local affiliates of the Auschwitz gatekeepers?

To Harper the purest illustration of the Left's moral bankruptcy was its opposition to the Iraq war. It's worth noting that Harper would never mention that war again after 2006, except when pressed by the Liberals and their eggers-on in the media and the universities. One of the enduring questions about the man is how he can reconcile his certainty about Iraq in 2003 with his silence, punctuated by the briefest possible equivocation, afterward. Another question is how he could be so reliably shocked by moral inconsistency on the Left and so willing to indulge in such inconsistency himself. Perhaps the flip side of moral nihilism is anaphylactic moral shock brought on by exposure to even trace elements of one's political opponents.

Many times since 2006 Conservatives have cited Harper's Civitas speech as the best expression of the new conservatism Harper was seeking to build. I am giving it this much space, this early in my narrative, because I have indeed found it to be a handy guide to understanding so much of his political action. But Harper's moral analysis is not a finer analysis than the Liberals'. It is merely a different analysis, appealing to a different audience. Perhaps that was all Harper would need.

———

Brimelow's 1986 book helps us understand the motive for a new Western Canada–based conservatism, rooted in a pervasive sense of betrayal at the hands of Trudeau Liberalism and its pale Progressive Conservative imitations. Righting that betrayal was the mission that first sent Stephen Harper and hundreds of other activists into electoral politics. Reform had burned itself out as a protest party and botched its first attempted transition into a governing party. Harper's Civitas speech indicated the mindset a new conservatism would have to adopt as a governing party: frankly social-conservative, with a strong focus on families, communities and crime-fighting, and with a "hard power" foreign policy.

Still another book from the archives can help us understand the operating philosophy of Harper's conservatism. Beyond telling us how a Harper government would think, it offers hints on how that government would function. Appropriately, it was written by the man who would become Harper's operational lieutenant after the 2006 election.

Ian Brodie's *Friends of the Court: The Privileging of Interest Group Litigants in Canada*, published in 2002, is a highly unflattering study of one aspect of Pierre Trudeau's legacy. But any serious politician learns from his opponents, and Harper later incorporated many of the techniques Brodie described into his governing style.

Born in Toronto in 1967, Brodie studied at McGill before taking his MA and PhD at the University of Calgary in the 1990s. He then accepted a post in the Political Science Department at the University of Western Ontario, but took a leave of absence a few years later to work for Harper after Harper became the Canadian Alliance leader. By 2005 he was Harper's chief of staff. After the 2006 victory he became the new government's chief enforcer of discipline. In 2008 he left to work in Washington.

Friends of the Court is based on his doctoral dissertation. Brodie's focus was the Supreme Court of Canada in the aftermath of the Charter of Rights. "A remarkably activist tribunal," he wrote. "In recent years it has forced Alberta to extend its human rights code to protect against discrimination based on sexual orientation. It has required Canadian governments to extend spousal benefits to same-sex couples. And it has disrupted resource management policies by extending aboriginal rights." This burst of activism in the 1980s was "unprecedented," and Brodie plainly found the reaction to it a little odd: even though a succession of governments and powerful interests had been dealt defeats at the Court's hands, its activism hadn't provoked a political backlash. Brian Mulroney and the premiers had spent the years since 1987 trying to change just about everything in the Constitution it was possible to change—except the Charter and the functioning of the courts.

The rise in judicial activism was matched by a rise in the sustained activity of interest groups: "groups representing feminists, civil libertarians, language minorities, unions, business and others" organized "to wage long-term battles in the courts." Such groups often claimed to be politically disadvantaged, he observed. Which may indeed be the case, except that state funding has been crucial to their formation, survival and their frequent court victories. The main vehicle for this funding was the Court Challenges Program, which provided money to civil-society applicants so they could challenge laws on Charter grounds.

Eventually it becomes clear that Brodie is describing a loose network of interests congenial to broadly Liberal goals which extends well outside the government or the Liberal Party. He cites two leading Calgary School academics, Ted Morton and Rainer Knopff, who had written a study of what they dubbed the "Court Party." This network included "social reform-minded professionals and academics in public interest groups, government departments, independent government agencies, the criminal bar, and the law schools." Irving Kristol would have called it Canada's New Class.

"Morton and Knopff's central observation is that the Court Party is a political minority in Canada," Brodie wrote. "Electoral politics is therefore not an advantageous arena for them. The Court Party prefers to advance its agendas through institutions that are insulated from electoral politics. The courts, quasi-judicial tribunals, and the administrative arms of government are arenas where the Court Party's professional skills and abilities can make up for their lack of electoral support."

Of course electoral politics was an advantageous arena for the Liberal Party through the first half of the 1980s. But the Liberals didn't dare wear their activism on their sleeve. They had to look like moderates. In this Morton–Knopff–Brodie view, the courts served as the advance guard of what Brodie calls a "post-materialist" vision.

Harper made it clear he had taken Brodie's argument to heart when he delivered an extraordinary news conference in the Centre Block lobby outside the House of Commons as opposition leader in 2003. Ontario judge Roy McMurtry had just handed down his landmark ruling permitting same-sex marriage. Harper argued that the Liberals had plotted for a very long time to produce precisely this result.

"They wanted to introduce this same-sex marriage through back channels," Harper said then. "They had the courts do it for them, put the judges in they wanted. Then they failed to appeal, failed to fight the case in court."

But, the reporters protested, McMurtry was a lifelong Progressive Conservative. He used to be Bill Davis's attorney general in Ontario. He was appointed to the court by Mulroney. "Well, he's a former Tory," Harper said. "But whether he's conservative or not is a matter of terminology."

After a brief stint as a junior political staffer in the Mulroney government in the mid-1980s, Harper worked in a succession of opposition parties for nearly twenty years before he formed a government. He clearly had no trouble holding two simultaneous thoughts about much of what he saw along the way: "This is outrageous" and "This will come in handy someday." The lesson he took from the behaviour of the Court Party was subtle. It wasn't "Stack the courts." It wasn't "Use the Court Challenges Program to fund Conservative-friendly legal challenges." One of the first things he did as prime minister was to cancel the Court

Challenges Program. He pretty much gave the courts up for lost as potential instruments of ever-broader Conservative hegemony, and events would show he was right to have done so.

The lesson he did draw was "Work your networks." A conservatism that operated only in the Prime Minister's Office and on the government side of the House of Commons would be like a plant without roots. It could not survive or flourish. But over time he would identify the "back channels" he could work through. Long after he became prime minister in a minority Parliament, electoral politics would rarely be an advantageous arena for advancing his goals. He would find others.

Harper was a keen student of Liberal outrages and Liberal weaknesses, but he was also uncommonly aware of shortcomings on his own side and in his own actions. Like most successful politicians he would be loath to admit error. But many times, as he approached, won and held power, he would quietly take stock of his own errors and vulnerabilities, and adjust his course. One such moment came in 2002, during the final weeks of the Canadian Alliance leadership campaign. Ted Byfield's little *Report* magazine, formerly *Alberta Report*, published a cover story that crystallized a glaring weakness in Canadian conservatism.

The headline on the story was "A Self-Hating Nation." Its author was Kevin Michael Grace, a regular contributor, a bit of an ornery cuss and no fan of Harper's. The story now reads as a period piece of immediate post-9/11 Canada, when shock over the World Trade Center massacre and widespread embarrassment about Jean Chrétien's plodding response brought a host of Canadian insecurities to the surface.

Grace's article opened with shock quotes from two prominent conservative writers. "When William Gairdner is asked for his opinion on the future of Canada, he chuckles—and then apologizes. 'Pardon the laughter,' he says. William Christian laughs too. 'A short story, is it?' he asks."

While 9/11 had provoked a tide of patriotic indignation in the United States, among Canadian conservatives it had provoked disgust at the country's perceived shortcomings. Canada was a den of terrorists. Canada was a politically correct hideout for the enemies of freedom. Canada was soft, weak, more worried about the White House than the Taliban. Grace's insight was to wonder whether this critique of Canadian shortcomings was distinguishable from outright contempt for Canada. "It is arguable that patriotism, let alone nationalism, is in short supply on the Canadian Right," he wrote. "A reliable source claims that a famous right-wing pundit, a star of the *National Post*, was heard to say, 'The *Post* has a problem. It was started to save Canada, but Canada isn't worth saving.'"

This raised a question, Grace wrote: "Does the Right hate Canada?"

While that issue of the *Report* was on newsstands, Harper became Canadian Alliance leader. He would discuss the *Report* story often with the people around him. Political parties everywhere wrap themselves in flags. The Liberals, who had built much of the apparatus of a modern Canada, did the same. It helped that they had designed the flag they were wrapping themselves in.

Harper had to take care not to make his contempt for the Liberal legacy read as contempt for Canada. Most opposition parties elsewhere didn't have to worry about such a thing. "Nobody believes that the Democratic Party in the U.S. is not an American party," one of his strategists said later. "In Australia, both of the major parties are recognized as legitimate parts of the debate."

For the longest time, Harper simply had to protest that he did not, in fact, hate his country. Of course it was easy to imagine where somebody might have gotten the idea he did. In what was intended as a lighthearted 1997 Montreal dinner speech to visiting members of a conservative U.S. group, the Council for National Policy, Harper got off this thigh-slapper:

"Canada is a Northern European welfare state in the worst sense of the term." In a bitter *National Post* op-ed after the Alliance lost the 2000 election, he wrote: "Canada appears content to become a second-tier socialistic country, boasting ever more loudly about its economy and social services to mask its second-rate status." In 2005, when he began the campaign that would take him to power, the first question he faced from a reporter was whether he hated Canada. "We didn't have a competing narrative," the strategist said. "What are the symbols people talk about when they talk about Canada? Health care. The Charter. Peacekeeping. The United Nations. The CBC. Almost every single example was a Liberal achievement or a Liberal policy.

"We had gotten to a point in Canada where the conservative side of politics had been marginalized—where we weren't even recognized as legitimately Canadian."

Shortly after he became Canadian Alliance leader, Harper had even briefly considered adopting red and white as the party's official colours. He finally decided the problem of patriotism wouldn't lend itself to a quick fix. Building a competitive conservative vocabulary of Canadian pride would take time. "We didn't have any illusions about displacing the Liberal vision and the Liberal narrative of Canada," his strategist said. "But we needed to give the conservative side something to rally around." Over time, Harper began to promote symbols Canadians could love even if they weren't (yet?) Conservative voters: symbols his opponents had neglected. "It's the Arctic," the strategist continued. "It's the military. It's the RCMP. It's the embrace of hockey and lacrosse and curling." It would become much more than that. Eventually it would include the monarchy, the War of 1812, the rechristening of public buildings with the names of Conservative politicians and, by 2011, a campaign podium for Harper that would feature the word CANADA across the front, as though man and nation were synonymous. Every time critics would say he was going too far, he would tell himself the Liberals went further, for decades, in offering their party as a synonym for Canada. All he was doing, he would tell himself, was righting the balance.

———

By the time he finally faced Paul Martin in a national campaign as Conservative leader in 2004, Harper had had almost no time to implement any of the lessons he had learned on his way to national leadership because he'd spent most of his time actually running in various contests. His platform was simply the arithmetic mean of the 2000 Progressive Conservative and Canadian Alliance platforms, exactly the sort of difference-blurring he had decried in his Civitas speech. Few voters knew him. His first ads showed him reciting some forgettable boilerplate into the camera and then pausing before saying, with weirdly intense emphasis, "My name is Stephen Harper." This information alone was news to many of the people seeing the ads. That was the point of them.

It was amazing that Harper managed to pull close enough to the Liberals to make them sweat. Most polls had him ahead of the Martin Liberals a week before the election. Then interview footage of Conservative candidates surfaced, sounding a little extremist.

"To heck with the courts, eh?" Randy White said, promising to undo same-sex marriage at the first opportunity. White, one of the original Reform MPs, wasn't running for re-election, but with this single disastrous interview, he had given everybody who was running something to remember him by.

Harper had time to learn one last lesson on the weekend before he lost the 2004 election. The Conservatives didn't run many negative ads in that campaign. The ads they did run in that vein were cheerful and pointless, such as showing trash collectors tossing tax dollars into the back of a garbage truck. "That was based on Harper's belief at the time that the public didn't like attack ads," one Conservative MP said later.

Martin, facing defeat, didn't have the luxury of worrying too hard about voters' sensibilities. In the last weekend of the campaign, the Martin Liberals released a wave of anti-Harper ads, mostly in Ontario, and the tenuous Conservative garbage-truck ad melted away like snow in rain.

Today, Conservatives who were active with the party in 2004 can tell you about one of the Liberal ads, a rapid-fire succession of shock images: aircraft carriers, factories belching pollution. "He'd sacrifice a woman's right to choose," the voice-over said, "and he's prepared to work with the Bloc Québécois." The image those Conservatives remember is a handgun pointed into the camera. The weapon quivers as its owner pulls the trigger.

That Liberal ad would help Conservatives justify to themselves every negative ad they would ever produce going forward. But Martin's campaign staff didn't think the gun-in-your-face ad was their most effective attack, and neither did Harper. The ad that took Harper apart was quieter and less scattershot. "Can you increase expenditures, lower taxes and still balance the books?" the ad asked. A photo of Brian Mulroney slid onscreen. "Prime Minister Brian Mulroney tried it. He left behind a deficit of $42 billion a year." A photo of Ontario Conservative premier Mike Harris, whose party had lost the provincial election a year earlier, appeared next to Mulroney's. Then Harper's photo appeared between the two older men. "Now Stephen Harper wants his turn."

During that final weekend, the modest gains Jack Layton's NDP had built vanished as skittish centre-left voters went back to the Liberals. They would not do so in any of the next three elections, but this time their return was enough for Martin to hold power. Harper watched and learned. Where almost everyone else in his party would remember the gun-in-your-face ad, Harper would remember the one that actually worked. The one that simply showed his face in the most unflattering possible context.

"He learned that if you're hit and you don't hit back, you always lose," the Conservative MP said. "That was a seminal event in the development of Harper tactics."

THREE

LES QUÉBÉCOIS OR, AS WE SAY IN ENGLISH, THE QUÉBÉCOIS

The Citadel in Quebec City was built in the 1820s by Lt.-Col. Elias Walker Durnford of the Royal Engineers. To this day it is both an active-duty Canadian Forces base and a monument to the utility of planning for multiple contingencies. Durnford built fortifications on every side of the Citadel. In the event of an attack from the west by Americans, the British garrison could use the fort to defend the good people of Quebec City, a few hundred metres to the east. And in the event the good people of Quebec City decided to revolt against British rule, the officers and men of the British garrison could use the fort to defend themselves against the neighbours. One never does know, does one? Even today, this brutish fortress, carved into a cliff face, is a major challenge to get into. On June 23, 2006, taxi cabs full of visiting reporters had to drive through two thick walls, along narrow streets, stopping three times so their passengers could wave press passes at earnest soldiers. Two dozen protesters waved placards outside the Citadel gate. They might as well have been on Mars.

Five months after his election, Prime Minister Stephen Harper and the ministers of his cabinet had come to the most impenetrable redoubt in the Dominion to celebrate Harper's close relationship with the people of Quebec.

It was the first federal cabinet meeting held in Quebec City since the 1950s. It was the eve of St. Jean Baptiste Day or, as Harper called it, Quebec's "Fête Nationale." On the day itself he would attend a picnic at the home of his industry minister, the strapping libertarian divorcé Maxime Bernier, in the Beauce. Compared to the Citadel, Bernier's house would be a model of openness and accessibility, although there would be a guest list and government staffers to control who got anywhere near the festivities.

But only the logistics of the event bespoke the prime minister's customary fever-pitch wariness at the possibility of being confronted by a surprise or a stranger. The tone of the official communications was jubilant. As indeed it might be. Harper had lasted five months, longer than Charles Tupper, John Turner and Kim Campbell had. Ian Brodie had staged a brief, jokey ceremony in the PMO to mark each of those benchmarks. By October, Harper would outlast Joe Clark, which would mean he need no longer fear going down as the shortest-serving elected prime minister.

What was more, he was building up a record to run on, whenever he would need to. The PMO communiqué from Quebec City noted that "great progress had been made on the issues that matter to Canadians." In "just under five months," the government had passed the Federal Accountability Act through the House of Commons; lowered the GST by one point; introduced legislation "to crack down on street-racing and gun and gang crime"; put in place the "Choice in Child Care" program, which would send parents $100 monthly cheques for each child under the age of six; extended the military mission in Afghanistan; and "ushered in a new era of open federalism, as evidenced by the recent agreement between the Government and Quebec that established a formal role for the province at UNESCO."

If anything, the list of achievements was modest compared to what Harper had actually accomplished to date. On February 21, twenty-nine days after the election, Harper had announced that Kevin Lynch, a former deputy minister at Finance and Industry, would become Clerk of the Privy Council, the head of the federal bureaucracy. Eight days later he confirmed Marshall Rothstein as the first Harper-appointed Supreme Court justice, following quick and genteel vetting of the nominee by a parliamentary committee. In March, Harper had visited Afghanistan, then flown to Cancún for meetings with George W. Bush and Mexican president Vicente Fox. He wore a sportsman's vest over his blue shirt during the photo op, a tour of a Mayan pyramid—precisely the same ungainly get-up Paul Martin had worn during the previous year's Three Amigos summit. The *Globe and Mail* assigned their columnist Leah McLaren to make fun of Harper on the next day's front page. "Stephen darling, can we talk?" the column began. It was the best laugh the press gallery had had since two days after the election, when Harper walked his kids to school and bid nine-year-old Ben farewell with a brisk handshake. Harper took careful note of the mockery. His revenge on the press gallery smart alecks would be a dish served cold and in bulk.

On April 21 Harper announced that Gwyn Morgan, the former EnCana CEO, would lead a Public Appointments Commission to provide "more open, honest and accountable government for Canadians." Three and a half weeks later he scrapped the whole idea of a Public Appointments Commission after the opposition majority backed an NDP motion to brand Morgan "unsuitable" for the job. You see, Morgan had donated to the Conservatives and helped raise funds for them. And he'd given a speech to the Fraser Institute. "The vast majority of violent, lawless immigrants come from countries where the culture is dominated by violence and lawlessness," he'd said in that speech. "Jamaica has one of the world's highest crime rates driven mainly by the violence between gangs competing for dominance in the Caribbean drug trade. Why do we expect different behaviour in Toronto, Ontario, than in Kingston, Jamaica?"

In Calgary, insulting Gwyn Morgan is just not done. Two hours after the committee meeting ended, Harper struck a blow for the oilman's wounded honour by announcing he was scrapping the appointments commission altogether. "Obviously I'm very disappointed with what I think is an irresponsible decision," he said. "Here you have a top CEO in the country and a number of his colleagues who are willing to work for nothing to clean up the appointments process. For partisan reasons, the other parties, the opposition parties, don't want to do that."

But the appointments commission wasn't going away forever. "We won't be able to clean up the process in this minority Parliament," Harper said. "We'll obviously need a majority government to do that in the future. That's obviously what we'll be taking to the people of Canada at the appropriate time."

Remember that last bit. Maybe circle that paragraph if you're not reading a library copy. We'll come back to it later—when there's a majority government.

But back to the cabinet meeting carved into the cliff face. It was artifice designed to portray something real, or something Harper hoped might be real. All by itself, the notion of a "cabinet meeting" in Quebec City was an alluring fiction. Already, Harper was rarely convening his entire cabinet as a deliberative body anywhere, and he would do so more rarely the longer he was in office. The Operations committee met on Mondays to put out fires. Priorities and Planning met on Tuesdays to try to plan stuff. The full cabinet did meet every day at lunch, no exceptions, no exemptions, to rehearse for Question Period. But as a decision-making body "the cabinet" was close to being a white lie.

Bringing them all to the Citadel was for a good cause, though. In these early days Harper was excited about his chances in Quebec. He knew his crew was still strange and new in parts of the province that were more used to voting Liberal or Bloc. He had been lucky so far. He meant to keep pushing his luck.

"The biggest story of the evening of January 23, anywhere in Canada, was the result for our party in the province of Quebec," he had told the Montreal Board of Trade on April 20. "Counted out by almost every observer at the outset, we gained more than a quarter of the Quebec vote, winning the ridings of the outstanding Members of Parliament we have here today, and finishing second in most of the rest."

How did it happen? "No doubt, Quebecers were attracted by elements of our platform," he said. "But I think it is more profound than that. I believe the population understood the real meaning of our slogan—that it is now more than just 'time for a change.' It is time for a new departure toward the future, time to turn the page on history."

The Conservatives' English-language election slogan had been "Stand Up for Canada." In French they had used "Changeons pour vrai"—"Let's Make a Real Change." The change, Harper told the Montreal business swells, was providing a real alternative to "a government that was directionless"—that would be the Liberals—"and an opposition that was useless"—the Bloc Québécois.

Harper estimated that Quebecers, by voting Conservative in modest numbers, had shown they wanted to "turn the page on an era of political polarization." The Liberals believed everything should be run out of Ottawa. The Bloc believed everything should be run out of Quebec City. "The truth is that Quebecers want neither the Liberal view of federalism nor the Bloc view of independence. They've had forty years to adopt one or the other and they aren't going to." As he spoke, the Bloc was just sixteen years old, but never mind. "Quebecers want a stronger Quebec in a better Canada," he said. "This is a message our government has heard. We are going to turn the page. Not just by rejecting separation . . . but by changing the debate, changing the agenda and changing the federation."

All of this was self-serving. It was a political speech, after all. But there was truth to it too, and the speech serves as a useful guide to significant changes Harper would pursue throughout his time as prime minister. It helps explain his attempts to expand the Conservative Party in Quebec, attempts that would often be tentative and hobbled by the way the province made him feel defensive and uncertain. But they also explain his adopted Albertan attitude toward the respective roles of federal and provincial governments, and the steps he would take to change those roles substantially.

First, Harper described his understanding of the "fiscal imbalance" and his plan to correct it. Young people today will have a hard time staying awake while their elders explain to them that in the early years of the twenty-first century every provincial government in Canada was worried about a mismatch between federal and provincial finances. The Chrétien Liberals had run a succession of surpluses. They had used them to increase transfers to the provinces—but only on condition that the provinces accept Ottawa-imposed mandates to run their social programs in ways that pleased Chrétien. Meanwhile most of the provinces were running deficits and didn't know how to dig out of them. Why couldn't the feds simply transfer money and responsibility to the provinces and butt out? "The money is in Ottawa," a succession of provincial treasurers would say, "and the needs are in the provinces."

The Chrétien Liberals said that notion was poppycock. The Martin Liberals said roughly the same. Harper campaigned on a promise to eliminate the fiscal imbalance. At his Board of Trade speech he outlined his plan. First, he would define the fiscal imbalance in ways that were congenial to him. Here he was mightily helped by the fact that the fiscal imbalance was a figment of a few premiers' imaginations. It described the temporary result of several governments' choices, and choices can change. If any of the provinces simply raised their taxes they would have more money without Ottawa's help, whereas if Ottawa cut its own taxes it would eventually run out of money to spread around.

Harper liked the sound of that last bit, the bit about cutting taxes. "Probably the most important fiscal imbalance in this country is between all levels of government and the citizens and businesses of this country, who are all overtaxed," he said. "Under the previous Government, billions upon billions of dollars were taken from Canadians through over-taxation—nothing more, nothing less." Over a decade, "roughly 100 billions of dollars in 'unexpected' surpluses poured into Ottawa." Some of it went to pay down debt, but much went to "off-budget, unplanned and poorly thought out spending, including literally billions in well-known examples of waste, mismanagement and scandal."

Why not leave the money in Canadians' pockets? It could have helped parents buy schoolbooks for their kids. This, Harper said, was why he would cut taxes ("not just the GST, but personal taxes, business taxes, capital gains taxes") in his first budget and as often after as he could.

Harper knew full well that helping parents buy schoolbooks wasn't quite what the premiers had in mind when they started beating the fiscal-imbalance drum. They wanted the federal government to inflate provincial coffers instead of its own, so that provincial governments could impress their electorates. But Harper would not be even a junior-league political strategist if he allowed others to define the problems he wanted to solve. The good news for the premiers was that, on top of tax cuts, he did indeed intend to shift the money balance between Ottawa and the provinces.

"But here in Quebec, fiscal imbalance has attained a significant importance," he said to the Board of Trade. "It is used by those who allege that federalism is detrimental to Quebec's interests. This squabbling has kept the Bloc alive—artificially. But under the new approach to federalism that I'm proposing, Quebec will have its place. And the Bloc? Not so much."

Cool. How?

Harper promised "specific proposals" for the fiscal imbalance within a year. "And let me tell you what those proposals will not include: they will not include increasing federal spending in areas of exclusive provincial jurisdiction."

This was significant. If Harper meant what he was saying—and in the years to come it would become clear that he did, mostly—he was signalling a major shift in federal priorities. Chrétien and Martin had increasingly made highly conditional health-care transfers the focus of their activity, Chrétien grudgingly, Martin with a sort of mad delight. Harper was planning to spend far more than they had on areas of exclusive federal jurisdiction, such as defence and criminal law. He had campaigned on a promise to follow Martin's plan for increasing health-care transfers at a genuinely hectic clip through 2015. But provincial health ministers would soon be delighted to discover he had no intention of policing the forest of strings Martin had hoped to attach to those transfers. Ottawa was out of the business of "buying change," a favoured Liberal-era euphemism for blackmailing provinces into compliance. It was now simply giving money to provinces as it was to parents, trusting in both cases that the recipients would find a good use for it all by themselves.

Harper also talked about providing a seat for Quebec at the Canadian delegation in UNESCO. Two weeks after the Board of Trade speech he would fly to Quebec City to sign an agreement with Jean Charest setting out the terms of Quebec's participation in UNESCO. The coverage of the UNESCO deal would be huge. The ceremony, in the ceremonial Salon Rouge of the National Assembly, would be front-page news. It's the little things that count. And in the mind of Harper's team, UNESCO was definitely a little thing.

"So this idea of the UNESCO thing," a senior Harper advisor said much later. "I don't know where the hell that came from. In a certain sense it was a very convenient idea. Because, really, on the Conservative side of the House of Commons, English-speaking MPs don't give a flying fuck about UNESCO. Really don't give a flying fuck about UNESCO." But Charest wanted to show he could get things done with a new team in Ottawa. So letting Quebec appoint somebody to be the Quebec person in Canada's UNESCO delegation was a fun way to put something nice in the window.

As a bonus, it was perhaps the only way to get English-speaking MPs to pay even passing attention to UNESCO. "The objective, then, in bringing an ambassador to UNESCO is to keep track of the Quebec guy," our senior Harper man says. That is, the Canadian government's UNESCO ambassador would keep an eye on Quebec's provincial representative.

But while the Outremont salon set was busy poring over the fine print of the UNESCO deal, the broadest, most durable elements of Harper's approach to federalism were getting little scrutiny. The GST cuts—a point in 2006, a second point on the way for 2007—durably chiselled away at federal government revenues. Continued transfers to the provinces, growing at a rate far ahead of the general growth of the economy, would take an ever-larger bite out of the feds' ability to spend on anything else.

In 2001, as president of the National Citizens Coalition, Harper, along with five other Alberta conservatives, had famously signed an open letter to Alberta premier Ralph Klein in the pages of the *National Post*. "It is imperative to take the initiative, to build firewalls around Alberta, to limit the extent to which an aggressive and hostile federal government can encroach upon legitimate provincial jurisdiction," this notorious "Firewall Letter" said.

Now, Harper's first two grand economic gestures worked together to implement a variation on the firewall agenda, not by shielding the provinces but by disarming Ottawa. Tax cuts—"the ultimate decentralization"—would ensure that less money ever got to Ottawa. Increased transfers would ensure less of it stayed there long enough to do anything that might annoy the kind of people who write firewall letters.

The Laval University economist Stephen Gordon has written that it was the Martin health-care transfer increases, phased in by Harper on Martin's schedule, and Harper's GST cuts that together eliminated the string of federal surpluses that began in 1998. The GST cuts alone, Gordon wrote, "blew a $12 billion hole in the federal balance that will have to be filled somehow." Or, you know, not. By 2010, federal revenues as a share of GDP would hit their lowest level since 1963.

Like just about every economist in Canada, Gordon was sharply critical of the Harper GST cuts because cutting value-added sales taxes is not the best way to boost productivity. But Harper was not interested in boosting productivity. He was interested in clearing a lot of money out of Ottawa fast. He wanted to do it in a way that would be noticed by voters every single time they acted as consumers; because those consumers had noticed, a future government from another party would not feel able to revoke that cut. If your objectives have more to do with federalism and elections than with productivity, a GST cut is a fine cut indeed.

In 2011, after I began to do some journalism about the combined long-term effects of tax-cuts-plus-transfer-hikes in sucking the activist air out of Ottawa, a long-time Harper associate sent me an e-mail. "You are correct on the PM's desire to reduce successive federal governments' ability to intrude in provincial jurisdiction," my correspondent wrote.

"This is due, in part, to his decentralist convictions (he has never renounced, or even qualified, the firewall letter, to my knowledge). But, more pertinently, it is about his desire to wean Canadians from the Liberal Party and others, like the NDP, who see a strong—and flush—federal government as their personal social-engineering playground. Politically this is working. Witness the last [2011] election, where any grand pronouncements on this front were greeted with the inevitable

'How are you going to pay for it?' The only answers are (1) raise taxes or (2) forgo other federal expenditures. Responses to either one are favourable political ground for the Conservatives—especially in dodgy economic times."

Much of the context for all these decisions came from two big elements of the Liberal legacy that Harper inherited: a healthy federal balance sheet and a huge measure of fatigue with federal-provincial summitry.

"Those were good times," a former senior bureaucrat says. "We were running surpluses and it was clear we were going to have another sizable surplus—probably close to ten billion I think in 2005; 2006 maybe it was thirteen billion-ish—which is pretty good. The government's coming in with this large agenda. It all seemed very affordable at the time, partly because we had this economy running faster than potential."

The result was something approaching giddiness among the new crew. "These were kids in a candy store that had a big allowance. They were saying, 'Well, we can do all this stuff.'" It didn't inspire a lot of caution. In fact there wasn't a lot of patience with people who sounded cautious notes.

"We prepared material on broader issues—productivity issues, fiscal federalism issues like the whole transfer stuff, economic issues," the former bureaucrat said. "They were just like, 'Okay, no, we want to implement our agenda.'"

The so-called challenge function is, of course, central to the work public servants do. A politician has a plan. A bureaucrat implements it—but first, he pushes back, tests the assumptions of the plan, makes sure the politician wants to do what the politician thinks he wants to do. "Fearlessly challenge and faithfully implement" is a watchword in the Canadian public service. With Conservative governments in particular, however, there is at least a veneer of suspicion on the political side about whether the challenges are valid or the implementation faithful: the "permanent government" of the civil service is presumed to be essentially a Liberal government.

But it's easy to overstate the level of animosity. During the Harper years individual Conservative politicians have often formed strong working relationships with their counterparts on the bureaucratic side. And the challenge function could often be exercised without penalty. One of the loudest internal voices pushing back against the Harper clan's early plans was a bright young associate deputy minister of finance named Mark Carney.

"This guy, he was never shy of speaking out," our former bureaucrat says. "I have huge respect for this guy. He was like, 'Do you really need to do the GST? Why not do other things?'"

They were not interested in other things. The 2005 federal budget, the last from Paul Martin as prime minister and Ralph Goodale as finance minister, had called for a series of small income-tax rate cuts. At the lowest rate of taxation, Martin and Goodale wanted to reduce the rate from 16 percent of income to 15 percent. But that cost money, and the Harper crew needed that money to be able to afford their GST cuts. So ironically, in a budget they trumpeted as a tax-cutting triumph, the Conservatives reduced the lowest rate only to 15.5 percent, cancelling half a point of income tax cuts. The Liberals raised a ruckus. But nobody was listening much to the Liberals at that point.

———

Through this intense period of redefining Ottawa's fiscal relations with the provinces, with municipalities and with every Canadian, Harper avoided what had become a familiar mechanism of federal-provincial relations: the big, formal First Ministers' Meeting at which the prime minister would sit down with the premiers while reporters and camera crews stood vigil outside. Harper's goal was that the provinces do more by themselves. He had no particular interest in working with them. On February 24, he had played host to the premiers at

24 Sussex Drive. The three-line news release did everything possible to lower expectations for the event. It noted that premiers would be in Ottawa anyway for a meeting of their own; it said photos could be taken only at the beginning of the dinner; and it used a peculiar verb to describe Harper's role, saying he would "entertain" his guests. When reporters finally caught up to Harper, two weeks after the dinner, he made it clear that any transformation in the relationship would take place on his terms. "I was glad I didn't have my chequebook there," he said of the dinner, "because there were a lot more potential bills being talked about than certainly I could possibly afford to pay or that the taxpayers of Canada could afford to pay."

One of his advisors said: "He had that meeting because he thought he had to, as a new prime minister, to meet everybody. But keep in mind that fresh in everybody's mind—I don't just mean in his mind, everybody in the party, everybody in the Federal-Provincial Relations Office, everybody in the PCO, everybody who would be mobilized for something like that—the most recent thing they had been through was the health deal to save medicare for a generation."

This would be the federal-provincial summit Paul Martin convened four months after the 2004 election. It turned into a bit of a marathon, with Newfoundland premier Danny Williams threatening to walk out. The premiers kept testing how much more money they could get from Martin; the answer was, generally, a little more. To be fair, the summit went a long way toward establishing federal-provincial peace on health funding where there had been little before. But it was still excruciating to watch.

Alex Himelfarb, the outgoing Clerk of the Privy Council, had sat at Martin's right hand in 2004. In 2006 he told Harper not to have another no-holds-barred federal-provincial meeting. "Alex could just barely contain himself with the 'Don't ever do this,'" the former PMO advisor said. Harper's staff told him he needn't worry. Having the gang over for dinner—"entertaining" them—was the closest thing to not having them over at all. "Stephen thought he had to meet everybody at once, if only just to say he'd done it, and he wouldn't have to do it again for a long time," the advisor said.

William Stairs, Harper's communications director (soon to be replaced by Sandra Buckler), was getting questions from reporters about what would be on the menu. He was told to say beef. Not because that was the answer—nobody knew what the chef at 24 Sussex was going to serve, and nobody wanted to bug him about it—but because it was the least interesting possible answer, and everybody around Harper wanted this to be the least interesting possible dinner.

After it was over, Harper implemented his preferred method for dealing with premiers, which was to meet them one at a time and with no fuss. "He made a decision when they came to see us, there wouldn't be any joint press conferences or anything. Nor were we going to have cameras in for photos, generally speaking. Because this was going to be businesslike. And there was going to be differences of opinion and sometimes conflict, and there was no point in playing that up as a great public psychodrama, because in the scheme of things, for most of these things, we were just going to manage through them," the PMO advisor explained.

But there will always be something a leader can't simply manage his way through. Harper's first serious curve ball as prime minister came to him from the Liberal Party. While Harper was making the decisions and establishing the work routines that would define his approach to federalism, the Liberals were holding a campaign to find a replacement for Paul Martin. They were taking their time about it. Harper and Brodie had assumed the Liberals would hurry to have a new leader in place by early autumn 2006. But the party booked a Montreal convention centre for December.

The front-runner was Michael Ignatieff, tall, preppy, handsome from the right angle. A BBC television host, author, journalist and former director of the Carr Center for Human Rights Policy at Harvard. A few Liberals had cultivated him as a sort of greenhouse experiment in twenty-first-century Liberal leadership. Ian Davey, Alfred Apps and Dan Brock had gone to Harvard to tempt Ignatieff into returning to Canada. Peter C. Newman had seeded the news columns of the *National Post* and *Maclean's* with word of his formidable intellect and passion, along with a reminder that the Liberal Party always chooses outsiders to lead it. Outsiders like John Turner and Jean Chrétien and Paul Martin.

To simplify, most candidates for party leadership build their sales pitch around one of three attributes: mastery, authenticity or revolution. A candidate offering mastery is telling party members he can navigate the thickets of Parliament and government better than any rookie. Jean Chrétien claimed mastery when he sought the Liberal leadership in 1990, as did Joe Clark when he returned to the Progressive Conservative leadership in 1998. A candidate offering authenticity is telling the party base he is one of them and will never betray their convictions. Stephen Harper in 2002 offered authenticity. But Ignatieff would have had trouble finding Parliament on a map, and he had supported the Iraq war, which pretty much blew up mastery and authenticity as selling points. So Davey and Apps, who had their own history of estrangement from a succession of Liberal establishments, decided to go with revolution. The Ignatieff team's sales proposition was that only from outside could the Liberal Party be properly shaken up. Accordingly, Ignatieff needed a few ideas that would constitute a proper shaking. Perhaps because he was out of the country when Brian Mulroney's attempts to amend the Constitution to please Montreal newspaper editorialists turned into the Meech and Charlottetown debacles, Ignatieff decided it would be a swell idea to try again.

He was shaky on the details. "To recognize Quebec—and Aboriginal peoples—as nations within the fabric of Canada is not to make some new concession," Ignatieff wrote in a policy book he published during the summer of 2006. "Nor is it a prelude to further devolution of powers." Got that? No new concession, no devolution of powers. A page later, Ignatieff wrote that he expected Canadians would be called upon to ratify "a new constitution" at some point. What would be in it? Hard to say. "The details that must be reconciled in a constitutional settlement are complex."

The Quebec wing of the federal Liberals, divided among several candidates but inclined to prefer Ignatieff's openness over Stéphane Dion's tidier view of federalism, called a special meeting to adopt a resolution endorsing a proposal to recognize Quebec's status that largely echoed Ignatieff's language. The Liberals seemed certain to debate the notion of Quebec as a nation on the floor of their leadership convention in Montreal in early December. Candidates lined up on various sides of the question, with Ignatieff most strongly in favour of recognizing Quebec somehow, in some form, and the essentially unilingual Gerard Kennedy, a late-arriving refugee from Ontario provincial politics, most strongly opposed to any sort of recognition.

There followed a few strange weeks of the kind that have transpired since on other national-unity files. Quebec-based newspaper columnists lined up to savour the corner Ignatieff had painted the Liberals into. What would the Liberals do? How could the Liberals reconcile the heritage of Pierre Trudeau's opposition to Meech and Charlottetown with Ignatieff's bold new initiative to recognize Quebec's "difference"? The spectacle the Liberals were providing was so fascinating to commentators that just about everybody forgot Canada had a government and that it was currently run by the Conservative Party. Stephen Harper, the Conservative leader who was currently serving as prime minister, had a solid track record on the question of recognizing Quebec's otherness. His position could not have been less of a secret. He was against it.

In 1997 the premiers of every province except Quebec had met in Calgary to discuss responses to Quebec separatism. They ended up producing something called the Calgary Declaration, an essentially trivial document that affirmed provincial equality four times before proclaiming that "the unique character of Quebec society" was "fundamental to the well-being of Canada." But the premiers took even that fantastically timid step over Stephen Harper's specific objections.

Harper, recently retired from politics after a single term as a Reform MP and running the National Citizens Coalition, and Tom Flanagan had written a letter to the *Calgary Herald*, published the day before the premiers met. "It's vital not to start drafting legislative resolutions to recognize Quebec as 'distinct' or 'unique' or anything else," they wrote. "No new declarations are needed. Quebec is an integral part of Canada and Canada's treatment of Quebec has been generous without comparison." Harper and Flanagan called talk of Quebec's uniqueness "code for distinct society, and 'distinct society' . . . code for special status."

They were plainly furious with the Quebec Liberal Party (PLQ, then led by Daniel Johnson) for encouraging such talk. "Much evidence suggests that the PLQ is still committed to the strategy that it has executed so successfully for three decades—brandishing the threats of secession made by the separatists in order to extract concessions beneficial to Quebec nationalism." Even today in 1997, they wrote, Johnson "still refuses to sign the Constitution, insists on Quebec's right to sovereign self-determination, and resists federal efforts to make any referendum process abide by Canadian law and the Constitution."

Given that background, Harper's position on the question of Quebec's nationhood might have seemed germane. But it went unasked by reporters and opposition politicians until November 2006, when Bernard Landry, the former Parti Québécois premier, wrote a newspaper article calling on Harper to follow Ignatieff's example. The Liberal pretender "paved the way for you," Landry wrote to Harper. It fell to the Bloc Québécois to force the question by putting the recognition of a Quebec nation to the House of Commons in a votable motion. This they were able to do on one of the regularly scheduled "supply days" when the Commons debates, and sometimes votes on, a topic chosen by an opposition party, not the government.

On November 21, Gilles Duceppe, the Bloc leader, tabled the wording of his motion: "That this House recognize that Quebeckers form a nation."

The following day Harper rose after Question Period, during the slot in the parliamentary day reserved for statements from ministers. "Mr. Speaker," he said, "tomorrow the Bloc Québécois will present the House with an unusual request that we here at the federal Parliament define the Québécois nation. As a consequence, with the support of the government and with the support of our party, I will be putting on the notice paper later today the following motion: 'That this House recognize that the Québécois form a nation within a united Canada.'"

His "preference," Harper said, was to leave it to Quebec's National Assembly to decide how Quebecers should be described. It needn't be Parliament's business, he said. "But the Bloc Québécois has asked us to define this. And perhaps that's a good thing, because it reminds us that all Canadians have a say in the future of this country." Forced to take a position, Harper would take one. "Our position is clear. Do the Québécois form a nation within Canada? The answer is yes. Do the Québécois form an independent nation? The answer is no and it will always be no."

When it came, the final vote would be overwhelmingly in favour. Every Bloc MP voted for Harper's wording. And every Conservative, except Michael Chong and Inky Mark, who abstained. Every Liberal leadership candidate in the House except Ken Dryden. In all, fifteen Liberals voted against the motion. Plus Garth Turner, whose colleagues had evicted him from the Conservative caucus for being a blabbermouth and who would soon join the Liberals.

What the hell happened?

"We'd had internal discussions about, you know, what do we do if Ignatieff brings a motion or the Bloc brings a motion? Will we get cornered on this? And there was nothing conclusive," a Conservative who worked with Harper on a response to the Bloc motion said. "This was discussions at the level of P&P"—the Priorities and Planning committee of cabinet—"or of a few key advisors." These included Dimitri Soudas, the press secretary from Montreal who had been with Harper since 2002, and Paul Terrien, a former Mulroney speech writer who was Lawrence Cannon's chief of staff. "And the tentative conclusion was that, you know, if this happens, we may bite this bullet. It wasn't a definitive decision but there was a feeling that, yeah, we don't want to get cornered on this."

Between the moment the Bloc released the wording of the motion and the moment Harper released his reply, there was about a day. That evening and the next morning Harper consulted with staff, colleagues, outside advisors. He didn't consult his intergovernmental affairs minister, Michael Chong, who spent the evening undisturbed at dinner in the Byward Market with some journalists from *Maclean's* magazine. Chong's job used to be a big deal. Stéphane Dion had it under Chrétien. Joe Clark held a comparable post under Brian Mulroney when that crew was trying to climb out from under the rubble of Meech. As a rookie minister in a rookie cabinet, Chong had gamely set about learning the intricacies of his government's position on the fiscal imbalance. He rather expected to be in the loop on big questions of federal-provincial relations. He was surprised to learn otherwise.

Harper, meanwhile, was warming to the notion of recognizing Quebecers as a nation. Well, not Quebecers, precisely. The Bloc motion had referred to "les Québécoises et les Québécois" in French, and "Quebecers" in English. Harper's version referred to "les Québécoises et les Québécois" in French and "the Québécois" in English.

Keen observers will note that "the Québécois" is not quite English. "Well, I think it means the francophone people historically rooted within the province of Quebec," the Harper advisor said later. "What I think in previous generations you would have called 'French Canadians.'

"What we didn't want to do, and what is, I think, consistent with the PM's history on federalism is, he didn't want to set up a situation where Quebec—as a province, as a legal entity—had a special status compared to anyone else."

The nuance between a "Quebec nation" that included everyone living on Quebec's territory and a "Québécois nation" limited to historic francophones will go sailing over the heads of most readers outside Quebec. But the largest part of the province's intellectual elite had learned, over many years, to insist that Quebec is a civic nation whose population is every person living in Quebec. A year after Parliament passed Harper's resolution, the former Parti Québécois premier Bernard Landry published an op-ed in *Le Devoir* rehashing this argument. It reads today as a sort of museum piece.

"The use of the word 'nous' to designate members of the civic Quebec nation is unavoidable: it encompasses every person of Canadian citizenship . . . living on our territory," Landry wrote. "Only 75,000 or so citizens have another belonging. These are the Amerindians and Inuit [who] have their own nations. . . . All other citizens of Quebec are part of our nation."

Good luck with that. Harper's wording flew in the face of the consensus Landry had spent most of his career trying to build. The Commons motion was a kind of play on words: in seeming to endorse the Bloc/PQ argument that "Quebec" is a nation (with one significant addition, the notion that this nation exists within a "united Canada"), Harper had actually endorsed a much older notion of nationhood. One which, handily, has no legal expression, as there is no "National Assembly of Francophone People Historically Rooted Within the Province of Quebec."

It fell to poor Lawrence Cannon to try to explain all this for the TV cameras. It didn't go well. A reporter asked him if the definition of Québécois could "include every resident of Quebec regardless of which boat their ancestors came over on."

"No, it doesn't," Cannon said. "It doesn't."

So did he mean anglophone Montrealers weren't Québécois? "I didn't say that they're not Québécois. What I'm saying here, and the reference that the Bloc Québécois has made is that they've made the francophone *pure laine*. That's the intention. The intention is to be able to divide. We are taking the same words and we are saying no."

It will do no good to attempt to find meaning in this. Cannon had begun by making sense while saying something deeply impolitic. He quickly changed course until he was safely making no sense at all. Meanwhile, once again we find we have let ourselves get sidetracked. While it's interesting to wonder which Québécois Harper meant to recognize, it's even more intriguing to ask how he could make any such gesture when he had railed against the possibility of such a thing in the not-distant past.

"He had obviously moved a considerable distance in accepting that there was a cultural specificity to Quebec that had to be recognized," the Harper advisor said. "And this was how he felt able to do that."

Were they worried about the flagrant contradiction? You bet. "I think we got away with that more easily than I would have expected. I thought there would have been more [questions like], 'Are we catering to an ethnic nationalism as opposed to a civic nationalism?' But I think just the shock and awe was so great that that debate never happened. People were just stunned that Stephen Harper would in some sense recognize Quebec as a nation. So it didn't get parsed as much."

But was there not a time, and a recent time at that, when Stephen Harper would have been among the people who would have been stunned at what Stephen Harper had done?

"I'm sure if Stephen Harper had [still] been in the National Citizens Coalition [in 2006] he would have been against it."

So how does the Stephen Harper who is no longer president of the National Citizens Coalition sleep?

My interlocutor deemed my question too cynical. "Harper actually has a genuine capacity for growth and change. It's one of his strongest qualities. It's not simple opportunism that he flipped on a dime. He decided, and the party decided a couple of years before, that he was going to have to take a different position on that question than the party would have taken in the '80s or '90s."

Most of the party decided that, anyway. Michael Chong resigned as intergovernmental affairs minister within days. "Everyone was surprised at the stance he took because he was seen as a Red Tory, Joe Clark type, and [pulling the Québécois nation motion out of a hat] was very Joe Clarkish." Harper worried for a while that Chong's resignation would launch him on a new career as an incorrigible backbench critic of the government, but the worry was misplaced. Having made his statement and surrendered his privileges as a cabinet minister, Chong promptly ceased to be any kind of gadfly or pain in the government's backside. And that was as bad as things got for the Conservatives over the Québécois nation resolution.

Coverage of Harper's gesture in Quebec for several days after he introduced the motion was strongly positive. As might be expected of a symbolic act that was designed to have no real-world consequence, this one had no real-world consequence: soon enough, the motion was all but forgotten. Given that the Bloc had hoped to set a trap that would hurt Harper badly, perhaps a transient benefit should be counted as a relative triumph.

As we ponder what led Harper to make a gesture Brian Mulroney might have made, we should consider that one of the strongest influences on him in his first two years in power was Brian Mulroney.

The charm that oozed in industrial quantities from the wily old man was the catalyst for the wary, tentative Harper–Charest friendship. "Mulroney was managing both sides of the relationship, for a whole bunch of reasons," another Harper advisor says, "because he likes Charest and feels an obligation to keep Charest whole for a long-standing loyalty going back to Lucien Bouchard's departure from the PC Party. There's a whole crew of Mulroney-Charest guys with crossover between the two. And Mulroney wanted to rehabilitate what he knows is his otherwise poor reputation in the federal party."

Harper had wanted to feature Mulroney as a keynote speaker at the first Conservative Party policy convention in Montreal in 2005. Mulroney couldn't come but he sent a video. "Stephen was very eager to have Preston and Brian on equal footing," this advisor said, "despite the fact that that was going to piss off some people on the Reform side." Here was an example of Harper's eagerness to ensure that the new party would not seem to be a mere extension of the Canadian Alliance. The same instinct helps explain, for instance, why so few Albertans made it into Harper's cabinet. Mulroney's career had ended poorly. Harper had never liked him in the days before the new party was born in 2004. But for thousands of members of Harper's Conservative Party, Mulroney was practically family, and Harper would treat him as such. Manning, whose supporters needed less flattering and reassuring, could wait.

In April of 2006, when *Corporate Knights* magazine decided to designate Mulroney as Canada's greenest prime minister, Harper ventured across the street from the Langevin Block to the Château Laurier to attend the event. It must have been excruciating. Harper could not have been less interested in having environmental activism recognized as any prime minister's standard of success. But it seemed that if it made Mulroney feel good he would fake it. Manning was holding an event for his Manning Centre for Building Democracy on the same night, in a different ballroom in the same hotel. Harper ignored it.

A few months later, in the summer, Harper invited Mulroney and his family to the prime minister's country residence at Harrington Lake. "This was like the final acceptance," the Harper advisor said. "And Mulroney and Mila and the kids were so effusively grateful to be asked back." It dawned on Harper's crowd, who had not been in power long and weren't sure they'd be in power much longer, what a refuge from the daily stress Harrington Lake was for long-timers. "The Mulroney kids had the fondest memories of Harrington. And they would have liked to have gone back [for a visit] in the Chrétien years, but there was no way Chrétien was going to have them. The family made a huge effort to get there for the weekend they were invited, and enjoyed it hugely. And Mulroney was very thankful to everybody."

Later, Mulroney told Marjory LeBreton, a senator he'd appointed who had gone on to serve in Harper's cabinet, what a wonderful gesture it all was. He told David Angus, another of his Senate appointees. He told Peter MacKay's dad, Elmer, who'd served in his cabinet. He told everybody who would listen how grateful he was to be invited back to his home-away-from-home by the current tenant.

Not all of it was social. Mulroney was far more sure-footed in Quebec than Harper would ever be. He still knew everyone. He persuaded Jean-Pierre Blackburn to run for Harper after a long period out of politics. He was in constant contact with Lawrence Cannon. The seat for Quebec on UNESCO was, as far as anyone could recall, Mulroney's idea. "Harper's Quebec lieutenant for quite a while," the former Harper advisor said, "was effectively Mulroney."

The old charmer's understanding of how people operate in positions of power was exquisite. He would know when Harper's people were having a lousy day. He would call to buck them up. LeBreton, of course, sometimes more than once a day, but Angus, and Rob Nicholson, the justice minister. Ian Brodie's phone rang once and it was Mulroney. "This must be a difficult day to be chief of staff."

Brodie was baffled.

"I just want you to know you did a superb job and Stephen's very lucky to have you." And with that, and a few more pleasantries, the chat was over, the legendary Mulroney hand had reached out, and Brodie was left to contemplate the life he might have led if he had worked for such an extravagantly empathetic boss.

But even a world-class schmoozer like Mulroney could work only limited miracles. Charest is often a loner. Harper usually is. Even a good catalyst can't encourage a reaction between inert elements. When Harper believed he had finally delivered everything Charest wanted, he learned he had not understood much about Charest at all. He didn't like the surprise.

The Harper government's second budget was designed to deliver on the promise of the first. Its title was "Restoring Fiscal Balance." Just as Harper had signalled in his Montreal Board of Trade speech, the budget defined fiscal imbalance broadly, so every move Harper and Jim Flaherty made could be interpreted as a solution to some aspect of the problem. If more money went from Ottawa to the provinces, Flaherty said it settled the imbalance. If money went zooming past the provincial capitals and straight into Canadians' pockets, that settled the imbalance too. If Flaherty announced no new plans in areas of provincial jurisdiction, that was good too.

The main element in the budget package was the recalculation of equalization payments to poor provinces. This had to happen anyway, as equalization payments are calculated for five years at a time and the old five-year plan was running out. So any prime minister would have had substantial news to announce in this budget. Harper had chosen to rejig the formula in ways that disproportionately benefited Quebec, something he could afford to do because British Columbia's improving finances were about to permit it to leave the ranks of equalization-receiving provinces. Harper added increases to the Canada Health and Social Transfer, in line with promises Paul Martin had made at the ramshackle 2005 federal-provincial health-transfer conference. The government threw in some new money for infrastructure programs.

In the end Quebec, with 24 percent of Canada's population, got 46 percent of all the new money Flaherty's budget transferred to the provinces. Ontario, with more than a third of the population, received 24 percent of new money. British Columbia wound up losing $1 million. Of course the reviews in Quebec were ecstatic. *La Presse* columnist Alain Dubuc wrote that the budget "settles the dossier of the fiscal imbalance." It sets out "stable, clear, predictable and equitable" funding and represents "an enormous change of course in Canadian political life." Indeed it did represent a change. Stephen Harper used to complain when governments distributed wildly disproportionate benefits to Quebec. Now he was running a government that was distributing wildly disproportionate benefits to Quebec, and he had no complaints.

At least, not until two days after the budget. That's the day Charest gave his own speech to the Montreal Board of Trade. There was an election campaign on in Quebec, and the Liberal premier was in deep trouble. For once it wasn't the Parti Québécois that was threatening him. It was Mario Dumont's party, the upstart Action Démocratique du Québec. This was Charest's first challenge from the right. He responded by announcing that, if he was re-elected, he would use the fiscal imbalance money from Harper to cut income taxes by $700 million.

"That," one of Harper's staff would say later, "was the end of open federalism."

The whole provincial pitch on the fiscal imbalance, led by Quebec, was that "the money" was in Ottawa, while "the needs" were in the provinces. So Harper sent hundreds of millions to Quebec, which in Charest's best estimation turned out not to have any needs except to cut taxes. The vision of tax relief, offered with the full knowledge that the gesture would be a slap to the Harper government, was not enough to secure Charest a clear win. His Liberals were reduced to a minority in the National Assembly and the ADQ formed the opposition. "From a political perspective, it looks like it didn't help Mr. Charest," Flaherty told *Policy Options* magazine. "It may have in fact harmed his party, and it was not helpful in the rest of the country, certainly from comments that were made across Canada."

The relatively close working relationship between Charest and Harper was shattered. The damage to their relationship was permanent: in the Quebec provincial campaign of 2008, the federal campaigns of 2008 and 2011, and the provincial campaign of 2012, neither would lift a finger to help the other. Harper had worked hard to present a province-friendly face, sharply decentralizing the federation. He had bent his principles into pretzels to appear specifically Quebec-friendly. He had cultivated a close working relationship with the man he often called "the most federalist Quebec premier of my lifetime." And it had led to a nasty surprise from a politically weakened premier.

Harper and Charest would still talk, but the special relationship was over. And soon, Mulroney's own past would come back to haunt him in a way that would lead Harper to shun his predecessor and, crucially, to stop seeking his advice about a province Harper otherwise did not know well himself.

As he often did, Harper gave this personal snub a partisan interpretation. Conservatives in Ottawa started to remind one another that most members of the Quebec Liberal Party voted Liberal federally as well. Maybe it was time to try a new partner.

On December 9, 2007, Harper gave a speech to a business crowd in Rivière-du-Loup, northeast of Quebec City. It was Mario Dumont's riding, and the young conservative opposition leader was present. Reaching out publicly to Charest's most prominent political opponent was more than payback. It was Harper's attempt to build a more genuinely conservative base for Conservatives in Quebec. But his streak of bad luck in that province hadn't run out yet.

FOUR
THE GREEN SHIELD

By Sunday afternoon, October 15, 2006, the candidates
for leader of the Liberal Party had been nice to one another all
summer and they had had just about enough of it. Party leadership
contests have a dependable story arc. They begin with protestations
of goodwill and end in appalling mudslinging. It's the arithmetic
product of human nature and the certainty that only one candidate
can have the prize.

On this particular sunny Sunday the candidates converged on Roy
Thomson Hall for their last official debate before delegates would
choose a new leader in December. The crowd that filled the King Street
concert hall to watch them fairly glittered. Toronto Liberals are always
different from Liberals elsewhere because more of them have gone
straight from power to money. Many have followed a tour of duty in
Bytown with a soft landing on Bay Street, at Queen's Park, or, at the
very worst, at Massey College, to pursue a genteel afterlife as a deal
broker, visiting fellow or general-purpose layer-on of hands.

Of the brochette of aspirant leaders on the Thomson Hall stage, Michael Ignatieff was the acknowledged front-runner, a fine-looking lug with a soft-focus reputation as a public intellectual with an international background in safari jackets and faculty lounges. But he had made things interesting by putting blood in the water. His own. In the summer a shooting war between Israel and Hezbollah in Lebanon had killed hundreds, including dozens of civilians in an apartment building in Qana, a village in south Lebanon. Ignatieff's first public comment on the slaughter was weirdly insouciant. "Qana was, frankly, inevitable," he told the *Toronto Star*. "This is the kind of dirty war you're in when you have to do this and I'm not losing sleep about that."When many Liberals managed to take that poorly, he essayed some equally clumsy damage control. On October 8, on the wildly popular French-language Radio-Canada talk show *Tout le monde en parle*, he buffed his credentials—"I was a professor of human rights, and I am also a professor of the laws of war"—before delivering what he apparently intended as an expert opinion: "and what happened in Qana was a war crime. And I should have said that. That's clear."

For his pains, Ignatieff lost the public support of a Jewish MP from Toronto, Susan Kadis, and he showed up at Roy Thomson Hall shaken and defensive. His rivals came with the sense that Liberals' allegiances were up for grabs in a way they hadn't been until now. They fell on one another like dogs.

During an exchange on foreign policy, Ignatieff inexplicably decided this was a good week to accuse his old college roommate Bob Rae of flip-flopping. On Afghanistan, Ignatieff said, "I actually don't know where you stand."

Rae drew himself up to his full five and a half feet. "For a guy that's changed his mind three times in a week with respect to the Middle East . . ."

With that the hostilities were engaged. The surprise scrapper of the afternoon was Stéphane Dion. The political scientist son of a political scientist, the owlish and intermittently comprehensible Dion had done yeoman work as Jean Chrétien's national-unity enforcer before recycling himself as Paul Martin's environment minister. Dion often presented as an A student on every subject in the world except English syntax and political strategy, but there was a clever design to his work that day. Appearing before the Liberal Party's landed gentry, he sought to position himself as the only real Liberal in a field that included a Harvard Yard expat, a Habs goalie and the man whose 1990 Ontario election victory had ended David Peterson's career as the province's first Liberal premier since the Second World War.

That would be Rae. It was okay "to make errors because you have heart, because you have a conscience," the former New Democrat said in reference to the smoking crater in which he had left the province's economy in 1995.

Dion saw his chance. "When Jean Chrétien and Paul Martin decided to put the fiscal house in order, they had compassion, Bob. They had compassion." Point made: Rae defended a failed NDP government. Dion defended Liberals.

Then Ignatieff, Dion and Ken Dryden faced off on the environment. Ignatieff had all kinds of proposals, including one for a carbon tax that would discourage burning fossil fuels by making it more expensive. Dion had adapted to his role as the Martin government's chief environmentalist with an ardour that was genuinely surprising. And while he had never put it this bluntly, he had long believed that if he was right about something, nobody else could be right about it too. So he was sure there was no need for what Ignatieff was proposing. Plus, today was "I'm a Real Liberal Day." "You need to pay tribute to what the former government has done," Dion told Ignatieff.

"Stéphane, we didn't get it done," Ignatieff said, accurately: greenhouse gas emissions had soared, instead of declining, since Chrétien had made Canada the ninety-eighth country to ratify the Kyoto Accord at the end of 2002. "We didn't get it done and we have to get it done and we have to understand—"

"This is unfair," Dion cut in. For a moment he appeared to have nothing more to say.

Flummoxed, Ignatieff repeated his point. "We didn't get it done!" he said, left fist hammering each word in the air.

"You don't know what you speak about," Dion said. "You don't know what you speak about. You think it's easy to make priorities?" The crowd erupted in applause, although perhaps they were applauding different things. Ignatieff's boldness? Dion's intransigence? Were some clapping to make this seem like a happy room and to make it harder for either man to say any more? Applause by itself offers only punctuation, not text.

———

The next morning in the Langevin Block in Ottawa, Patrick Muttart had a brief chat with Ian Brodie. Muttart had pulled Greg Weston's *Ottawa Sun* column about the Roy Thomson Hall debate from the morning press clippings. Weston was one of the media voices Brodie's PMO paid close attention to. He was no great admirer of the Harper government, but he had an unerring ability to spot what mattered in the daily avalanche of stuff that never would. Muttart had circled the seventh paragraph of this morning's Weston column and showed it to Brodie: "But most of all, over the course of two hours, the Liberals provided ample television footage the Conservatives can use to smear the next Liberal leader—whoever it may be—in an election probably only months from now."

Muttart, a methodical man, had already set his staff to archiving video of the debate, time-logged according to speaker and target. Perhaps it would come in handy.

The Conservatives watched the protracted Liberal leadership race with a kind of amazement. Harper had been elected with the weakest minority in history, thirty seats shy of a majority—rather, twenty-nine once the Liberal Peter Milliken returned as Speaker. Harper had a cabinet of rookies. Surely he was vulnerable. Surely, sensing this, the Liberals would replace Martin as quickly as possible. In the early days Brodie had worried that Martin would reconsider his retirement—or that the party would turn again to Jean Chrétien.

Instead, the Liberals took nearly a year to find a replacement for Martin. So by the time Dion became Liberal leader on the fourth ballot on December 2, 2006, the Conservatives were ready for the new leader.

Well, they would have been if the Liberals had picked Rae. The Conservatives had really hoped the Liberals would pick Rae.

"I was surprised when we did the research at how much people knew, or remembered or thought they remembered—what a strong view people had of what Bob Rae was like as a premier," one of Harper's advisors said. "Even outside of Ontario." Rae ran a rookie one-term NDP government during a deep recession with high unemployment. Near the end of his run, he managed to alienate the NDP voter base with tough public-sector cost-containing measures, so that by the time he was turfed in 1995 just about nobody in Ontario liked him. There were good reasons why Ontario had been a hard province for anybody to govern in the early 1990s, but the one who had the job was Rae and he was still paying the price in public perception.

Dion, on the other hand, was a near unknown. After more than a decade in public life he had led few Canadians to form an opinion about him. "And we were worried," said the Harper advisor. "For the people who knew him in the public—which was, again, a small chunk—they thought he was basically honest. 'Corrupt Liberals' was a critical piece of branding for us. So the fact that he was basically honest and not involved in any of the sponsorship stuff in any way was a huge threat to our brand against the Grits."

The few who knew anything about Dion were more likely to admire him. Francophone voters in Quebec, the Conservatives found, were willing to hear Dion make a case for himself. Ontarians were always worried, more than Canadians in other provinces, about Quebec's place in or out of Confederation. "People [in Ontario] who were potential Liberal voters but could be Conservative voters under different circumstances, they thought, 'Oh well, they've got a franco guy and he's a serious player on the national unity file. We've gotta give him a chance to show his thing.'"

Taken together, these two vague notions that a few voters had about Dion contained the seeds of trouble for the Conservatives. A Dion-led party would be harder to depict as crooked. And it would be seen as one that could defend Canada in a unity crisis. "It's a very small piece of the population," the Harper advisor continued. "But if those had grown, we were in trouble. And so we had to get ahead of that. We had to get ahead of that."

Somebody was going to tell Canadians who Stéphane Dion was, and the Harper crew decided it was going to be them. "We had to create the persona of Stéphane Dion," the Harper advisor said. "Like, we were going to do it or they were going to do it."

The party Dion had inherited was strongly counselling him to do the defining, and fast. In an article in the November 2008 issue of *Policy Options* magazine, Steven MacKinnon, a former Liberal Party national director, wrote that a group of party brass had handed Dion a proposed transition plan almost immediately after he became leader. In the report, Liberal admen recommended that the new leader "undertake an immediate advertising campaign to 'introduce' himself or herself to Canadian voters, define his or her priorities and contrast his or her record with that of the governing Conservatives," MacKinnon wrote. "This recommendation prophetically predicted that the new leader would face a 'race to the frame' against an anticipated Conservative onslaught of negative advertising." The Liberals had the resources to make such a move: the Liberals ended 2006 "firmly in the black," MacKinnon wrote, thanks largely to convention revenues.

And the race to define Dion was truly a race, because the Conservatives were beginning from a standing start. They had had the elements of an anti-Rae campaign in place before the December convention. The ad scripts wrote themselves. Dion took more study, and the first ads against him did not run until January 28, 2007, nearly two months after he won his new job.

The ads were simplicity itself: footage of the Ignatieff–Dion confrontation at Roy Thomson Hall, with Dion's lines spelled out on the screen, partly because the Conservatives believed most listeners wouldn't understand Dion's accented English. "This is unfair," the words on the screen said, and "Do you think it's easy to make priorities?" A stern voice concluded: "Leaders set priorities. Leaders get things done. Stéphane Dion is not a leader."

Soon after the ads started running, the Canadian Press reported on a Decima poll about perceptions of the Conservative image campaign. The article suggested that the poll showed the ads were a dud, but it's hard to read the numbers that way. A week after the ads began, 38 percent of respondents reported seeing them. That's a huge number. Of course seeing isn't always believing. Only 22 percent of respondents said the ads were fair, and only 26 percent said the ads would affect their vote. Perhaps some people who saw the ad decided they would never vote Conservative again. Probably most of the rest who said the ad would affect their vote were already going to vote Conservative and had simply had their choice confirmed. But the goal of any single campaign tactic is not to change each of the next hundred voters' choices. It's a good day at the office if you can shave off one or two in a hundred. Large clusters of ridings can swing from one side to another on margins of a few hundred votes out of tens of thousands.

In the end, Dion would ignore the party panel's advice. There would be no Liberal ads to define the new leader. The frame he sat in would remain the one designed and built for him by the Conservative Party skunkworks.

But the "not-a-leader" ad has been talked to death elsewhere. At least as important in Harper's response to Dion's rise was a quiet ceremony at Rideau Hall on January 4, 2007, nearly a month before the ads hit the air.

"The public's been clear to us, they want [the environment] to be a priority," Harper told reporters outside Rideau Hall after his first cabinet shuffle. "I think it should be a priority, a priority for my children and grandchildren as much as anyone else's."

He would not actually have grandchildren for years, if ever. But today he had a new justice minister, Rob Nicholson. Vic Toews had moved from justice to president of the Treasury Board. Monte Solberg and Diane Finley had swapped portfolios, so she was now in charge of immigration and he took over human resources. And more significant than any of that, John Baird was his new environment minister.

Harper shunted Rona Ambrose, the incumbent in the environment portfolio, to intergovernmental affairs to make room for Baird. As Mike Chong had already discovered, being intergovernmental affairs minister in Harper's government was tantamount to not being a cabinet minister at all. For the next two years, teams of bloodhounds would have trouble finding any trace of Ambrose.

In Harper's eyes Ambrose, a poised and efficient Edmontonian not yet forty, had done nothing wrong. But understandably enough, she had become associated with the Conservatives' environmental policy. That policy had essentially no fans. The Conservatives now faced an opponent who would lead with his environmental policy. Ambrose had become inconvenient.

"Our initial plan was to focus on pollution as opposed to carbon emissions," a senior Conservative who worked on the Harper government's various early environmental policies said. "Focus on NOx and SOx"—nitrogen oxides and sulphur oxides—"and the actual pollutants that cause smog. Bring in a much more vigorous program on that, [a program] we felt people actually cared about more because it affected people directly."

What the Conservatives soon discovered was that reducing industrial pollutants brought few political rewards at considerable economic cost. Environmental groups had had to fight hard enough to get Chrétien, and then Martin, to take the Kyoto Accord's targets for aggressive reductions in carbon emissions seriously. They were not impressed by a government that proposed to ignore carbon and go after airborne pollutants instead. "We would have been charging a lot of chemical companies, coal producers, and so on huge dollars to make these [pollutant] reductions," the senior Conservative said. "And we would not have been getting any credit from environmental groups."

Unfortunately the Conservatives figured all of this out after Ambrose had made her big move. In October 2006 she introduced her Clean Air Act, Bill C-30. Every opposition party announced it would vote against the bill. Ottawa went through one of its periodic frenzies of election speculation. Jack Layton persuaded Harper to send the bill to a special committee for review. There it was amended until it was unrecognizable, as the combined majority of opposition MPs wrote whatever they liked into the bill. Eventually it would become clear that Ambrose's Clean Air Act, like her career as the government's environmental champion, was over.

Baird wasted no time arguing that his appointment indicated Harper was now going to take the environment seriously. In an interview on CBC Radio's *The House* two days after the Rideau Hall ceremony, he called climate change "one of the biggest challenges facing the world. . . . It requires collective action. It requires Canada to do its part."

Many Canadian voters, and many Conservative supporters among them, were certain there was no long-term trend toward warmer temperatures. Others believed that if there was, human activity had nothing to do with it. Still others believed that even if the sum of human activity was warming the atmosphere, nothing a small population like Canada's could do would change things. Around the cabinet table itself, a Harper advisor said, "there was a mix of views, some of them quite grey," on the validity of climate science.

But Baird would have none of that skepticism. "I think the overwhelming majority of the science, you know, says that this is a huge problem. We accept that and we want to take action."

Within days, Baird was in Vancouver meeting with the leadership of Canada's environmentalist movement, including Greenpeace Canada, Pollution Probe, the Pembina Institute and the David Suzuki Foundation. The news release announcing the meeting was full of chirpy quotes from the minister. "Environmental groups are important to Canada's New Government's efforts to achieve shared environmental goals," he said. "Furthermore, the millions of Canadians who are members of these organizations are instrumental in helping Canada develop environmental citizenship across the nation."

A month after his appointment, Baird was in Paris to receive the Fourth Assessment Report of the Intergovernmental Panel on Climate Change. This in itself was quite a turnabout. One of Ambrose's first acts as environment minister had been to remove previous IPCC reports from Environment Canada's website. Now Baird had penetrated the sanctum sanctorum of global-warming orthodoxy. "It is clear that the science is speaking to us," he said in Paris. "It is saying that climate change is real, and that climate change is here. I get it."

Whether he got it was actually pretty much beside the point. The point was that the leader of the opposition wouldn't stop talking about climate change and Baird and Harper were worried people were listening. In Hollywood, Al Gore, who had won the popular vote in the 2000 presidential election, was nominated for an Oscar for best documentary for his climate-change movie, *An Inconvenient Truth*. "This has become a bigger problem," Baird said in his CBC Radio interview, "not just environmentally but also with the general public."

So until the extent of the Dion menace was clear, Harper would change his tune on global warming. The goal was not to persuade committed green voters that their next vote should be Conservative. It was to blunt the combined opposition parties' attack.

The environment, a senior staffer for one Conservative minister said, was a classic shield issue for the party. Harper and much of the government's senior staff talked in terms of "sword" and "shield" issues. "Issues that we can win on, those are sword issues," the staffer said. "There's issues that, even if we're talking about them, they're largely defensive issues that if we're not careful, you lose on them. Crime, jobs, the economy, managing government, all that stuff is sword issues. First nations, environment, health, health care, human resources, unemployment insurance, those are shield issues." Normally, the rule with shield issues was simple: stay away. "You start talking about that shit, no good's going to come from it." But a shield must sometimes be raised to fend off an opponent's attack. This, they felt, was one of those times.

Baird was handy with a shield. In Question Period he was quick with a snippy rejoinder to any opposition question, and while it was almost impossible to get actual information from him during the daily forty-five-minute jousting sessions, it was equally hard for Liberals and New Democrats to rattle him. Most important, he had paid his dues. In 1984 he had fought in the battle to select a Progressive Conservative nominee for the federal election in Nepean-Carleton, supporting Kay Stanley, whose sister was Marjory LeBreton. Stanley lost the nomination but Baird had tasted enough of politics to know he loved it. In 1995 he ran provincially in Nepean. He won and became the youngest member of the Ontario legislature just as Mike Harris became premier. By 1999 he was in Harris's cabinet. It's probably fair to say that during his stint in provincial politics he became more conservative: although in 1985 he had supported Roy McMurtry, the most moderate of candidates to succeed Bill Davis as Ontario Conservative leader, in 2003 he supported Jim Flaherty, the most conservative of the candidates to replace Harris.

Perhaps it's significant that candidates Baird backed didn't often win. A losing streak is handy in politics, because it cements conviction and toughens the hide. It may raise questions about your judgment, but at least it suggests that you're not in politics for the sole purpose of hitching your wagon to the next sure thing. And it does wonders for your sense of gratitude when you finally discover you've managed to pick a winner. In 2006 an old acquaintance of Baird's spotted him on his way into Hy's and asked how he had managed to land such key roles in Harper's government. Baird's reply, as recounted by this acquaintance: "I just said yes to everything that I was ever asked to do."

When Harper ran for the leadership of the united Conservative Party in 2003 and the Harper campaign asked Baird to introduce Harper at a campaign event, Baird said, sure thing. The moment had more significance than it might seem to. Baird's colleague in the Harris cabinet, Tony Clement, was running against Harper. His old boss, Mike Harris, supported Belinda Stronach. Baird was siding with Harper against his own Ontario network. When Harper asked him to serve as Ontario co-chair for the leadership campaign, he agreed to do that too. In 2006 he agreed to run for Parliament. By then, with John Tory leading the Ontario Conservatives nowhere in particular, Baird was looking for somewhere else to shine. Finally, when Dion made environment the most delicate portfolio in government, Baird didn't hesitate to accept Harper's latest request. And if the moment demanded that Baird become someone who "gets it" about "one of the biggest challenges facing the world" as he helped Canada "develop environmental citizenship across the nation," well, who was he to say no?

Only five years earlier, when Baird had been Ontario energy minister, he'd showed up at a Queen's Park reception thrown by an anti-Kyoto lobby group, the Canadian Coalition for Responsible Environmental Solutions, which was organized by a former Mike Harris chief of staff now working for National Public Relations, Guy Giorno. A Greenpeace activist who snuck into the reception wrote in Toronto's *Now Magazine* that "a particularly passionate" Baird "made his anti-Kyoto rallying cry." But that was then. Times had changed.

Leaders who demand loyalty, and followers who display it, are easy to mock because loyalty necessarily involves giving up a measure of freedom. There can be no grace in a politician who always hurries to endorse whatever the boss just said. But loyal followers are the only force-multiplier a politician has. They can go where he can't, see what he doesn't, spread his message, amplify his action. Harper had particularly good reasons to put loyalty ahead of other virtues in deploying his lieutenants.

First, he had that lousy minority. Others might forget how weak his numeric position in the Commons was. He never would. His caucus would have enough trouble even if it stuck together.

Second, the writings of Brimelow and Kristol had taught him to expect he would be surrounded by a New Class of bureaucrats, academics and pundits, casually and implacably opposed to anything he wanted to do. The first several months in Ottawa hadn't done much to suggest to him that Brimelow and Kristol were wrong.

Third, if by the late 2000s anyone should have learned the value of loyalty, it was a Canadian prime minister. There were plenty of examples of how badly things could go wrong if a leader couldn't trust his people. Chrétien and Mulroney had been able to survive against all external adversaries. But each was brought down by a challenger from his own ranks. Mulroney brought Lucien Bouchard into politics in 1988 to serve as his Quebec lieutenant. Two years later, Bouchard blew up Mulroney's Quebec caucus and wrecked his party's electoral chances in Quebec, and if it was conviction more than ambition that made him do it, that was slim consolation to Mulroney or to Progressive Conservatives. Chrétien and Paul Martin made a formidable team for twelve years after Chrétien stomped Martin on the first ballot at the 1990 leadership convention. When Martin finally got tired of waiting for the top job to open up, he turned the Liberal Party against its leader. The infighting wound up costing the party more than a fresh face was worth. Harper concluded he must never let a Paul Martin rise too high within his own party.

Finally, Harper knew the damage a disloyal lieutenant could do to a leader because for years that was the kind of lieutenant he'd been.

Preston Manning's memoir of his years as Reform Party leader, *Think Big*, is in part a chronicle of Stephen Harper's troublemaking years. At almost every turn, if Harper felt that Manning was making a bad decision, the young renegade felt free to agitate against his leader, whether through rebellious action or indiscreet communication. When Manning took a long time deciding whether to support the Charlottetown constitutional amendments in 1992, Harper, who was sure Manning shouldn't, chafed at the boss's indecision. "When these internal disagreements were eventually leaked to the media—as such disagreements invariably are—they gave our opponents fresh ammunition," Manning wrote. "'Friendly fire' invariably attracts 'enemy fire.'" When Manning hired Rick Anderson, a Liberal-connected Charlottetown supporter, as Reform's national campaign director, Harper objected and was "prepared to air his objections in the media."

In 1994 two *Globe* columnists, "fed by a disgruntled caucus member," wrote columns that alleged Manning was abusing his parliamentary expense account. During the Easter break from Parliament, "Stephen Harper and several other caucus members went public with their criticism," Manning wrote. "Even though procedures existed for handling any complaints . . . Stephen went to the media."

There followed a special caucus meeting and several rounds of internal finger-pointing. Manning's relations with his wife, Sandra, at whom "part of Stephen's attack had been directed," suffered. She felt he hadn't done enough to defend her.

"This whole issue—which really wasn't about expenses at all—was the most painful experience our family had endured to date," Manning wrote. "What made it particularly hard to endure was that it was initiated not by an external opponent, but by one of our own." If being a Member of Parliament meant his family would be attacked, Manning wanted no part of it. "That night, I took off my House of Commons pin—given only to MPs—threw it into my briefcase, and never put it on again until the day I left Parliament."

So yeah, Harper liked Baird, because for all his pluck, the thing he resembled least was a young Stephen Harper.

Within four months Baird had developed a new environmental policy that, at least rhetorically, reversed the order of priorities in Ambrose's doomed attempt. In Toronto on April 26, 2007, he released "Turning the Corner: An Action Plan to Reduce Greenhouse Gases and Air Pollution." At last the Conservatives were giving climate change top billing. Baird said his plan would "force industry to reduce greenhouse gases and air pollution."

Canada "needs to do a U-Turn," Baird went on, "because we are going in the wrong direction. Since the Liberals promised to reduce greenhouse gases in 1997, they have only gone up." He promised "tough industrial regulations" as a centrepiece of this effort. Finally, the rubber was going to meet the road. No messing around. Real business. Really. No fooling. Total serious face.

It was all baloney. What I'm about to write will ruin the suspense, but in October 2011, Scott Vaughan, the federal commissioner of the environment and sustainable development, released a report called

"Climate Change Plans Under the Kyoto Implementation Act." Vaughan found that Baird's 2007 release of "Turning the Corner" was the high-water mark of federal rhetorical ambition on greenhouse gases, and that Baird and his successors had proceeded methodically to ratchet down their ambition and action ever since.

The centrepiece of "Turning the Corner" was those tough industrial regulations Baird mentioned, in the form of the proposed "Regulatory Framework for Industrial Greenhouse Gas Emissions." It would have been so amazing, guys. It would have set short-, medium- and long-term targets for "emission intensity," a measure of emission per unit of energy output. It would have provided compliance mechanisms that gave firms a range of options for meeting their targets. This unprecedented— really, magical—mix of tough targets and comfy enforcement was, Vaughan wrote, supposed to reduce greenhouse gas emissions by about 164 million tonnes by 2012.

In the end it would never be implemented. After an extended display of bravado, Environment Canada finally announced in 2010 that it would ignore its own promises regarding a Regulatory Framework "due to a decision to align Government of Canada actions to address climate change with those of the United States." By then, it was clear that the Obama administration's actions to address climate change would be sufficiently close to non-existent that Canada could safely align with them.

In addition to the 164 million tonnes of reductions from the framework that was never implemented, Baird in 2007 was counting on a further 80 million tonnes of reductions from a $1.5-billion Clean Air and Climate Change Trust Fund, which, Vaughan wrote after the money vanished without a trace, was designed to provide "federal funding to provinces and territories for GHG emission reduction measures." Again in 2010, Environment Canada finally admitted a pretty big design flaw in the Trust Fund: "Because the fund was established on an arm's-length basis, provincial and territorial governments were not required to report to the federal government on how the resources were used,"Vaughan wrote. "Therefore the impact of the fund on GHG reductions could not be assessed."

So the Framework provided no framework and the Trust Fund displayed a culpable excess of trust. In the end, the Trust Fund functioned as the much larger GST cut had done: it succeeded in getting money out of Ottawa. What happened after it left was, to Harper's mind, none of Ottawa's business. It should have been called the Decentralized Federalism Trust Fund, but in 2007, making it sound green was important for the purposes of shield politics.

The most generous possible measure of the Harper government's ambition on climate change—the friendliest way to measure whether Harper "got it," whether his government was providing "environmental citizenship" as a priority for Harper's children and grandchildren as much as anyone else—was the total amount of its own greenhouse gas reduction targets. This is not even a measure of actual reductions; it's just a record of how much the government said it wanted to reduce emissions. Vaughan found that between 2007 and 2010, the Harper government's total expected greenhouse gas emission reductions had fallen from 282 million tonnes to 28 million tonnes, a reduction of 90 percent.

Eight weeks after Vaughan released that report, Canada formally withdrew from the Kyoto Protocol.

But now we are well ahead of ourselves. Through 2007, John Baird would tell you he was a full-bore environmental crusader. Dion, in contrast, was trying to figure out his own climate change policy.

———

It was one of Dion's particularities that if you suggested something to him that was not already on his mind, he would disagree immediately and forcefully. Most times he would also say you were reckless to propose whatever you had just suggested. It was entirely possible that, after retreating to his corner to think for a bit, he would change his mind. But first he had to persuade himself that the idea he had rejected was not only an excellent idea, but that it was his own.

The Liberal leader spent the first half of 2007 going through this odd dance with regard to the most important issue he could imagine, global warming. There was no record of climate change skepticism in Dion's past, no indication that he had surrounded himself with global warming deniers, no doubt that he really did believe this was a challenge that faced this generation and engaged generations to come. But there remained the question of what to do about it.

During the leadership campaign, Ignatieff had proposed a carbon tax. As policy tools go, this one is simplicity itself: for every tonne of hydrocarbon-based fuel you burn, you pay a set supplementary cost. Businesses doing what businesses do, trying to contain costs, will suddenly become way more interested in burning less carbon and figure out ways to accomplish that goal. Dion didn't like the idea, largely because it came from Ignatieff. He preferred a cap-and-trade system. It's a little trickier. Everybody in a given sector is given a limit to the quantity of hydrocarbons they can burn. A business that exceeds its limit can buy permission to keep going by purchasing carbon credits from another firm that hasn't yet hit its cap. This produces a commodities market in which the commodity being traded is the right to burn fuel. Burning fuel is free, or at least devoid of supplementary cost, until the moment you hit your cap. Then it becomes expensive. As an extra incentive, if you ensure you'll never hit your cap, you can sell your unused permissions to some more profligate neighbour.

Dion, as a former environment minister who had named his family dog Kyoto and built his leadership campaign on environmental awareness to such an extent that his supporters at the convention wore green scarves, had thought this all through and decided what the best policy would be, and that was that. Just kidding. No, what he really did was spend the first half of 2007 sending out mixed messages.

On March 1, as he left the Commons after Question Period, Dion was asked whether he was considering a carbon tax. "We have a set of possibilities, and it's a possibility," he said. The next day his office sent out a news release. It promised that whatever Dion proposed would be "bold," but added, "What we are considering is not a carbon tax."

On March 16 he proposed a modified cap-and-trade system. Instead of allowing open-market trading of emissions credits, a Liberal government would set fines for each tonne of emissions over a business's cap. The money would go into an account to finance green projects. What was the cap? Nothing gentle here: the cap would be 6 percent below the 1990 emissions level for the largest industrial sectors. When would the system be implemented? January 1, 2008: in less than a year.

The date contained a built-in assumption: that an election was imminent. It had been a constant assumption on Parliament Hill at every moment from 2006 forward. The new wrinkle in this spring of 2007 was that many thought Harper would do something to provoke the election himself. A "poison pill," maybe, something crazy in the budget that the opposition parties couldn't stomach. Something.

As is so often the case when everyone in Ottawa knows something, it wasn't true. Three years of minority government had given the capital a case of chronic jitters that had blown out the Hill's political radar, to the extent it has ever had one. Harper's interest lay not in hurrying an election but in delaying one. The Conservatives' research showed that voters they considered gettable in 2006 but who hadn't voted for them had resisted, in many cases, because they worried about a hidden Conservative agenda. Those worries were receding at a glacial pace as Harper showed his governing style. As a handy bonus, while he was calming swing voters, he was getting to make the dozens of decisions a day that only a prime minister can make.

Others could have their revolutions. Harper had never had the luxury of overwhelming force, but he had no faith in its efficacy in any case. He had seen revolutions—most recently Mike Harris's in Ontario—undone. He was an incrementalist to the bone, a Burkean conservative who had come of age in the Alberta of Lougheed and Klein, a diligent student of how Liberals win and make change. He would make his own change, not by revolution or even really by evolution, but by erosion.

There were a lot of other details to Dion's climate change plan—with Dion, there were always a lot of other details—but the modified cap-and-trade system was the gist of it. "It's time for us to be a leader again," Dion said.

But being a leader was really hard. Not for "us," but for him. As the spring of 2007 gave way to summer, Dion found it increasingly difficult to establish himself as the Liberals' leader. A brief period of rosy polls turned out to be a sugar high from the party's excellent Montreal convention. The Conservative ads that quoted Ignatieff heckling Dion at Thomson Hall had the desired effect, grinding a few points off Liberal support. Ignatieff's presence in the ads produced a handy side effect, one that Conservative strategist Patrick Muttart had very much intended: it kept Dion loyalists wondering whether Ignatieff could be trusted, and most other Liberals wondering whether there was any point being a Dion loyalist when Ignatieff was handy.

The summer of 2007 was not conducive to renewed Liberal solidarity. The leadership candidates had spent themselves into wild amounts of debt, so they all worked the summer barbecue circuit doing debt-retirement benefits. Which meant that most weeks, if Dion wasn't in your hometown, Rae or Ignatieff or Gerard Kennedy might drop by.

For the leader that steady annoyance was relieved in September when he was given something worse to worry about.

The venue was Outremont, a mostly refined and leafy enclave north of downtown Montreal, an area the Liberals had held since time immemorial, except for a Conservative interlude from 1988 to 1993. The riding's incumbent, broadcaster Jean Lapierre, quit politics to return to his first love, schmoozing, almost as soon as Dion became leader. Harper called by-elections for September 17 there and in two other Quebec ridings.

Dion was deluged with free advice about who his candidate should be in Outremont. Liberal grandees told him he could bring the riding's old standard-bearer, former justice minister Martin Cauchon, back. Marc Garneau, the astronaut, made it known he'd love the riding. But Dion had his own idea: he would find a bespectacled academic. Who didn't love a bespectacled academic? Dion appointed Jocelyn Coulon, a foreign-policy analyst and former writer of columns for *Le Devoir* that even *Le Devoir* readers didn't read, as the party's candidate. When the ballots were counted, Coulon had lost by more than four thousand votes to Thomas Mulcair, a prickly veteran of Quebec provincial politics who became Montreal's first NDP Member of Parliament.

Denis Lebel, a former mayor of Roberval running as a Conservative, managed to take his riding from the Bloc Québécois. The Liberals couldn't even scrape together 10 percent of the vote there or in Saint-Hyacinthe–Bagot, the other by-election riding, where the Bloc candidate won.

Dion had to move quickly to stem nasty infighting caused by the defeats. So he waited a month. Then he asked Denis Coderre, a Montreal MP, to replace Marcel Proulx from Hull-Aylmer as his Quebec lieutenant. Coderre said he'd think about it, then called Proulx to discuss how the transition might go. Unfortunately Proulx didn't know he was leaving. He quit in a huff. Coderre decided he wanted no part of this mess and refused the assignment. So did Dion's second? . . . third? . . . well, anyway, next choice, a dapper Montrealer named Pablo Rodríguez.

Dion wound up rummaging through the Senate to come up with Céline Hervieux-Payette, a Trudeau-era utility infielder who had run and lost in 1984, 1988 and 1993 before Jean Chrétien finally put her where the voters could not trouble her further. Now her job was to enforce discipline on Dion's behalf. It worked roughly as well as if he had been enforcing discipline for her.

What floored me, when I returned from a year abroad and started covering Dion close up again in early 2008, was that the people who worked for Dion saw his judgment—his political gut instinct, which in the end is all any politician ever has—as a problem to be managed, not an asset to be deployed to best advantage. "He doesn't know what he doesn't know," one long-standing Dion supporter told me. "He won't give a stump speech. He had a good speech a while ago about poverty. Caucus said to him, 'All right, give that speech thirty times across the country.' He wouldn't do it. He said, 'My views on poverty are known.'"

In Question Period he would, by the middle of his second question every day, be shouting. It made sense; there was much about Harper's government that would make any adversary angry. But soon the anger seemed rote, because there was not the faintest glimmer of a strategic sense in Dion's manner of deploying it. Daily outrage in Question Period—and hourly outrage in news releases, always written in identical format and e-mailed to the tiny colony of Ottawa reporters—was not matched by any concerted effort to explain to Canadians why the Liberals thought Harper should outrage Canadians.

The relatively robust party bank account Dion had inherited in 2006 was now gone, spent on routine party operations without healthy fundraising to replenish it. The Liberals raised one-third as much money in 2007 as the Conservatives did. Even if he had had money to spend, Dion was not sure what to spend it on. "I told him we should run an ad that says three things about Harper," one of his helpers told me at the time. "[Harper] wanted to take us into Iraq; he wanted to participate in George

W. Bush's missile defence program; he wants to keep our soldiers in Afghanistan. This is when I thought we were going to be against extending the mission. That wouldn't be a negative ad. It would be purely factual. And it would frame Harper for a year to come. Dion wouldn't do it."

Despite the evident difficulty Dion had in making serious trouble for the Harper government, the Harper Conservatives proved well able to make trouble for themselves by themselves.

On November 18, 2007, Atomic Energy of Canada Limited shut down the National Research Universal nuclear reactor at Chalk River, 180 kilometres northwest of Ottawa in the Laurentian Hills near the Ontario–Quebec border, for routine maintenance. Inspectors from the Canadian Nuclear Safety Commission declared that two of the reactor's cooling pumps lacked the type of emergency power systems the site's operating licence required. The emergency power systems were the sort of thing that would come in handy if the plant's main power system ever went offline during, say, an earthquake. Keeping the pumps pumping would prevent a meltdown. An inability to prevent a meltdown would be a problem.

AECL extended the reactor's shutdown so they could install the emergency power systems. But this created its own problem: Chalk River produced most of the radioisotopes used for medical treatment around the world. The Harper government quickly introduced emergency legislation to start the reactor back up, with only one of the two recommended power systems in place. Natural Resource Minister Gary Lunn and Health Minister Tony Clement both proclaimed the reactor to be safe. The emergency legislation passed the Commons and Senate the way most of Harper's bills passed—with very little trouble and with substantial opposition support, indeed in this case from every party. The bill became law on December 12, a scant three weeks after the crisis began. By then Lunn had announced the resignation of AECL chairman Michael Burns. The AECL would be turning over a new leaf. It was time, Tony Clement said, to give AECL better management after this lamentable episode.

This, in turn, created its own problem, nested inside the others like a Russian doll. Burns hadn't actually quit over Chalk River. He'd handed in his resignation letter on November 29, he promptly told a *Globe and Mail* reporter, and for "an entirely different set of reasons," never defined. Appearing to blast him out the airlock as part of the Chalk River political cleanup was "a clumsy piece of political opportunism," he said.

But repurposing Burns's resignation was nowhere near as clumsy as what Harper did next. On December 11, the day the emergency reopening bill roared through the Commons at high speed, Ignatieff led the Liberals in Question Period in place of Dion, who was travelling. The Liberals would support the bill. Indeed, by the end of the day their votes would help ensure its speedy passage. But Ignatieff still had questions. Why would the CNSC have no oversight role on this reactor once the plant was open again, he wanted to know. "Why does the government believe AECL, which was in flagrant violation of its licence, is competent to decide whether the reactor is safe to operate?"

Something about this line of questioning got right up Harper's nose. Perhaps it was the snippy tone from a party that was going to support the bill anyway. Perhaps it was simply the refreshing chance to take a poke at Ignatieff instead of Dion. "Mr. Speaker, the government has independent advice indicating there is no safety concern with the reactor," the prime minister said. "On the contrary, what we do know is that the continuing actions of the Liberal-appointed Nuclear Safety Commission will jeopardize the health and safety and lives of tens of thousands of Canadians."

It was a stretch to suggest that "tens of thousands" of lives were at stake because of the Nuclear Safety Commission and its chair, Linda

Keen. But what was more surprising was the way he was connecting her to the Liberals.

On the next round of questions, he acknowledged that Keen's actions might be "within [her] legislative authority." But they were "not in the public interest. It is in the public interest to get this reactor back online and get these medical radioisotopes produced." He called on the Liberals to "stop protecting their appointee and get on with getting these medical isotopes produced."

Again with the suggestion of a Liberal connection to the safety commission.

Ignatieff chose to ignore that. "Mr. Speaker, since when is the Prime Minister of Canada an expert on nuclear safety?" The Liberal benches roared their approval of this actually not terribly clever line. Ignatieff had delivered it promptly, ad lib, and in comprehensible English. The sound Liberal MPs were making reflected relief at the change from Dion more than admiration of Ignatieff's rapier wit.

But Harper did not like seeing happy Liberals under any circumstance. He let his temper shape his response. "Since when does the Liberal Party have a right, from the grave through one of its previous appointees, to block the production of necessary medical products in the country?"

The evidence for Harper's assertion that Keen was a Liberal partisan of any stripe was shaky. Keen had been born in Alberta, had worked for Conservative Alberta governments, and had entered the public service while Brian Mulroney was prime minister. She had indeed joined the CNSC while Jean Chrétien was prime minister. But there would never be any evidence that she was carrying out Liberal orders by remote control. But then, that wasn't really what Harper had in mind. What he had in mind was two things.

First, Keen was plainly, on the face of things, one of those people—the Kristol–Brimelow New Class of mandarins—academics, lawyers and teachers and journalists and assorted smarty-pants—whose patron saint, Count Michael Ignatieff of Harvard Yard, was even now getting up in Harper's grill. Well, if Roy McMurtry could turn out, retroactively, to have been a cog in the Liberal machine as soon as he endorsed gay marriage, then it only made sense that Linda Keen would be diagnosed as a Liberal predator drone as soon as she stuck her head up.

Second, Keen had triggered another old instinct in Harper, a vintage bit of Brimelovian resource-sector atavism. The people who ran the nuclear plant wanted to make the nuclear plant go. And here was this dame saying it should stop. Just as Trudeau had said the West mustn't rise. Just as a global cartel of scientists and socialists had said the very source of Canada's wealth and power, burning hydrocarbons, must somehow be treated as a pestilence and a source of—yet more!—tax revenue and a pretext for—yet more!—regulatory burden. The very thought of this technocrat trying to tell him how to run a power plant made him rage.

One more thing. Harper might simply have had the notion of partisan appointees carrying out partisan agendas on the brain, and if that was the case, it would be no great surprise. As Tim Naumetz reported later for Canwest News, cabinet records showed that eight days before he called Keen a Liberal zombie spy, Harper had appointed Ronald Barriault, a former Progressive Conservative candidate in the 2006 New Brunswick provincial election, to the Nuclear Safety Commission. A psychologist would say Harper was projecting.

Name-calling in the House was not sufficient revenge against Keen. In January, Lunn wrote a letter to Keen saying he was thinking of firing her. The *Ottawa Citizen* got its hands on the letter and published its contents. After a week of controversy, late in the evening of January 15, the government dismissed Keen. The next morning, she and Lunn had been scheduled to testify about the whole mess before a parliamentary committee. Now her services would not be required.

On the substance of things, Keen's behaviour is open to debate. Much later she finally did testify to a parliamentary committee and said she had thought the chances of a Chalk River meltdown to be tiny, on the order of a thousand to one. But safety standards required that the risk be closer to a million to one. So to her, the risk was a thousand times greater than it needed to be. To Harper, opposing her was a safe bet, because the likelihood that nothing untoward would happen was 99.9 percent. It was never Keen's job to make a bet. It was her job, as head of the safety council, to be obsessive about safety. She'd done what the job required. So Harper fired her.

The AECL controversy would soon be nearly forgotten as a series of more titillating revelations superseded it. But in retrospect, and in the context of this chapter's broader discussion of environmental policy, the Linda Keen firing begins to look like what poker players would call a "tell," an unconscious reaction that betrays a player's state of mind. From the day Dion became Liberal leader, Harper had sought to portray the Conservatives as cautious custodians of the nation's environmental conscience. But it was clear that when Canada's natural resources were at play, he was strongly inclined to view counsels of restraint, caution and prudence as troublemaking.

––––––––––

The Keen firing said much about how Harper viewed his responsibilities in government. Two of the spring's other cow-pies seemed also to offer insight into how he ran his party. Yet another featured a gorgeous woman with ties to biker gangs.

At the end of February the *Globe* ran a story about a new book by Vancouver journalist Tom Zytaruk. The book was a tribute to Chuck Cadman, a former Canadian Alliance MP who lost the Conservative nomination in 2004, ran as an independent anyway and won his Surrey North riding. He died of skin cancer shortly after he voted to support Paul Martin's Liberal government in the spring of 2005. His vote helped keep the Martin government from falling until months later, long after Cadman himself had died.

That Cadman's vote had been hotly vied for at the time was known. What Zytaruk's book revealed was that two Conservative operatives had sought to secure his vote for their side. "The Tories actually walked in with a list of offers written down on a piece of paper. Included in their proposal was a $1-million life insurance policy—no small carrot for a man with advanced cancer," Zytaruk wrote.

Cadman's widow, Dona, was by 2008 the designated Conservative candidate in Surrey North. In a phone interview with the *Globe* she corroborated Zytaruk's account. "Chuck was really insulted," she told the paper's reporters. "He was quite mad about it, thinking they could bribe him with that."

After Cadman died, Zytaruk had learned that Harper was paying a visit to Cadman's widow and interviewed the future prime minister in the driveway of Cadman's home. His book contained excerpts from that interview. "Of the offer to Chuck, it was only to replace financial considerations he might lose due to an election, okay," Harper explained. He said the two who had approached Cadman "were legitimately representing the party," but that Harper had told them they'd be "wasting their time. I said Chuck had made up his mind he was going to vote with the Liberals."

It's really illegal to offer an MP a financial inducement to change his vote. When the story came out, the Conservatives said Zytaruk had misquoted Harper. Zytaruk produced a recording of the interview. The Conservatives produced experts who said the tape had been altered. Months later, a court-ordered analysis would find that none of the sections of the tape that contained quotes from Harper had been edited. Meanwhile Harper served Dion a notice of intent to sue for libel for statements about the Cadman affair that had appeared on the Liberal Party website. The suit served its purpose, scaring the Liberals away from an attack on Harper's personal credibility. For a while, in a rare display of cheek, the Liberals' youth wing hired a car to drive around downtown Ottawa playing the tape of Zytaruk's interview with Harper. That stopped right away after the lawsuit was filed.

In their defence of the suit, the Liberals sought legal advice from Peter Russell, a University of Toronto law professor. "This use of legal action to silence the opposition is characteristic of authoritarian governments," Russell wrote. "It is incompatible with democratic government." Russell's opinion was correct insofar as no prime minister had ever sued an opposition leader. But he neglected to mention a case where a cabinet minister had sued an opposition leader. It was a case that might have been expected to occur to him, since in 2005 Stéphane Dion had sued Gilles Duceppe, the Bloc Québécois leader, for publishing a pamphlet that tried to connect Dion to the Liberal sponsorship scandal.

What nobody was ever able to explain was how the Conservative Party could even have procured life-insurance coverage for a man who was, as a matter of public knowledge, dying of cancer. It remains the one big stumper in this whole saga. Through the spring of 2008 Harper and other Conservatives argued that all that had ever been discussed was defraying the normal costs of Cadman's campaign for re-election.

It was an odd claim. During the period in question, Cadman was weeks from the grave. He never suggested he wanted to run again. The two Conservative operatives who visited Cadman, it emerged, had been Tom Flanagan and Doug Finley. Flanagan's book *Harper's Team* included an account of his and Finley's visit to Cadman's office. Flanagan wrote that they were trying to influence Cadman's vote. He nowhere suggested that he and Finley were trying to get Cadman to run as a Conservative in an election Cadman was inclined to avoid and would, in the end, never live to see.

As I mentioned, Harper has never spoken to Flanagan since the publication of Flanagan's book, which Harper sees as a breach of trust.

Conservatives close to Harper often mention that the first draft of Flanagan's book contained far more surprising revelations, which Flanagan removed before publication in an attempt to mollify Harper's office. For whatever reason, he does not spell out what he and Finley offered Cadman. His account of the episode concludes: "That Doug and I made this last desperate try with Cadman shows how we were all caught up in the attempt to force an election. . . . It's an excellent example of how the passions of politics lead to decisions that later make you scratch your head."

The Conservatives would have occasion to do more head-scratching on April 15, 2008, when the RCMP raided the Conservative Party headquarters in Ottawa at the request of William Corbett, the commissioner of elections. The Conservatives share an office tower with a lot of other tenants. One of them called a reporter when the cops showed up, and by the time the search was well under way, the hallway outside the office was filled with reporters and TV camera crews. The hallway crowd also included a Liberal Party staffer with a video camera.

The subject that so fascinated the elections officials was the so-called in-and-out affair. After the 2006 election, local Conservative candidates across the country submitted receipts for advertising and sought reimbursement from Elections Canada. When the agency investigated, it found that the local campaigns hadn't incurred the expense. The national Conservative campaigns had sent local candidates money; they had returned the money to the national campaign; and they had booked, as local, expenses that had in fact been incurred at the national level. The goal of the whole thing was to get around caps on total national campaign spending. In the end the party had managed to exceed the national advertising limit by more than $1 million with this shell game.

Typically, the Conservatives had responded to the Elections Canada queries by stonewalling. Few candidates answered questions about their money management. But those who did described what looked like a nationwide effort to increase centralized campaign spending while decentralizing the evidence. Hence the RCMP raid to procure evidence the party would not part with willingly.

––––––

The last springtime headache for Harper was practically care-free compared with the others. It began with the welcome news that somebody in the Conservative caucus was thought to be sexy.

At the beginning of May the *Hill Times*, a tabloid newspaper for the parliamentary precinct, published its annual survey of hotness and not-ness in Ottawa. Peter MacKay, the minister of defence, had won the Sexiest Male MP for nine years running, but suddenly he was dethroned by Maxime Bernier, the foreign minister. It made sense. MacKay had his charms, but Bernier, the rookie MP from the Beauce, was a rangy, loping horndog with legs like a gazelle's, a chest that could repel machine-gun fire and a gimlet eye for a well-turned ankle.

It was not so much that Ottawa had been slow to warm to him as that a summer cabinet shuffle had forced a communal recalibration: arriving for his swearing-in, Bernier had tumbled out of a staff car outside Rideau Hall and held out his arm to a stunning new companion, a wild-haired brunette whose sundress revealed an even more impressive rack than his own. "Maxime Bernier's date helped," *Hill Times* editor Kate Malloy told reporters. "I think the pictures taken of last year's swearing-in ceremony added a lot of glamour."

The world loves a lover, and Bernier would have had no further trouble if reporters had not started inquiring into rumours about his date's background. On May 7, Lloyd Robertson told the CTV News audience the latest. "CTV News was handed documents showing that the minister's former girlfriend had a connection with organized crime and she was not given an RCMP security check."

Bob Fife had the details. It turned out the magnificent woman in the sundress was named Julie Couillard. "One live-in boyfriend had ties to Hell's Angels boss 'Mom' Boucher," Fife said. "He was later murdered. She then married an enforcer for the Rockers, the farm team for Boucher's gang." The RCMP really hadn't done a background check. Bernier, who by then had moved on from Couillard, apparently had no clue about her history. Single men who had seen the sundress pondered this part of the story and knew it to be credible.

But the Bloc and the Liberals wouldn't stop asking questions. On May 8 Harper paused as he left Question Period to say something to the TV cameras. This almost never happened. "I hear that one of my cabinet ministers has an ex-girlfriend," he said in French. "It's none of my business. It's none of Mr. Duceppe's business, none of Mr. Dion's business. Mr. Duceppe and Mr. Dion are quite a group of gossipy old busybodies." Then he repeated the remark, verbatim, in English. We had our clip.

But Couillard had spent a fair amount of time with men whose business dealings were both complex and occasionally lawless, and the more the forensic reporting came out, the more the story dragged on in the headlines. Finally, on May 26, after nearly a month of this, Harper announced that he had accepted Bernier's resignation. Bernier had left classified documents in Couillard's home. "Let me be very clear," Harper said, first in French and then in English. "This is not to do with the minister's life or the life of a private citizen, 99 percent of which I think is completely off bounds."

The documents, it was soon revealed, had been left in Couillard's home in April, before the stories about Couillard's past had broken. Perhaps at some point she simply got tired of being in the headlines because she had selected a flattering dress, and decided to hang Bernier out to dry. In the end it mattered little. She was out of his life, he was out of cabinet, and

Harper was left to contemplate how much more frequently damaging revelations came from his own team than from the hapless Liberals opposite.

———

Dion could be an extraordinarily quick learner when he thought something was worth learning. For his first eight years in politics he had no reputation as an environmentalist, but after Martin turfed him from cabinet in 2003, he made himself a formidable expert on the subject in a matter of months. But Dion always believed politics was something odd that other men did. He never lowered himself to learning how to do it. He believed he had won the Liberal leadership because Liberals shared his vision on the environment. His own staff told him the only reason he had won was that in the third round of voting at the leadership convention, Gerard Kennedy had delivered a bloc of delegates intact.

Through the middle of 2008, visitors to Dion's office, part of an impressive suite reserved for the Official Opposition one flight of stairs up from the prime minister's Hill office and the cabinet room, were astonished to discover the grand old room was barren. There was only a small photo of Mackenzie King over the mantel, a bust of Wilfrid Laurier in one corner, and Dion. He did not believe a Liberal should be in the opposition leader's office. So for a year and a half he refused to move in.

But at least he had his convictions. At least he knew what he wanted to do. Or so you'd think. But when he was not putting out political fires, or simply watching in bemusement while they burned, he spent much of his time in that empty, unloved office doing a one-eighty on his plan for fighting climate change.

He did not do it out of fecklessness or inattention. Dion had no end of free advice from backseat drivers eager to tell him he would only improve his environmental plan if he replaced cap-and-trade with a proper carbon tax. Elizabeth May, the Green Party leader, said as much on the day he became leader. But he had been categorical, calling a flat levy on hydrocarbon burning "simply bad policy," in part because "for Albertans, it's a non-starter."

The free advice wouldn't stop. Jeffrey Simpson, the most serious man in Canada, used a *Globe* column five weeks after Dion got the top job to say Dion wasn't serious about the environment. "Okay, the first thing Mr. Dion should do is talk to the man he defeated, Michael Ignatieff, whose ideas for improving Canada's climate-change record were far better than those Mr. Dion peddled, and is still peddling."

Simpson said Dion's vanquished rival even knew how a carbon tax could be peddled to wary voters: by trading new revenues for forgone revenues from other tax sources. "Mr. Ignatieff properly called his measures 'tax shifting,' and described them as 'the need to shift taxes toward emissions and pollution and away from labour, income and investment over the long term.'"

Dion continued to get such counsel for a year. There's a broad current of opinion, to which I subscribe, to the effect that it was correct counsel: if you want people to burn fewer hydrocarbons you should make burning hydrocarbons more expensive. It is radically simpler than other methods and will, as price signals always have, inspire feats of ingenuity. And a tax raised over here can always be matched against a tax lowered over there. The challenge lies in persuading voters that, in every case, the "over here" and "over there" will align so their wallet isn't conscripted to cover the difference. But to say that is to wander into politics, and before Dion ever began to think about that, he was seduced by the policy design.

In the fall of 2007, John Roy, a Nova Scotia businessman, held a weekend meeting in Merrickville, Ontario, near Ottawa. Scott Brison and John Godfrey, two Liberal MPs, attended, along with figures from business and the public-policy community. They thought hard about how to control carbon and decided, as folks often do, that price signals through a simple tax were the best mechanism. "John Godfrey came with good arguments," Dion, who hadn't attended, told *Maclean's* reporter John Geddes, who first reported about the meeting. "Scott Brison has been very insistent, I must say."

Similar sessions elsewhere reached similar conclusions. Dion finally stopped resisting after a real-world example of a carbon tax appeared. British Columbia's finance minister, Carole Taylor, introduced the province's 2008 budget in February. It included a modest tax on fossil fuels. It would start low, then build up over four years to $30 per tonne of carbon emissions, and be offset by tax cuts elsewhere. "I think British Columbia is doing for climate change what Saskatchewan did for medicare," Dion told reporters during a Vancouver visit.

And so it came to pass that on June 19 just about the entire Liberal caucus crowded into one of the largest committee rooms in Parliament's Centre Block to face a crowd of reporters. This was the unveiling of the Liberals' "Green Shift," a plan that was "good for the planet, and good for the wallet," Dion said. Loosely modelled on the B.C. tax shift, Dion's new plan called for a tax on fossil fuels that would rise, over four years, to $40 per tonne.

If the tax was modest, the compensating income-tax and business-tax cuts were minuscule. That was partly because Dion wanted to use part of the carbon-tax windfall to pay for public transit and for a range of benefits for families and low-income earners. To Dion that meant his plan was revenue neutral. He even planned to ask the auditor general to verify that every dollar a Liberal government collected would be returned in tax cuts or new programs.

Harper was unimpressed. He seized on Dion's change from cap-and-trade to a carbon tax. "Mr. Dion went around the country for years claiming he would never impose a carbon tax," the prime minister said in Huntsville, Ontario. "He couldn't be believed then and he cannot be believed now."

Conservative research showed that voters gave Harper more credence on economic matters than Dion. That advantage conditioned the Conservative response to Dion's new plan. Instead of playing defensive on the environment, the Conservatives would play offensive on economic management. The message was not that Dion was bad on the environment or that the Conservatives could be better. It was that he was lousy on the economy and just about anyone would be better. For a week before Dion spoke, the Conservatives had been running TV and radio ads decrying Dion's "Permanent Tax on Everything." (The Conservatives knew about almost every move Dion wanted to make well in advance because they read about it in Jane Taber's column in the *Globe and Mail*. Dion's caucus was divided, and chatty caucus members were prone to such leakage.) The TV ads, and a new website (willyoubetricked.ca) linked to the Conservative Party's home page, featured a mascot, a cheerful black cartoon oil stain with human eyes. The ads and websites all used the same photo of Dion, head cocked quizzically, arms straight out in an epic shrug. Not a Leader.

The ads were devastating because they resonated with suspicions about Dion that were everywhere in the country, including Ottawa offices occupied by Liberals. Both Rae and Ignatieff had privately urged Dion to force an election now, this June for a July vote. All he had to do was take his entire Liberal caucus into the Commons for a money vote and join the NDP and Bloc, who almost always voted against the government, in doing the same. Rae said the Couillard and in-and-out scandals had weakened Harper and it was time to strike. Ignatieff said the only way to force Canadians to concentrate on the choice they needed to make was to start an election campaign and turn the five-week writ period into a study session on policy alternatives. It would, in the end, turn out to be a stubborn Ignatieff theory about Canadian politics: that Liberals would do better during a campaign than they had before it. He would eventually get to test the theory himself.

Dion resisted. He wanted to spend the summer pitching his Green Shift to voters. "You want to know why I'm happy with this?" he said to me that summer. "I'm happy because people are talking about it. This policy assumes cynicism won't win. The cynicism that says, 'Oh, people will never believe a politician who says if we raise one tax we'll lower another. They'll just hear the first half and then walk away.' I think we in the politico-media class—people in your line of work and mine—are far more cynical than most people. A lot of people will vote because they believe in somebody."

At the beginning of August, Harper and his Conservative caucus met in Lévis, across the river from Quebec City, to plot strategy for the fall parliamentary session. They capped two days of meetings with a rally on a fairground in the small town of Saint-Agapit. Outside the hall where Harper spoke, folks were lining up for a chance to shake Maxime Bernier's hand. He might as well indulge them and bask in his popularity; he would be sleeping in the doghouse for a few more years before Harper began to forgive his indiscretions.

Inside the hall, Harper essentially called Dion a chicken. One of the prime minister's less temperate remarks had been that a carbon tax would "screw everybody across the country." Dion had called for an "adult" debate. Fair enough, Harper said now. "If Mr. Dion wants a real debate—not just among politicians, but a debate open to everybody—all he has to do is follow through on his latest threat to force an election."

It wasn't the first time Ottawa had been on election alert, Harper said. And it was all quite tiresome by now. "Canadians deserve to have a Parliament that works. They want the government to keep governing, to address the issues that matter to them, to keep the country moving forward. So Mr. Dion must decide to either fish or cut bait."

Two weeks later, Dion took a seat in the National Press Theatre on Wellington Street, with a row of maple leaf flags behind him and four rows of reporters in front of him. He had, he revealed, just come back from summer vacation. "I cut bait. I caught fish. I won the competition. It tasted like victory. All this because I struck at the right time."

Ooh. A metaphor. Time for reporters' questions. Was Harper correct to say Parliament had become dysfunctional?

"The truth is when the Parliament has difficulties, it's because the Conservatives are delaying committees," Dion said.

Was he thinking about forcing an election?

"I'm considering different possibilities," he said, "and one is to stop strategic voting when we disagree with the government." In other words, Liberals would turn out in full force, instead of sending in a corporal's guard for confidence votes. It would, at that point, suddenly no longer be up to the Liberals to decide whether they should force an election. It would be up to the other opposition parties to decide whether they had the stomach for one.

"Timing is important in politics," Dion said. "Like for fishing!"

He said he wanted to make Canada "Richard Peregrino." Or at least that's the way I kept hearing it. Explanation is in order. In the spring I had brunched with a Liberal friend who was working on the Liberal platform. "What do you think of this for a campaign slogan?" she asked. "Richard Peregrino."

I stared blankly. "It's a bit . . . opaque."

It took me three minutes to figure out that what she'd actually said was, "Richer, Fairer, Greener." Which was what Dion wanted to make Canada. But the imaginary name stuck in my head, so now once again Dion seemed to be saying Canada should be more like this guy Richard Peregrino.

One reporter asked whether, if Harper ever asked for an election, Michaëlle Jean could refuse to dissolve Parliament. There was, after all, a fixed-election-date law on the books. There was not supposed to be an election until October 2009. Surely the governor general could say no?

Dion found it an uninteresting question. "In my opinion, the governor general does what the prime minister asks her." Nobody in the room realized it was foreshadowing, and with regard not just to the election's start but to its aftermath. At this point Harper had been prime minister for two years and seven months, longer than nine of his predecessors, including Paul Martin. Watching the Dion news conference on television, Harper saw an upstart pipsqueak daring to talk as though the choice of an election date should lie with him. Harper didn't like that kind of talk. Not one bit.

FIVE

EXCELLENT BUYING OPPORTUNITY

A few days after Dion held his news conference to discuss the burden of the decision he thought he had to make, a video production crew disembarked at the prime minister's Harrington Lake country residence, a short drive from Ottawa in Quebec's Gatineau Hills. Over the years different prime ministers have used Harrington Lake for different things. Margaret Trudeau grew a vegetable garden there. Kim Campbell lived there for the entire summer she was prime minister; she never did get to see the inside of 24 Sussex Drive as anything but a guest. Jean Chrétien used it to get the capital out of his head. He almost never invited PMO staffers or cabinet colleagues to visit. A 2000 campaign ad that showed Chrétien strolling with Paul Martin through the woods near the residence, waving at schoolchildren, could not have been more marvellously fictitious if the two rivals had been depicted rehearsing a piano duet or shucking oysters.

Stephen and Laureen Harper used Harrington Lake frequently, especially in the summer. They often invited friends, a list mostly curated by

Laureen that included staffers, cabinet colleagues and people most denizens of Parliament Hill would never have recognized. But on this late August day, the guest list was short and the agenda was strictly business. Narrowly defined, the day's goal was to get usable footage of Harper for some television ads. More broadly, Harper's ambition was to yank Stéphane Dion's shorts so far up his backside the Liberal leader would never walk the same way again.

At some point over the summer, between the June launch of Dion's Green Shift and the August news conference where Dion hinted clumsily at being ready to force an election, Harper had decided an election was coming. He was sure Dion would vote no confidence at an early opportunity to silence Liberal naysayers by demonstrating strength. The Bloc Québécois would vote the same way, because in Quebec, Dion was not strong. The NDP would complete the opposition's common front because outside Quebec, Dion was not strong. So, despite very different motives, their actions would finally align.

Despite its numerical weakness, Harper's was already the longest-lasting minority government in Canada's history. Now at last it would fall. In June his plan had been to hold on for as long as possible. Over the summer he decided he might as well move before his opponents could.

The fish-or-cut-bait speech to the Conservative caucus at Saint-Agapit was for show. It was not up to Dion to decide whether there would be fishing or bait-cutting. Harper had already decided there would be an election. The decision came as news to his staff, but they adjusted. The Conservatives had to scramble to pull together a platform and ads, but at least they scrambled. Dion thought he had the advantage. He spent the last month of summer savouring it instead of using it. When the campaign finally began, the Conservatives and the NDP would be more prepared than he was.

There remained the small matter of the election's seeming—but only seeming!—illegality. Harper's government had passed legislation providing for fixed federal election dates. The bill amended the Canada Elections Act to add this language: "Each general election must be held on the third Monday of October in the fourth calendar year following polling day for the last general election, with the first general election after this section comes into force being held on Monday, October 19, 2009."

Crystal clear. But this new paragraph came after another new paragraph that was nearly as clear and said, in effect, that the bit about fixed election dates was almost meaningless: "Nothing in this section affects the powers of the Governor General, including the power to dissolve Parliament at the Governor General's discretion."

Now here's the thing about the governor general's discretion. She had none. Or rather, ever since the 8th Earl of Elgin had signed the Rebellion Losses Bill in 1849—and with the exception of the 1926 King–Byng crisis, an exception only romantics mistake for the rule—generations of governors general had so construed their discretion as to make it synonymous with the prime minister's. So, taken as a whole, the fixed-election-date law amounted to saying there would be an election in 2009 unless Harper decided he would rather not wait. With this prime minister it was always a good idea to read the fine print. Especially when the fine print and the headlines were the same size and a paragraph apart.

Still, many of Harper's advisors were worried about a voter backlash. Harper had, after all, advertised fixed election dates, and the accountability legislation as a whole, as a change from business as usual. Now he would be displaying electoral opportunism, the purest expression of business as usual. At the very least, his handlers worried about days or weeks of process questions from the sticklers in the press corps distracting from Harper's campaign messaging.

In the end they needn't have worried. The more sanguine voices around the table pointed out that very few voters even knew a fixed-election law had been passed. Canadians had never voted in a federal election whose date had been known months or years in advance. So they would miss the next—first—fixed election about as much as they would miss anything else they had never had long enough to miss, such as a third arm or a new internal organ that spontaneously generated cheeseburgers. As so often happens in Canadian politics, the calmer voices would turn out to be right.

And so Harper settled into a wingback chair in a Harrington Lake study while a small knot of senior staffers, including Patrick Muttart and the Conservatives' Toronto-based admaker, Perry Miele, read to him from a long list of questions. They had no script as such. Harper might briefly discuss the gist of a possible answer with his helpers before launching into a full-blown monologue. If he stumbled he would start again. If they liked an answer he would repeat it a few more times in hopes of a better performance. But mostly he was riffing on themes.

The Conservative leader was wearing a navy sweater vest over a lighter-blue dress shirt. Nobody in the video crew wanted him in a suit. They wanted something softer. The sweater vest was what was in his dresser. "He doesn't have an unlimited wardrobe," said someone who was there.

Harper's answers to the many questions were much like his getup: improvised, but with a goal. Later the campaign team would pore over hours' worth of digital video recordings to find, and then display for voters, evidence of a gentler Stephen Harper.

The ads, when they ran, were tiny perfect imitations of real moments. There were three of them. Each opened with a shot of a maple leaf flag flapping, then cut to Harper in his sweater vest conversing with his off-camera visitors. In one ad he talked about his children. "You know, the time is precious. But being a father is the best experience of my life." In another he marvelled at the importance of immigrants' contribution to Canada. "We can build this country together."

The third ad offered Harper's gratitude to veterans. "What you always remember when you meet a Canadian veteran is that everything we have in this country was earned. And those men and women went out and put their lives on the line for this country. Never forget what they contributed. But more important, never forget how precious it is—how precious what we have is."

It would be easy to miss the significance of the most telling detail in the ads if you didn't know to look for it. In each of the three versions, after Harper finished delivering his folksy homily, the soundtrack's string orchestra swelled and a closing message appeared over a blue background: "Canada: We're Better Off With Stephen Harper." This was new. Until 2008, Harper had never been popular enough for it to be worth making his persona the centrepiece of his party's campaign pitch.

In 2004 voters barely had a clue who he was. So he appeared in those hilariously contrived ads in which he complained about the Liberals, offered some kind of solution, and then paused and added, slowly, "My name is Stephen Harper." Viewers came away wondering about his speaking style but pretty sure that, whoever this guy was, his name must be Stephen Harper.

When the next campaign began, at the end of 2005, Harper had been opposition leader through two years of constant electoral brinks-manship. It hadn't helped him much. The Conservatives' research showed that Harper, personally, was not a popular guy. Voters were intrigued by the notion of getting rid of the Liberals, but telling them they would be handing power to Harper didn't generate much excite-ment. So even in ads in which Harper appeared, the party took care not to tell you who he was.

This practice reached its surreal pinnacle in an ad that featured vari-ous people talking about the leader without ever naming him. An unidentified blonde-haired lady whom experts would have identified as Laureen Harper sat next to . . . some fellow . . . on a sofa. "He works long hours," she said. "He works very hard." A voice-over described the same . . . fellow . . . as "a leader who looks more like one of them" and as "a leader who will not just bring the country together but finally take it forward." Great. And what was his name? The ad was not helpful on this score. "Stand up for Canada," the voice-over said.

But that was 2006. Two and a half years in power had made Harper the party's best asset. The new ads reflected their voter research. The election was his decision. The vote would be a referendum on his record and the alternative. And the mistakes, when they came, would be his own.

As the Harrington Lake ads began going to air in the last week of August, Harper's new communications director, Kory Teneycke, started taking reporters out to lunch. My turn came on Thursday, August 21, at a fabulously cheap and plentiful Chinese buffet on Albert Street. Teneycke ladled himself some wonton soup, swore me to secrecy, then announced that Harper had concluded, at some point during the summer, that getting anything done in the current Parliament was like "swimming in molasses." He would meet the opposition leaders soon. Very soon. "We're not talking weeks here." Unless one of Harper's opponents promised to refrain from voting no confidence, Harper would ask the governor general to dissolve Parliament and call an election.

A day later, Teneycke decided he'd be warning reporters about a fall election until Christmas if he did it one lunch date at a time. So he summoned representatives from all the Ottawa news bureaus to a briefing room inside the Langevin Block. "An election would clear the air and give a government—ours or a Liberal government—some open water to manoeuvre in," he said, still off the record. Why bring all these reporters in to tell them the plan? "If you have to guess, you may guess wrong," Teneycke said. "So I'm telling you so you'll guess right."

There followed several days of kabuki theatre. One by one, the opposition leaders visited 24 Sussex while reporters and camera crews waited outside. Each came out warning that Harper was desperate to have an election and announcing that they wondered why he was in such a rush.

So nobody was really surprised when Harper's motorcade took the two-minute drive from his house to Rideau Hall on the morning of

September 7. He disappeared inside Michaëlle Jean's residence for half an hour and emerged for a short stroll from the front door to a podium in the Canadian Heritage Garden.

He was wearing a standard-issue two-piece suit and tie. But his remarks, oddly jovial and grandfatherly, made it clear he was still in a mental sweater vest. "*Bon matin*, good morning," Harper said. He made a little show of pausing to peer at the journalists clustered before him. "I guess I never realized until now how many of you there really are." He smiled bashfully. Just a regular fellow.

"Between now and October 14, Canadians will choose a government to look out for their interests at a time of global economic trouble," he said, reading his prepared text. "They will choose between a clear direction or uncertainty, between common sense or risky experiments, between steadiness or recklessness."

Reporters, always on the lookout for surprises and missteps, pay little attention to such bland statements. But here was the entire argument of the Harper campaign in two sentences. Twenty months earlier, a Conservative vote had represented a risky experiment, even for some who had cast such a vote—certainly for many who had considered doing so but decided against it. Now Harper was hoping he could be seen as the reassuring alternative to risk.

"Canadians know that I'm not one for big talk or grand slogans," Harper said. "I believe we show who we are, and how much we care, by what we do." What he had done was get government out of your wallet. "Today, Tax Freedom Day—the day you stop working for the government and start working for yourself—arrives eleven days earlier than it did in 2005." Against that kind of simple fiscal restraint stood "an Opposition whose increasingly strident criticism attempts to mask unclear and risky agendas."

That much was, by now, familiar rhetoric from Harper. What followed really wasn't. Harper announced a desire to conclude on a personal note.

Then he recited some homey-sounding thoughts Muttart had written for him. "Over the past two and a half years I've had a tremendous opportunity," he said. "An opportunity for which I will be forever grateful. The opportunity to serve as the prime minister of the best country in the world." With that he closed the clipboard that held the text of his speech, took a sip of water and waited for questions.

One of the first was about the Harrington Lake sweater-vest ads. Harper explained, accurately, that his staff was behind this sudden confessional burst. "They feel that voters don't yet know me the way they"— his staff—"know me, the way my caucus knows me. And we should probably go out of our way to highlight the non-podium parts of the job.

"You know, people say it must be tough to balance your family life with being prime minister. In fact, if I didn't have this family life, I don't think I could stay balanced as prime minister. As you all know who have been dads, once you become a dad, that's pretty central to your character and your life."

All of this cozy *mise en scène*—the sweater-vest ads, the Prime Minister Dad shtick—served a strategic purpose. Muttart had long felt that while mothers in large middle-class families should represent a pool of Conservative support, other women were harder to reach. "When we did the demographic stuff, we'd always sort of written off non-married women who had less than two kids in any situation," one senior strategist recalled.

But the summer of 2008 had been a time of rising economic uncertainty, and the Conservatives began to see opportunity among voters most preoccupied by economic concerns. During the campaign's first week, one independent pollster was in the field finding results that matched the Conservatives' research. Environics found the Conservatives leading the Liberals 38 percent to 28 percent, with the NDP at 19 percent. Among men the Conservatives led 41 percent to 28 percent. But the lead among women was almost as strong: 35 percent to 28 percent.

This latest poll capped a six-month trend during which Environics found ever-increasing Conservative advantage among women. "I find this an extremely interesting development," Environics' Donna Dasko told reporters from *Maclean's* after she released the poll. "I can't quite figure out why it is. There certainly has been a traditional advantage for the Liberals in women's votes."

If Environics' numbers were accurate and held, they would mean trouble for Dion. "If the Liberals don't have an advantage among women, they do not win," Liberal Party pollster Michael Marzolini told *Maclean's*. "Especially women over fifty-five—that is over 25 percent of the entire electorate."

But as the campaign began, Dion pretty much had his pick of troubles to choose from. As Harper was leaving the Rideau Hall grounds, Dion walked into the House of Commons foyer with his wife, Janine Krieber. "The next thirty-seven days will be some of the most crucial in our history," the Liberal leader said. "There has never been a federal election that has more clearly provided Canadians with such a stark choice between two visions for our country." Harper, he said, had "formed the most conservative government in history."

But beyond drawing stark contrasts with his main opponent, Dion was plainly relieved that the campaign had begun. "I am excited about this election that will give me the opportunity to have a direct dialogue with you," he said. "And for the first time, you will be able to learn more about who I am and what I stand for."

It was amazing that such a belated introduction was even necessary. Dion had been an MP for more than a dozen years, leader of the opposition for nearly two. Now he hoped he could accomplish in five weeks what he had so far never managed: persuade Canadians to share his opinion of himself. And some of the necessary repair work was right at home, among his fellow francophone Quebecers, among whom he had not exactly caught fire.

"My friends, I am as proud a Quebecer as Gilles Duceppe," he said in French. "The role that we can play—that we should play—in this Canada that we have built is more important than ever before. . . . Nothing is too big, nothing is too ambitious for the hearts of Quebecers." He closed with a similarly sweeping appeal to the broader Canadian population. "My fellow Canadians, we Liberals will speak to your great minds and your big hearts about our vision," he said. What lay ahead "may well be the most crucial election campaign in our history."

With that, Dion walked out of the Centre Block to a waiting campaign bus. There was no Liberal campaign airplane. Dion would not have one for three more days. His staff had not managed to book one in time. The mismatch between the Liberal leader's rhetoric and his means was jarring. Dion hoped to make history, but Canadians didn't know him, Quebecers didn't trust him, and airlines wouldn't rent to him. Harper was seeking to broaden his coalition. Dion was trying to hang on to his.

——

Harper's first campaign stop, hours after the writ drop at Rideau Hall, was in Quebec City. "It's true that not everyone in Quebec agrees with everything I've done," he told a crowd at the Hilton. "But you know, not everyone in Alberta agrees with everything I've done either." And yet, he said in another confessional moment, he tried to earn Quebecers' support by "speaking your language." His French might not be perfect, "but I hope that every day it's getting better. . . . Because a prime minister must be able to transmit your pride to the world." The party already had ads running in Quebec, feel-good images of Harper and his Quebec cabinet ministers chatting around a sunlit table. "*Le Québec prend des forces,*" the ads' Quebec-only slogan said. Quebec is gathering strength.

The most resounding rebuttal to the Conservatives' Quebec optimism came first, not from the Bloc or the Liberals, but from Jack Layton's NDP.

The party went into the campaign with something it had never had before in a general election, an NDP incumbent in a Quebec riding. Thomas Mulcair was a former Quebec environment minister who had left Jean Charest's cabinet rather than accept a new post he perceived as a demotion. After flirting with other federal parties, including the Conservatives, Mulcair had thrown in his lot with Jack Layton and defeated Dion's hapless candidate in the 2007 by-election in Outremont.

Only once before had a New Democrat won in a Quebec riding: Phil Edmonston in Chambly in 1990. But Edmonston was a prickly fellow who did not get on well with his colleagues, and he had decided not to run for re-election in 1993. Without him the NDP had promptly lost his riding. So Mulcair, smart, urbane and hot-tempered, looked more like Quebec momentum than anything the party had ever seen. Step one in consolidating that momentum, the New Democrats decided, was to drive up the number of undecided voters by carpet-bombing the Conservatives. The result was the most starkly terrifying broadcast ad in the history of Canadian political campaigning.

Shot in black-and-white, the French-language ad featured a nightmarish surge of dissonant music in the background and a montage of animated and archival images. "A vote for the Conservatives . . ." a woman's voice, barely a whisper, intones. The screen goes blank for an instant before words rush toward the camera: "RETROGRADE IDEOLOGY AUTHORITARIAN INTOLERANT." The narrator finishes her thought: ". . . is voting for narrow thinking." A featureless cartoon father and child hurtle toward the viewer in silhouette. Suddenly the child's head disintegrates, then its shoulders, thorax and abdomen. Perhaps it is because of radiation from the nuclear power plant now rushing at the camera behind the dissolving child. "For cuts to culture," the woman says. "It's voting against Kyoto." While the voice-over is saying this, cloudy newsreel footage of Harper's face runs on the left side of the screen, while footage of George W. Bush runs on the right. "It's a pro-war vote that makes us the slaves of the oilmen." Animated black-clad armies fill the screen as two arms, encased in chains, bisect the screen.

Suddenly, sunlight. Orange-tinted sunlight. A balding man with a moustache appears. Jack Layton! "A single act and all that can stop," he says in pretty good French. "Join us! Vote NDP."

At the end of the 2006 campaign Paul Martin's Liberals had produced ads warning that a vote for Harper was a vote for armies in the streets. The Liberals had backed down from broadcasting such dark messages, or thought they had: a copy of an ad leaked and became a symbol of Liberal panic. But the Liberal spot was a walk in the park next to these new NDP ads.

Conservative pollsters followed their impact over the next several days. They found that the ads had accomplished only half their purpose. They drove voters away from the Conservatives. But not toward the New Democrats. These were not ads that put voters in a mood to take a flyer on something new. Wherever they aired, support for the most familiar choice, the Bloc Québécois, went up.

From Quebec City Harper flew to Vancouver for a night's rest at an airport hotel and an early morning breakfast-table chat with the Huang family in suburban Richmond. The Huangs—Edwin, Fei, their toddlers Renée and Eric—didn't say much, but they should have been flattered. The prime minister of Canada had flown across the Rockies for a photo opportunity with them. He would fly back over the Rockies without speaking to anyone else.

At the time it looked like an exquisitely calibrated message: send leader to Quebec City, slingshot him back over half a continent and insert him into an appropriately multiethnic breakfast nook, evacuate. In retrospect it would not look so clever. It's a lasting anachronism of the modern cam-paign that it actually does matter which cities and towns party leaders visit. You would think the multimedia modern world would make the leader's physical presence obsolete, but it doesn't. There is no substitute for the local coverage an aspiring prime minister draws. It ratchets attention up and, normally, translates into significantly improved polling performance for the local candidate. But to make that effect last, a leader needs to stay in the area for a while. Harper's toe-touches in Quebec and British Columbia were his last visits to either province for more than a week. In the end the Conservatives would post unimpressive results in British Columbia, and worse in Quebec. (For the 2011 campaign there would be adjustments.)

Meanwhile it was on to Saskatchewan and the gleaming, unscuffed farm of Kevin and Kenda Eberle, a short drive outside Regina. Here again Harper did his new come-all-ye-bold-Canadians thing. It was starting to freak out the reporters on the campaign plane a bit.

"Now let me just end with this, my friends," he said at the end of a speech that had been mostly devoted to complaining about Dion's carbon tax. "It has been an unbelievable experience, the experience of a lifetime, to be your prime minister. You get to see this country in a way no one else gets to see it. You get to travel across the country, to see the true breadth of our country, you get to meet people in every corner and from every background in this great country. And you get to travel the world. And you get to see other people and the situations they live in, and the difference and the advantages that we have here.

"When I come to Saskatchewan, even on a beautiful day like this, I never cease to be amazed. To look out and to think—especially as that cold wind whistles across the prairie in the wintertime—to think how tough the people who came here had it. To break the land and to build everything that we have today. How tough it must have been for the Aboriginal people before that, to live in that environment.

"But I also never forget this: there are very few places in the world where you can look out as far as the eye can see and see land that is rich, land you can grow things on, land you can build your families on, land that is full of potential. That's what people see in this country when they come from every corner of the earth. They see opportunity as limitless as the horizon of Saskatchewan. That's what we're building here."

For two and a half years, just about all the nightly news from Ottawa had told the Eberles' neighbours that this fellow Harper was a pure son of a bitch. And now here he was among them, and those who hadn't come to the farm—because of course only loyal Conservatives had been told to show up—would see him on their news, and what they would see was that the prime minister of Canada suddenly sounded like a touring production of *The Vinyl Café*.

In Winnipeg he had a photo op and a morning press conference in a frigid warehouse where vegetables were stored waiting for trucks to take them to market. Diesel trucks. Harper announced he would cut the excise tax on diesel fuel. The cut would "benefit consumers who buy virtually anything that moves by truck, train, ship or plane," he said.

What it would also do, of course, was sharpen the contrast with Dion's Green Shift, which sought to pay for income-tax cuts by imposing a carbon tax. Dion, the Conservative lore said, would make life more expensive. Well, Harper would make it cheaper. As a sort of bonus, his diesel-tax cut drove economists batty. "This is unfathomably stupid," economist Stephen Gordon wrote on his blog. "In one stroke, it takes two serious and pressing problems—the deteriorating fiscal situation and greenhouse gas emissions—and makes them both worse."

The diesel-tax cut was also a returned favour to Canada's trucking associations, which had done yeoman work whipping up antipathy to Dion's proposed Green Shift. On doorsteps across Canada, Conservative campaign workers were dropping off flyers that featured the local Conservative candidate's name next to a photo of Stéphane Dion shrugging. The largest words on the flyer were "THIS MAN WILL COST YOU MONEY." A handy arrow pointed to Dion, so you wouldn't think it was the Conservative candidate who would cost you money. Dion was carrying a sack of groceries with the words "PLEASE PAY MORE" crudely Photoshopped onto the bag. But it was the fine print that completed the sale. "As a result of [Dion's] carbon taxes, prices of consumer goods and food would rise," the flyer quoted Peter A. Nelson, executive director of the Atlantic Provinces Trucking Association, opining. "The average consumer would see this rise in the form of paying $8 for a head of lettuce at your local grocery store."

Yikes! Eight-dollar lettuce. This would mean the price of lettuce had quadrupled. The arithmetic on this was not obvious. Dion was proposing a $10 tax per tonne of carbon emissions. It was hard to imagine the truck that would belch out 0.6 tonnes of hydrocarbon waste for every head of lettuce it carted unless the truck was built and operated by Druids with torches. I could also point out that Dion's plan did not call for any tax on gasoline until the third year of a by-now highly hypothetical Liberal government—but now we are getting lost in a level of detail the Conservative flyer was not made to convey.

Peter A. Nelson, incidentally, knew a good line when he saw it. As the blogger BigCityLib pointed out, Nelson had already announced the end of cheap lettuce twice before. When the State of Maine had considered a toll road to the New Brunswick border, Nelson had predicted $8 lettuce. When the Marine Atlantic ferry service mooted a fuel surcharge, Nelson's prediction spiked to $10. God put Peter A. Nelson on this Earth so Peter A. Nelson could predict expensive lettuce. It is what Peter A. Nelson does. But BigCityLib's blog has a few hundred readers. Peter A. Nelson's prediction was on every doorstep in the nation.

In the end, Harper's diesel-tax cut would be poor payback for trucking services rendered. The Conservatives put the cost of the Winnipeg promise at $600 million a year. When, very late in the campaign, Harper finally released a platform, the diesel-tax cut accounted for fully half the dollar value of all Conservative spending promises. And after the Conservatives were re-elected, the diesel-tax cut was never heard of again. Not only was it never passed into law or regulation; it was simply never mentioned. The biggest promise Harper made in the campaign vanished without a trace afterward. Actually, there was a kind of poetic justice to this. Harper had fixed Peter A. Nelson's imaginary lettuce tax with a make-believe diesel-tax cut.

Yet in the moment, in that frigid Winnipeg warehouse, it was a pleasure to watch Harper defend his imaginary policy. Was he encouraging fuel use by making fuel cheaper? No, because fuel use is so crucial to the fabric of modern life it is impossible to encourage or discourage, he said. "The kinds of thing diesel is used for—which is primarily for commercial transportation—this has to be done. This has to be done. You know, my opponent says he wants to tax things that are bad. Heating your home: is that bad? Taking groceries to market: is that bad? Allowing airplane transportation, the shipping of goods across the continent and around the world. Business and passenger transportation. Are these bad things? No, these are essential things for the economy."

Meanwhile, the reporters on Dion's bus had noticed they weren't airborne yet. In the spring, NDP strategists had started a bidding war with the Liberals for the last available Air Canada charter plane. The Liberals, short on cash, pulled out and started casting about for an airplane they could rent on short notice. They finally found one, not exactly brand new, from Air Inuit, a northern Quebec company. But it wouldn't be ready for days. In the *National Post*, Don Martin called the Liberal campaign "a funeral procession."

Later, a senior Conservative said his side was floored by the lack of focus in the Dion campaign. "They were going to ridings that were the safest Liberal ridings you can imagine. No campaign plane, no message. At the end of every speech you give in a campaign, you state the ballot question. I defy you to find a ballot question in anything Dion said in the first week. And I was watching, trying, but he didn't make any sense."

———

It is worth emphasizing that this thing Dion was trying to do was always going to be difficult. Not just because he went about it badly, but because it was just an inherently unlikely task. Not once since Confederation had a newly selected opposition leader defeated a newly elected prime minister.

Canadians tend to give their heads of government time and the benefit of the doubt. Since Confederation, only three elected prime ministers have been defeated after a single victory at the ballot box: Alexander Mackenzie, R.B. Bennett and Joe Clark. Each was defeated, not by a new opponent, but by the veteran he had beaten in the previous election. Sir John A. Macdonald beat Mackenzie. William Lyon Mackenzie King beat Bennett. And Pierre Trudeau came out of retirement to beat Joe Clark. It was far more common for a new prime minister to be re-elected.

Nor did Dion have a strong hold on his party's leadership. On the first ballot in the Montreal convention in 2006, he won only 18 percent of the vote. Voting went to four ballots; Dion didn't lead until the third. This was novel in an important way. The Liberals had been holding delegated leadership conventions since Mackenzie King won in 1919. And ever since then, every leader of the party had led the field on every ballot at every leadership convention. Dion was the first come-from-behind winner in the history of the party. It's a compliment to him, but it meant he needed to consolidate his hold. He didn't. He had fewer admirers within his own party than Michael Ignatieff and Bob Rae did. Neither rival plotted behind his back, or not much. But it was an inherently destabilizing situation.

Early in the campaign, as part of what might be called the Sweater-Vest Initiative, Harper let Teneycke talk him into sitting down for breakfast with travelling campaign reporters for an on-the-record session. Not just croissants and coffee, but cameras and boom microphones. When the meeting happened in an east-end Toronto hotel, reporters were so surprised to get this close to Harper that their questions were unaggressive. Harper was on his guard—he ate nothing and drank only water. Yet something about the unaccustomed setting made him open up. He wound up delivering detailed comments on strategy, his read of the electoral map, the flaws in the other parties' game plans, and his own evolution as a politician.

"Every campaign we've had, whether it was a leadership campaign or a national campaign, don't kid yourself," he said. "We might come out and say to you that everything went fine. But in private, we sit down every time and we go through what did we do right, and what did we do wrong. And we do it brutally, frankly. And every single time we've made changes in terms of strategy. We've made changes in terms of personnel. And I've tried to make changes in myself."

He had read somewhere that leaders keep making the same mistakes until, sooner or later, those mistakes catch up. He had decided he wouldn't let that happen to him. "And what I've vowed to myself, at least in this position as leader of a national party, is that we will look at our mistakes and try to make sure we do it differently the next time."

Nothing was sacred. Everything was open to re-examination. Nobody was indispensable.

Of course there was a measure of self-flattery about all this. Campaigns aren't gearboxes that allow you to pop out a component and pop in a fresh one. They are more sociology than engineering, and in important ways a Harper campaign would always look like a Harper campaign. But with that caveat in mind, Harper often showed great flexibility in staffing and strategy.

The summer of 2008 had provided another example. Ian Brodie, the soft-spoken but sometimes ruthless organizer who had seemed pivotal to the Harper operation, left on Canada Day. He probably took one big regret with him. If he had it to do over again, he would have been less chatty on budget day in February.

The day before Jim Flaherty delivered the 2008 budget, Brodie had been in Washington discussing the extraordinarily entertaining Democratic presidential primary. Hillary Clinton and Barack Obama were going at each other hammer and tongs. Since much of their fight was in the declining industrial Midwest, they had taken turns criticizing NAFTA as a drain on U.S. manufacturing jobs, mostly south to Mexico. Might one of them reopen the trade deal if elected?

At the Canadian embassy Brodie heard somebody say that wasn't a real danger. "We have heard this from one of the campaigns," the same somebody said. Brodie assumed it was the Clinton campaign that was claiming to hold different private and public opinions about NAFTA.

The next day, February 26, Brodie was back in Ottawa for budget day. On such occasions, reporters enter a big room at the Government Conference Centre across Wellington Street from the Château Laurier Hotel, where they trade in their smartphones in return for copies of the budget. They get hours to read the documents and prepare their stories; in return, they don't get to leave until the minister of finance rises in the house to begin talking.

As a bonus, representatives of the government and bureaucracy are in the room to tell reporters how excellent the budget is. Brodie was one of these. Harper had a communications director, Sandra Buckler, who might normally have been expected to spin reporters. But both of their roles had evolved. Buckler was on poor terms with most of the press gallery and rarely had much to tell them. Brodie was on excellent terms with a few senior journalists, chosen more for how much fun he had talking to them than for any ideological compatibility; he took great pleasure debating politics with them. And so it came to pass that, while chatting with a CTV reporter about the budget, he had thrown in some fresh gossip from Washington to the effect that the Democrats' rust-belt NAFTA trash talk should not be taken seriously.

This, CTV decided, would be way more fun to cover than the budget. So the next day a CTV reporter phoned Michael Wilson, the former Mulroney-era finance minister who was serving as Canada's ambassador in Washington. What was Brodie on about when he said the Clinton campaign spoke with forked tongue on NAFTA? the reporter asked.

Here things get a little muddled and silly. Wilson hadn't heard any such thing from the Clinton campaign. But he had seen a report from the Canadian consul general in Chicago, who'd been chatting with Austan Goolsbee, an Obama economic advisor. Goolsbee, the report said, "cautioned" the Canadians that all Obama's anti-NAFTA talk "should not be taken out of context and should be viewed as more about political positioning than a clear articulation of policy plans." The report added that "going forward"—diplomat-speak for "in what we hope will be a nice change from the gong show of recent days"—"the Obama camp was going to be careful to send the appropriate message without coming off as too protectionist." The Chicago report was classified and should not normally have been fodder for chats with reporters. Wilson wouldn't normally have mentioned it to CTV, but he thought they were on the wrong trail asking about Clinton.

By now the whole business was looking like a typical iteration of the children's campfire game Telephone, and it was ending the way it usually does. Goolsbee said something to a Canadian in Chicago, who sent a memo to Washington, where somebody gossiped with Brodie, who chatted with CTV, who broke the story in mutually contradictory dribs and drabs over the next several days. Inevitably the next step was an attack ad. The Clinton radio ad in Ohio was designed to sound like a news story, which it really wasn't:

"This is an election news update with a major news story reported by the AP. While Senator Obama has crisscrossed Ohio giving speeches attacking NAFTA, his top economic advisor was telling the Canadians that was all just political maneuvering. . . . How will Ohioans decide whether they can believe Senator Obama's words? We'll find that out on election day. Paid for by Hillary Clinton for President."

Clinton wound up winning the Democratic primary in Ohio. Exit polls showed she was the overwhelming choice of late-deciding voters. The whole business about the Goolsbee memo and the prime minister's chief of staff leaking misleading stories to TV, the whole indigestible mess, received blanket news coverage in the United States, where Clinton vs. Obama was the season's best political story. Suddenly, just about the only thing millions of Americans knew about the Canadian prime minister was that his minions were meddling in a U.S. election. And it wasn't even true.

Harper went out to do damage control. He called the original stories about Obama's apparent NAFTA double-talk "blatantly unfair" to the Illinois senator. "There was no intention to convey, in any way, that Senator Obama and his campaign team were taking a different position in public from views expressed in private, including about NAFTA," he said. He appointed his most senior bureaucrat, Privy Council Clerk Kevin Lynch, to figure out what the hell had happened. Lynch reported at the end of May. "There is no evidence that Mr. Brodie disclosed any classified information," Lynch wrote. Brodie hadn't heard about the Chicago report on Goolsbee until he had gotten the whole story rolling with his budget lock-up chat with the CTV reporter. He'd just been spitballing, is all.

To Harper that must have seemed even worse. His chief of staff, the architect and feared enforcer of Conservative message discipline, had locked himself up with a roomful of bored reporters and flapped his jaw to spout fresh gossip on a story that had nothing to do with the news the government was trying to make. Five weeks after Lynch filed his report on the mess, a new chief of staff showed up for work at the Langevin Block.

The new guy was Guy Giorno. He had held the same post for Mike Harris in the late days of Progressive Conservative government in Ontario. Like Harris and a substantial number of Ontario Conservatives, he had supported Belinda Stronach in the 2004 Conservative leadership race, preferring a photogenic Ontarian to yet another Calgarian. But Giorno surprised Harper with an extraordinary article he wrote for the *National Post* in March 2005. The article delivered flattery when Harper was short on flatterers. And it also showed that Giorno's analysis of the Conservatives' situation was close to Harper's own.

At that point, midway between elections, Harper had been leader long enough to draw public criticism. Giorno wrote to tell his fellow Conservatives to knock it off. His text showed the sometimes obsessive attention to details and numbers that would be a hallmark of his political career. It was the Liberals who should be ashamed, he wrote, while the Conservatives had formed "the sixth-largest Official Opposition caucus in history." He accused Harper's detractors of making "five strategic errors."

First, they hadn't learned from the 2004 defeat, when Conservatives lost in the home stretch because "they became the issue instead of the Liberals." Second, they were showing a lack of discipline. (There has never been a time when Harper did not welcome hearing from somebody who wants Conservatives to show more discipline.) Third, Harper's detractors would, if they succeeded in turfing the leader, simply reward Liberals for sowing doubt about Harper. "It is foolish to believe that changing the truth of one's positions will stop others from lying about them," Giorno wrote. "Opponents will find new policies to twist, while the public will be confused by inconsistency." Fourth, the naysayers were letting themselves get rattled by a few bad polls. "Even a championship sports team will lose some games during the regular season. Imagine the folly of rewriting the playbook after a single loss. The result would be chaos, and many more losses."

But it was Giorno's final argument that revealed him to Harper as a potential asset for the future, not just a defender in a rough moment. "The fifth mistake," Giorno wrote, "is buying into Liberal stereotypes. I refer to the error of assuming that voters think the way Liberals and the media say they think."

This showed that, even though he had supported the most Liberal-friendly candidate in 2004 (Stronach would, in fact, leave the Conservatives to join the Liberals two months after Giorno wrote his op-ed), Giorno understood that Harper was seeking to build a new Conservatism on a different client base from the one the Liberals had built and Mulroney had sought to appropriate.

"It has become fashionable to dismiss Mr. Harper for failing to understand the 'urban vote' and 'ethnic vote'—as if those groups are monolithic and true to stereotype," Giorno wrote. "Ethnic voters and urban voters (I fit both categories) have their own minds, thank you very much, and don't take direction from the *Toronto Star*. What is disrespectful of these communities is to assume a Liberal party monopoly over them."

On the strength of that op-ed, Harper had brought Giorno in as a member of the 2006 campaign staff. Now, he promoted this advocate of discipline and consistency to be his most senior lieutenant.

Giorno wanted a new communications voice. Sandra Buckler had mastered a defensive game that consisted mostly of fending off reporters' queries. Her tight-lipped approach kept Conservatives from shooting themselves in the foot, but it had limited their ability to get their message out. They were like a hockey team with nothing but goalies. On Giorno's counsel, Harper replaced her with Teneycke, who had worked with Giorno in Ontario politics. Teneycke was tall, slim, blond, a former campus Progressive Conservative who had quit his party for Reform in the late 1990s, long before such defections became fashionable.

When he moved into his new office in the Langevin Block, Teneycke decorated the walls with three laminated posters. One was a Ronald

Reagan "Morning in America" re-election poster from 1984. The second was a Preston Manning poster from Manning's doomed attempt to fend off Stockwell Day for the leadership of the then-new Canadian Alliance in 2000. The third was most illustrative. It was a reproduction of a Canadian morale poster from the Second World War. It showed a soldier with a machine gun, a factory worker with a rivet gun and a female farmer brandishing a hoe, all in profile wearing the same expression of grim determination. "ATTACK," the poster said, "ON ALL FRONTS."

That slogan offered the best available summary of Giorno and Teneycke's operating philosophy. As in a game of chess, Giorno and Teneycke would try to attack with every move. They would use all the tools at a modern government's disposal. This included communication. Teneycke was less prone than his predecessor to play the defensive game of withholding information. He preferred to push it out, leavened with substantial doses of pro-Conservative spin. Giorno told senior staff the Conservatives had spent enough time demonstrating their competence at delivering dispassionate governance. Now they should leave most routine decisions to the public service. The Conservatives' job was to be Conservatives, and to win, the coming election. Let the permanent government run the permanent government.

One other appointment in early 2008 had helped Harper plan for growth in the Conservative vote in the election. He put Jason Kenney, the young Calgary MP, in charge of outreach to ethnic communities. It was a long play. The Liberals had spent decades courting ethnic voters, so Kenney often met polite indifference or worse. But Kenney was patient and diligent, and Harper trusted him. He scored an early victory with the immigrant constituency when he persuaded Harper to abandon visa requirements for visitors from several ex-Communist countries in the European Union.

The eastern European diaspora in Canada contains millions of voters, Kenney told his boss in March. They would notice this gesture. "These visa restrictions are going to be dropped someday. The department wants us to do it after the Americans and after the election. Why not do it before the Americans—and before an election?"

Harper liked the sound of that. A bureaucratic delegation from Foreign Affairs had toured Europe after Christmas and was months away from reporting. Harper didn't bother waiting. He dropped the restrictions in the spring. After that, the website of the Canadian Polish Congress was sometimes so full of cabinet ministers' photos it looked like the Conservative Party website. The head of the Polish association, Wladyslaw Lizon, would eventually run, in 2011, for the Conservatives.

In May 2008 Canada became the first country to recognize the Soviet-inflicted Ukrainian famine of 1932–33 as a genocide. James Bezan, the Conservative MP for Selkirk-Interlake, introduced the bill. The opposition parties hurried to get behind it. It passed quickly and unanimously. But the idea and the initiative were the Conservatives'. It got noticed.

———

The election player whose result was hardest to predict was Jack Layton. His ambitions were through the roof, but they weren't baseless. He had posted steady progress in two previous elections. In 2000, under Alexa McDonough, the NDP had won just over a million votes. Under Layton that score had grown in 2004 and again, to 2.5 million, in 2006. When pollsters asked whom voters liked as prime minister, Layton kept coming in second, behind Harper—but ahead of Dion.

At an NDP convention in Quebec City in the summer of 2006, Layton had told party members he intended to campaign for the job of prime minister at the next election. When he made the announcement, Layton's caucus counted twenty-nine MPs. His vow to become prime minister received almost no coverage because the reporters there dismissed it as fantasy. Now he made every effort to act as if he was putting his promise into action. On August 31, when Harper invited him to 24 Sussex Drive in the long prelude to the election call, Layton had told reporters as he left the meeting that whenever Harper decided to "quit," he would "apply for his job." On the first day of the campaign, Layton flew, using the campaign plane he had managed to rent because he was not Stéphane Dion, straight to Harper's Calgary riding.

On Wednesday, September 17, Harper and Dion found their campaign itineraries bringing them close together, which made it easy to compare their styles. The battleground of the moment was south-western Ontario, a Chrétien Liberal stronghold that veered sharply Conservative in 2006. Harper's destination, Welland, was about 160 kilometres away from Dion's event in London. The ideological and strategic differences on display were much further apart.

Dion was at the University of Western Ontario to talk about universi-ties. "Nothing could stop me from coming to Western," he said. "I would have jogged here." He proceeded to list a bunch of changes to student aid. A Liberal government would replace a range of student credits and benefits with an upfront education grant payable every three months. Dion would add 100,000 "access bursaries" for Aboriginals and other under-represented groups. He would increase funding for the indirect costs of university research by 60 percent. And he would borrow $25 billion to bankroll needs-based bursaries for two decades to come.

Taken together, Dion's promises on this one day of campaigning would tally perhaps $1 billion, in addition to the increase in federal debt that would pay for his bursary endowment. Eventually his proposals for stu-dent aid would earn the Liberals an A-minus from the Canadian Federation of Students. But good luck to any Liberal candidates trying to explain his plan at the doorstep. It was a morass of acronyms and program amendments. And Liberal candidates received no pedagogical material to make the plan more comprehensible to voters. They were on their own.

Almost at the same instant, Harper stepped behind a podium at the Casa Dante restaurant in Welland and vowed to ban tobacco products that were flavoured to taste like bubble gum and cotton candy. "These products are packaged as candy, and that's totally unacceptable," he said. Clearly the products were marketed to children. "This can't continue." To top it off, he would ban sales of cigarillos in packages of fewer than twenty.

Taken together, the promises Harper announced on this day would cost little more than the price of the photo opportunity. Their effect on tobacco use among children would be hard to measure. And, a Conservative campaign official revealed much later, the tobacco promises were invented only a few days ahead of the Welland announcement because Harper's staff decided he'd already gone too many days without a visually appealing photo op. To be fair, the re-elected Harper government actually did implement this ban on candy-flavoured tobacco. So the promise met a better fate than the diesel-tax cut did. But the candy-tobacco ban had little to do with a concerted strategy against tobacco. It was a bauble at a moment when the Harper campaign needed a bauble.

"Dion was announcing $100 million a day. Harper was announcing $2 million a day. And on the evening news we would play them to a tie," a Conservative campaign insider said.

Periodically during the 2008 campaign, Dion would mention his bold new vision for Canada. When such remarks played on television, they invariably drew chuckles in the Conservative war room, the insider said. "We're so cynical, we laugh at him. Like, internally. We're so focused on small, limited, targeted initiatives that we say, 'Well, that's not gonna work.'"

As part of their effort to get maximum pop from minimum campaigning, the Conservatives devoted far more of their ad budget than in 2006 to television with a large female audience, such as the Food Network, HGTV and the doctors-in-love drama *Grey's Anatomy*. Several days into the campaign, a Harris Decima poll showed that 22 percent of respondents, both male and female, reported seeing "a great deal" of Conservative advertising. Only 8 percent said they'd seen a great deal of Liberal advertising; for the NDP the figure was 3 percent. The same firm's polls showed the Conservatives opening an early lead over every party among rural women and those over the age of fifty. The Tories and Liberals would trade the lead among younger and urban women throughout the campaign, but simply being competitive in that market constituted a breakthrough for the Conservatives.

Dion, meanwhile, was pushing back at every attempt by his staff to make either his policies or his discourse digestible or relevant to disengaged voters. At the heart of his problems was the Green Shift and its carbon tax. Brian Topp, an NDP strategist, called it a "very big anchor" for the Liberals.

Michael Marzolini, the Liberals' chief pollster, would not have used different language. In the spring he had tested every argument for and against the Green Shift with focus groups. Some people say it's an intrusive, big-government tax grab: what do you think? Some people say it's our chance to do our bit for a twenty-first-century economy in a greener world: do you agree? Support for the arguments in favour was "fairly middling," a Liberal familiar with the research said. Support for the arguments against the Green Shift was "incredibly strong." Marzolini told Dion the policy would be electoral suicide. Weeks later it was the centrepiece of Dion's election plan.

Of course it is good to believe in things. But Dion's campaign staff urged their leader to sugar the pill a bit, or at least to accompany the Green Shift with policies that might make environmentalism easier to understand and embrace. A ban on dumping sewage in waterways? Dion wasn't interested. Plant trees at every stop? A gimmick, he said. Phase incandescent light bulbs out in favour of fluorescents? "We had that before John Baird did," a Liberal source said, but it was Baird who announced the end of incandescents instead of Dion. (The shift to fluorescent bulbs, like most of the rest of the Conservatives' environmental agenda, would be delayed repeatedly after it was announced.)

By mid-campaign, the Liberal team was receiving frantic memos from all over about the leader's performance. At his law office in Toronto, national campaign co-chairman Senator David Smith said that in less than an hour he'd received calls from two former cabinet ministers, Herb Dhaliwal and Anne McLellan, and from Heather Chiasson at the National Women's Liberal Commission. Were they happy calls? Long pause. "Well . . . they're happy in the sense that the family is there," Smith said. "There's some good positive ideas." So no, they weren't happy calls. One B.C. organizer said later he was drawing inspiration from the Jude Law war movie *Enemy at the Gates*. The harrowing battle sequence at the beginning of that film depicts Soviet Red Army regulars so desperately besieged that they don't even have enough guns to fight off the German invaders at Stalingrad. An officer hands a rifle to every second grunt. "'The one with the rifle shoots. The one without follows him,'" the organizer said, quoting the hopeless officer. "'When the one with the rifle gets killed, the one who is following picks up the rifle and shoots.' I say that every morning at the staff meeting."

Dion arrived in Vancouver and promised to spend $250 million against the mountain pine beetle. Marzolini, vexed, sent a memo to the Liberal campaign office. It landed at five o'clock the next morning. "Canadians do not care about the size of funding announcements," he wrote. "Each should be announced because Stéphane Dion cares about the average Canadian and shares their values." With their leader touring the country with lists of problems and dollar figures in his hand, the Liberals looked like "cold-hearted accountants."

But suddenly the Conservatives could not take much pleasure from the Liberals' discomfiture. They had serious trouble of their own. It came from Quebec.

Early in August, Canwest News had reported that the Harper government was cutting a $4.7-million program designed to send artists abroad to promote Canadian culture. When Canwest's reporter David Akin called the PMO for comment, he was told the money had been going "to groups that would raise the eyebrows of any typical Canadian." Those included the "general radical" and former CBC broadcaster Avi Lewis, and a Toronto band named Fucked Up. "I think there's a reasonable expectation by taxpayers that they won't fund the world travel of wealthy rock stars, ideological activists or fringe and alternative groups," Akin's source said.

Within a week various news organizations were pegging the total cuts to assorted arts programs at $45 million. The culture-war overtones of the PMO's political defence went down particularly badly in Quebec. By late August hundreds of artists were staging protests in Montreal and Toronto. "They don't want to recognize the existence of art in our society, and that's appalling," actress Marie Tifo said in Montreal. "I'm here with all my peers to say 'no,' we exist, and [culture] is an essential good." A satirical video appeared on YouTube, showing pop singer Michel Rivard facing a thuggish panel of Ottawa arts bureaucrats who get his French lyrics all wrong and won't give him a grant. The ad, which was funnier than I've made it sound, went viral, logging hundreds of thousands of views. Layton and Duceppe organized their campaign tours so they could attend a Montreal concert protesting the cuts. The Conservatives want to "turn off the floodlights on our stories, on our hearts, on our souls," Layton told the crowd. "We say that creative industries are an enormous part of our country's future."

In Saskatoon Harper's political radar let him down. Perhaps playing to the Western crowd he saw before him, he called the cuts "a niche issue for some."

Then he elaborated. "You know, I think when ordinary, working people come home, turn on the TV and see . . . a bunch of people at a rich gala all subsidized by the taxpayers, claiming their subsidies aren't high enough when they know the subsidies have actually gone up, I'm not sure that's something that resonates with ordinary people."

Francophone reporters asked Harper to repeat the comment for French-language TV and radio, a routine request. Perhaps he hadn't liked the sound of his remark as it escaped his lips. For whatever reason, he declined. But the Conservatives' Quebec problems were only beginning. The Bloc soared up toward 40 percent in Quebec polls. The Conservatives, who had been flirting with 30 percent support or higher, collapsed to 20 percent or lower. At those levels, Harper could forget about picking up seats in Quebec. The challenge now would be to salvage the ones he already had.

———

Dion, meanwhile, was finally learning how to deliver a campaign speech. His belated journey up the learning curve could not have come any later. On Friday, September 26, the midday tracking poll from Nanos Research showed the worst result of the campaign for the Liberals. The Conservatives led nationwide with 40 percent to 25 percent for the Liberals and 19 percent for the NDP. Those numbers made a Harper majority possible. The Liberal number was three points lower than John Turner had won in 1984, up to now the party's lowest share of the popular vote since Confederation.

As Dion prepared for an event at a farm in Belmont, Ontario, word of Harper's morning event started to arrive. With banks failing in the

U.S. and a global liquidity crisis fast advancing, the Liberals had been hitting Harper hard on his handling of the economy. Now Harper had accused Dion of "trying to drive down confidence in the Canadian economy without foundation—and quite frankly sitting on the sidelines virtually cheering for there to be a recession."

Dion was furious, and huddled with Jim Munson, a former CTV news reporter turned Chrétien-appointed Liberal senator, and Herb Metcalfe, another veteran Liberal organizer. The two men thought Dion's anger might be an asset. They told him to let it show when he addressed the crowd.

So Dion let loose. At the Belmont farm and again in a rally in London that night, he ditched the teleprompter he had been using for his speeches and simply vented. "He lied today in order to make cheap shots," he said of Harper. "This is unacceptable. And it says a lot about him and nothing about me." He said he would debate the economy any time with Harper "if he wants to discuss it as an adult."

The crowds at both events loved it. Dion led local newscasts in London, Hamilton and Kitchener. "You did what you were supposed to," Munson told him. For weeks Munson had been trying to get Dion to understand that the emotive line wasn't necessarily a betrayal of the intellectual line.

"Well, sir," Munson would ask Dion, in Socratic fashion, "what does enhanced productivity mean?"

Dion would ponder the question at some length. ". . . Jobs?"

Here was progress. "Well, why don't we say that?" Munson would reply. "And what do jobs mean?"

". . . Hope?"

"Well, we could say that too."

The night after the Belmont speech, Dion took time off from campaigning to spend an evening at home at Stornoway. Metcalfe came for dinner, armed with new numbers from Marzolini's overnight polls.

He told Dion: "Your numbers are starting to move because people are starting to see passion and conviction." Dion would need both: the leaders' debates were now only days away.

There had already been considerable preliminary debate over the format of the debates—and the attendance list. Dion and Elizabeth May, the Green Party leader, had a non-aggression pact. He had announced in April 2007 that he would run no candidate against her in Central Nova, the Nova Scotia riding where she had chosen to run against Peter MacKay. Their alliance was not purely tactical; they clearly got along well. She often said she would greatly prefer Dion as prime minister over Harper. Dion called her "courageous" for saying so.

That was all the evidence Harper needed to conclude that May and Dion were objective allies. Only one of them should be allowed in the debates. They were free, he said magnanimously, to decide which one of them it should be. Conservatives also persuaded Layton's campaign staff that it was to the NDP leader's benefit to keep May out of the debates. In a crowd Layton could not hope to stand out, they argued. With only Dion and Layton representing alternatives to the Conservatives outside Quebec, Layton might hope to marginalize Dion. The Conservatives were sure they had persuaded Brian Topp, Layton's campaign director, of the logic of this argument. But when May began to complain that she was being frozen out, Layton heard an earful from NDP supporters from coast to coast. Ordinary New Democrats were not inclined to think strategically. They figured the more people onstage who didn't think like Harper, the better. E-mails to the party ran overwhelmingly against keeping May out. Layton couldn't get his daily campaign message out because reporters only wanted to know about why he thought May shouldn't be in the debates. So Layton caved. May would be welcome, he said.

Four hours later, Harper abandoned his opposition to May's participation. Privately he viewed Layton's capitulation as further proof that the New Democrat leader was more interested in being a nice guy than in winning. In Harper's eyes it was an unforgivable flaw.

The debate was turning into a swamp for Harper. He would now have four people attacking him, not three. He was vulnerable on May's defining issue, the environment. Worst of all, she was a woman and he had a temper.

"It circles back to the women-vote thing and the need for women to be reassured, that they want someone calm," a Conservative close to Harper said. "A lot of time was spent in debate prep on getting Stephen ready about how to look at and treat and react to Elizabeth May."

So Michael Coates, the CEO of Hill+Knowlton Canada, had one preoccupation as he started preparing Harper for the debates. No matter how much the other leaders tried to kick sand in Harper's face, the Conservative leader must be calm and reassuring. The debate prep team told Harper to keep staring at Elizabeth May with what one advisor called "the icy blue eyes of love."

It was a profoundly defensive strategy. "He knew," the advisor said, "that how he reacted and dealt with her could potentially, in one wrong move, one wrong look, one wrong word, one wrong reaction, be captured and just drive away that vote that they worked so hard to get."

Immediately before a leaders' debate, campaigns often release some juicy bit of news to rattle and demoralize their opponent. These "destabilizers" are usually uncovered months ahead of time by party research offices. There comes a day when you find something embarrassing about the other party. Instead of pushing it out immediately, when nobody is paying attention and your opponent will have all the time in the world to recover, you sock it away for debate day. Sometimes it's not even something secret. Days after Dion became Liberal leader he appeared on Don Newman's CBC *Politics* show, where he told his host he would win the English-language leaders' debate when it came. The Conservatives' eyebrows raised and somebody put the clip aside for the right moment. On the day before the first debate of the 2008 campaign the party sent the clip to the television networks so the pre-debate shows would be full of footage of Dion looking arrogant.

Here at least, in the search for campaign destabilizers, the Liberals had the Conservatives soundly beat. On the morning of the first debate, Bob Rae had a foreign affairs speech scheduled in Toronto, complete with a surprise. While Rae watched from his podium, onstage TV monitors showed a speech Harper had delivered on the eve of the U.S. invasion of Iraq in 2003. Next to Harper were images of John Howard, then Australia's prime minister, giving a speech of his own thirty hours before Harper's.

They were the same speech.

Sentence after sentence, somebody had lifted Howard's arguments and given them to Harper to parrot. The effect of the side-by-side videos was extraordinary. On a major foreign-policy issue, here was Harper speaking another man's words. It reinforced the notion that Harper got all his foreign-policy ideas from conservatives in other countries. It undercut a cherished element of the Harper mythology, that he was his party's leading thinker and his own best speech writer. And it just made him look silly.

Hours after Rae spoke, a long-time Harper speech writer, Owen Lippert, confessed to the plagiarism and resigned from the campaign. The Howard tape didn't really affect the campaign, except to launch teams of researchers from every party into an orgy of Google searching to try to catch other parties in similar patterns of plagiarism. One Conservative in the Harper war room started running every Harper speech through plagiarism-detection software in case the Liberals had another such salvo ready to fire. The rest of Harper's speeches came up clean. But the lifted speech did transfer a little good morale from Harper's camp to Dion's. And that's where things stood as the French debate began on Wednesday night.

Harper smiled doggedly. Alone among the leaders, he referred to his opponents by their first names. Duceppe accused him, three times in the first five minutes of the debate, of "enriching the rich oilmen." Layton said his environmental policy would be great for Exxon. Dion reminded Harper of every insult he had ever sent Dion's way, such as the time he'd called Dion a fan of the Taliban for asking about prisoner abuse. Duceppe told Harper that by letting Michael Fortier, an unelected senator, parade around Quebec telling voters it was a waste of money to vote for the Bloc, Harper was showing "contempt for democracy."

The prime minister looked trapped. Trapped and weirdly happy. There was no getting that smile off his face. Still, he looked besieged. By agreeing to a seated format, he had consented to a format that made everyone look the same. Since it eliminated his height advantage, he wound up looking small and docile. He had not ever wanted to look small and docile in his life.

Something else happened too. Dion kept turning toward the camera, an unnatural behaviour that, thanks to the tight angle of the TV camera shots, gave him an intimate contact with the camera that the others lacked. He spoke in quiet, conversational tones. The others, with their tunnel-vision attacks on Harper, let him talk. And Dion, alone among the leaders, brought something new: a "thirty-day plan" for dealing with the economic turbulence. It was nothing fancy, basically just a plan for meetings. As prime minister, Dion would meet the premiers, some private-sector economists, and the heads of the Bank of Canada and other federal agencies, as soon as he could. He'd put out an economic update. He'd speed up some infrastructure spending.

The flimsiness of Dion's plan would end up sharply limiting its useful shelf life. But for now at least he had a set of ideas about what was turning into some truly nasty global economic turbulence. Harper didn't, as far as anyone could tell. He had identified economic turmoil as a major campaign issue as early as his trip to Rideau Hall on Day One. He had asked the broadcast consortium that was broadcasting the debates to lengthen the economic component of this debate from twelve minutes to thirty. He'd been reminding every crowd he'd spoken to that he was an economist. But he'd brought nothing to this debate but icy blue eyes of love.

"At a moment when heads of government around the world are acting to address this crisis, Mr. Harper seemed passive," Radio-Canada commentator Michel C. Auger told the network's viewers later. Over at TVA, Jean Lapierre had even more surprising news. Among viewers who had called and written to the network with an opinion, Dion was the clear winner.

On Thursday came the rematch in English. Outside the National Arts Centre, young Conservatives waved blue candidates' signs, pursued by mobs of young Liberals chanting "Ozzie Ozzie Ozzie, Oi Oi Oi!" Because Harper had delivered a John Howard speech. Get it?

Inside, this time, Harper brought an offensive game. His staff had spent the morning scripting and rehearsing an opening charge against Dion. "What leaders have to do is have a plan and not panic. Last night, Stéphane, you panicked." Canada's economy wasn't the same as the one south of the border, he said, and ours wasn't doing too badly.

It was the sort of thing that sounds clever until you say it. The debate wasn't five minutes old and Harper had already managed to sound more blasé in English than he had sounded all night in French. "The economy is not fine," Layton shot back. "Now, either you don't care or you're incompetent. Which is it?" Layton wouldn't stop needling Harper. Every other party had released a platform, Layton pointed out, except the Conservatives. "Where is it?" he asked. "Under the sweater?"

Mostly the debate was a mess. And Harper had not managed to dispel the impression he was a bit out of it. Later, during the post-mortem exercise Harper had bragged about during the fake breakfast with reporters in Toronto, the campaign team would decide they had made a serious mistake in preparing for this debate. In handing debate prep to Mike Coates and a bunch of other people who had no daily involvement in the rest of the campaign—competent as they were—they had ensured that Debate Harper would be subtly different from Rest-of-Campaign Harper. Different body language, different catchphrases, different tone. Which was great if they wanted to convey, to the largest audience they were going to get in the campaign, that the Conservative leader had been captured by body snatchers. And if not, not. Next time, Harper's regular campaign staff would coach him for the debates.

When Frank Graves of the polling firm EKOS Research Associates did a quick survey after the 2008 debates to check viewer perceptions, he found something curious. When he asked who had won the English debate, 26 percent said nobody had. Harper came in second with 23 percent; May followed with 18 percent; Layton with 15 percent. At 10 percent, Dion came dead last, except for Duceppe. When asked who had lost the debate, respondents were as likely to name Harper as Dion, at 25 percent each. This meant only that Harper was a polarizing figure, with fans as well as detractors. With a tie for top loser and a fourth-place berth out of five in the winners' circle, Dion could not claim to have had a stellar night.

But then EKOS asked respondents whether anything they had seen would make them reconsider their vote. Eighteen percent said yes, a pretty high number. And who were they thinking of voting for? Among the vote-changers, the highest number—22 percent—said they were thinking of voting Liberal. Harper's Conservatives had attracted only 7 percent of vote-switchers.

This helps explain why coverage of debates is such a lousy predictor of their political effect. Journalists covering debates are trying to declare a winner. Everyone else is looking for a prime minister. A lot of people watching the debate had decided Dion didn't win it. But a significant fraction among them had decided he might make a good prime minister anyway.

The Liberals were back in the game. At first Dion even seemed to have some vague awareness that this was the case. But he had a much better plan for the thirty days after the election than he did for the twelve days left before it.

The next day Dion was in Montreal to address the Board of Trade along with a similar group representing young people in business. He was obviously on a bit of a high, full of obscure asides and literary allusions. "I'm always wary when I hear about 'la relève,'" he told the young entrepreneurs in French, using the term that means a rising generation. Its literal translation would be "the next shift" or "the ones who take over." "I'm always reminded of what Gilles Vigneault said whenever he heard it: 'What, did somebody fall?'"

This was the day the U.S. House of Representatives would pass a reworked version of the US$700-billion bank bailout package it had rejected, in a particularly nasty afternoon of infighting and finger-pointing, four days earlier. "We need a plan," Dion said. "A plan made in Canada, not in Australia." Applause, none too raucous, from the business crowd. "One thing that is certain: Stephen Harper is an economic risk Canadians can no longer afford," Dion said.

It was not a bad speech, but neither was this business lunch the kind of foot-stomping rally Dion needed to fan the weak flame of hope he had finally lit for his campaign. By Saturday in Dieppe, New Brunswick, Dion was finally sounding like a bit of a populist. He said he wanted a Canada "where not only the rich go to university," a potent distillation of the indigestible seminar on student aid he had delivered early on at Western. He wanted a Canada "where nobody has to sell their house to pay for their medication."

"He's beginning to feed off the crowds that he sees," Munson said later, after a brief stop on Prince Edward Island. The Conservatives had been saturating the tiny province with its four Liberal seats for a year—radio ads, mailers to every household, visits by half the cabinet. Dion needed to shore up Liberal support. Still playing defence. "He's beginning to pay attention to the simpler messaging that he could be using."

Wasn't it perilously late?

"Well, it is. Absolutely. But it's happening. That's the good thing. It's happening," Munson said.

But it was happening in the middle of nowhere. After New Brunswick, incredibly, Dion went to Nunavut, then to the almost equally isolated town of Churchill, Manitoba. Harper was actually taking the day off. But the election was ever closer, the surprising debate performance another day further into the past. Dion was doing nothing useful to push his advantage. Yet almost despite him, support for the Conservatives was starting to fall in the daily tracking polls. Nanos, which had put the gap between the two largest parties at fifteen points only nine days before, now had it down to four.

On Tuesday the Conservatives finally released their platform. The election was a week away. The plan had always been to drop a platform near the end of the campaign. It would not announce a glorious future because Harper was supposed to be the candidate of stability pointing out the nonsense in everyone else's plan for a glorious future. Policy for the Conservatives had been very much an afterthought this time around.

Harper's problem now was that the economy and his shaky debate performance had made at least some voters wonder whether he was still up to the job. His platform, designed as a show of confidence from a party whose old ideas worked fine, now looked like confirmation that it was out of new ideas. As Dion's chartered Air Inuit plane flew from Victoria over the Prairies, Dion's advisors pored over the Conservative campaign document.

At a rally for candidate Anthony Rota, the Liberal leader shared the fruits of his staff's research. Harper's forty-four-page document made no reference to poverty, climate change or fiscal discipline, Dion said. But it mentioned Harper a hundred times. "We have a platform of sixty-six pages," he said. "We mention the leader six times." The Liberal platform had one picture of Dion. "It's a very nice picture." Harper's platform had twenty-two pictures of Harper. "Beyond the words, it's all about him. It's me, myself and I," said Dion. "It's his navel. It's about his job. Our plan is about your jobs." The crowd of four hundred roared. It was the kind of rally Dion could have used four days earlier, to capitalize on the momentum coming out of his performance in the debate.

While the Liberal leader was at pains to depict Harper as out of touch with ordinary Canadians, Harper seemed eager to help him. Speaking to reporters after his platform launch, Harper was relaxed and expansive, delivering long, thoughtful replies to the questions from the press gallery. This turned out to be a problem. "I think there's probably some great buying opportunities emerging in the stock market as a consequence of all this panic," Harper said. Certainly there was panic: the S&P/TSX Composite Index was down for the fifth straight day.

That night Harper appeared on the CBC to be quizzed by Peter Mansbridge. The CBC had labelled their leaders feature "Your Turn," and its conceit was that this was supposed to be a chance for ordinary Canadians to ask leaders the questions. Only one leader had refused that format. Guess which one. Harper would take questions from Mansbridge alone, the CBC had been told, or he would not show up.

As it happened, it did not much matter who asked the questions that night. Harper was determined to dig himself deeper. "We always know that when stock markets go up, people end up buying a lot of things that are overpriced and when stock markets go down people end up passing on a lot of things that are underpriced," he said. "I think there are probably some gains to be made in the stock market."

Mansbridge was incredulous. "Do you really want to be heard saying that?"

Publicly, Harper's team insisted the leader's comments were innocuous. Privately, the remarks hit the Conservatives like a lightning bolt. Ever since the Lehman Brothers collapse on September 15, barely eight days into this campaign, a few Conservatives, including Muttart and Teneycke, had been nervous. They had designed a campaign suitable for sitting on a comfortable lead, one that depended on a calm electorate. But Harper's reassuring tone had, for some time, been an increasingly lousy fit for the voters' mood. Before the debates, the campaign's road team and headquarters staff had convened in the dining room at 24 Sussex Drive to discuss the progress of the campaign. Doug Finley, Jenni Byrne, Teneycke and Muttart were among the participants. They all told Harper that the Conservatives' slide in the polls was real. The participants agreed to show more empathy on economic concerns and make sure the focus stayed on Dion.

But in the days after the debate it became clear that the Conservative campaign wasn't swift or agile enough to adjust to changing circumstances. And the leader himself seemed, simply, not to get that he was much of the problem. Later, many Conservatives would point out that early October 2008 was, in fact, a period of excellent buying opportunity in the stock market. None of them thought Harper should have said so. "This was Harper being Harper the pundit," one said. "Harper the pundit is a fantastic pundit. He's a very interesting pundit. But you don't get to be a pundit when you're the prime minister."

Now, finally, Harper tried to hammer home the idea that the alternative to him wasn't bliss, it was Dion and Layton and Duceppe. In Victoria on October 8, for the first time, he raised the possibility that a coalition of opposition parties might wind up in power. "If you get Prime Minister Dion, either directly or by the opposition parties helping him take power, interest rates are going to go up."

Events in the real world were accelerating as the campaign sped toward its conclusion. On Wednesday, October 8, the Bank of Canada joined the European Central Bank and central banks in the United States, Sweden, Switzerland and the U.K. in announcing a simultaneous half-point cut in their base rates. China followed suit hours later. It was a nearly worldwide expression of concern about the flagging global economy, conjured by the fates as if to underscore Harper's contention that voters must not view this as an ordinary election.

But this late in the game, a change in tone might not be enough to improve Harper's trajectory. "We weren't running on our ballot question," one of his advisors said later, "and we weren't fighting a campaign against a real person." How bad was it? "I think it was possible to lose."

Somebody needed to make the choice real again, and turn the comparison to Harper's advantage. That task fell to Stéphane Dion.

In Halifax, Dion made what is nearly an obligatory call for campaigning leaders who want to reach a wide Atlantic audience: the studio of veteran ATV supper-hour news anchor Steve Murphy. The interview was pre-taped, as most of these things are. Anchor and party leader sat facing each other.

"If you were prime minister now," Murphy asked, "what would you have done about the economy and this crisis that Mr. Harper has not done?"

Who among us is rock-solid on questions phrased in the conditional perfect tense in our second language? "If I would have been the prime minister two and a half years ago?" Dion responded, uncertainly.

"If you were the prime minister now," Murphy said, "and had been for the past two years."

The look of bewilderment on Dion's face was plain. Perhaps by now he understood the question but was seeking to reframe it to his advantage. "If I'm elected next Tuesday," he said. "This Tuesday." He was trying to explain what he would do, starting the morning after an election. The whole point of his thirty-day plan was that it was about the future.

But Murphy was asking about the past. Murphy wanted to refight the past. Murphy wanted to know what Dion would have done if he'd been in Harper's shoes when the crisis hit. Dion ignored this, or perhaps he still did not understand it. He pressed ahead. "I would start the 30-50 plan that we want to start the moment we have a Liberal government."

Okay, that wasn't great. It wasn't even what Dion had meant to say. He had meant to put in a plug for his thirty-day economic plan. The 30-50 plan was his anti-poverty agenda, which he didn't want to talk about right now. Dion tried to correct himself, then thought better of it. "Can we start again?"

This sort of thing happens in television, which after all most often seeks to present an idealized simulation of reality. Mistakes happen. When the broadcast isn't live, as this wasn't, there are all kinds of chances to fix mistakes. Often an anchor screws up the intro or the question and asks his production crew and his guest for their indulgence while he restarts. It's less common for the guest to request a Mulligan, but it's not unheard of. So Dion and Murphy restarted. Murphy asked the question again. But even then, Dion still didn't know where to situate himself, the question, and the fate of the nation in time and space. Dion's press secretary, Sarah Bain, off camera, tried to explain the question to him. Dion asked for yet another restart. It all went downhill from there.

In what follows, it's worth remembering that Murphy had agreed to a do-over. He had not said, "No, Mr. Dion, your answer must stand!" So it was highly unusual for him and the CTV management to decide, later, to air the false starts. Just as it was odd that the whole tape found its way onto coast-to-coast cable via Mike Duffy's CTV Newsnet show. Both choices—to air Dion's false starts and to take them national (well, national-ish; the supper-hour Ottawa cable news shows hardly have huge audiences)—would be criticized by other journalists for a long time to come.

The decision was made during a lengthy phone call between Halifax and Toronto whose participants included Robert Hurst, CTV News president. The journalists decided one do-over was permissible (and had been permitted by Murphy), but a chain of fumbles was a story. "My personal sense is if we had to restart the interview once, you and I wouldn't be talking about this today," CTV Atlantic news director Jay Witherbee told Susan Newhook, an assistant professor of journalism at King's College School of Journalism, two weeks after the election. "Somewhere between that and an aide jumping in to explain the question, and a few other do-overs, we got ourselves to the situation that we're in."

The following May, the Canadian Broadcast Standards Council would rule against both CTV and Duffy for their behaviour on this campaign Friday. But of course, by May, it would be altogether too late.

The upshot was that Dion was seen on TV looking like a goof on the very issue he had hammered Harper on for a week. "Isn't this great?" a Conservative war room staffer told me at the moment the news broke. "It's so great on so many levels."

The Conservatives' only worry was that the Dion interview would remain stuck in the viewership ghetto of CTV's Atlantic affiliate and its cable news show. Travelling with Harper in Winnipeg, Teneycke made a quick decision: get the leader back out in front of the TV cameras. Everybody would have to carry the prime minister's comments. And they would also have to carry the interview footage to put the comments in context.

"When you're managing a trillion-and-a-half-dollar economy, you don't get a chance to do do-overs, over and over again," Harper said. "I don't think this is a question of language at all. The question was very clear. It was asked repeatedly. But what's important in the end, after all the times the question was put, the answer was, from Mr. Dion, that he does not have a plan, that if he is elected he would spend thirty days trying to create one."

To call this entire display disingenuous would be like calling the Pacific Ocean moist. Harper had been the only party leader to show up at the televised debates without a platform. The platform, when it did land, was mostly a photographic celebration of Harper's physiognomy. He would never implement large parts of the plan he did put before the voters. And he would wind up swiping much of the plan from Dion that he claimed Dion didn't have—the meeting with premiers and leading economists, an early economic update . . . but again we are getting ahead of ourselves. For now it is worth pointing out that Harper's attack on Dion's credibility presumed a good deal more credibility on Harper's own part than he had earned in this campaign. But it mattered little. For more than a year the Conservatives had warned voters that Dion was "Not a Leader." Now Dion had acted in a way that tended to confirm those suspicions. The resulting television footage would be the last image of him millions of voters would see before they voted.

The last image of Harper was one the Conservatives had chosen. After the debates, at the campaign meeting where it became clear Harper had pretty much screwed up in framing the election as a choice between economic stability and Liberal chaos, his staff had decided to shoot some new ads and make sure they landed in front of swing voters' eyeballs. Now on TVs across the country, whether they were tuned to HGTV or the Food Network or maybe some other channels, the last-ditch ads began to appear. They showed a young mother in a pantsuit in what was, frankly, her gorgeous, sprawling new kitchen. She looked worried. She picked up the paper. "Markets Unnerved," the headline said. The mother put a protective hand on her daughter's shoulder. There were no live males in this house, only televised images from the TV hanging in the corner of the immense kitchen. In fact, there was Stéphane Dion now. The mother listened and frowned. "He worries me," she said in voice-over. "He promises money like it grows on trees. Keeps promising this carbon tax. We can't afford more debt. I can't afford more taxes."

Mother and daughter cast a glance at each other over the sprawling marble-topped island in front of the immense spice racks. "Dion's just not worth the risk," she said to herself as the Conservative party logo appeared at the bottom of the screen.

The Conservatives did a bigger buy with that ad in targeted swing ridings than with any other of the campaign. "Our lead with women had slipped away a bit, but it's coming back," Marjory LeBreton said. "I always say women are the most worried about things, they're worried about stability."

When the final returns were in, the Conservatives had won again. The party's share of the popular vote inched upward 1.38 percentage points, to 37.65 percent. Given the lower voter turnout, it meant fewer Canadians had voted for Harper's party in 2008 than in 2006, although the same was true of all the major parties. What mattered, it seemed, was that Harper would return to the Commons on a more stable footing. He had 124 seats, up 16 from the 2006 elections. Layton's NDP, with voter support a shade higher than in 2006, picked up 7 more seats, for 37 in all.

Dion's Liberals lost 18 seats and not quite 4 percentage points in the popular vote. It was a smaller decline than the Liberals had suffered in 2006 and, it would turn out, smaller than they were in for in 2011. It was still plenty bad: the lowest share of the popular vote for the Liberals since Confederation.

Dion's leadership was destroyed. He would, astonishingly, spend six days alone with his family at Stornoway before finally emerging to admit as much. He would, he told reporters, resign the leadership as soon as his party could find a replacement.

Harper's election-night speech to supporters at Calgary's TELUS Convention Centre was becoming a tradition. This was his third such speech since he had become Conservative leader in 2004. "Tonight, Canadians have voted to move our country forward and they have done so with confidence in the future," he said. Even accounting for rhetorical flourishes it was a lousy choice of words. Canadians had almost never felt less confidence in the future. "These are challenging times in the world economy," Harper said. "Canadians are worried right now and I understand those worries. But I want to assure Canadians that working together we will weather this storm."

He announced three priorities. "First, we will continue to govern on behalf of all Canadians." And because, despite its electoral gains, the government's "scope is not as wide as it should be," Harper promised "an inclusive and responsive government."

Second, he vowed to "continue to respect the principle that government is accountable to the people's representatives in Parliament." To that end he asked the opposition parties to work with him on the problems facing the country.

And third, he promised to "keep our promises. We will do what we said we would do."

So much still lay ahead, but there was time for Harper to run one victory lap. Four weeks after the election, the Conservatives held a national policy convention in Winnipeg, the first they had permitted themselves since 2005. Holding a convention on the heels of an election campaign was a formidable and entirely optional logistical feat. They could have delayed the thing. But Harper wanted to underscore his victory. From its tenuous beginnings, Harper's tenure as prime minister had now outlasted those of nine others, including Paul Martin. By early 2011, if he could keep fending off the opposition parties, he would have outlasted Alexander Mackenzie, and then Lester Pearson, and then R.B. Bennett. His residency at 24 Sussex Drive was changing from something that had happened to something that would matter.

"Let us pause for a moment to truly reflect and appreciate how far we have come in such a short time," Harper told the assembled delegates. "Five years ago, the conservative movement in this country was divided, defeated and demoralized. The government of the day ridiculed us, the pundits discounted us, the public said, 'Don't bother talking to us until you've got your act together.' Worse, a political juggernaut was poised to take over the Prime Minister's Office."

There was a knowing laugh from the crowd. Once they had feared Paul Martin. But Harper and Peter MacKay had merged their parties and the Conservatives had fought one election to cut into the Liberals, a second to take them down and a third to consolidate victory. Referring to the election just finished, Harper said: "We made important inroads with women voters and new Canadians. We welcomed our first Conservative MP from the Northern Territories in two decades. We swept large parts of Ontario and made gains in the Greater Toronto area. We broke the Liberals' twenty-year stranglehold on Prince Edward Island, we picked up seats in British Columbia, New Brunswick, Nova Scotia and right here in Winnipeg. The Conservative Party is once again Canada's Party."

Of course that last was an applause line, but now Harper would transform it into the theme of his speech. Not long ago Conservatives' critique of the Liberals had seemed, even to some Conservatives, interchangeable with contempt for Canada. Harper had gone into the 2006 election facing questions about his love for his country. The rest of his speech would show how far he and his party had come from that untenable position.

"It is not by chance that Canadians of diverse backgrounds, communities and experiences have renewed their faith in our party at this critical time in our history," he said, "because the Conservative Party has always been Canada's Party. We are the party that has been there for Canada since the beginning. We are the party whose legacy movements have built and renewed our country. It was Conservatives who founded the Canadian federation in 1867, creating one of the most durable political arrangements anywhere in the world. Conservatives bound this country together with the Canadian Pacific Railway. Under Conservative prime ministers, women and Aboriginal people got the right to vote for the first time. This is the party under whose banner we elected the first Chinese, Black, Japanese, Muslim, Hindu-Canadian members of Parliament. We are the party with the first female cabinet minister, the first Aboriginal senator. We are the party that not only proposed electing a Senate—something all the other parties oppose—we have actually named elected senators. We are the party of Canada's first Bill of Rights, the party that first gave Aboriginal people living on reserves the same rights as other Canadians. This is our history. This is the truth, past and present. No other party has a better record for bringing Canadians together and of standing up for their country's interest—because the Conservative Party is Canada's Party."

There were still, there would always be, millions of Canadians who would find Harper's claim silly or obscene. Millions more might even vote Conservative but would reject, or never pause to consider, its new-found claim to synonymy with the national soul. But one narrow requirement for success in politics has always been the ability to say an audacious thing with a straight face. And one of the goals Harper had set for this party was that it would, someday, stop playing defensive on matters of the heart. Introducing him that night, Laureen Harper had told the crowd that her husband had always been willing to interrupt any meeting to take a phone call from their son, Ben, or daughter, Rachel. She said he had seen the movie *High School Musical* four times. She was methodically patting an undertaker's shovel on the caricature of Stephen Harper as a cold or distant father. Now he was staging his own funeral for the notion that the Conservative Party was an unwelcome or unwilling guest at the table of proud Canadians.

"We will succeed because Conservative values are Canadian values," he said. "Love of country. Commitment to community. Devotion to family. Respect for peace, order and the law. Reward for risk and hard work. These are the values on which our country was built and, in this way, the Conservative story is Canada's story. It is a story about people from all walks of life joining together to work toward common goals.

A story about harnessing the ingenuity and talents of a diverse population to overcome any challenge that may come our way. It's about building together what we could never have built alone."

This part of his speech, about "common goals" and "building together," could have been delivered by Tommy Douglas. Suddenly Conservative values were collectivist values too. No matter. He was on a roll. "We acknowledge our enormous debt to those who came before us. The Aboriginals who created Canada's first communities in a beautiful but harsh land. British settlers who brought with them political traditions and institutions we have moulded to make our own. And all the others from every corner of the earth who have made the difficult decision to leave their families behind and to build a better life. And especially all those here who have made the great sacrifice, our veterans, to stand up for our values.

"Canada is their legacy to us, and it is our duty to them to uphold the legacy of our forebears, to secure the future of our descendants. We will do so. Because the Conservative Party is Canada's Party."

The crowd roared its approval. The celebration would continue long into the Winnipeg night. The greatest political crisis of Stephen Harper's life was two weeks away.

SIX

THE SHORT SECOND ELECTION OF 2008

The prime minister of Canada sat alone in his office, staring at a four-page memo, the instrument of his undoing.

It was Monday afternoon, December 1, 2008. Forty-eight days earlier, Stephen Harper's Conservative Party had won re-election. A small increase in the popular vote had given them 143 out of the 308 seats in the House of Commons. Not a majority, sure, not technically. But it was sixteen more seats than Harper had controlled in the previous Parliament. Nine more than Paul Martin had after the 2004 election. Enough to govern, surely.

The other parties had seemed to agree that it was enough. For seven weeks Harper had been doing the things a prime minister gets to do. Nobody had said boo. Nobody tried to stop him. God knows they'd had plenty of chances to pipe up, if they thought they had a case. He'd appointed a new cabinet. Met with the premiers. Travelled abroad and spoken for Canada at summits of the mighty. He had trooped into the red Senate chamber along with everyone else and listened while Governor

General Michaëlle Jean read a Speech from the Throne full of plans and projects for his Conservative government. He had watched the Liberals, led by Stéphane Dion, vote for that Throne Speech fair and square, which meant they had signed on to this notion of a Conservative government. A Throne Speech vote is like a Chinese finger trap: you stick your thumb in and you can't pull it out, everybody knows that; and Dion's thumb was in the trap and he'd told the world he was retiring from politics anyway; and of course he was, because Stephen Harper had handed him his teeth rattling around in a zip-lock bag on election night—lowest popular vote in Liberal history, lowest seat count in Liberal history, and what the hell was Dion supposed to do but skulk back to the University of Montreal and teach half-term graduate seminars on how to be a great big loser? So of course Dion and the rest of them were going to let Harper keep governing. Nothing else was possible.

Except here's the thing. Damnedest thing. Funny thing. Stéphane Dion was about to take Harper's job away from him. That's what it said right there in the astonishing document in Harper's lap.

Alone in his office on the third floor of the Centre Block of Parliament in Ottawa, he stared at his copy of the news release of an agreement Dion, Jack Layton of the New Democratic Party and Gilles Duceppe of the Bloc Québécois had signed in a public ceremony a couple of hours earlier. Its pussy-footing, shit-eating title blackened Harper's mood even further: "A policy accord to address the present economic crisis."

The first paragraph of the text, under the heading "Preamble," gave the game away. "The new Government is supported by parties that share a commitment to fiscal responsibility, a progressive agenda and a belief in the role of Government to act as a partner with Canadians and Quebecers. Where appropriate, these goals should be pursued in full partnership and consultation with the provincial and territorial governments."

The new Government. A new government. A new government that wouldn't be Stephen Harper's government, but a cabal of his tormentors.

The signatories of this accord had conspired to kick Harper out of his office. They would form a government to take the Conservatives' place. Stéphane Dion would become prime minister. Jack Layton would sit in Dion's cabinet. Gilles Duceppe would promise that no Bloc Québécois mischief would unseat them. "The Liberal Party of Canada and the New Democratic Party of Canada will adhere to this agreement until June 30, 2011 unless renewed," their contract accord said.

Fuckers.

There was a knock at the door. Ray Novak let in three guests. As Harper's principal secretary, he controlled access to the prime minister. He was present at most important meetings. Even before he had been promoted to this new role on July 1, Novak had always played on files. His advice had always mattered to Harper. But now he had a title that matched the awesome clout that had accreted around him through years of managing not to screw up in the boss's presence. One cabinet minister said that when you couldn't get something done through ordinary channels you went to Ray. But only if you really had to. Novak could help or end a Conservative career in Ottawa as surely as Harper could. Usually it was impossible for an outsider to tell the difference between the master's actions and those of the apprentice. This cabinet minister called an e-mail of complaint to Novak "the nuclear option."

The three men Novak ushered into the boss's presence late that afternoon were ministers in Harper's government. As today was Monday, the Cabinet Operations committee had been holding its weekly meeting down the hall. The government had two central co-ordinating committees. Priorities and Planning met on Tuesdays and attempted to plan the government's action over the long term. Since the long term is regularly pre-empted by one damned thing or another, Ops met on Mondays to try to help the government win its immediate battles amid the chaos of any given week. Ops was for putting out fires. As luck would have it, here was a nice toasty fire now.

"Don't forget, Operations Committee was created by Mulroney, right?" a senior Conservative said much later. "He created Operations Committee, and the idea of Operations Committee was supposed to be that it was the political committee. That's where you put your most political ministers, your hardcore political guys. When Ops was first created there were no staff. It was the committee to which you threw the 51–49 political decisions. It was the Machiavelli committee. Still is."

All the members of Ops had heard the news that Statist and More Statist, propped up by Wants-an-Independent-Statist, had come together to launch a bicycle-clip junta. But the news had broken too late to make the agenda. So the committee had worked through the written order of business feeling more than a little ridiculous. "Okay, well I'm looking for permission to consult on the next phase of the drug patent legislation and I'm here seeking government's approval to support this Private Member's Bill," someone later said, paraphrasing the surreal ordinariness of the proceedings. "And the whole time we're just like, 'What the fuck are we doing?'"

So when the Ops meeting broke at five-thirty, and somebody reminded the assembled ministers that the next scheduled meeting was Monday a week hence, everyone laughed darkly. The way things were going, they would not have to worry about that meeting.

As their colleagues left, three ministers lingered. They discussed the real business of the day, which was the abyss. After a few minutes they decided to share some ideas with the prime minister.

———

Of the three visitors at the door, Jim Prentice was the chair of Ops. In the Mulroney days, that role had gone to the deputy prime minister. Prentice didn't have the title but he still had the responsibility. A handsome and meticulous Calgary lawyer, Prentice came from the Progressive Conservative side of the Conservative Party. He had boundless ambition, had run for the PC leadership and would, it was generally assumed, run to replace Harper someday, but he was cautious by nature. Jay Hill was Prentice's vice-chair, a Reformer from Prince George–Peace River in British Columbia. Like Harper, he had come to Ottawa in 1993 with Preston Manning's astonishing bumper crop of rookie Reform MPs. Harper had left politics from 1997 to 2002. Hill never left. He would never have Prentice's polish, but he had seen strange sights and he knew how to count. The third man, James Moore, was the youngest minister in cabinet, just thirty-three, built like a bear, an avid reader, a hell of a talker. Despite their disparate backgrounds, the three now occupied the same state of high anxiety.

After Novak ushered them into Harper's presence, Prentice laid out the Ops guys' consensus: Harper should ask the governor general to prorogue Parliament, suspending the legislative session almost before it had begun. It was for the good of the country, Prentice said. It would give everyone a chance to cool down.

Other visitors earlier in the day had given Harper similar advice. But Harper was tempted by another path. Let them win, he said. Let Stéphane Dion try to run the country, with Jack Layton tugging him to the left and Gilles Duceppe exercising a perpetual veto. The coalition will fall apart in six months. We'll pick up the pieces in the next election. Come back stronger than ever.

James Moore cut in. "It might be good politics to let them govern, screw up after three months and then we can go back to the country and win two hundred seats. That might happen." But he also pointed out that it might not. Given a choice between staying together in power and facing the voters in an election, the coalition would stick together for as long as possible. Meanwhile they would be shovelling the Harper government's secrets out the front door for the press to feed on. "But even if they do do well," Moore added, "they'll do well in their context. And that's bad for Canada. A three-headed government, led by a wonky and weak Stéphane

Dion. Being bullied by a strong-armed separatist whose real goal is to be premier of Quebec." Moore went on in this vein for a minute. "This is bad for Canada, boss. You can't do that. You have a bigger obligation."

The prime minister was unconvinced. It fell to Jay Hill to make the most direct appeal. "Prime minister," he said quietly, "if you give up power now, I don't know if you can survive as leader of the Conservative Party of Canada."

So that was late Monday afternoon. By then the gravest political crisis of Stephen Harper's career was four days old.

But let's back up.

Foresight probably shouldn't count if you don't know you're displaying any. In his first budget speech as minister of finance, on May 2, 2006, Jim Flaherty gave a bullish description of the economy his party had just inherited from the Liberals. This took some finessing. "Mr. Speaker," Flaherty declaimed, "Canadians have reached a level of accomplishment few other countries can rival. Our economy has shown great resilience, and in spite of a heavy tax burden, Canadian workers and business people have shown the world what talent and hard work can do." In fact, as he listed the bounties from across the land, Flaherty . must have spared a moment to wonder once again how the Liberals had managed to blow the election. Unemployment was at a thirty-year low. Corporate profits were at record levels. Nominal GDP was beating six-month-old projections by $20 billion.

It's at moments like this that speech writers like to insert a to-be-sure passage so the speaker can acknowledge difficulties and not come off looking like some kind of loopy Pollyanna. And here came that caveat now. "The challenges we need to watch for are still mostly external," Flaherty said. "Uncertainty about commodities prices. The risk of a sudden correction in U.S. house prices. And the impact of a higher dollar on our manufacturers."

More than two years later, when the Western economy started to fall apart, money nerds would spend endless hours debating whether anyone had seen this coming. Everyone knew "the risk of a sudden correction in U.S. house prices" was one of "the challenges we need to watch for." Nobody planned for it, is all. Flaherty spent the rest of the 2006 budget speech giving away the year's surplus, and future years' surpluses, in tax cuts.

And not much more was heard from the gods of bad luck until well into the 2008 election campaign. As he launched that campaign on September 7, Harper was banking on a little economic uncertainty to make the idea of changing from the Conservatives to the Liberals look risky. "Between now and October 14, Canadians will choose a government to look out for their interests at a time of global economic trouble," he told reporters in the Canadian Heritage Garden on the grounds of Rideau Hall.

If anything, Harper was understating the economic trouble at hand. He had spent the summer getting apocalyptic updates from Bank of Canada governor Mark Carney and from finance department officials. "That was one of the reasons that he wanted to have the election in fall 2008 rather than waiting," a former Harper advisor said later. "He was worried that the collapse had [already] happened."

A week into the campaign, Lehman Brothers declared bankruptcy. The markets went off a cliff. Harper and Flaherty couldn't co-ordinate their messages. Harper claimed the battered stock markets offered "some great buying opportunities." Three days later, Flaherty took over $25 billion of bank-held mortgages. Harper's opponents hammered him for being passive during a global crisis. They didn't stop him from winning, but maybe they planted a doubt in voters' minds.

After the election Harper moved quickly to show he was concentrating on the economy. He met with the premiers in Ottawa, for the first time in two years. On October 30, he swore in a new cabinet, promising: "The central responsibility of our new mandate will be to ensure Canadian families and businesses have the security they need to weather any global economic storm."

During the campaign he'd been categorical: his government would allow no budget deficits going forward. "Our election platform is not full of grandiose, costly promises," he wrote in the *Toronto Star* on October 14. "It's a prudent approach. We can afford it. We'll never go back into deficit."

October 14 was election day. By October 17, three whole days later, previous certainties no longer held. Funny what victory can do to rattle a man's convictions. In Quebec City, asked whether deficits were on the way, Harper said, "I don't think we're in a position to know all of the information. And I think it would be premature to speculate in that regard."

When swallowing yourself whole, keep swallowing. "One message was very clear," Harper told reporters after meeting with bank economists in Toronto on November 7. "Don't be afraid to run a deficit if the deficit is in the best interests of the economy." The government wouldn't "force a surplus" if a surplus was "clearly not in the economic interests of the Canadian economy." Having run as the man to protect Canadians from deficits, Harper was now protecting them from surpluses.

"Already, governments around the world have been responding with large budgetary actions," he told the Commons on November 20 in his address in reply to his government's Speech from the Throne. "China has announced a half-trillion-dollar package to bolster domestic spending. The United Kingdom and the United States, though already deeply in deficit, are moving ahead with additional fiscal stimulus. In short, world governments have resolved that they will undertake whatever financial, monitoring and budgetary measures are necessary to cope with the crisis. And, let me be clear: this is also the position of the Government of Canada."

Was he just giving China and Britain and the United States a hearty clap on the back as they dug themselves into deficit holes? Nope. He was preparing to join them. "We will undertake whatever short-term fiscal measures are necessary to be part of a global economic solution to a global economic problem."

All of which takes us most of the way to Flaherty's Economic and Fiscal Statement, which he was to deliver in the Commons on Thursday, November 27. The fall update is a staple of the federal budget cycle. Halfway between one spring budget and the next, a finance minister tells MPs, and through them the nation, how the economy is doing. It is always a big day. This year it would be crucial, because the fiscal woods were on fire.

But first Harper had to spend a weekend in Peru. The 2008 Asia-Pacific Economic Cooperation summit was in Lima. Harper's main public solo event was a speech to the affiliated APEC CEO Summit on Saturday, November 22. Listening now to the audio recording of that speech, it is possible to hear how uncertain Harper was over the fix Canada was in, and over the proper way forward.

A speaker always needs an opening joke. "Some have observed to me recently that winning re-election right now is a bit like winning a vacation in the Caribbean during hurricane season," he said. Heh-heh. But seriously, folks: "As everyone here knows, the financial crisis has become an economic crisis, and the world is entering an economic period unlike, and potentially as dangerous as, anything we have faced since 1929."

What should countries do? Canada had already done a lot, Harper said, recasting the tax cuts of 2006 as prudent fiscal stimulus instead of as raiding the pantry to reward the electorate for dumping the Liberals. But now it was starting to look as though more fiscal stimulus was needed. "These are, of course, the classic circumstances under which budgetary deficits are essential," he said.

"Now, I say this with some reluctance." Here he departed from his written text for emphasis: "In fact, some great reluctance." He'd helped create the Reform Party of Canada twenty years earlier in part to fight long-term structural deficits, he said. "So whatever short-term fiscal stimulus or government spending our government pursues, we will ensure that Canada does not return to long-term, structural budgetary deficits."

The way he spoke it, the sentence didn't make a lot of sense. Whatever government spending our government pursues? And in fact, the printed script he was reading from said: "whatever deficit spending." He had inserted "government" in place of "deficit" unconsciously. The word was in his speech but he couldn't bring himself to pronounce it.

But despite his reluctance, he was working himself into not just arguing for deficits, but preparing to deliver them. Since his written promise never to spend more than the government took in was only five weeks old, this took some mental contortions. Harper's new thesis: the greatest economic crisis of the twentieth century was pushed along by a mindless allegiance to fiscal discipline. Not for the first time, or the last, an observer would have wished for nothing better than to watch the latest Stephen Harper debate a Stephen Harper visiting from the recent past. On November 7 and again on November 20 and 22, Harper had spoken, with clarity rising to urgency, about the need to ignore budget balance in the rush to stimulate the economy. His examples, China and the United States and Britain, had already spent big and would spend further. It had become impossible to watch the prime minister and not conclude that he was sorely worried about the economy; that he saw major fiscal stimulus as the response; and that time was wasting.

This is why Flaherty's fall update came as such a surprise and a disappointment.

———

Ottawa is never a good town for keeping secrets. On Wednesday, November 26, the day before Flaherty's fall update, Don Martin's *Calgary Herald* column began: "Like it or not, MPs will personally feel the economic squeeze this week. Federal politicians of all parties, along with senior civil servants, will be tapped for sacrifices in Thursday's fiscal update—with moves expected to include a freeze in their pay, a cut in their discretionary spending and a clampdown on travel and assorted parliamentary perks."

Martin's sources were calling the undefined moves "a dramatic and symbolic gesture to capture public attention" and "reflect Ottawa's empathy" for ordinary people hit by the bad economy. Best yet, the cuts inside the Ottawa bubble would be "almost impossible for opposition parties to oppose without appearing petty."

Martin quoted Kory Teneycke, Harper's relentlessly partisan communications director: "It will set the tone for government, Parliament and the bureaucracy. It will happen at a leadership level and affect political parties and politicians across the board." But Teneycke was more eager to marvel at how awesome the government's move would be than to describe it comprehensibly. He did say MPs' salaries wouldn't be touched, nor their generous pensions. All he would say beyond that was, "There will be much bleating from political parties, but it will hit the government disproportionately. It will be deeper and broader than anyone expects. The other thing I will predict is that the public doesn't care—in fact, they want it."

Teneycke's comments would wear their desired aura of mystery through most of Wednesday and then his office distributed another round of leaks. By dinnertime, the Conservatives' plans were making headlines. At 8:32 p.m. the Canadian Press moved a story from reporter Julian Beltrame under the headline, "Tories expected to slash party funding." It said that "a political grenade—ending the $30 million public subsidy to parties" would be a "highlight" of Thursday's economic update:

"Finance Minister Jim Flaherty will ask the five political parties to give up the $1.95-per-vote subsidy they get to pay for staff and expenses. Opposition parties are likely to see the measure as a declaration of war only weeks after the election because of the Conservatives' commanding strength in fundraising. The president of the Treasury Board rejected that suggestion. 'It would hurt us the most,' said Vic Toews, although he refused to confirm the measure publicly."

Beltrame's story spelled out the consequences. Cutting per-vote subsidies would cost "the cash-strapped Liberals" $7.7 million, the NDP $4.9 million, the Bloc Québécois $2.6 million and the Conservatives fully $10 million. "But proportional to revenues raised last year, the taxpayer subsidy represents 37 percent of the totals raised by the Tories. That's far less than the 63 percent chop for Liberal coffers, 86 percent for the Bloc and 57 percent for the NDP."

The story accurately predicted the opposition's reaction to the surprise move. A Postmedia reporter asked NDP MP Pat Martin what he thought of the rumoured change to party funding. "This means war," Martin growled.

Where did the idea of eliminating the per-vote subsidy come from? A broad consensus within the Conservative Party that taxpayer money shouldn't prop up a fading party. Where did the decision to announce this now come from? One man: Stephen Harper. "There had been backroom discussions about this idea of doing something with party finance," one former Harper advisor said. "But most people thought this was going to be something that was going to happen in the next budget, not something that was going to happen in the statement. There had been a discussion about, well, do we cap it? Do we phase it out over four years? You know, what do we do with it?"

The Conservatives' beef with the per-vote subsidy was as old as the subsidy itself. On February 11, 2003, Jean Chrétien introduced an array of changes to party funding as a bill in the House of Commons at a time when the sponsorship scandal was a source of daily headlines alleging that government contracts to promote Canadian unity in Quebec had gone to promoters who were willing to kick back a portion of their windfall earnings to the Liberal Party of Canada. As damage control, Chrétien moved to sharply limit corporate and personal political donations. In return the government would pay each party a small sum for each vote it received in the latest general election.

After Chrétien introduced the bill, Harper spoke as leader of the Canadian Alliance opposition. "Obviously, the biggest beneficiary is the Liberals and they will benefit regardless of how people's views of them may change in their performance as a governing party," he said. The Liberals had no culture of raising serious money in small increments from legions of highly motivated donors. They were addicted to big corporate donations. Cut off that revenue line and only one hope remained for the Liberals: guaranteed taxpayer funding.

Now Harper could do something about it. Just before Flaherty's fall statement was to go to print, only a few issues remained for Harper's final approval. He made those decisions in Lima, during the APEC summit. Jeremy Hunt, Ray Novak's replacement as Harper's body man, phoned the PMO with the boss's final call: "We're eliminating party finance."

This was a big surprise, even within the PMO, for two reasons. First, eliminating the vote subsidy was not part of any public debate. The Conservatives were less than two months past a national election campaign in which they hadn't breathed a word about the issue. And then there was the way they were planning to do it. No cap, no phasing out of the subsidy over years. It would simply be cut. "The PM made a unilateral decision to, you know, 'Let's just go for it,'" the former advisor said. "In the end everyone said, 'Okay, well, the PM has made up his mind, let's just go do it.' I think the assumption was—and this is the fatally flawed assumption—that the NDP would not be enthusiastic supporters of this but would go along with it, seeing it as a way of weakening the Liberals and furthering their long-term objectives."

It was indeed a flawed assumption. In his book *How We Almost Gave the Tories the Boot*, NDP strategist Brian Topp says he received an e-mail from Jack Layton just before six p.m. on Wednesday. "CTV is reporting that the per-vote public financing scheme is to be cancelled in tomorrow's update," Layton's e-mail said. "I believe that the Liberals could be tempted by our earlier proposition, faced with such a catastrophic proposal. Self-preservation could provoke out-of-the-box thinking."

The "earlier proposition" was the notion of replacing the party that won the most seats in an election with a government formed by a coalition of smaller caucuses. Topp reveals that an NDP committee whose members included Topp and former Saskatchewan premier Allan Blakeney had met repeatedly to discuss such options throughout each federal election campaign since Layton became leader: in 2004, 2006 and again in 2008. Every time, the nameless group—Topp retrospectively dubs it the "scenarios committee"—based its calculations on the obvious fact that the relative size of each party caucus would affect an opposition coalition's chances of success.

Ten days before the 2008 election, Topp writes, the scenarios committee met. "I suggested that the best possible outcome would be an election result that gave the Liberals and the NDP in combination a majority of the house." Blakeney agreed that would be a wonderful outcome. But it probably wouldn't happen. If the NDP and Liberals fell short, the Bloc Québécois's support would be needed. "Blakeney considered a direct deal with the Bloc to be political poison,"Topp recounts, "and preferred that the Liberals, who would benefit by leading the government, pay the price of obtaining that support."

On October 14, the election results added up to a severe case of Blakeney's scenario: 77 Liberals, 37 New Democrats, 49 Bloc, 143

Conservatives. "Nonetheless, Layton gave it a try," Topp writes, but his election-night telephone pitch to a dejected Dion got nowhere. Even then Layton didn't drop the notion, and he directed Topp to open a line of communication with David Smith, the veteran Liberal senator and campaign organizer.

Harper knew none of this. "Had we known that, I think we might have reacted differently," the former Harper advisor says. "Our working assumption was that Jack Layton wanted to replace the Liberals as the principal opposition, and position the NDP as the principal party of the centre-left. That was his overriding objective, and therefore we had common interests." Harper was hoping to play one opposition party against another. He did not believe he would set them all against him.

Harper also had the unanimous support of his MPs. Shortly after he returned from Peru, the Conservatives held a special evening caucus meeting in the Railway Committee Room off the Hall of Honour in Parliament's Centre Block. The room was a holdover from Confederation's early days, when the railway was the connecting thread for a young nation's transport, communication, economic development, patronage and more. As one of Parliament's largest and most ornate meeting rooms, it usually holds enough chairs for the weekly Conservative caucus meeting. But tonight there was standing room only. Flaherty outlined his fall update, including the party-funding measure Harper had decreed only days before. "Everybody applauded," somebody who attended the meeting said. "Everybody thought, 'Yes, good good good, because that's a Reformer-ish thing. It's a little more red meat, we want some more red meat. Tough times are coming, and this is the chance to turn the knife and bankrupt the other parties.'"

A Conservative MP said, "Despite all the navel-gazing afterwards, there wasn't a voice against it in caucus. Amongst MPs, as you walked around the government lobby"—on the day of Flaherty's update—"everyone thought, 'Right on. This is fantastic. This is the right thing to do.'"

On that same Thursday morning, the Liberals were having an emergency caucus meeting to decide how to respond to the threatened attack on their funding lifeline. They settled on a clever communications strategy. Instead of decrying the change to party funding, they would link it to a broader story about Harper's sleepy, useless response to the global economic crisis. Going into the meeting, the chief object of their concern was their own imperilled backsides; on the way out they wept for the orphaned nation. "Stephen Harper is playing silly politics," Liberal MP Gerard Kennedy said. "While world leaders are bringing their parliaments and their parties together to work on economic problems, Stephen Harper is playing silly divide-and-conquer games to further his political agenda."

This would have been a ridiculous talking point if the economic update had contained the immediate fiscal stimulus Harper had described as "essential" on several recent occasions. It didn't. Given the economic near-panic in the land, the 132-page Economic and Fiscal Statement Jim Flaherty delivered on Thursday afternoon still stands as one of the more witless documents the Harper government has ever produced.

Its title was "Protecting Canada's Future." The thrust of it was that everything that needed doing to protect Canada's future had already been done in the past. The Goods and Services Tax cuts and the modest increases in infrastructure spending of 2006 and 2007, it turned out, were the work of a clairvoyant government that had blunted the effects of the crisis years in advance. Without mentioning, until now, that that was what they were trying to do. How modest of them.

The document listed no new measures regarding fiscal stimulus. The word "deficit" appeared not once in the main economic update document. Nor was the move on party financing the only bit of jiggery-pokery in the update. There was a provision to suspend the right of public sector unions to strike until 2010, and another that removed the right of women to complain to the Canadian Human Rights Commission over pay equity. All of this is hard to square with Conservatives' later claim that they hoped the NDP would support the government on the elimination of party financing. The economic update was a whole, and there was no way the NDP could support it with all this stuff in it.

The former advisor offered this explanation: "The PM, because of his interactions with the G-20 and so on, had decided that everyone was going to do stimulus and Canada was going to play ball. But he didn't want to do it in a haphazard way. It was thought that the natural time to do that was going to be the 2009 budget, and basically he wanted the November 2008 fiscal statement to be a base-setting exercise, just to strictly lay out the numbers and hint at more action to come."

Flaherty's speech tried to set that tone. "Today's statement lays out a plan that keeps our budget balanced for now. However, in the weeks ahead, we will determine the extent to which we will inject additional stimulus to our economy, joining the efforts of our international partners. Any additional actions to support the economy will have an impact on the bottom-line numbers in our next budget. These actions, or a further deterioration in global economic conditions, could result in a deficit."

But that was all vague, conditional and somewhere down the road. The party-financing stuff was now. After Flaherty finished, the other parties had a chance to react. The important question was whether any party would support the government. The Liberal finance critic, Scott Brison, was scathing but noncommittal. Duceppe and Layton said they would vote against the update. Dion took his reaction outside to the TV cameras waiting in the Commons foyer. "We will vote against this plan," he said. The scrum around him instantly shrank as reporters backed away to file their dispatches by Blackberry.

Harper had made a career-threatening miscalculation. What saved him was that Ottawa had other leaders tempted by folly too.

The Conservatives could not have predicted that the economic update would produce something very close to jubilation among their opponents. Glen Pearson was a Liberal MP from London, Ontario, who kept a blog. His account of the atmosphere in the House after Flaherty spoke remains striking. "No sooner was the speech ended than the Prime Minister and his Finance Minister left the House, along with half of the Conservative caucus," Pearson wrote. "The faces on those that remained told the story in vivid detail. Listening to the response from the three opposition parties, you could tell from their countenance some kind of line had been crossed.

"In the Opposition Lobby, I saw things I had never witnessed in my two years here. Bloc members were 'high-fiving' NDP caucus members, and some women from the Bloc were embracing their counterparts in the Liberal caucus. It was incredible to watch."

CTV reporter Rosemary Thompson had asked Dion whether he had talked about a coalition with the other opposition parties. "Well, the option now is for the prime minister," Dion said, as he launched into a long answer that didn't answer. The correct answer, if he had cared to give it, was yes. He had already talked to Layton by telephone that morning. "I intend to meet him tonight to start the process," Layton wrote in an e-mail to his chief of staff, Anne McGrath, and Topp.

Indeed, meetings were happening all over Ottawa. One line of communication was between two party veterans, Ed Broadbent and Jean Chrétien. Brad Lavigne, a senior Layton advisor, explained the rationale: "We're not really sure who the Liberal leader is right now." Dion had announced his resignation, effective after a successor could be chosen. Michael Ignatieff, Bob Rae and New Brunswick MP Dominic LeBlanc planned to run to replace him. "Chrétien's almost the only guy whose calls get returned by every Liberal faction," Lavigne said. "So we asked Ed to reach out to him."

The reaction of the opposition was obviously huge trouble for the government. But another surprise awaited Harper. The very substance of the economic update was coming under fire from ordinary Canadians. "We were getting the shit kicked out of us in our ridings," one Ontario Conservative MP recalls. "I had hardcore Conservatives calling, screaming and hollering at me, and e-mails. These are Plus 14s, Plus 12s. That means they'd donated, taken lawn signs." The MP was referring to the internal Conservative system for identifying supportive voters in a riding and ranking the level of their fervour.

"They weren't angry because they wanted to preserve this sacred cow called the political subsidy. Most people hadn't even been aware it existed. It was that the world was going to hell, Bush was bailing out financial institutions, Lehman Brothers had collapsed, the auto industry was in free fall, people were watching their stock portfolios tumble by 30, 40 percent. It looked like economic Armageddon out there. And folks just wanted us to do something. Now, they weren't even sure what something was. It wasn't that they knew we needed a stimulus or something. But they wanted us to be doing something. And then we came out with this irrelevant, extraneous subject of the political subsidies, which had obviously no bearing. So folks were just enraged that this whole political game was starting when the rest of the world was going down in flames. It was like 99 to 1 against. And from across the spectrum."

The House was scheduled to vote on a Ways and Means motion on Monday. It was also a scheduled supply day, which meant MPs would spend most of the day debating a motion from an opposition party, in this case the Liberals. The motion would be votable. So in only ninety-six hours, the Liberals would have two chances to vote down confidence in the government.

Harper's first move was to try to stick the pin back into the grenade he'd just dropped into his own lap. On Friday morning, government officials told reporters the party-financing provisions wouldn't be included in Monday's Ways and Means motion. Almost immediately, Liberals and New Democrats said they would vote against the government no matter what happened to the party-financing rules. Shortly after lunch on Friday, the Canadian Press moved the text of the Liberals' supply day motion. "This House has lost confidence in this government and is of the opinion that a viable alternative government can be formed within the present House of Commons." It was on. The Liberals planned to propose an alternative coalition government to replace the Conservatives.

Three hours after the CP story moved, Harper walked out of the House of Commons to a microphone in the foyer. Dozens of reporters were waiting. A Conservative media advisory had said he would speak between 5:00 and 5:30 p.m. It was now 5:38.

The prime minister's substantive message was that he was pushing the Ways and Means motion, and the supply debate, to December 8, a week later than scheduled. Everyone he was talking to knew that if the opposition's resolve held, he would not be in less trouble then than now. So he began in earnest to engage the battle over perception. "Less than two months ago, the people of Canada gave our party a strengthened mandate to lead Canada during the most serious global economic crisis in generations." He listed his government's actions on the economy, almost all of which predated Flaherty's update. But Harper promised to add to the meagre tally soon. "These actions represent our first steps. In the next couple of months, the government will present a budget that outlines our next move forward." That budget would include "expected stimulus measures."

From that sketchy defence, he moved to the attack. "While we have been working on the economy, the opposition has been working on a backroom deal to overturn the results of the last election without seeking the consent of voters. They want to take power, not earn it. They want to install a government led by a party that received its lowest vote share since Confederation. They want to install a prime minister, Prime Minister Dion, who was rejected by the voters just six weeks ago. They want to install a coalition that they explicitly promised not to support. The Liberals campaigned against the coalition with the NDP, precisely because they said the NDP's policies were bad for the economy. And now they plan to enter into the very same coalition under the guise of strengthening the economy. Stéphane Dion and the NDP plan to make this happen by accepting the support of a party that wants to destroy the country. The opposition has every right to defeat the government. But Stéphane Dion does not have the right to take power without an election."

Harper called on Canadians to "make their views known" on this matter to MPs. Reporters started to holler questions. Harper said, "Thank you very much and I hope you will all have a good weekend," and turned on his heel, retreating back inside the Commons. "Sir," one reporter called after him, "did you make a mistake?" Harper didn't pause to respond.

While Harper was talking, his chief of staff, Guy Giorno, was putting the final touches on an e-mail to Conservative MPs. Giorno, a veteran of Ontario Conservative politics in the days when Mike Harris was premier, reinforced Harper's fondness for political attack. It was "absolutely essential that we use every single tool and medium at our disposal," Giorno wrote, to warn Canadians against the opposition's "crass political opportunism." The memo included a proposed script for television and radio interviews. The script repeated almost every detail of Harper's statement in the Commons foyer, complete with scripted ad libs so MPs could be sure their comments sounded natural and unscripted: "This is what bothers me the most" and "I mean, I follow the news" and "And I wish the media would be more clear on this point." The script ended with a nod to the constitutional and parliamentary gamesmanship that could lie ahead. It suggested MPs say: "I don't want another election. But what I want even less is a surprise backroom Prime Minister whom I never even had the opportunity to vote for or against."

Taken together, Harper's Friday statement in the foyer and the Giorno memo point toward four decisions the Conservatives had taken almost before they knew they were in a fight.

The first decision, really more a reflex, was that when attacked they would attack right back. By now this was such an obvious part of the Harper modus operandi that a more contrite or passive stance would have been surprising. The second decision was to waste little time fussing about factual accuracy. As constitutional scholars would soon remind everyone, when Harper said the opposition wanted to "overturn the results of the last election," he was talking humbug. The election had returned 308 Members of Parliament. It was up to them to select a government among them and show their support for it by voting confidence in it. There was a forest of rules, traditions and conditions surrounding the exercise of that selection, but there would be nothing illegal or unconstitutional about a Dion-led coalition government. If a majority of MPs supported the project, Harper could not stop it.

Of course, Harper knew this. And of course, before he was in government, he had made the same argument. Before the 1997 election, Harper announced he would not run again as a Reform Party candidate. In an interview with TVO, the Ontario government educational network, he speculated on what would happen if Liberal support declined. "I think you're going to face, some day, a minority parliament, with the Liberals maybe having the largest number of seats," he said, "and what will be the test is whether there's then any party in opposition that's able to form a coalition or working alliance with the others."

Such a coalition would have been created in defiance of the party with the largest number of seats in the House, just like the one that threatened to take Harper out in 2008. And it is impossible to imagine that Harper didn't expect the Bloc Québécois to participate in such a coalition back when he was bruiting it about. At the moment he spoke to TVO in 1997 the Bloc had fifty seats. Reform, the Progressive Conservatives and the NDP had sixty-one seats among them.

Harper's apparent support for a coalition alternative to the governing party was even clearer in 2004, after Paul Martin's Liberals were reduced to a minority. Harper, Duceppe and Layton showed up in the National Press Theatre across Wellington Street from the Commons on September 9, 2004, to present a joint opposition agenda for the new Parliament. And they revealed that they had sent a letter to the governor general of the time, Adrienne Clarkson. "We respectfully point out," the letter said, "that the opposition parties, who together constitute a majority in the House, have been in close consultation. We believe that, should a request for dissolution arise this should give you cause, as constitutional practice has determined, to consult the opposition leaders and consider all of your options before exercising your constitutional authority."

"There has been some informal chitter-chatter around the Hill," Harper said when reporters asked him what the letter was meant to accomplish, "that if a prime minister were weakened by his own party or defeated in the House that he could just automatically call an election. That's not our understanding of how the constitutional system works, particularly in a minority Parliament."

So the defeat of a government need not mean an election? No, Harper said. If the government was defeated, "the governor general should first consult widely before accepting any advice to dissolve Parliament. So I would not want the prime minister to think that he can simply fail in the House of Commons as a route to another general election. That's not the way our system works." But that was 2004. This was now.

Harper's third decision was to begin preparing contingencies for a defeat on a confidence motion. If he could not avoid a confidence vote, and if he lost it, he would ask the governor general to dissolve Parliament and call another election. The other parties would plead with Michaëlle Jean not to send their coalition proposal to the electorate. The "I don't want another election, but . . ." talking points anticipated that fight.

The fourth decision was the most important. Outnumbered in the Commons, Harper was seeking a wider arena. He did not have the people's representatives on his side, but he could appeal to the people. He had no guarantee of success. Only seven weeks earlier, more Canadians had supported the coalition parties than the Conservatives. He had to persuade at least some of them that what they were heading toward wasn't what they had asked for.

During the long wait before Harper's statement in the foyer, Teneycke chatted with reporters. "We are going to stand our ground on principle," the PM's message man said. "I'm saying we're not backing down." But as the crisis headed into the weekend, the Conservatives backed down some more. On Saturday morning, Baird made a flurry of phone calls to reporters to tell them the government was abandoning the party-financing provision that had got them into this mess. He showed up at the CBC building on Queen Street in Ottawa to make the same vow on camera. In a conference call with reporters on Sunday, Flaherty said the pay-equity and right-to-strike restrictions would be removed too. Since there had been very little in the economic update besides the measures the government was now abandoning, the tactical retreat amounted to a blanket repudiation of a major statement by the finance minister. It would not have been astonishing to see Flaherty resign over the disavowal. He stayed on. This was not a fight over the proper care and feeding of ministers of the Crown. It had become bigger than that.

Opposition negotiating teams were camped out in three downtown hotels—Liberals and Bloc at the Château Laurier, NDP and Bloc at the Marriott, Liberals and NDP at the Sheraton. The negotiators showed up at the annual press gallery dinner at the Museum of Civilization on Saturday night flushed with excitement. In the cold outside the museum, Doug

Finley, Harper's dour Scottish campaign manager, stood cradling a Scotch and taking a smoke break. One reporter suggested Harper's options came down to "fight" or "contrite."

"Oh, we won't be contrite," Finley said.

On Sunday, the Conservatives made their best attempt to shut down the coalition, with Flaherty throwing off ballast in that conference call with reporters. To their astonishment it had no effect. So the Conservative Party released a recording of a conference call Layton had held with NDP MPs on Saturday. One of the newest NDP MPs was Linda Duncan, the party's lone Alberta caucus member. Instead of sending her office the instructions for the Layton call, the NDP had mistakenly sent them to Conservative MP John Duncan. So the Conservatives were able to dial into Layton's call, unbeknownst to the NDP.

During the call, Layton addressed worries that the Bloc would be unsteady supporters of the coalition. "I actually believe they're the least of our problems," he said. "This whole thing wouldn't have happened if the moves hadn't been made with the Bloc to lock them in early because you couldn't put three people together in three hours." To the Conservatives, this sounded like what it was: proof the coalition had been in the planning since long before Flaherty's botched fall update.

"We thought that releasing the tapes would kind of blow the whole thing apart," the former PMO advisor said later. "There would be Liberals that would be horrified by this, and that this was going to be the bomb that was going to stop the momentum. And it didn't at all. Everyone kind of rallied around." Even Dion's Liberal leadership rival and probable successor, Michael Ignatieff, wasn't publicly offside. "That's when we really realized that we were against it, because you know, basically everyone—Ignatieff was quiet, and everyone else was completely on board with going forward with this."

Monday morning, November 30, "the prime minister was sick as a dog," one former MP recalls. "He was pale, he was morose, and I don't think at that moment he knew what to do." Part of it was simple illness. The food in Lima had been treacherous. Of the eight thousand delegates at the APEC summit, more than a hundred developed upset stomachs or worse. The Peruvian government put out a news release blaming the weather in Lima, "characterized at this time of year by midday heat, but cool breezes in the mornings and afternoons," for "upset stomachs" among "unprepared diners." Stephen Harper was one of the victims. The APEC food had caught up with him as soon as he landed back in Ottawa and its effects had lingered, mutating into a sullen and thuggish flu.

The day began with a Tactics meeting at Langevin. The PM's senior staff reviewed what was in the press: their imminent defeat. They reviewed what was likely to come up at Question Period that day: their imminent defeat. As one participant recalls, Harper said to the room, "I've decided I'm going to let this confidence vote happen and let them try to form the government. They'll screw it up so badly, they'll be so disorganized, that within a few months we'll be back into another election."

Almost all of Harper's team thought this was a bad idea. Conservatives can name few exceptions. Jason Kenney was one. The forty-year-old Calgary Southeast MP, a full member of cabinet since only a month earlier, found the "let them screw up" option tempting. So did Pierre Poilievre, eleven years younger than Kenney, the Calgary-born MP for Nepean-Carleton near Ottawa. The two men were Conservatives in the Harper mode, bookish and eloquent but viscerally sure of themselves and certain their opponents would be unmasked and undone by the pressure of power.

More experienced ministers were certain Harper could not win later if he let himself lose now. In varying assortments through the day, they visited his office, or buttonholed him in the government lobby just outside the Commons chamber, and told him he needed to fight. Lawrence Cannon, the foreign affairs minister, and Tony Clement from

Industry, told him he must get the governor general to prorogue Parliament. Then the current session of Parliament, barely begun, would be cancelled and Harper could prepare a new session. The clap-trap opposition cabal would fall apart. As a student at the University of Toronto, Clement had seen the provincial Liberals and New Democrats unite to form a government after the Ontario Progressive Conservatives won a plurality of seats in 1985. As a result, the PCs languished for a decade before they could get back into power, Clement told Harper.

Harper wasn't feeling it. He could do the math: the other guys had his side outnumbered. When MPs filed into the Commons for Question Period at two p.m., he watched glumly as Liberals, New Democrats and Bloc MPs stood to give Stéphane Dion a long standing ovation.

"Instead of introducing an economic stimulus package in his fiscal update last week, the prime minister decided to play politics," Dion said, "ignoring difficult economic times Canadians are facing. Does the prime minister still believe that he enjoys the confidence of this House?"

Harper delivered a disjointed, weirdly nonchalant answer, reading from notes. "Mr. Speaker, in the fiscal and economic update, the min-ister of finance announced, among other things, the fact that he would be providing EDC and BDC additional money to extend to manufactur-ing and auto sectors, that there would be special help for retirees who are dealing with problems of losses in the stock market. He announced the fact that there would be numerous measures to strengthen our financial system. And Mr. Speaker, of course . . ." He checked his notes again, pausing for quite a while.

In their usual place behind Harper and a little to his right, so they would line up properly in the shot from the fixed Commons television camera, sat three senior female caucus members, Helena Guergis, Diane Ablonczy, Lisa Raitt. They sat bolt upright, staring at his back, waiting for an applause line. None was forthcoming. Guergis had nodded tentatively at the news about help for retirees.

Harper found his place in his notes: ". . . he announced that we would be doubling infrastructure spending over the next year to a record high. Um." Guergis began to clap. Ablonczy and Raitt weren't ready to do that yet. "Mr. Speaker, when the honourable, uh, gentleman speaks about playing politics, I think he's about to play the biggest game in Canadian history." Now the Conservatives stood as Harper sat, but they applauded without particular enthusiasm. Their leader had given a lousy answer. It acknowledged that the game was Dion's to play. It defended without attacking. And the basis of the defence was a fall update the government's own supporters found deeply unimpressive. If this was the best Harper could do, it was game over.

It seemed to be the best he could do. In French, after Dion's second question, Harper found himself asking for the population's indulgence and the population's patience. His party had governed for three years, he said, "even though it may not have been perfect." As for what came next: "My personal opinion is that they should at least wait for the budget to determine the future of a government recently elected by the citizens of Canada." His personal opinion. But you know, to each his own. He switched back into English and his mouth turned to soup. "Mr. Speaker, let me say quite simply in terms of what we all, uh, know the honourable Leader of the Opposition is up to," he said, staring at the floor. "And I understand he, uh, wants to be prime minister. It's a great honour. A great experience, but I can just tell you, Mr. Prime Minister—" Wait, that wasn't right. "Or Mr. President." That neither. The Speaker is called "le président" in French, but right now Harper was speaking English, sort of. The other side started to chortle. "Oh, grow up!" Helena Guergis shouted across the aisle.

Harper tried one more time. "I can just tell you, Mr. Speaker, I would certainly not want to find myself governing this economy today, and in this position, under a situation where I was required to follow social—socialist economics and to be at the behold—and be at the behest of the veto of the separatists." The rest of the Conservative caucus rose, unsteadily, to applaud whatever the hell Harper had said as he collapsed back into his seat.

Harper slouched and mumbled his way through another half-hour of this mess, then retreated upstairs to his office. It was at that very moment that the gods of political opportunity decided to smile on him.

———

As reporters arrived in the Railway Committee Room for a 4:30 p.m. press conference announced by the leaders of the opposition parties, they saw that three chairs and microphones had been laid out. For whom? Dion, Layton and Duceppe, MPs gathering for the event said. A few reporters thought this odd. Surely Duceppe, who was pledging only to support the coalition government, not to contribute MPs to serve as ministers, was not being presented as an equal party to this coalition? It turned out that indeed he was. Martha Hall Findlay, a Liberal MP, rolled her eyes when reporters suggested this might be a very bad idea. The Bloc's been around here for ages, Hall Findlay said. We're past that old paranoia.

In his book, Topp says the only person on the coalition side who said out loud that it might be a bad idea to give Gilles Duceppe equal presence was Gilles Duceppe. To his credit, Topp notes that nobody, including himself, gave the matter any thought. It was not until the three leaders came in together, signed the accord together, gave opening statements in turn and took questions as a team that the impact of what was happening began to register. Their words were confident and offered no hope of appeal.

"Prime Minister, your government has lost the confidence of the House and it is going to be defeated at the earliest opportunity," Layton said, speaking to the cameras as if directly to Harper. "I urge you to accept this gracefully." Harper was indeed watching, one floor up in his Centre Block office. But as he took in the words, he also began to parse the damning imagery of his adversaries sitting together as equals.

Still, it took time to sink in. Harper was still unsure of his course when Prentice, Hill and Moore trooped into his office minutes after the Ops meeting ended. When Moore and Prentice left Harper's office to provide some comment for waiting reporters in the Commons foyer downstairs, they had no idea what conclusions Harper would draw from their conversation, so the two ministers said as little as possible to the media. All options were on the table, Prentice said. Whatever that meant.

Something was happening in the land. "The day the coalition thing was signed, I remember it was eerie," the Ontario Conservative MP said. "I called my staff because I was constantly asking my correspondence lady, 'What are we getting? What are people saying? Who's writing? Where do they fall in our databases of supporters?' And they said, 'We're not getting anything.' The mail just stopped. And the phone calls just stopped. I think folks were just confused."

Much later, Topp would admit what the Conservatives had realized before him: Duceppe's presence was the key. As soon as trouble started brewing, Patrick Muttart, now Harper's deputy chief of staff, had started polling. He didn't have time to design and field his own poll, so he reached out to Conservative-connected professionals in the market-research community who were already in the field. They may have been polling about consumer preferences on corn syrup. Whatever. The Conservatives had the pollsters add a few incongruous questions about the coalition. Muttart had reported his findings at the Monday morning senior staff meeting.

"He said three things that were interesting," someone who was there recalled. One, the angle that Jack Layton and the NDP would impose socialist economics in a time of crisis didn't matter to people. They weren't afraid of Jack Layton. I guess we should have taken that as a sign." (Of the moment nearly three years later when Layton would become the biggest surprise in Canadian politics.) "Second thing was that people did not like the idea of a Prime Minister Stéphane Dion—but that was not the thing that worried them the most. Overwhelmingly, and across political affiliation in English Canada, the thing that shocked everyone was the notion that somehow the Bloc Québécois would be part of the government."

For the umpteenth time, Muttart had given the Harper Conservatives the words. It fell to Stockwell Day, the international trade minister, to add music. The clumsy former Canadian Alliance leader had handed Harper a Canadian Alliance that badly needed saving in 2002, but Day still had clout with social Conservatives and the party's base in Alberta and British Columbia. For seven or eight minutes, he spoke with genuine emotion about the need for a patriotic, anti-separatist message to rally the country, or most of it, against the coalition. Day's speech, an observer said, crystallized the message from Muttart's polling data.

Sick, embarrassed, outnumbered and rocked back on his heels in a way he had never known since he had become prime minister, Harper took nearly a day to digest the messages from his helpers and ministers. When he went home to 24 Sussex that night to prepare for the Conservatives' annual Christmas party, he was still visibly morose. When he and Laureen showed up together at the Westin Hotel, he didn't seem to have changed his mood. In a kitchen off the main event hall, with a few staffers listening in, Laureen told him the party needed their leader to lead. Now more than ever. Harper took her words in silently, then took to the podium.

"He got up," says one party-goer. "He was meek. He was exhausted. And he got this, like, ten-minute standing ovation. And it entirely changed his psyche."

Harper had brought a prepared text. While he usually stays close to his scripts, weaving in an extra sentence or sharpening a phrase on the spot, that night he simply ignored what his staff had written and delivered a kind of defiant roar. "I mean, the PM does not give barnburners," said another observer. "It's a shame that this one was to a private-party-only audience, because it was really one of the most extraordinary performances he's ever had. Everyone sort of went out of there pumped up, you know . . . 'We're going to fight.' I think at that point, it became obvious that the PM was going to prorogue. There was continued discussion about prorogation versus other options, but at that point that was the default option."

———

Tuesday, December 2. Topp's meticulous hour-by-hour account of that astonishing week contains no mention about the previous day's Question Period, which had nearly finished Harper off, and no hint that the coalition partners gave a second's thought to how they would handle Question Period now, after they had announced to the world that they were taking over. It would prove to be a fatal oversight.

They could have simply skipped QP, for instance. The daily question session is an occasion for the opposition to beg for scraps from the government. The government routinely refuses to hand those scraps over and mocks the little guys for asking. In every detail—the thirty-five-second countdown clock for each question and answer; the way the government always speaks last—the ludicrous little ceremony is rigged in the government's favour. A creative, agile, cohesive new parliamentary coalition simply could have decided not to lower itself by showing up for such a debasement of its new role. This lot was none of those things.

So they all filed into the Commons and waited their turn, and Stéphane Dion stood up and put on his tiny perfect Stéphane Dion scowl, and asked his defiant Stéphane Dion question. He read from an old quote about how "the whole principle of our democracy is the government is supposed to be able to face the House of Commons any day on a vote." Failing to face a confidence test, he said, still reading the old

blind quote, was "a violation of the fundamental constitutional principles of our democracy." And here came his question:

"Can the prime minister inform the House who said these words?"

Oooh, let me guess. It was Stephen Harper, right? Here was a favourite Dion tactic. Put your opponent's words to him. Make him face his
contradictions. It was neat and clever and about five times too subtle
for the moment at hand, because what Harper did was pull himself up
to his full height, button his suit jacket, lean forward across the aisle of
the Commons, and bite Dion's head clean off.

"Mr. Speaker, the highest principle of Canadian democracy is that if
you want to be prime minister, you get your mandate from the Canadian
people, not from Quebec separatists." This time Ablonczy and Guergis
and Raitt behind him knew what to do, as did the rest of the Conservative
caucus. They leapt to their feet as if prompted by cattle prods. A gut-
tural roar went up from the applauding Conservatives. Lawrence
Cannon, standing next to Harper, shouted a word that was probably
supposed to be "Oui" but came out as if he'd suffered a back-alley
appendectomy. "WAAAAAAAAEERRGH!"

Harper wasn't done. "Mr. Speaker, this deal that the leader of the
Liberal Party has made with the separatists is a betrayal of the voters of
this country." His index finger jabbed downward. "A betrayal of the best
interests of our economy." Another jab. "A betrayal of the best interests
of our country. And we will fight it with every means that we have."

The end of his response was drowned in another roar as the
Conservatives jumped back to their feet. Over the next half-hour they
would spend about half their time on their feet, bellowing their defiance
of their tormentors.

The roar from not quite half of the throats in the House of Commons,
every time, was a physical thing. People in the visitors' gallery above felt
the wood furniture shake in sympathetic vibration. Dion squeaked out
one more question, took another thumping, sat blinking as Harper

rounded on Layton and then on Duceppe in turn. Finally, near the end of the session, Dion stood to ask another set of questions. He might as well have saved his breath.

The show Harper put on was at times jaw-droppingly demagogic. He answered Layton by claiming that when the three opposition leaders had signed the deal a day earlier, "they would not even have the Canadian flag behind them. They had to be photographed without it. They had to be photographed without it because a member of their coalition does not even believe in the country."

This was not true. Baffled editors of news websites dug out day-old photos of Dion and the others in front of ten provincial flags and two maple-leafed Canadian flags and reposted them. But Harper was not interested in passing factual muster. He was here to do some walloping.

"It wasn't until Mr. Harper made indisputably false claims about the flag and Mr. Dion that the proceedings truly turned," Aaron Wherry wrote on his *Maclean's* blog that night. "At that point, for all intents and purposes, Question Period ceased, giving way to a remarkable clash between the two men who seek a claim to high office. Dion could barely maintain the control necessary to form words, screaming across the aisle at the Prime Minister. Harper challenged and goaded him on."

When it was over, the Conservatives trooped out to the government lobby, which is behind closed doors in the space just outside the Commons chamber. Royal Galipeau, the MP for Ottawa-Orleans, led MPs and staff in "O Canada." The Ontario MP whose office had been deluged with criticism over the voter-subsidy stuff in the economic update checked in for the latest. "My correspondence lady said, 'It's all on your side now.' Nobody even remembered the political-subsidy issue. It just vanished in twenty-four hours."

Another member of Harper's government said, "There are moments when this government talks to the country, to our supporters and our networks. This wasn't that. This was the country talking to us. Immediately after the [three-leader coalition] press conference it was a kind of electric shock. Every phone line, every e-mail, every blog, every radio commentary lit up like Vegas on jackpot day."

The ungainly creature the opposition had sewn together would continue to lurch forward for a few more days, but Harper had now wounded it beyond repair. Later, there would be learned political analysis from some quarters to the effect that Harper was peddling a set of fictions nestled each within the other. There had been a Canadian flag. The separatists weren't part of the coalition, they had merely promised to vote with it for a year and a half. A government doesn't get its mandate from the Canadian people. It gets it from Parliament, and the confidence vote Harper wanted to avoid would be the right measure of Parliament's judgment. In the heat of the moment, none of that mattered.

————

After Harper got his prorogation and the coalition fell apart, after Michael Ignatieff became the new Liberal leader and took to threatening the Conservatives about what might happen later rather than making any attempt to take power from them now, it would become fashionable to criticize the Canadian people for letting Harper get away with a swindle against parliamentary convention. Peter Russell and Lorne Sossin, two constitutional scholars, wrote a book called *Parliamentary Democracy in Crisis*, in which all the right people lamented the decline of Canadian wisdom about the rightness of the Dion–Layton *démarche*. "Widespread public uncertainty and confusion about the principles of government evident during the crisis revealed a grave lack of understanding about the mechanics and legalities of parliamentary democracy on the part of Canadians," they wrote.

These analyses forgive nothing Harper did and everything his opponents had done. But the notion that democratic legitimacy boils down to an arithmetic majority in a vote in the Commons is pretty sterile. We have not often heard it argued since the 2008 confrontation; the Harper Conservatives have won dozens of confidence votes as a minority government and, since 2011, as a majority government. If Commons voting arithmetic is the only test of legitimacy in our democracy, then this will be a short book because, under this peculiar theory, no criticism of most of what Harper has done is possible. Nor was it a notion the coalition partners thought to share with voters during the 2008 campaign. Nobody, not even Layton, campaigned on a promise to form a government with other parties if they found their own party outnumbered. Dion explicitly rejected the idea three times: first, as a hypothetical question, when reporters put it to him on the campaign trail; second, on the phone with Layton once the results were in; and finally, when he announced he would resign from politics after winning the lowest share of the popular vote in Liberal Party history.

If the Liberals had won nearly as many seats as the Conservatives, Dion could have made a better case of it. Or if the Liberals and New Democrats had together outnumbered the Conservatives, which was the preferred scenario of Topp's secret committee. Or again if the Liberals and New Democrats had needed only a few Bloc MPs to complete their hand. But to pull a coalition off, Dion would have needed essentially the entire Bloc caucus to prop his government up, so Liberal MPs would be a minority, not just in the Commons, but in their own government's caucus support.

It was a mess, and the opposition parties would not even have attempted it if they had not been interested, first of all, in saving their own hides. But even then Canadians might have backed the coalition in numbers sufficient to give heart to the plotters, if they had been angry enough at Harper, if they judged his misstep on the economic update sufficiently damning.

Pollsters already in the field were starting to hear otherwise. But the main players in this drama still had a chance to make their case directly to Canadians. On Wednesday morning, December 3, Harper announced that he had asked for network broadcast time that evening. The networks offered reply time to the opposition leaders.

Dion waited until late that afternoon to record his statement. He had it done by a Liberal staffer who did not have professional equipment and whose video camera, as luck would have it, had a busted autofocus. There was no time to fix the lousy footage. The Liberals had to rush the recording to the parliamentary press gallery for broadcast. Unfortunately, they neglected to check where it was supposed to go, and the delivery crew took it to the wrong address first. So, a half-hour late and comically out of focus, Dion delivered his pitch. On the substance of their messages, nobody had anything new to say. Harper said the people's will was being thwarted; the others said Parliament's will must be expressed and respected.

The first decision would be made by Michaëlle Jean. On Thursday morning just before 9:30 a.m., Harper's motorcade drove the short distance from 24 Sussex Drive to Rideau Hall, taking care to sweep right past the nest of reporters in front of the main entrance so that Harper could use a smaller entrance where no cameras waited.

Two hours later, Harper came out. The governor general had granted his request to prorogue, he announced. Parliament would meet again on January 26. Parliament had always been scheduled to meet on January 26; all that was changing was that it would stop sitting immediately instead of on December 12. There would be no confidence vote until the New Year.

What on earth took him so long in there? What could they have talked about? Not much, it turns out. "He spent very little time with her," Guy Giorno said in an interview. "And then she left and returned after a delay." So she made him cool his heels alone for almost the entire two hours? "She can speak for herself," Giorno said, then added, "Well, she ought not, as a matter of constitutional convention."

Another Harper advisor suspects the delay was a way of asserting a power Jean had no intention of using. Still, the decision was hers, and she left the meeting room to press that point home, then returned and granted what the prime minister had requested. The overwhelming weight of the constitutional advice the PMO had gathered in the days leading up to the meeting had suggested she would do just that.

What if Jean had said no? What if she had let Parliament keep sitting despite his request? In his 2010 book *Harperland*, Lawrence Martin quotes Teneycke on other options Harper might have had. "Well, among them, the Queen," Teneycke said.

Could Harper really have asked the Queen to countermand the governor general? Giorno argues that the question is simply meaningless because what Harper was asking for was not something any governor general would have refused. "I don't want to contradict my good friend, my very good friend," Giorno says now, referring to Teneycke, "but I can only believe that Lawrence took Kory down a path where Kory was wildly speculating. Because that's not, I'm sorry, that's . . . how do I say it? Not only did it not happen that way. There's no conceivable reality from which one could conceivably come to that conclusion."

Giorno isn't even sure what "going to the Queen" would entail. "Ask the Queen to come over and rule the country directly? Fire the governor general? I don't think it works."

In the end, simply by acceding to Harper's wishes, Jean concocted an exquisitely simple stress test for the Dion-led coalition. If this was indeed a durable realignment of forces within the four walls of the House of Commons, proroguing wouldn't change it. A confidence vote that didn't end Harper's career on December 8 could do so on January 30 or in February. All the opposition parties had to do was stick together.

That didn't happen. Michael Ignatieff, Dion's likely successor as Liberal leader, had stayed mum throughout the crisis. But in a Liberal caucus meeting that began minutes after Harper's Rideau Hall media statement ended, Ignatieff said there was nothing to gain by pushing the coalition now. The government's defeat could lead to two outcomes: Michaëlle

Jean handing power to an untested new Liberal-led government—or an election. He did not think an election would go well for the Liberals.

As the poll numbers began arriving, they bore out Ignatieff's hunch. Boy, did they ever. Polling on December 2 and 3, EKOS asked: "If a federal election were held tomorrow, which party would you vote for?" Nationally 44 percent said they would vote Conservative, to 24.1 percent for the Liberals and 14.5 percent for the NDP. EKOS also asked which option respondents preferred as a solution to the impasse. A plurality, 37 percent, favoured "Parliament taking a break for a month or so to see whether the Conservatives can get the confidence of parliament when it comes back into session." Fewer, 28 percent, wanted to give the coalition a chance to govern. Only 19 percent wanted an election.

Strategic Counsel, on December 5: Conservatives 45 percent, Liberals 24 percent, NDP 14 percent.

Ipsos Reid, same day: Conservatives 46 percent, Liberals 23 percent, NDP 13 percent.

All three polls put the Conservatives in majority-government territory, with support nearly one-fifth higher than in the election only a month earlier. There were important regional variations, of course: the coalition was far more popular in Quebec than elsewhere, for instance. But the implication was obvious. The reaction of the opposition parties had succeeded in producing the clear referendum Harper had sought and failed to obtain in the election campaign. Canadians were realizing the available choices came down to a government composed of Conservatives and led by Harper, or a government composed of Liberals and New Democrats, supported by the Bloc, and led in the next several weeks of a global economic crisis by Stéphane Dion. In the main they supported Harper. If forced to vote, they appeared ready to do so in a way that would put his job out of reach of the combined opposition. It was over.

On Monday, December 8, Dion announced he would resign as Liberal leader as soon as his caucus could find an interim leader. It didn't take long. On Wednesday, Michael Ignatieff became the new interim Liberal leader. There was no suspense to what followed. On CTV's *Question Period* on December 7, speaking even before Dion had announced his resignation, Ignatieff had left Harper all kinds of room to avoid a further confidence-vote showdown. "Coalition if necessary but not necessarily coalition," he told CTV. "I think it's very important for Canadians to have the coalition option so that if Mr. Harper presents a budget which is not in the national interest we can present to Canadians a coalition alternative to spare us a national election." This was fantasy: if the opposition had not been able to take power while avoiding an election at the beginning of December, they would not have more luck at the end of January. The first choice facing the new Liberal leader-of-sorts would be whether to submit the coalition notion for the voters' approval in a winter election. And thanks to the polls, Ignatieff already knew how they'd respond.

"Public opinion was crucially important," Mark Cameron, Harper's former policy advisor, said later. "You know, there were protests and counter-protests going on. I think if public opinion polls had shown that 60 percent of the population thought that Harper was on the wrong track and the coalition was a good idea, and if only they'd put Bob Rae there instead of Dion, then people would embrace it, the result would have been different. I don't think Harper would have been able to do what he did if public opinion wasn't behind it. Because I'm sure the governor general was looking at public opinion polls too."

This thought led directly to another, more surprising one. "In some ways, the events of that two-week period were the real election campaign of 2008," Cameron said. "The election was kind of a bland issueless election, despite the fact that you had this economic crisis going on all around you. In some ways, the real election was the swings in public opinion of that two-week period."

This short second election of 2008 was a watershed moment for Harper. He could never be sure before now that a working plurality of Canadians would prefer him to the alternative in a direct comparison. Suddenly and quite against his wishes, circumstances had conspired to produce such a direct, binary choice. And more Canadians had preferred Harper to the alternative. He knew that, when it came to it, the country would have his back.

The lesson was not lost on Harper. After Christmas he sat down with Ken Whyte, the editor of *Maclean's* magazine, for an interview. The opposition coalition, at least theoretically still a menace hanging over his government, was much on his mind. "Obviously, if we had an election today somebody will have a majority," he said, "because it will be either Canada's Conservative government or the coalition."

Whyte was plainly surprised by the notion. "So you think they'd actually run as a coalition?"

"I don't think they have any choice: if they defeat us as a coalition they have to run as a coalition, and I think those will be the real choices before the electorate. The electorate will know that if you're not electing the Conservative government you're going to be electing a coalition that will include the NDP and the separatists."

The election Harper was thinking about was the one that still loomed as a possible consequence of the 2009 budget, now only weeks away. In the event, Ignatieff would back away from a confrontation, a manoeuvre with which he would soon become wearyingly familiar, and Harper would live to fight another day. But Harper would hang on to his plan to run the next election as a clear choice between a Conservative majority and an opposition coalition. He would make no secret of it, repeating that line dozens of times, until eventually senior ministers repeated it too. The opposition parties had more than two years' advance notice of Harper's strategy for the next election. Surely with that much warning they could confound him. Surely.

SEVEN

MESS UNTIL I'M DONE

Stephen Harper had called the 2008 election hoping to calm
the opposition by thumping them soundly, so that he could concentrate
on governing instead of on survival. Fat chance. The election's outcome
led straight to the crisis that nearly ruined him. And after Michaëlle Jean
prorogued Parliament and the coalition had fallen by the wayside, he
had to keep on patching holes.

Harper had appointed no senators since he had put Michael Fortier
in the Red Chamber immediately after winning the 2006 election. He
had run, after all, on a promise to get senators elected, not appointed.
Steady attrition meant that more and more Senate vacancies were
opening up. Harper didn't care. But during the coalition crisis he'd
learned that Stéphane Dion had been preparing to fill those vacancies
with Liberal, NDP, even Green Party senators who, once they were
in, could not be removed before they turned seventy-five. It was one
of those moments when you realize you're vulnerable in a place you
hadn't even been looking. If Dion had succeeded, a bulwark of Liberal

hegemony would have been fortified durably, no matter what Harper managed to do later. To Harper that was unacceptable.

So on December 22, while the House was prorogued, he appointed eighteen senators, hailing from eight provinces and the Yukon. Many, like the party fundraiser Irving Gerstein, were loyal Conservatives of long standing. One of them, a high-strung young Algonquin from Maniwaki, Quebec, named Patrick Brazeau, was meant to symbolize the success the Conservatives were having in winning support among some off-reserve Aboriginal Canadians. Two of the new appointees were stars of television journalism, Pamela Wallin and Mike Duffy. Duffy had made no secret of his desire for a Senate seat since long before the Conservatives were elected. Word of his appointment came seven weeks after he aired footage of Stéphane Dion flubbing an interview.

Announcing his newly made senators, Harper said he would continue to work for a reformed Senate. "If Senate vacancies are to be filled, however, they should be filled by the government that Canadians elected rather than by a coalition that no one voted for." That made tactical sense. It also made a mockery of convictions some might have thought Harper held dear. But he had no conviction dearer than the need to keep winning. Having managed to leap off the train tracks an instant before the coalition locomotive would have rolled over him, he was in even less of a mood to play nice than usual.

The dangers his government now faced were myriad, as any government's always are. But we can divide the important challenges into two broad contexts and two new interlocutors. The contexts were global economic upheaval and a shooting war in Afghanistan that grew nastier by the month. The interlocutors were a pair of Harvard liberals: Michael Ignatieff (PhD in History, 1976) and Barack Hussein Obama (Juris Doctor, 1991).

In some ways Ignatieff looked like a more formidable opponent by far than Dion. At the Montreal leadership convention in 2006 he had led on the first ballot, the position every previous Liberal leader had occupied. A trick of alliances spoiled his victory, a mishap that had finally been corrected. The caucus liked him. If there is one myth about Ignatieff that was never true, it is that he is frosty or arrogant. Up close, chatting with anyone at all, he is a gentle and attentive listener. He speaks both English and French well. He had written all those books. He was almost dashing. This last is hard to remember, but there is documented evidence. There is, for instance, a 2004 novel by the Toronto journalist and author Patricia Pearson called *Playing House*. Its main character runs into the Harvard academic and essayist Michael Ignatieff at an Italian restaurant in New York City. She's briefly smitten. "He was, I mused, everything that I'd ever dreamed suitable," Pearson's narrator says. "Accomplished, bold, socially gracious, a touch mischievous, emotionally pent-up in a wonderfully provocative way. One could sense real excitement within that crumpet. I was half in love with him by the time he'd analyzed the Middle East and the tartufo had arrived."

The problem with Ignatieff in politics was that, for the first time in his life, the tartufo never seemed to arrive. Alf Apps and Ian Davey had brought him back from Harvard as a man of ideas. In journalism, especially as it is practised at the BBC, he knew what that meant: say something provocative about big issues. But every time he did that in political life in Canada, he got into trouble. He spent the years from 2006 to 2009 repairing self-inflicted damage to his reputation.

In August 2007, for instance, he published a story in the *New York Times Magazine* called "Getting Iraq Wrong." His goal, transparently, was to get on the right side of the Iraq war. This was a challenge because he had been one of the war's pre-eminent academic cheerleaders. The magnitude of the circle he needed to square was clear in every line of the piece. Parts of it were nearly incoherent, as if Google-translated from Finnish. The "unfolding catastrophe in Iraq," he wrote, had "condemned the judgment" not only of George W. Bush but of "many others, myself included, who as commentators supported the invasion." How had this happened?

Ignatieff spent much of the rest of the article asserting a difference between "professional thinkers," who could pretty much just say whatever sounded good, and politicians, who had to get stuff right.

"Politicians live by ideas just as much as professional thinkers do, but they can't afford the luxury of entertaining ideas that are merely interesting. They have to work with the small number of ideas that happen to be true and the even smaller number that happen to be applicable to real life," he wrote. "In academic life, false ideas are merely false and useless ones can be fun to play with. In political life, false ideas can ruin the lives of millions and useless ones can waste precious resources."

In his previous submission to the *New York Times*, barely two years earlier, he had laid out the arguments he was now disowning. "A relativist America is properly inconceivable," he wrote then. "Leave relativism, complexity and realism to other nations. America is the last nation left whose citizens don't laugh out loud when their leader asks God to bless the country and further its mighty work of freedom. It is the last country with a mission, a mandate and a dream, as old as its founders. All of this may be dangerous, even delusional, but it is also unavoidable. It is impossible to think of America without these properties of self-belief."

Now Ignatieff was saying that those had been "merely interesting" notions, "fun to play with." One presumes he would have been miffed if anyone had made that claim against him in 2005. It was on the basis of such idle riffing that his Liberal recruiters had called him up for a run at the party's highest post.

But his goal now wasn't to make sense. It was to insulate himself against future attack, to have something on record that he could point to when anyone complained about his earlier positions. A similar motivation sent him to Holy Blossom Temple in Toronto on April 14, 2008, to apologize to a who's who of Toronto's Jewish community for having said, in 2006, that the Israeli Air Force bombing of Qana was "a war crime." The evening's moderator was Aurel Braun, a political scientist from the University of Toronto, who brooked no critique of Israel's efforts to defend itself.

His remarks that night were lengthy and often tinged with self-pity. "How many of you feel that nothing Israel says is listened to, because so many people have stopped listening at all?" he asked. "It also happens to be the way I feel I am perceived in some parts of the Jewish community." He blamed his Qana comment for his perception problem. He called his remark about war crimes "the most painful error of my political life." Since he was now a politician and thus confined, by his own analysis, to the smaller number of ideas that happen to be true, we can infer he thought his Qana comment was more painful than his stance on the Iraq war. But such quibbling ignores the point of the exercise. Ignatieff had checked, or done his best to check, another item off the list of amends he felt he needed to make.

To Ignatieff's supporters these periodic *mea culpas* should have been preoccupying. But in declaring his past sentiments inoperative, he was only doing what he had done all his life.

A diplomat's son from a storied Russian-Canadian family, Ignatieff had pursued studies in three countries by the time he turned thirty. Afterward he honed an unusual mode of career advancement, showing up at the gate of some exclusive fortress—the BBC or the New England foreign-policy *nomenklatura*—and finding a way in. He never stormed the ramparts. In such genteel institutions, that would not have worked. Instead, he ingratiated himself with the gatekeepers through observation and deft mimicry. He studied the way people in these clubs talked, the subjects they favoured, the attitudes they prized or scorned. Soon enough he began to speak like them. He did nothing to shake up the BBC, for it was not seeking a Canadian to shake it up. He simply became the kind of fellow the BBC liked to hire. He didn't revolutionize the liberal-interventionist school of American foreign policy; he simply ducked into a broom closet and emerged saying the sort of stuff that would make the Brookings Institution lads chuckle and nod. Outsiders may join exclusive clubs only on the clubs' terms, not their own. Long before he moved to Ottawa, Michael Ignatieff was a world champion shucker-off of old flesh.

If nationality was an obstacle, he could camouflage that, too. In the preface to his 2000 book *The Rights Revolution*, Ignatieff included a few lines written specifically for his Canadian readers. "This book may seem like a report by a visitor from a distant planet," he wrote. "I want to alert readers that I am a Martian outsider." Further on, he added what seemed to be a reassurance: writing this book had "deepened my attachment to the place on earth that, if I needed one, I would call home." Editions of the book released after 2005 omitted these lines.

His skill as a chameleon would cost him in politics, not because it emboldened his opponents but because it bewildered potential supporters. In 2006 I wrote in *Maclean's* about Liberals—not Conservatives—who complained about Ignatieff's "pronoun problem," his tendency, when sitting in the U.K. or the United States, to use the pronoun "we" in reference to countries that weren't Canada. Since the 1960s the Liberals had come increasingly to believe theirs was the party that best embodied Canadians' aspirations, perhaps the only one that bothered to try. It was not a mere curiosity that they had found a leader whose attachment to Canada, both geographical and emotional, was so tenuous. It was a fundamental weakness. Harper would not fail to exploit it.

But meanwhile Ignatieff had more pressing concerns. When he became Liberal leader the party was still proposing a Bloc-supported coalition with the NDP to take power. Ignatieff had signed the same letter all his colleagues had signed, petitioning the governor general to consider the option. But he had taken care to be the last Liberal to sign—as if that made a difference—and, as he later told Peter C. Newman, he didn't like the whole notion. "I had very substantial objections from the beginning," he said. Once he took over the party, met Layton and "listened to

Canadians," he said, "my initial feelings that this was the wrong move were redoubled." He needed to climb down from an adventure he had never liked. The 2009 budget offered an off-ramp.

It was a straightforward stimulus budget, seeking to pep up the sagging economy with a multi-billion-dollar Keynesian sugar high. Jim Flaherty's spending plan featured modest income-tax relief, incentives for home improvements, and billions for major public infrastructure projects. He called for a $33.7-billion deficit in the 2009/2010 fiscal year, and $29.8 billion the year after. There was not a word about public financing of political parties. The Bloc and NDP hated it all. It broadly resembled what they had nearly brought down the government in order to implement, but Layton in particular now preferred a clear path to NDP cabinet seats over policy consistency.

Ignatieff convened the scribes at the National Press Theatre for a formal news conference instead of the no-frills scrum opposition leaders usually used to reveal their budget reactions. Stimulus spending was all well and good, he said, but Liberals would be "watching like hawks" to make sure the money actually got out. "We are putting this government on probation. We've put down a very clear marker. This government has to get the money out the door. If this government fails to meet these targets, it will not survive for long."

Concretely, what the Ignatieff Liberals proposed was an amendment to the budget bill. The Liberals would support the budget if the government promised to report to Parliament at the end of March, June and December on "the actual implementation of the budget." Each report would be subject to a confidence vote, so the opposition could bring the government down any time. In particular, the Liberals demanded information on "the protection of the most vulnerable in Canadian society, the minimizing of existing job losses, the creation of the employment opportunities of tomorrow," and "the provision of economic stimulus in a manner fair to all regions of Canada."

It took about an hour for Jay Hill, the government House leader, to say the Conservatives would support that amendment. Probably Harper and Hill had taken that long to get their breath back after turning cartwheels in the cabinet room. The coalition uprising had forced Harper to spend billions of dollars quickly, something most governments are tempted to do anyway. Now Ignatieff was requiring Harper to explain, frequently and in detail, how he was spending those billions and how Canadians were benefiting. Twist my rubber arm, was Harper's reply. Within weeks, the Conservatives had developed strategies and graphic designs and Message Event Proposals for the many hundreds of sod turnings, ribbon cuttings and profoundly convivial chamber-of-commerce luncheons their economic action plan would entail. The Liberal-mandated quarterly stimulus reports would not be sullen reports to the teacher; they would be full of colour photos and zippy charts. Their none-too-subliminal message every time would be, What kind of fool would want to stop this fun and hold an election?

All this would become clear later. For now Ignatieff had saved his party's hide. Jack Layton was furious, because the Liberals' assent to the budget marked the effective end of the coalition experiment. Harper had finally come out as a deficit-spending Keynesian. Eventually he would be criticized, from left and right, for his spending binge. It would be silly criticism. The spending binge was the single condition of his survival as a political leader. After 2010 he would wind the spending down sharply, retiring most of the stimulus programs; the auditor general would even congratulate him on the care he and his officials had taken in ensuring that the proper rules were followed in disbursing the money. The only real surprise, perhaps, was how much he enjoyed the spending binge while it was happening. Glossy reports. Signs everywhere with jaunty, upward-pointing arrows. TV commercials praising Ottawa's munificence. It was a heady time for a small-government guy, as long as he showed a little flexibility.

The other pressing project of Harper's winter was securing and preparing for the visit of the man who had suddenly become the world's most prized social guest, Barack Obama. The forty-fourth president had been sworn in a week before Flaherty delivered his stimulus budget. Harper's PMO was deeply worried about screwing up this new relationship with the new leader of Canada's most important neighbour. It would not be hard to do. There was a long history of shaky relations, with gusts to open hostility, between presidents and prime ministers of different party stripes. Kennedy thought Diefenbaker was a buffoon. Trudeau thought much the same of Reagan.

Jean Chrétien got along famously with Bill Clinton, but when George W. Bush came to office, the relationship started off badly and never recovered. In the sort of snub only Canadians ever notice, Bush became the first president of the modern era (defined, in this instance, as "since Ronald Reagan") to visit any other country before Canada. Of course there were extenuating circumstances: Bush was a Texan whose state bordered on Mexico. Visiting Mexico was easy and automatic. No matter; the Conservatives' Canadian Alliance forebears had heckled Chrétien mercilessly for missing the big get. Then came the terrifying 9/11 attacks and Bush's speech days later to a joint session of Congress. Britain's Tony Blair sat in the VIP gallery next to Mrs. Bush. Chrétien was not even in town. Then came Chrétien's decision to stay out of the Iraq war followed by Paul Martin's decision to stay out of Bush's continental missile-defence project. From the standpoint of bilateral relations, none of it was pretty.

Harper had been a keen student of every step in this deteriorating relationship. He was quite sure he could do better. On May 28, 2002, he had made Canada–U.S. relations, and more specifically the proper bond between presidents and prime ministers, the subject of his first speech to the House of Commons as leader of the Canadian Alliance opposition. The occasion was a doomed opposition motion of no confidence against the majority Chrétien government condemning Chrétien's "failure to persuade the U.S. government to end protectionist policies."

The reason things were going badly with Washington, Harper said, was "the consistent and complete inability of the present Canadian government to make our case to American authorities, to Congress and especially to the Bush administration." Chrétien was so lost he kept making trade trips to China instead of concentrating on Washington, Harper claimed. "The Prime Minister went back to the future. He tried to revive the failed trade diversification of the 1970s, the Trudeau government's so-called third option strategy, which did not work then and is not working now."

Harper pointed out that if Brian Mulroney had understood nothing else, he had understood the Americans. The lesson from Mulroney: "The United States is our closest neighbour, our best ally, our biggest customer and our most consistent friend. Whatever else, we forget these things at our own peril. . . . We will be unable to get the U.S. administration on board unless whoever is in the White House and leading members of congress value and respect what our Prime Minister brings to the table."

So it was striking that on George W. Bush's last day in the White House, when his spokesperson released a list of the farewell telephone calls the two-term president had made to the leaders he had most enjoyed working with over the years, Harper's name was not on the list. Bush spoke to Brazilian president Luiz Inácio Lula da Silva. He spoke to British prime minister Gordon Brown. He called Denmark's Anders Fogh Rasmussen, France's Nicolas Sarkozy, Georgia's Mikheil Saakashvilli, Germany's Angela Merkel, Italy's Silvio Berlusconi, Israel's Shimon Peres, Japan's Tarō Asō, Russia's Dmitry Medvedev and his boss Vladimir Putin, and South Korea's Lee Myung-bak. Bush did not need to phone Australia's John Howard; the Howards were in Washington visiting the Bushes. He called the former Mexican president, Vicente Fox. He didn't need to call Felipe Calderón because Calderón had just visited with him.

But Bush didn't call Harper. There's no way of knowing why not, but the omission seems significant. One possibility: Bush's most important foreign-policy adventure, certainly the defining project of his presidency, was the war in Iraq. He and his advisors cannot have failed to notice how quickly Harper backed away from Iraq as he approached power.

In January 2003, Harper had stood in the Commons to remind MPs that as early as the previous October, he had noted: "there is no doubt that Saddam Hussein operates programs to produce weapons of mass destruction. Experience confirms this. British, Canadian and American intelligence leaves no doubt on the matter." Therefore, Canada must help depose Saddam Hussein, he said. Failure to do so "is not fitting with the greatness of our history or with our standing as a nation."

On March 26, 2003, six days after the American tanks rolled into the Iraqi desert, Harper told the Commons: "We should be there with our allies when it counts against Saddam Hussein." That August, he said to *Maclean's*: "Canada remains alienated from its allies, shut out of the reconstruction process to some degree, unable to influence events. There is no upside to the position Canada took."

This is prehistory in relation to the scope of this book, but it is necessary background for understanding what happened next. As soon as the Iraq adventure went sour, Harper put as much distance as he could between himself and the allies he had insisted Canada must support: Bush, Tony Blair and Australia's John Howard. This may have been smart politics, but that is not how it would have looked to Bush, Blair and Howard. They stuck with their policy after it became unpopular. Harper cut and ran.

By late April 2004 there had been more than eight hundred coalition fatalities in Iraq. On April 25 on CTV, Harper was asked about sending Canadian soldiers into the battle. "Given our limited military capacity and the extent to which our people are already over-committed across the world, I don't think that's feasible." Campaigning in Barrie, Ontario, several weeks later, he said his 2003 stance "was about putting pressure on Saddam to comply with UN resolutions." If Canada had helped to apply that pressure, "we could have avoided a war." That's nice, but it does not square with the public record. The war was six days old when Harper said "we should be there . . . when it counts." A year later he was claiming that when he said that, it no longer counted.

By December 2005, campaigning for votes once again, Harper was hurrying to correct U.S. conservatives who were too eager to embrace him as an ally on Iraq. A *Washington Times* columnist called him Bush's best supporter. Harper paused from the campaign trail to send the staunchly right-wing little paper a letter: "While I support the removal of Saddam Hussein and applaud the efforts to establish democracy and freedom in Iraq, I would not commit Canadian troops to that country."

In January 2006, Harper became prime minister. He worked fine with Bush. But there were no chummy photo ops, no visits to the ranch in Texas. By settling a long-standing dispute over softwood lumber exports, Harper had early success at ensuring that bilateral relations remained cordial and productive. They were never warm.

At intervals, for reasons having nothing at all to do with foreign policy, the Conservatives convene focus groups with undecided voters, seeking their impressions of the government and of other party leaders. These groups may include handing participants a picture of a party leader and a stack of photos that might evoke a strong emotional response: a bag of money, an army tank, a mother hugging her child. One of the cards portrays an American flag. Group convenors have noticed that the flag card is never perceived as a compliment when it is laid next to a party leader's photo. It always evokes a criticism: "Too close to the Americans." The longer Harper was prime minister, the less often participants associated him with the Stars and Stripes in this game of associative tarot. Harper went into power thinking he needed to be close to the American president. He realized that keeping power required keeping his distance.

Now Bush was gone and Obama was coming. In person. The newspapers brought the glad tidings on Sunday, January 11, 2009, that the new president's first foreign trip would be a hop up north soon after his inauguration. The *Toronto Star* called it "the result of days of behind-the-scenes contact between Ottawa and the president-elect's transition team."

There were reasons to hope the two leaders would get along. They were from roughly the same generation, younger than many world leaders. Both had run as outsiders who wanted to shake up their respective capitals. I know this is thin gruel, but Harper's communications staff peddled it with admirable relish to reporters in Ottawa. They needed to hope the meeting would go well. All Obama had heard about Harper before the election was that his former chief of staff had babbled something to TV reporters about NAFTA that wound up casting doubt on Obama's credibility. "Would they be the sort of people who'd remember something like that?" one PMO source wondered. "We certainly would have." If Obama remembered and carried a grudge, Harper would be toast.

Attitudes aside, the trip was hobbled by lackadaisical planning. Later, a former ministerial staffer who had worked on the Obama visit said the Harper PMO was so eager to land Obama first that they never got around to thinking too deeply about what the visit might actually accomplish.

"Once the word went out that Obama was coming to Canada, then it was time to do some serious pre-meeting meetings," this source said. "Set the table so to speak. It was pretty peculiar, because you couldn't really find out who was doing that work for Harper. Giorno was reported to be doing some work with [Obama's chief of staff, Rahm] Emanuel, chief to chief. It was suggested that Patrick Muttart was doing some of the work. Patrick's a good guy, but he's hardly a policy wonk. [Bruce] Carson was sort of neither here nor there."

It became "pretty clear," this source continued, that unlike the first Mulroney–Reagan meeting in Quebec City in 1985, there was little concerted sherpa work around the Harper–Obama visit. Mulroney believed that unless they were very careful, Canadians would always get the short end of the stick in negotiation with the Americans. "We're small in scale and we're largely captive to their market," the source said. "So we take conditions, we don't make conditions. We take a price instead of setting price." To compensate for that tendency, "there has to be a high level of engagement from people who are known to be serious in terms of speaking on behalf of the PM and that the PM is engaged with the President. He is calling, they are talking." But this time, "none of that went on and we drifted into that meeting."

Shortly before Obama arrived, I visited the Langevin Block with my *Maclean's* colleague John Geddes to meet a Harper advisor. It was clear from that conversation that Harper had no intention of troubling the president of Canada's overwhelmingly powerful neighbour with suggestions for an agenda. "We're not the new guy, he is," the advisor told us. "We're here to listen."

In the middle of a global economic crisis, with Obama trying to get U.S. troops farther into Afghanistan and right out of Iraq, and both countries pondering a massive investment to prop up the faltering General Motors, Harper took a remarkably passive approach to summit planning. Since no meeting of heads of government can be counted a success if it produces no paper, at least a memorandum of understanding, our inside source says, "the Americans slapped on what was the cookie cutter of the day. The cookie cutter for 2009, Obama-style, were bilateral clean energy MOUs, clean energy dialogue."

So, when Obama came to Ottawa on February 19, he toured the House of Commons and held a joint media availability with Harper. "We are establishing a U.S.–Canada clean energy dialogue," Harper told the scribes, "which commits senior officials from both countries to collaborate on the development of clean energy science and technologies that will reduce greenhouse gases and combat climate change." The announcement included a clean energy fund, work to study carbon capture and sequestration, and a plan to study the creation of an energy-efficient "smart grid" for power distribution.

Nine months later, Obama and the Indian prime minister, Manmohan Singh, announced "enhanced co-operation on Energy Security, Energy Efficiency, Clean Energy, and Climate Change," including a clean energy fund, carbon capture and smart grids. In January 2011, Obama and China's Hu Jintao announced "Cooperation on Climate Change, Clean Energy, and the Environment." Four months later, Obama and Polish premier Donald Tusk "welcomed new momentum in the two countries' cooperation on energy and climate security." Soon Obama was in Canberra to release a "Statement on Energy Cooperation" with the Australians.

For Obama, handing out memos of understanding on clean energy was the equivalent of a bantam hockey player handing out mugs with crests on them to families he's billeted with at tournaments. Jim Prentice, the environment minister at the time, tried to make the thing sound exciting in an interview with *Policy Options* magazine. "On a scale that has never actually been achieved previously, we will be working together with the United States on these working groups, and one of them is very specifically focused on new technologies." Prentice and his U.S. counterpart, the Nobel-winning physicist Stephen Chu, who served as Obama's energy secretary, reported back to their leaders about the dialogue in September 2009. Chu delivered a second report with his new Canadian counterpart, Peter Kent, in February 2011. Prentice had by this point given up on federal politics and gone into banking. Chu and Kent promised to report further to their bosses in "spring 2011." They finally got around to it fifteen months later.

Nobody cared. If the best that can be said of the Obama–Harper relationship is that it lacks animosity, that is still a credit to both leaders because it bucks a long-established trend. The feuds between Diefenbaker and Kennedy, Reagan and Trudeau, Bush and Chrétien are part of the shared history of the two countries. In their turn, between these two, there has mostly been apathy. In the end it wasn't their age or their outsider status that Obama and Harper shared. It was this: neither man had any personal friendships with foreign leaders of the kind Bill Clinton and Brian Mulroney cultivated in their day. These two, Obama and Harper, found their human warmth closer to home to the extent they found any. In their meetings they briskly ticked off items on a to-do list. They even managed to get some big projects accomplished. They bailed out General Motors and kicked off an apparently endless negotiation to enhance the continental security perimeter. Then they parted company and returned to other matters they actually cared about.

———

On March 10, 2009, Harper went to Brampton to deliver his first Liberal-mandated quarterly update on his Economic Action Plan in a speech before an invited audience at the Pearson Convention Centre. Shame about the name of the place. CANADA IS WEATHERING THE STORM, the finance department news release read. "Ladies and gentlemen, in times like these I'm reminded of a quote by investor Warren Buffet," Harper told his audience. "He once said, 'It is only when the tide goes out that you know who was swimming naked.' The global economic crisis has revealed quite a few skinny dippers but Canada is not one of them." Hee-hee. The release accompanying Harper's speech also bragged about EXTRAORDINARY AND UNPRECEDENTED ACTION. The word "Action" appeared fifty times in the release. This was a surprise, as Parliament had not yet even passed the budget implementation bill that would allow money to start flowing. But it looked impressive. Who could want to stop all this action, or at least all this mentioning of action? Guess.

"I must admit I have been very frustrated with the opposition since the election," Harper said. They had "formed a coalition to try and prevent us from even bringing our budget forward." Now they were daring to ask questions and propose amendments. Harper asked his audience to "send them a message: Stop the political games!"

A day later Ignatieff announced he had finally realized it might not be the best idea to let the Conservative fox issue quarterly updates on the quality of its henhouse management. The Liberals would henceforth release their own reports. When he was asked why Harper was still blaming the opposition for stuff, he replied, "My only hypothesis is this economy's falling like a stone and he'd like you to write about something else."

At the end of March a few thousand Liberals repaired to Vancouver for a leadership convention to rubber-stamp Ignatieff's takeover of the party. A tribute to Stéphane Dion went hours over schedule. The departing loser's speech was interminable. Louise Arbour, the former Supreme Court justice turned United Nations high commissioner for human rights, was inexplicably present at the convention. Probably somebody thought she'd make a fine Liberal leader someday. Her speech had been scheduled after Dion's, and was broadcast late at night to a country situated, for the most part, assorted time zones to the east. Arbour's coming-out as a Liberal person of interest played mostly to insomniacs.

On May 12, with Ignatieff formally ensconced as leader and guaranteed not to go anywhere any time soon, the Conservatives released their attack ads against him. "Why is Michael Ignatieff back in Canada after being away for thirty-four years? Does he have a plan for the economy? No," the trademark snarky voice-over intoned. The ad featured footage of Ignatieff blowing kisses to supporters. The screen flashed quotes from his writings. "Horribly arrogant." "Cosmopolitan."

"With no long-term plan for the economy, he's not in it for Canada—just in it for himself. It's the only reason he's back. Michael Ignatieff: Just Visiting."

Muttart, the ads' architect, had the Conservatives register a website in Montenegro so its URL could read www.ignatieff.me, reinforcing the aura of egotism around the Liberal leader.

The content of the ads would have been uncontroversial to many Liberals, as they had been expressing the same sentiments back in 2006. The notion that Ignatieff's long sojourn out of the country should count pretty seriously against him was a common topic among Liberals—until he became their leader. Now that Harper was making it the focus of an ad campaign depressingly reminiscent of the one that had put lead in Dion's wings, Liberals were outraged.

Outraged but unwilling to do anything to respond. On CTV, Steve MacKinnon, the party's former national director, proclaimed that the most important effect of the Just Visiting ads was to boost donations to the Liberals. A member of the party's national executive leaked me an internal memo, written by party president Alf Apps, detailing a plan to create a $25-million annual war chest to respond to such attacks. "I believe the advertising campaign undertaken by our opponents last week has created the opportunity to galvanize the entire Party," Apps wrote, "around a reinvigorated fundraising effort now, even before the summer commences."

He was wrong. The Liberals never came anywhere close to raising the kind of money Apps was talking about. Two years would pass before they would buy any ads, on the eve of the next election. In the interim, having watched the Conservative ad machine take Stéphane Dion apart, they chose to repeat the experience.

"I don't think we really understood how effective it would be if done over a sustained period of time between writ periods," Dan Brock, one of Ignatieff's aides, said after the 2011 election. "We thought, 'Canadians are going to reject this, because this is just over the top. Canadians are going to say, "You shouldn't be doing this."' And that's exactly wrong. Canadians aren't going to say that. They're too busy living their lives. They pay a little bit of attention to [politics], and if that little bit of attention is dominated by a particular message, effectively delivered and repeated over and over again, it's going to sink in. And it did."

But it's not quite accurate to say Ignatieff had no response to the ads. He waited almost two weeks, though, then delivered an empty threat. In Gander, Newfoundland, near the end of May, he told a partisan crowd he had a message for Harper. "If you mess with me, I will mess with you until I'm done." The next day in Dartmouth, Nova Scotia, he tried again. "Don't trifle with me," he said. "Don't try this rough stuff with me."

Here we see another example of Ignatieff as anthropologist, Goodall among the apes, peering through the foliage and scratching observations into his Moleskine notebook: These creatures sometimes establish social hierarchy through displays of bravado. Very well, then. In order to gain their trust, I too will engage in chest-thumping behaviour. Unfortunately, he was new to this particular stretch of veldt and had not yet observed the consequences of conspicuous failure to deliver on a threat. An ape who threatened too often to attack without following up on that threat was, in fact, revealing weakness. Soon enough the rest of the band would tear him up.

The Liberals had launched a website, onprobation.ca, featuring photos of empty fields where the Conservatives had announced infrastructure projects. But the funny thing about probation is that it's a binary state of existence. If you're not failing, you're passing. Every day the Liberals declared themselves Harper's probation cop and didn't bust him, they were effectively endorsing him. This Parliament was custom-designed to be brutal on Liberals. They were up first in Question Period. They appeared to be holding Harper's fate in their hands. But Ignatieff could not stop Harper alone and he could not ally with the NDP and Bloc to stop him without triggering acid flashbacks from the coalition crisis. Ignatieff's response was to keep talking tough, doubling down on a bluff.

He was aided, if that's the word, by Ian Davey, a slouching and cheerful Toronto lawyer who was making an elaborate show of hating every minute he spent in Ottawa running the Office of the Leader of the Opposition. Davey and Apps were lifelong Liberals whose shtick, ever since John Turner's leadership, had been to stand outside the party's power hierarchy and remark loudly on how badly the Proper Liberals were screwing everything up. Davey's dad was Keith Davey, the fabled Rainmaker, the guy who kept Pearson viable, taught Pierre Trudeau how to play rough, and had done his best to save Turner. To call Keith Davey an insider was like saying eggs taste eggy: true, but it understated things. Ian adored his dad, but his enduring gesture of rebellion was to affect an outsider stance. He'd sit there in his fourth-floor office, kitty-corner from Ignatieff's, roll his eyes and tell a visitor he hated the place, hated the town, hated the games, but what's a guy to do?

Davey's hunch was that the Liberals need to own a patch of the waterfront stretching from the business-friendly centre all the way over to a brand of economic populism most New Democrats could endorse. Ignatieff had the centre nailed down, everyone hoped, but he needed help on the left, so Davey encouraged him to talk up employment insurance. EI was fantastic Big Ottawa stuff, real Rainmaker Liberalism, just like the old days. Times were tough. People needed help. Government would send them a cheque. Harper hated the program, thought it made people lazy. Ignatieff would champion its fast expansion.

Improving EI was "the most effective, rapid and targeted form of stimulus the government can offer our economy right now," Ignatieff wrote in the *National Post* on May 23, 2009. Expand the rolls by 150,000 EI recipients and you'd have "money flowing into communities that have been hit the hardest by this recession. That's the kind of immediate, targeted and effective stimulus we need right now." The fields of infrastructure were empty. Big Ottawa could help communities "directly, right now, by improving access to EI."

The EI thing reliably led Harper to call Ignatieff another big-government big spender. Ignatieff pushed back. "My party has an unimpeachable record in fiscal responsibility," he said in the Commons. Unfortunately, millions of Canadians didn't believe that. Ian Brodie, nearly a year out of his job as Harper's chief of staff but still loyal, told a conference at Carleton University that the Gomery Commission's 2005 investigation into political corruption had durably blown the Liberals' brand advantage as fiscal managers. "The idea that the Liberal party has a brand as a fiscally responsible organization—I never once saw a single piece of market-research evidence to support that," he said. "Never."

Of course that's the sort of thing Ian Brodie would say. Corroboration for his claim came the same week, however, in a new poll by the EKOS firm, whose director, Frank Graves, was generally thought to be fond of Liberals. The poll showed that respondents gave Harper the edge over both Ignatieff and Layton on decisiveness, patriotism—and economic management. The economy stuff was hard on Ignatieff's pride, and suggested he would have a harder time shielding himself against accusations of irresponsibility than he hoped. But the truly striking gap was on the response to the question about which leader respondents regarded as "a patriotic Canadian." Harper's advantage there was thirty-four points, nearly double his next-widest margin.

Shortly before EKOS released that poll, I received an e-mail from a Harper advisor:

ON BACKGROUND . . . IF YOU CHOOSE TO USE . . . "SENIOR CONSERVATIVE" IS FINE.

The simple fact that we are debating the "Canadianness" of the Leader of the Liberal Party of Canada is a victory for Conservatives.

Iggy is now playing defence on the #1 brand attribute of the Liberal Party. Even after the sponsorship scandal the Liberals still owned being the "Canada Party." The party with the pan-Canadian vision. The party best able to keep the country together. The party with the independent foreign policy. Having a Liberal play defence on his "Canada" credentials is as bad as a Republican having to defend his commitment to the U.S. military or a New Democrat having to defend her commitment to the labour movement. Attacks on Iggy related to "arrogance and elitism" (e.g. the "arrogance spot") and/or "tax and spend" (e.g. the "economy" spot) are standard operating procedure—the personalization of negative brand attributes associated with the party itself. But the attacks on Ignatieff's long-term commitment to the country are much deeper and much more problematic for a Liberal.

Ignatieff had hurried to write a book about the Canadian side of his prominent family and his travels in his native land, plainly designed, like the *New York Times Magazine* article and the trip to Holy Blossom Temple, to patch his leaky viability. The title of the book was *True Patriot Love*. At least there was no fooling him about what needed patching. The Conservatives had his number. Muttart and Finley had pored over his extensive writing with a vengeance. Canadian Conservatives had visited the BBC tape archives in London, which featured hundreds of hours of Ignatieff having fun playing with merely interesting ideas. They had rented an airplane to fly low over Ignatieff's summer home in the south of France, snapping photos. One Conservative marvelled in private at the news that, as far as anyone at the party could ascertain, Ignatieff had made it to his sixty-third year on God's earth without obtaining a driver's licence. What a freak. "How can you know the country if you've never driven through it?"

On May 28 in the House of Commons, Ignatieff was blustering about how Harper should fire Jim Flaherty. "I cannot fire the Leader of the

Opposition," Harper rejoined cheerfully. "And with all the tapes I have on him, I would not want to." It was the simple truth. Ignatieff would remain Liberal leader for nearly two more years. Twisting.

On Thursday, June 11, Harper went to Cambridge, Ontario, to release his second quarterly update on what it pleased him to call his Economic Action Plan. How could Ignatieff give Harper a pass? How could he stand in front of the money train? Ignatieff scrummed in Montreal, careful to say nothing that would commit him one way or the other, then limped home to Stornoway for the weekend, and brainstormed. On Monday in the National Press Theatre he pleaded with Harper to throw him a bone. Of course that's not how he phrased it. It was time for another ultimatum! He demanded a meeting with Harper. He wanted details from him on EI. He wanted to know how the government planned to produce medical isotopes in the wake of the Chalk River debacle. He wanted to know the precise amount of stimulus money the government had spent to date. And he wanted to see a plan for getting out of budgetary deficit.

So he was demanding answers? "I don't need to see all the answers this week," he replied. Wait . . . what?

He went to Question Period. Harper rarely showed up for Question Period, but today he made an exception. Somehow, however, Ignatieff made it through the hour without asking whether the prime minister would meet the four demands he had just listed for reporters. Bemused, Harper strolled to the National Press Theatre to announce he'd be happy to meet Ignatieff. They would meet the next day on Harper's turf, at his Langevin Block office. Harper was unimpressed with Ignatieff's threat because, like everyone else, he was having a hard time figuring out what the threat was. "You usually say, 'Do X or else,'" Harper told reporters. "You don't just say 'Or else.'"

When Ignatieff showed up in Harper's office on Tuesday, June 16, it took the prime minister about three minutes to realize the Liberal leader had no specific request to make. What do you want? Harper asked after the opening pleasantries. I want to see that you're serious about making Parliament work, he was told. But what would that look like? What specific changes? Eligibility times, enhanced benefits, changes to premiums?

After two months of riding the EI hobby horse most days in Question Period, Ignatieff was not particularly *au fait* with the details of the program's design. They would not have been able to reach a deal that day even if Harper had felt like it. The prime minister suggested, How about some kind of working group to spend the summer looking at the thing? Ignatieff loved the idea. Yes! A working group! And if it spent the summer working, as a group, there was no way Ignatieff could pull the plug on the government. So the sword of Damocles would remain suspended until September. This was fine with Ignatieff. He kept telling everyone the sword was over Harper's head. But if Ignatieff had looked up, it was pointing down at him.

He had no trouble selling the notion to Liberal caucus the next morning. Remember that election you've been dreading after our rout in the last election only seven months ago? Postponed! Reporters waiting outside the Liberal caucus room heard shouts of joy—from the Conservative caucus room, down the Centre Block hallway. Surely Harper was regaling the troops with tales of conquest? "Appearances can be deceiving," an MP told me later. In fact Chuck Strahl and some of the other caucus members had put together a barbershop quartet. They'd sung a tune for their colleagues, and brought the house down.

Ignatieff emerged from his own tuneless caucus meeting, backed by a dozen of the most photogenic Liberal MPs. This was a good day, he said. He did not mention that of his four ultimatum items, Harper had ignored three and sent the fourth to a committee. "Do I look like I've been steamrolled?" he asked rhetorically. Well, yes. Yes, he did.

The Liberal–Conservative EI working group spent the summer

getting nowhere. Harper sent Diane Finley, the minister responsible for EI, and just coincidentally the toughest bird in cabinet, and Pierre Poilievre, a young MP from Eastern Ontario with a rare knack for getting under Liberals' skin. They made a great show of listening intently to the Liberal envoys, retreating to their corner, and returning without having adopted a single comma of the latest Liberal proposal. This was no peace delegation. It was an extension of war by other means. Eventually the meetings ground to a halt.

June became September, and with it the prospect of yet another stimulus report. By now Ignatieff might as well just poke his own eyes out with barbecue tongs. Instead, he decided to follow his logic to its dreary conclusion. He had warned Harper three times. Surely his word must mean something or it would mean nothing. In Sudbury for the Liberals' annual Labour Day weekend caucus retreat to plan the parliamentary session, he announced that if it were up to him there'd be no session.

"After four years of drift, four years of denial, four years of division and discord—Mr. Harper, your time is up," Ignatieff told his caucus and the television cameras. "The Liberal Party cannot support this government any further. We will hold it to account. We will oppose it in Parliament.

"We can choose a small Canada—a diminished, mean, and petty country," he said. "Or we can choose a big Canada. A Canada that is generous and open. A Canada that inspires. . . . We can be the smartest, healthiest, greenest, most open-minded country there is—but only if we choose to be."

Canadians rallied around this bold vision.

Kidding again.

Within days, the Liberals started to drift gently downward in the polls as support for the Harper Conservatives inched upward. From a rough tie, Ignatieff's Liberals soon trailed Harper's party by fourteen points. It was the same phenomenon as in 2008: Canadians carried no torch for

Harper, but if the choice was between him and the only alternative, they'd stick with Harper, thanks. Nor could Ignatieff even hope to appeal to voters directly in a campaign. The NDP had voted against the Conservatives dozens of times since 2006, secure in the knowledge that it would be harmless chest-beating as long as the Liberals propped the government up. Now the NDP voted against Ignatieff's opposition motion.

The story Ignatieff had been telling himself since January now lay in tatters. He was not Harper's probation cop. He had no credible threat to make. Within weeks Ignatieff fired Ian Davey and most of the senior OLO staff. As if any of this were their fault. The new head of the leader's office was Peter Donolo, a former communications director to Jean Chrétien. Donolo had been a big player in Chrétien's Ottawa, a key enabler for Chrétien's Happy Warrior shtick. Maybe he'd bring some of the old mojo with him. Donolo coaxed a bunch of Toronto and Montreal Liberals of the same vintage to join him. He built a much more formal organizational structure than Davey had done. The mid-evening beer seminars among OLO staffers ground to a halt. There was work to do, and for once everyone knew their assignment. One of the conditions Donolo set for his return to politics was that, to the extent this sort of thing could be controlled, he wanted a year's peace before Ignatieff would even think about trying to call another election.

On October 3, the National Arts Centre held its annual fundraising gala. It was precisely the sort of black-tie arts gala Harper had denigrated during the 2008 election, in fact the grandest such date on Ottawa's social calendar. The orchestra's big guest that year was Yo-Yo Ma, the legendary American cellist. The Bytown swells in their tuxes and gowns were having their customary moderately good time. Then came a bit of fussing as stagehands adjusted a piano near centre stage. A lumbering fellow in a dark suit with an open-necked shirt appeared. It was Stephen Harper. It was the prime minister of Canada. It was Stephen Harper, the prime minister of Canada, sitting at the piano and belting out a creditable rendition of the Beatles chestnut "With a Little Help from My Friends."

Laureen Harper had been honorary chairwoman of the NAC's gala committee since 2005. The longer the government lasted, the more the arts centre's wily CEO, Peter Herrndorf, worked on solidifying the institution's relationship with Laureen. As long as she enjoyed her increasingly frequent visits to the arts centre, perhaps it would be safe from a government whose affection for orchestras and theatre was otherwise rarely demonstrated. Stephen Harper's game efforts at the keyboard, on the other hand, were not a PR contrivance. He really did have guys over to 24 Sussex fairly regularly to play. At some point every amateur musician feels ready for an audience, or is pushed in front of one by loved ones whether he's ready or not. Jean Chrétien, a less than convincing valve-trombone player, had squeezed out a few notes on occasion at Liberal caucus parties. A generation earlier, Chrétien's mentor, Mitchell Sharp, was a very occasional guest pianist at the NAC. So it does little good to parse Harper's coming-out on the piano too closely. Was it canny self-promotion? Exuberant self-expression?

The answer, of course, is that it was some of both. What made the appearance resonate was its moment. A year earlier, Harper had come close to engineering his own downfall at the hands of the combined opposition. In the days before he hit the stage, his most prominent opponent, Ignatieff, had struck again and missed. Harper was finally beginning to look like something more than an accidental prime minister. He might last long enough in the job to learn to enjoy it. The NAC gala had about it the mood of a belated victory party.

Trouble did not stay away long. Four days after Harper's NAC debut, on October 7, the Military Police Complaints Commission investigating claims of abuse of Afghan prisoners suspended its public hearings in Gatineau, across the river from Ottawa, while lawyers argued over the hearings' proper scope. That same morning, an affidavit from a former mid-ranking diplomat in Afghanistan, Richard Colvin, was sealed by court order at the instigation of government lawyers. Colvin's affidavit claimed widespread abuse of prisoners taken by the Canadian Forces in Afghanistan after the prisoners had been handed over to Afghan authorities.

The move to seal the affidavit drew widespread public attention, and did not stand long. On October 14, the complaints commission, or MPCC, unsealed the affidavit. In it, Colvin had written that he had become aware of serious problems within a month after landing in Afghanistan in April 2006. "I soon became aware of a number of what, in my judgment, were problems in Canadian policy and/or practice, including regarding Afghan detainees," he wrote. "I spent considerable time on the detainee file and sent many reports on detainee-related issues to Canadian officials." Colvin had seen nothing that looked like a response to his concerns.

It was an explosive allegation. Harper's government had insisted since 2006 that it had no evidence of Canadian soldiers knowingly handing over prisoners to be tortured. If there had been any, the Canadian soldiers involved would have been complicit in war crimes. Gordon O'Connor, the veteran soldier who was Harper's first defence minister, had been shuffled out of the job in August 2007, five months after he had to apologize to the House for inconsistent and misleading answers about the Red Cross's role in ensuring detainees' proper treatment. Since then the military complaints commission had been pecking away at the story. All along, Harper had hoped a lid could be kept on the allegations. Colvin's affidavit put an end to that hope.

And the magnitude of the government's effort to stonewall became part of the story. On the same October day that he unsealed Colvin's affidavit, Peter Tinsley, the commission's chairman, announced he was suspending hearings indefinitely. The government had already lost a court challenge to shut the commission down, and since March had consistently refused to hand over a single document the commission had requested. The commission wasn't digging into this out of idle curiosity: military police implicated by allegations of abuse needed the documentation to organize their defence.

"This is how we find ourselves where we are today," Tinsley said, "forced to adjourn the proceedings out of fairness to the subjects, since obviously they should not be the ones to suffer because of the government's conduct."

But there is more than one way to put a microphone in front of a diplomat who wants to talk. The opposition still had a majority on a special Commons committee examining Canada's role in Afghanistan. On November 18, Colvin testified in front of the committee, live on television.

"As I learned more about our detainee practices, I came to the conclusion that they were contrary to Canada's values, contrary to Canada's interests, contrary to Canada's official policies and also contrary to international law. That is, they were un-Canadian, counterproductive, and probably illegal," he said. A committee member asked how widespread was the practice. "According to our information, the likelihood is that all the Afghans we handed over were tortured," Colvin responded. "For interrogators in Kandahar, it was standard operating procedure."

Weeks of turmoil ensued. Good reporters at a dozen news organizations produced a gusher of stories that dominated the nightly news and the newspapers, using documents they had obtained through leaks or through access to information, testimony from secret sources or public comments from Colvin and others. Hardly a day went by without fresh revelations. Harper and his defence minister, Peter MacKay, were taking questions on the allegations almost daily in the House of Commons.

Questions about detainee abuse had dogged Harper for almost as long as he had been prime minister. It had already cost him one minister he liked, O'Connor, and there was no guarantee that on any given day it wouldn't swallow up another. "We were always fighting ghosts," a trusted Harper advisor said later. "There was a lot of friction internally on how to handle this issue, as to whether it was an inside-the-beltway press-gallery-type issue, or whether it was something that was resonating with Canadians."

That distinction is always crucial with Harper. He survives politically in large part because he is uninterested in debates that are of concern only to people who live within ten kilometres of Parliament's Peace Tower. He doesn't always guess right about which issues those are, but his instincts have consistently topped his opponents'. On detainees, he made one early decision, then issued a directive straight from him: nobody in the government was to refer to the possible victims of abuse as "Afghan detainees." They were to be called "Taliban prisoners." Ministers who slipped into language that might suggest, or permit, sympathy for the detainees would get a testy call from the PMO. The sentiment among Conservatives was that they were on the soldiers' side and that critics of government policy were therefore critics of Canada's troops.

The feeling ran deep. O'Connor was a former army general; Harper had insisted that the opposition had no right to question his judgment, right up to the moment he took O'Connor out of the defence portfolio. In conversation with me at the end of 2009, Teneycke referred derisively to Graeme Smith, a *Globe and Mail* reporter who had spent more time on the ground in Afghanistan than almost any other Canadian journalist, as "a guy whose sources are the Taliban." This was true, or part of the truth: Smith talked to Taliban fighters among many other sources in an infernally complex theatre. But this was hardly the only instance where the Canadian soldiers themselves seemed more open-minded about things than Harper's circle. On a trip I took to Afghanistan in December 2009, I received a briefing from a Canadian Forces officer who used a map of Kandahar that Smith had published in the *Globe*. "This is Graeme Smith's map, not ours," the officer said. "Ours are classified, and Graeme's is pretty good."

But regardless of how the detainee issue was playing across the land, the Harper advisor told me, the government took no joy from trying to handle it. "Every day there was a sense among some of us that we were going out and not having all our ducks lined up." This was a simple function of the nature of war. It is chaotic, the stakes are as high as they can be, and information is always partial and contradictory.

Few soldiers had a better view of the chaos through more of Canada's combat deployment than Lt.-Gen. (ret'd) Andrew Leslie. He was deputy commander of the International Security Assistance Force in Kabul in 2003. By the spring of 2006 he was chief of the Land Staff. The promotion came just as Canadian soldiers completed the move from Kabul, a relatively secure assignment in an urban setting where the burden was shared with troops from dozens of countries, to the wild, open Pashtun desert of Kandahar. As the brutal luck of war would have it, the Taliban picked that spring to dramatically increase the intensity of their military activity. The nature of the conflict changed from mopping up sparse resistance and helping restore civilian authority to full-bore and non-stop combat. Canadians weren't the only foreigners taken by surprise. Every country with skin in the game was rocked by the ferocity of the new combat environment. The consequences were deeply unsettling, especially in the south. From the beginning in 2002 through the end of 2005, eight Canadians had died in Afghanistan. Thirty-six more died in 2006 alone. The pace of the fatalities would be slow, but by mid-2013, the total Canadian death toll would stand at a hundred and fifty-eight. Harper telephoned the family of every soldier who fell. He was making far more calls than he would have anticipated.

In an interview in 2013, Leslie told me that back then, in 2006, Canadian forces were feeling their way: "We had almost no experience in actually handling detainees, and didn't have processes set up. We didn't have the attention to detail that comes with many years of experience of scooping up people who have been trying to kill us, and trying to figure out, at what point do you turn them over to the local authorities?"

For most of the time Canadians were operating in Kandahar, from 2006 at least until Obama sent serious U.S. reinforcements to southern Afghanistan in the second half of 2009, the Canadian numbers were badly insufficient for the task. In some ways the hopelessness of the task wasn't obvious. In any direct confrontation, Canadians defeated the Taliban and other enemy fighters handily. "The enemy were never more than 5 to 6 percent of our size," Leslie says. But winning firefights was only a small piece of a larger goal, which was to safeguard an environment of general calm so that everyday life could establish itself for ordinary Afghans, without constant insurgent harassment. That would have taken far more troops.

In 2008 John Manley, the former Chrétien-era Liberal cabinet minister, produced a report for Harper calling for an additional battalion, about a thousand troops, in Kandahar. The Americans pretty quickly provided that battalion. The problem was that a battalion was a teardrop in the desert. "I'm not sure where Mr. Manley got that number," Leslie said, "because a battalion disappears into three villages. What was needed was three brigades"—closer to thirty thousand troops. "Whoever told John Manley that a battalion was needed should be taken out and spanked." After his 2009 inauguration, Obama sent three brigades and more into the Kandahar desert. The scale of the transformation, by the time I went there for the last time in 2010, was vast. It probably came too late to save the country. It certainly came after more than three years in which Canadian soldiers and civilian development officials were barely hanging on in one of the deadliest parts of Afghanistan.

So, during the period covered by the Colvin memos, Canadian troops were combat-green and run ragged. In the transfer of prisoners from temporary Canadian authority to longer-lasting Afghan detention, there were frequent "stops and starts," Leslie said. There would be allegations of torture. The detainee transfer process would grind to a halt. The allegations would be investigated. Sometimes procedures would change. Transfers would resume. "The various operational commanders had the authority to decide [to halt transfers] on their own because you didn't want a political spin put on it," Leslie said. "In the final analysis it's the people wearing the uniform who are subject to [accusations of] war crimes. We take all that very seriously."

Leslie gave me the strong impression that military commanders didn't like having to handle the challenges of ensuring proper treatment of detainees on top of the need to protect the population of Kandahar—and to keep from dying—during those chaotic years. But, he added, "I think a bunch of the oversight and investigations, and the legal scholars who were swarming all over the armed forces in that period, did some good work in trying to keep everybody focused on what we were supposed to be doing right, and what we were doing wrong."

Further demonstrating the gap between the Conservatives and the military on questions of openness, Leslie said he wishes the Harper government had simply been more forthcoming about the challenges of warfare. "In retrospect, if someone had stood up and said, 'We're new at this and admit we don't have all the answers, and we're willing to take all criticisms—and by the way, Lawyer A and Human Rights Person B, why don't you come over and give us a hand?'—that might have been a better solution than circling the wagons and shooting outwards." But the imaginary government Leslie was describing, frank and modest and willing to admit flaws, was never going to be Harper's government.

Much later, in June 2012, the MPCC released its final report into the allegations of detainee abuse. It found the original 2008 complaint, which had been brought by Amnesty International and the B.C. Civil Liberties Association, "unsubstantiated." It found "no grounds" to suspect that the military police officers who were the object of the original charges had breached their duty. Their behaviour "met the standards of a reasonable police officer."

The report contained a full chapter on the government's refusal to provide needed evidence. "The doors were basically slammed shut on document disclosure," the report said. And not just the doors to the MPCC. In mid-December, just weeks after Colvin's explosive testimony, rumours started circulating in Ottawa that Harper was thinking of proroguing Parliament, putting an end to the current session and restarting the legislative agenda with a new Throne Speech in the new year. The move was plainly designed to cool down a Parliament grown suddenly too hot over the detainee allegations for Harper's taste. On December 30, after the House had risen for its regularly scheduled Christmas break, Harper telephoned Michaëlle Jean and asked her to consent to a prorogation. He obtained it without delay. Parliament would reconvene at the beginning of March. Harper's spokespeople framed the delay as an attempt to ensure that nothing distracted Canadian citizens from the Vancouver Winter Olympics in February.

Now, governments prorogue Parliament from time to time. Jean Chrétien had done it a couple of times himself. Harper had done it in 2007 and very few people noticed or minded. But this time it felt, to Harper's opponents, like an echo of his trip to Rideau Hall to save his political hide at the height of the coalition crisis, barely a year earlier. Ignatieff, Layton and Duceppe were furious. Two hundred thousand people joined a Facebook group to protest the shutdown of Parliament. Anti-prorogation rallies across Canada on January 23 drew more than twenty-two thousand people.

At first the Conservatives figured the protesters and Facebookers were just more of the usual suspects. Fewer than 38 percent of voters had supported Conservatives in the 2008 election. It would be easy enough to find a few tens of thousands of sensitive souls out of the other 62 percent. But over time it was becoming clear that this wasn't just an issue that offended the sensibilities of people who would never vote Conservative anyway. The House of Commons was empty. People expected their MP to show up for work, and that wasn't happening. An EKOS poll just before the rallies suggested that Conservatives and Liberals now stood at a virtual tie. Ignatieff had consistently failed to lay a glove on Harper. But Harper had managed, once again, to hurt himself.

The beautiful pageantry of the Vancouver Olympics did fill part of the news vacuum Harper had created by shutting down Parliament. The return of Parliament in the first week of March brought a measure of normalcy and, with it, put a floor under the Conservatives' decline. The opposition parties pressed for documents relating to the detainee crisis. The Conservatives stonewalled, citing national security needs. Peter Milliken, the Liberal MP who had served for more than a decade as the well-liked Speaker of the House, ruled that the government must come up with the documents within weeks. The government kept stalling anyway, while insisting that it was following Milliken's orders. The drama dragged out over half of 2010.

If the detainee issue showed Harper's determination to keep a secret even when greater openness might have helped, another 2010 controversy showed how important it was to him to reward and reinforce the right-wing base of his party, even when it meant leaving centrists baffled or furious. This was the decision to destroy the long-form census.

That's not the way the government announced it. In fact, it wasn't announced at all. On June 17, an order-in-council (a cabinet decision implemented, as many such decisions can be, without recourse to

Parliament) stated that the only mandatory census questions in 2011 would be the very basic questions in the short-form questionnaire. By default, the much more elaborate long-form census would become voluntary. There would be no penalty at all for failing to fill the long form out. In an apparent bid to compensate for people who wouldn't bother, the now-voluntary long form would be sent to more houses. The decision appeared in the *Canada Gazette*, the official record of government decisions, on June 26, 2010. Canadian Press reporter Jennifer Ditchburn reported on the move three days later. She quoted an anonymous source at Statistics Canada: "It will be a disaster. A lot of policy across Canada has been based on that long form."

She also quoted a spokesperson for Tony Clement, the industry minister, and responsible for Statistics Canada: "Our feeling was that the change was to make a reasonable limit on what most Canadians felt was an intrusion into their personal privacy in terms of answering the longer form."

Right off the bat, it was easier to find people who thought the decision was a disaster than people who had felt intruded upon. "There is no exaggerating the boneheadedness of this decision," Stephen Gordon, a Laval economist, wrote on his widely read blog. "It's not often that sample selection bias becomes an issue of national importance, but then again, it's not often that census sampling design is outsourced to drunken monkeys." Making the questionnaire voluntary would result in greater compliance among some parts of the population than others, Gordon wrote. And there'd be no way to know which groups it was, because there was no baseline against which to compare the new data. And incidentally, once the 2011 data set was compromised, returning to a mandatory census in the future wouldn't fix the 2011 data.

Before long he had company. The Canadian Association of University Teachers protested the move, and a group representing business economists, and the editorial boards of the *Edmonton Journal*, *Victoria Times-Colonist* and other newspapers ("The census is us," the *Toronto Star* proclaimed). The controversy quickly snowballed. Well, it wasn't much of a controversy, actually; it was more of a mauling. Three weeks after the original CP story, my *Maclean's* colleague Aaron Wherry produced a partial list of organizations opposing the end of the long-form census. They included:

. . . the town of Smith Falls . . . provincial governments in Manitoba, Ontario, Quebec and Prince Edward Island, representatives from the United Way, Canadian Labour Congress, Toronto Board of Trade, Canadian Nurses Association and Canadian Public Health Association, city officials in Edmonton, Calgary and Red Deer, Ottawa city council, former clerk of the Privy Council Alex Himelfarb, the chief economist of the Greater Halifax Partnership, the French Language Services Commissioner of Ontario, the executive director of the Société franco-manitobaine, the *Canadian Medical Association Journal*, the Canadian Jewish Congress and the Evangelical Fellowship of Canada, the Marketing Research and Intelligence Association, the Quebec Community Groups Network, the president of the CD Howe Institute, the Canadian Council on Social Development, the Association of Municipalities of Ontario, the director of Toronto Public Health, Mr. Census, the Statistical Society of Canada, the Federation of Canadian Municipalities, the Inuit Tapiriit Kanatami, the Canadian Marketing Association, the Canadian Federation of Francophone and Acadian Communities, the Executive Council of the Canadian Economics Association, the director of the Prentice Institute at the University of Lethbridge, the senior economist at the Canadian Centre for Policy Alternatives, the Canadian Institute of Planners, the Canadian Association for Business Economics, the co-chairman of the Canada Census Committee, Ancestry.ca, the Canadian Association of University Teachers and the former head of Statistics Canada.

Within days after he compiled that list, it grew by dozens of other names.

Against that list of organizations outraged by the end of the mandatory census, the government was able to cite precisely two complaints from individual Canadians to the privacy commissioner about the 2006 mandatory census, and twenty-two expressions of concern to Statistics Canada.

The list of those protesting the change soon included Munir Sheikh, Canada's chief statistician until he resigned from his post on July 21. Sheikh was no troublemaker. He had been a public servant for thirty-five years, and was well familiar with the notion that bureaucrats offer advice and governments do what they want with the advice. Sheikh had stood by his department and kept mum about his minister's choices for nearly a month, until he read the *Globe* on that morning of July 21. What he saw there wasn't Tony Clement taking responsibility for the census change. What he saw was Clement claiming he had been following Sheikh's advice.

"The impression we've got from your comments over the last few days is that Statscan is A-OK with this," the *Globe*'s Steven Chase had said to Clement. "Right," Clement responded, "and I do assert that. When an agency of government reports to its minister and gives that minister options, I am entitled to assume that they are comfortable with those options."

That afternoon, Sheikh wrote his resignation letter. "I want to take this opportunity to comment on a technical statistical issue which has become the subject of media discussion," he wrote soon afterward to Statscan staff, "the question of whether a voluntary survey can become a substitute for a mandatory census. It cannot."

The *Globe*, which was having a pretty good July 21 thanks to Clement and Sheikh, ended the day with a story on the bureaucrat's resignation. Sheikh's departure "threatens to deal a fatal blow to Conservative efforts to sell their census changes," the story said.

And indeed, pretty soon this was the consensus among the makers of consensus. "Canadians are confronted by the spectacle of a wounded prime minister leading a gang that can't shoot straight," James Travers wrote in the *Star*.

"Having lost the argument," former Mulroney speech writer L. Ian Macdonald wrote in the *Gazette*, "the government should be looking for a way out, for some kind of Canadian compromise."

On August 12, six weeks after the controversy began, Charles W. Moore surveyed the wreckage in the *New Brunswick Telegraph-Journal*. "I've been mystified by Stephen Harper's willingness to squander so much political capital on an issue as trivial as the long-form census," he wrote. "Only slightly less so by the media's piling on, treating this as a matter of great national importance, and by the level of emotional investment so many apparently attach to census-gathering. I don't get it. It's just not that big a deal either way."

What few observers had done during the whole business was to investigate why Harper might have bothered. Those who did look would have found a deep vein of census mistrust among conservatives in Canada and outside, reaching back many decades. They might then have understood that this was a very big deal for Harper, and, as a result, for his opponents too.

Even as Harper was seeking to eliminate the mandatory long-form census, the Republican National Committee was calling for an end to the long form's U.S. equivalent, the American Community Survey. The RNC passed a resolution saying the U.S. Census Bureau behaved "exactly as a scam artist would, asking very personal questions," and spending "millions of tax dollars to violate the rights and invade the personal privacy of United States citizens." A divided Congress and a Democratic president made it hard for the GOP to get its way, so the issue has never died in the U.S. In May 2013, a Tea Party congressman from South Carolina, Jeff Duncan, introduced a bill that would eliminate all data collection by the Census Bureau except for a decennial population count.

Duncan and the latter-day Republicans spring from a rich heritage. In 1977 Ronald Reagan, then preparing for his second run at the presidency, devoted one of his daily radio broadcasts to census excesses. There was no justification for the questions these "snoops" were asking, Reagan told his audience. "They are invading our privacy under threat of punishment if one says it's none of their business. And it is none of their business."

Reagan didn't invent census suspicion. It has popped up, in one way or another, every time a government has sought to count its citizenry. In 1940, a Republican senator from New Hampshire, Charles W. Tobey, led a nationwide protest movement against Franklin W. Roosevelt's plan to run the most elaborate census yet. There was a war on. America wasn't yet in it. Tobey correctly suspected Roosevelt of wavering in his resolve to keep the country on the sidelines, and he was pretty sure the census was designed to smoke out draft-worthy young men. "Many people are writing to me they are forming local anti-snooping clubs," Tobey told the New York Times. If FDR insisted on "this snooping campaign," he continued, "there won't be jails enough to hold the people who will have the courage to cry 'Hold! Enough!'"

The obvious counter-argument—that census data allows the thoughtful construction of public policy that properly reflects the contours of a complex society—is often of little interest to the person who greets a stranger knocking at the door. Such a character made a brief appearance in the world of art as Wash Hogwallop's gun-toting son in the Coen brothers' movie O Brother, Where Art Thou? The kid squeezes off a couple of shotgun blasts at George Clooney and his associates as they approach the Hogwallop residence. The shots miss, but the boy is proud to announce he had better luck with an earlier visitor: "I nicked the census man!"

Nor was suspicion about the census high only among American conservatives. In 1981, as the first United Kingdom census during her tenure as prime minister approached, Margaret Thatcher summoned the head of the U.K. census office and the minister responsible for the census, Patrick Jenkin. She proceeded to grill both men on every line of the census form.

"She demanded to know why each question needed to be asked," Jenkin wrote later. "She struck out several questions as too intrusive; she reluctantly accepted that others should remain in, even though they, too, seemed to seek very personal information. Throughout the discussion, she saw the exercise from the point of view of the citizen, not the bureaucracy."

In Canadian political folklore, census suspicion is not a common feature, but it does make the occasional appearance. In the summer of 1996, when Harper was a young single-term Reform Party MP, George Jonas devoted four of his *Toronto Sun* columns to complaining about the census. "I find the whole concept of the modern census oppressive and offensive," Jonas wrote. "By now the census has evolved from ordinary stock-taking on the part of the community to a tool of government intrusion. It has come to be conducted with damnable arrogance and no regard for privacy."

But "the worst thing" about the census, to Jonas, was not its manner but its aim. "By the government's own admission, the census is used to foster plans of social engineering. This inevitably includes plans that a citizen may view as inimical to his private as well as to the public interest. (I certainly do. Over the years I've considered at least half of all government programs injurious both to my interests and the community's.) Compelling people to provide information that may be used against them, personally or collectively, is unconscionable."

This is the thread of argument that drove Harper to act. A list of thoughtful organizations as long as your arm tried to point out to him and his government that proper information has no ideology, that critiques of the state can be built on evidence just as the state was. Harper was uninterested. As I have been trying to tell you, at intervals throughout: Harper has more than a conservative analysis or a Conservative label:

he has a conservative gut and he pays it some attention. Thatcher and Reagan and Jonas didn't like the census. That was all Harper needed. And he was not alone. I first heard of the Conservatives' concerns with the census in 2007, when a public servant mentioned to me that Maxime Bernier was "horrified" to learn that as industry minister in the first months after the 2006 election, he was in charge of Statistics Canada. Why was this horrifying? "Because to him, Statscan asks intrusive questions and then governments use the answers to build intrusive programs."

With this, Jonas and Bernier probably got closer to the real reason for ransacking Statistics Canada than did Reagan and Thatcher. The problem, from Harper's perspective, is not that people from the government were poking into people's lives with questions. It is that they would eventually return with answers—in the form of big, complex, tax-sucking programs that would limit Canadians' ability to lead their lives as they liked. It's worth noting that in the United States, one of the most consistent loci of census suspicion has been associations of parents who home-school their children. Some of those parents worry the state will come and take their children away. They would prefer the state knew as little as possible about them.

The most persuasive rationale for Harper's census crusade came, not from any accredited member of the government, but from Stephen Taylor, a young blogger with such impeccable Conservative connections that it was not always easy to tell where the Harper government ended and Taylor's own opinions began. Taylor had organized the big Parliament Hill protest against the Dion-led coalition in 2008. On July 22, 2010, he published a blog post under the headline "Census Change Is about Smaller Government."

"'If you measure it, it matters' is the motto of those net tax-receiving organizations who only matter if they can make their case," Taylor wrote. Harper "has tried the ideological argument against these groups for years. But ideology is by its nature debatable; removing the framework of debate is his shortcut to victory."

Come again?

"If one day we have no idea how many divorced Hindu public transit users there are in East Vancouver, government policy will not be concocted to address them specifically," Taylor wrote. And indeed if there were an organization representing those folks, "they'd be against the census change." Harper's "greatest challenge," Taylor concluded, "is to dismantle the modern welfare state. If it can't be measured, future governments can't pander."

Taylor was making his argument at an odd moment in the history of the Harper government, so the notion that Harper was in the business of dismantling anything might have been hard for some observers to swallow. The government was still spending tens of billions of dollars more than it had in 2008, running up really big deficits to punt the economy out of a ditch. Conservative MPs were pasting on their best smiles so they could hand out big fake infrastructure cheques to dazed Chamber of Commerce presidents in towns across the country. Harper had just finished playing host to the most expensive G-8 and G-20 summits in the history of international schmoozing. The welfare state, or at least the bloated state, looked just fine, thank you. But soon there would be cuts, in waves, to dozens of programs. Statistics Canada's ability to keep track of the changes in Canadian society caused by those cuts would soon reveal itself to be much weakened. Not incidentally, the agency itself would see its own budgets for other data-collection programs cut again, repeatedly. Those later cuts would get far less coverage than the pinprick that ended the mandatory long-form census. But Harper's changes were real whether the press covered them or not.

––––––

As 2010 progressed, Ignatieff seemed finally to be getting the hang of this opposition leader business. Under Donolo's tutelage, he sought to give the impression that he was setting an agenda rather than being dragged along by someone else's. In March he had convened a "thinkers' conference" in Montreal, with Liberals and friendly experts gathering to discuss the economy, social policy and global affairs. Being Ignatieff, he could not merely judge the meeting to have been pleasant or stimulating. "We are trying to think of new ways for this society to govern itself," he said as it wrapped up. "I think we've renewed our democracy this weekend."

From there the Liberal leader spent much of the summer on a tour bus grinding out the miles between barbecue rallies in one small town after another. Here the Harvard man would learn the niceties of retail campaigning. Reporters dutifully followed along and recorded his progress. He rolled up his sleeves. He shook hands. All was good. The summer tour ended. A fall tour began. The party called it "Open Mike." He was Mike. He was open. He would show up anywhere and talk about anything. Unlike the other fellow.

The other fellow was having a rough autumn. On October 12, at the United Nations General Assembly in New York, Canada withdrew its bid for a temporary seat on the Security Council after two rounds of voting made it clear we couldn't win. It was the first time in the organization's sixty years that Canada had sought a Security Council seat and failed to win it. Three weeks later, Jim Prentice, who had entered Harper's government as the closest thing it had to a deputy prime minister, got tired of playing make-believe environment minister and announced he was quitting politics to help run a bank.

On November 10 Harper admitted that he would keep more than a thousand troops in Kabul to train the Afghan army after the Kandahar combat mission ended in 2011. It was a complete flip-flop. He had argued strongly in the 2008 campaign for a clear end to Canada's military involvement. At one point Hillary Clinton had stopped by Ottawa to argue for Canadian troops to stay past 2011; Harper and his ministers nearly ran her out of town. "We just want to be absolutely clear that Canada's military mission in Afghanistan ends in 2011," the PMO had said in an e-mail to reporters in August. Three months later, it was absolutely clear it wouldn't.

On December 9, Bev Oda, the minister of international development, admitted that a memo from her department recommending a $7-million grant to Kairos, an ecumenical aid organization, had been altered clumsily to make it seem to have recommended the opposite. Really clumsily. Under RECOMMENDATION, the memo said, "That you sign below to indicate that you approve a contribution." Someone had pencilled the word "NOT" before "approve." It would take Oda a little longer to admit she had ordered the alteration herself. This was pretty much what Tony Clement had done to the chief statistician on the census: try to make faceless officials take the fall for a political decision.

This list doesn't even begin to exhaust the controversies that rattled the Harper government as 2011 approached. As was reliably the case with Harper, most of the damage was self-inflicted. Ignatieff's challenge was how to respond. He made two mistakes. That was all Harper needed to finish him off.

The first mistake was to abandon a promising line of argument the Liberals had begun to put forward on October 18. "We had a good day," Ralph Goodale, the Liberals' wisest strategist, wrote afterward on the party's website. "In four coordinated events—Scott Brison at the Empire Club in Toronto, Marc Garneau at the Montreal Chamber of Commerce, Michael Ignatieff at an Open Mike event in Guelph and my speech to the Economic Club in Ottawa, we sent a message: The Liberal Party regards the economy—and the concerns of middle-class families—as our nation's top priority."

Here was a promising change of pace for the Liberals. Since 2004 they had questioned much about Harper: his patriotism, his sense of fair play, his candidates' positions on abortion, his love of the arts, his respect for parliamentary procedure. What they had not done was develop a sustained critique of his economic management. *Sustained* would be the important word here. As time went on, Harper had worked hard to project the image of a prudent leader with a sure hand on the levers of the economy. Especially after the rocky 2008 campaign and the coalition crisis that followed, fuelled by the perception that Harper had taken his attention off the economy, the Conservatives had multiplied their appeals to pocketbook issues. The Liberals appeared to have finally decided to push Harper off that position of strength. They believed a series of decisions had suddenly made it easier to do so.

As a Liberal, Goodale wrote, he believed "hard-pressed middle-class families are being left to fend for themselves by this Conservative government. On everything from family care, to the high cost of higher education, to adequate pensions for a decent retirement, the Tory response is: Let them eat cake." Worse than that: not only were Conservatives ignoring families (so the Liberals proclaimed), they were obsessed with an odd assortment of other projects. "Conservatives prioritize a more costly & less reliable census, stealth fighters, bigger jails and an extravagant G20 weekend," Goodale wrote.

For six years Harper had portrayed the choice facing Canadians as one between a party that cared for hard-working families and one that had lost touch. Now Ignatieff was attempting some judo: the choice was precisely that, he and his colleagues were saying, but it was the Liberals who cared for families. The Conservatives were intrigued by the change, and a little bit worried. "If they'd kept that up, it might have been effective," one Harper strategist said about the Liberals' attempt to paint themselves as the truest friend of Canadian families. "We might have had to adjust."

But in the end they didn't have to. The constant flood of mini-scandals gave the Liberals a target-rich environment, and they fired at everything. Detainee documents, Oda documents, the cost of new jet fighters, the Conservatives' virtuosic skill at denying the opposition new information on any of it. The Liberals' one-day blitz on the economy failed to turn into a sustained line of argument. The Conservatives got over their initial mild alarm.

The second mistake was narrower, less subtle, and devastating. In the endless game of poker over election timing, the Liberals tipped their hand.

Late in the autumn *La Presse* ran a column by Vincent Marissal in which he quoted senior Liberals who said they didn't intend to let the next Harper budget pass a confidence vote if they could help it. The Conservatives took Marissal's column as gospel, and pounced.

Jim Flaherty had delivered the 2009 budget on January 27, a not unusual time. In 2011 he waited and waited before finally conceding he would deliver one on March 23. The two-month gap before the budget was a hole the Conservatives had consciously opened up in the winter political calendar. They proceeded to fill that space with an even longer and heavier-by-far anti-Ignatieff advertising barrage, the longest they had ever run against any Liberal. Earlier ad blitzes had run a few weeks. "This one went on for part of January, all of February and almost all of March," a Harper strategist said. He called the decision to leak the timing of the Liberals' next election attempt one of the worst strategic blunders in the history of that party.

The arrival of new Conservative attack ads gave the Liberals yet another chance to respond. For once, some of them were tempted to do so. Bob Richardson, a Toronto lobbyist who would be in charge of campaign advertising, figured the campaign was on as soon as the Conservatives fired a shot, and was eager to fight back. Donolo had the same instinct. Gordon Ashworth resisted. Ashworth was Ignatieff's campaign manager, a role he had played for Jean Chrétien through the 1990s. He didn't want to blow the Liberals' budget before an election.

In the end, the Liberals finally produced some ads to counter the Conservative barrage. So did the NDP, figuring as Bob Richardson had, that the campaign was, for all intents and purposes, already under way. But the Conservatives weren't putting up ads to set the scene for a campaign. They were seeking to end it before it began; the resources they allotted were commensurate with that ambition. In the weeks before the budget, a Liberal strategist said, the Conservatives bought airtime to run 1,600 ads. "We had 131, and the NDP had, like, 25 or something," the Liberal said. "It was a massacre."

EIGHT
REMEDIAL READING II

Let us pause from the rush of events and consider this fellow Harper. The hope for this book is that his response to events reveals much about him. But if we examine his administrative style for the length of a chapter we may learn more. Doing it now will help us understand what came next.

"Let's go through a typical day," somebody who works in the Langevin Block suggested. "He wakes up and he will do various media reviews with his wife, just by himself. And then he will come into the office for around 8:30–8:40 a.m. and he will meet with his senior staff. And they will then proceed to give him a media review. But he will have a sense of what some people have written already."

This is striking because Harper has often protested that he doesn't read the newspapers. He gets what he needs to know, he says, from his staff and the enormous bureaucracy that feeds it. But sometimes he is ahead of them when he arrives at work. Laureen Harper reads the papers, the blogs and Twitter. She will often mention reporters' work to them when she bumps into them at receptions around town. A recommendation or condemnation from her is probably a big influence on Harper's reading.

After the media review, senior staff convene a meeting with Harper focused largely on the issues of the day rather than long-term planning, with a strong emphasis on communications. "He will give broad assent and feedback. He may make some comments on memos that have been submitted to him in the days prior. And that will be sort of his morning meeting, which lasts about an hour or so."

A typical workday for the prime minister is hard to define because there can never be such a thing. Sometimes a visitor will show up—Justin Bieber or the recipients of the Canada Vanier Scholarships. Sometimes there is a trip to a factory or a meeting with a world leader. It's a complex job. But on quiet days, "there is mainly a mixture of meetings in the office; but really there's work time, where he's reading memos. The main way he prefers to be briefed is via a memorandum. Obviously, you meet with him and talk to him. But if you want to pitch something to him, a short note is how he likes to be briefed. One or two pages maximum."

This sounds all right as a way to function until you remember that before a weekly meeting of the Priorities and Planning committee of cabinet, Harper might have fifty such memos to digest. "And then he will engage with you on that basis. So he spends the day on a few notes, reading things, writing speeches. And then whatever events or round-tables with people outside of the government that get added to his calendar. And then the day ends and he goes home to his family."

In his early days as prime minister, Harper would scribble substantial notes in the margins of the memos sent to him by the bureaucrats. The memos would return to the Privy Council Office dotted with comments. Bureaucrats took the running commentary as evidence that Harper reads closely documents that nobody expected would receive his personal attention.

Once Harper wanted Canada Post to issue a commemorative stamp to mark the anniversary of the Montreal Canadiens hockey club in 2008. A memo came to him explaining that the prime minister does not normally request specific subjects for stamps, because it is important to keep Canada Post above the partisan fray, or beneath it—or in any event away from it. Note in margin of memo: "I don't care. I want the stamp." Sometime later another memo returned to the effect that this sort of thing just wasn't done, and perhaps somebody on the PMO staff could designate a suitable arm's-length surrogate who would ask for a Habs centennial stamp. Probably he needn't fuss anyway, because this was the sort of stamp Canada Post would normally produce on its own. Harper's note in margin: "Who is not reading my comments?" Today on the Canada Post website you can still purchase an impressive set of 100th-anniversary Habs commemorative stamps.

After a few years in office, Harper's staff decided the marginal comments left too many hostages to fortune: they might provide proof, for posterity or the Conservatives' opponents, of Harper's direct involvement in a file. The handwritten comments disappeared thereafter, although on each page of a memo Harper has reviewed there is still a checkmark and the initials "SH."

If Harper can be imperious with the mostly faceless strangers of the public service, he is surprisingly collaborative with his partisan political staff. Several people who have worked for Harper say hierarchies tend to flatten in his presence. Just as almost any minister can get up in Question Period and answer a question on almost any file, similarly, job titles and formal responsibilities matter little within the confines of his office. Hierarchies snap back into place as soon as everyone leaves, but if you are in the room he wants to hear from you. This helps explain how Ray Novak, who began life as a gopher for Harper, wound up as his chief of staff. He was in almost all the meetings. Nobody told him not to talk.

I almost never speak with the prime minister. I do not react well to the elaborate ceremonies that both his office and my own colleagues have erected around his news conferences, and to say the least, there aren't a lot of chances to run into the guy on an informal basis. But I used to speak with him occasionally, before 2006, and still manage it on the odd occasion. For instance, I chatted with him in 2012 at a summer garden party for journalists at 24 Sussex. There is normally one such party every June and another, inside the residence, shortly before Christmas. He asked me about the economic crisis in Europe. I responded with platitudes. "No," he said. "You've lived in Europe. You pay a lot of attention to what's going on over there. What do you think will happen?" I realized that Harper would rather get some added value out of his afternoon than trade small talk about the weather. I felt flattered by the attention and pressured to come up with something smart. I forget what I told him.

I checked my impression with people who speak to him more often, and who knew his predecessors. There's a pretty robust consensus: a conversation with Stephen Harper is a real conversation. He listens, is curious, asks questions, responds with something that relates to what you said, contests your conclusions if he disagrees, shuts up if you know more. This is rarer than it probably sounds. A conversation with Jean Chrétien is largely a series of anecdotes from Chrétien about his many adventures. It is reliably great entertainment and educational to boot, but a half an hour later you realize you didn't say much. A conversation with Brian Mulroney is an audience at a baroque monologue, played at half speed and an octave down, about Mulroney's courage and honour in the face of grave injustices inflicted on him. Paul Martin will quiz an interlocutor until he can find something in his own background that matches the other person's life story. The unspoken theme of a conversation with Paul Martin is, "You know what? We're a lot alike."

So, in an encounter with the prime ministers I've known, you are actually least likely to come away from a conversation with Harper muttering, "What the hell was that?"

Sometimes he's just a guy. "I was walking into work," one former Langevin Block denizen said, "and you go in the west doors. And that's where the PM pulls up." A motorcade, several black sedans and minivans deep, will arrive from the south and sidle up to the Metcalfe Street curb. "And there's a family there, and it must have been tourists. They were an Aboriginal couple. And the PM gets out with the RCMP—it's a big deal if you haven't seen it before—and they [the tourists] are taking pictures. The PM stops to talk to them. And he brings them into the office and shows them around and spends ten or fifteen minutes talking to them. And I thought that was very touching."

There was a pause in our interview. "He does like junk food." Any favourites? "Skittles, I think."

This person also commented on Harper's sense of humour. Many people do, although for the life of them they can almost never cite examples. Once, at the annual dinner of the parliamentary press gallery when he was in opposition, Harper performed an uncanny impression of John McCallum, then a Liberal cabinet minister, who talks a bit like Elmer Fudd. As soon as Harper became prime minister he stopped going to the gallery dinner. Reporters assumed this was because he hates us, and there is probably a lot to that. But another reason was that he didn't want to give a speech at the dinner without being funny, and he didn't want to devote the necessary staff and rehearsal time to speech preparation, so he decided not to bother.

(I checked the story about bringing the tourists up to the office with someone else. "That sort of thing would have been the exception, not the rule," I was told.)

"I didn't know him at all when I got there," said the person who reported the fondness for Skittles. "People ask me what he's like and I say, 'He's exactly what you think he's like.' Very serious, inscrutable. The closer you get to him, the more he yells at you. We use that as a barometer. The new guy always gets a free ride."

One does get a glimpse of the temper. Several people report that he doesn't yell at a staffer until the staffer has been around for a while. Clearly, then, he has some control over his behaviour. Swearing blue streaks at a staffer thus becomes a sign of trust. Nor is it wise to try too hard to implement whatever instructions he barks when he is feeling shouty. Sandra Buckler, his first communications director, used to take his tirades as her marching orders. A few days later and several degrees calmer, Harper would issue contradictory instructions. Soon, a colleague says, Buckler learned to take Harper's tantrums as "cathartic," not as an expression of his truest self.

Though they change, his moods often last several hours at a time. "He comes into the office sometimes in a bad mood and that will affect how he sees things throughout the day. And if he comes in in a good mood no one can do anything wrong." The surprising moments of bridge-building and clemency from this government usually come directly from Harper. So do the truly dark outbursts of vengefulness.

When he first became prime minister in 2006, he built a staff that could handle the ordinary flow of routine government business. He has replaced almost every component of that team again and again, like George Washington's axe in the old joke—three new blades and two new handles—often replacing a staffer with somebody very different. Yet the tone of the government changes little over time. The office delivers routine. The prime minister delivers surprise, for good and for ill.

He can carry a grudge. "He will refer to things that were said in Conservative caucus when he was first an MP, when he was first elected as a backbencher, and will use that as a basis for judging that person forever. If he forms a negative impression of someone, he retains it more than a decade after the fact, even if it's based on a trivial encounter."

Since Tom Flanagan wrote his book spilling many of the secrets of the early Harper years, Harper has continued his grudge against him. He probably won't change his mind on that. More than two years later, Flanagan turned up at a Calgary Stampede event at which Harper was to address the crowd. While he was speaking, the prime minister caught a glimpse of his former chief of staff. Later, in the "green room" set aside for Harper's use a short distance from the main event, he was livid. "Who the fuck let him in?"

For all the frequent displays of temper, Harper does not, his staff insists, forbid contradictory viewpoints. He asked Bruce Carson to direct the production of the 2006 election platform because, as he told Carson, "You're a little to my left politically." ("You've got that right," Carson replied.)

"Obviously you can't be contradictory for its own sake," the staffer who recalled Harper's ability to carry a grudge said. "But I feel like part of what I'm paid to do is to sort of beak off with my own opinions, especially when I'm challenging his. I do it respectfully with the PM, but I don't hesitate for a second to say what I think. And I would say others at the table—everyone does it differently, but there are always more than two people who, if they feel strongly about something, will find a way of making their views known to the PM. It may not be a full-frontal assault, it may be, 'Maybe we should canvas public opinion on that to see how it will go down,' or 'Maybe the following people will not react to that and we should care if they react poorly because of this,' rather than sort of telling him, 'You're wrong.' But I don't feel censored. I don't feel that I don't have the luxury of expressing my views."

When reminded by staff, Harper will make phone calls to staff members to mark significant moments in their lives. Nobody believes this behaviour comes naturally to him, but he has learned to do it and gotten better at it, and the very fact that it takes an effort means it is appreciated when it happens. "He's said complimentary things about Jenni [Byrne]," the noticer of the Skittles said. "He's very generous to Guy [Giorno]." When an employee leaves or a member of his cabinet decides not to run again, Harper often spends a few minutes with them on their last day. The photographer comes in, there's a handshake photo, and a few minutes to chat and reminisce. On at least three occasions, he has told departing ministers that they are leaving the best job they will ever have.

Doug Finley, the Conservative senator who died of cancer in May 2013, ran the campaigns of 2006 and 2008 and organized the government's defence during the 2008 coalition crisis. He was behind most of the party's fundraising efforts until 2011, when his serious health problems returned. His wife, Diane, is one of the government's senior cabinet ministers. I had the chance to ask him for some insights into Harper's personality. "I don't really know Stephen Harper," Finley said. "I don't socialize with him."

"He has a profound ability not to care about being hated," one former ministerial staffer said. He is indifferent to most criticism, and takes considerable pleasure from some, especially if it comes from the academic-media-legal New Class that Kristol and Brimelow warned him about so many years ago. But there was one exception to this general observation. The guffawing that greeted the photo opportunity when Harper took his son and daughter to school a few days after the 2006 election upset him durably. The photos and TV footage showed him shaking his son Ben's hand, as though they had concluded a real estate deal. Ben was a shy kid, as his father would have been forty years earlier, and it is hard to do anything the way you normally would when you are being followed by a gaggle of photographers. As it happens, I have since had occasion to drop off children at the same Ottawa school many times. Almost none of the parents hug their kids. They're dropping the kids off at school, after all, not ushering them into the French Foreign Legion. They'll see them again in a few hours.

The snark about the handshake took Harper by surprise and, having nothing to do with his work as a political leader, hit him hard. "The notion that he might be a distant or uncaring father hurt him," a former advisor said. "It's the only thing I ever saw that did."

But let's return to his office, which, depending on the events of the day, could be the one in Langevin Block or the smaller one on the third floor of the Centre Block. Harper works effectively with his staff but he likes to be alone for much of the day. "In terms of his work habits," the person who described a typical day told me, "he is most at home when he is either reading or commenting on memos, watching BNN or Sun News Network or Fox News—but mainly BNN—working on speech drafts. Other things get added to his schedule if they are worthwhile. But a case needs to be made for them."

What's his speech-writing process like? My source named the four-person speech-writing staff, led in recent years by the former *Calgary Herald* columnist Nigel Hannaford. There has been a lot of turnover in the speech-writing office. It doesn't sound like rewarding work. Harper "likes his drafts early and he likes to spend a lot of time reading over and commenting on drafts, especially on speeches. He likes to have a lot of time. He likes to go back and forth and make a lot of changes." It is the speech-writing staff that serves in this tennis match. Harper likes a draft he can react to. Then he reacts in detail.

"I think the 'Harper as micromanager' notion is wrong in a number of ways, but at the speech writer end it's definitely that. It's not that he likes to deliver deep and profound speeches. It's really rare that he will deliver a really meaningful speech."

I suggested that perhaps, because it is still hardly clear to anyone—including members of his own cabinet—what Harper conservatism really is, Harper takes pains with his language because whatever he says becomes the song sheet for an entire movement. No, my source said. That's not it at all. Harper doesn't spend his afternoons trying to find potent expression for his ideas. He works at removing memorable turns of phrase and identifiable ideas from his speeches. He puts great effort into flattening the prose.

"I find that oftentimes he makes his speeches more platitudinous rather than more [potent]. A good portion of his edits are taking out either superfluous phrases or ideas that people are trying to put into his mouth. . . . He tries not to make news with his speeches, even with speeches with which we would want to make news. I can't explain it because I don't understand it."

I had a hunch. Another former advisor confirmed it. "All the stuff that sounds good in speeches—'We must,' 'I will never,' 'Mark my words'—all that becomes a line in the sand. It gets held against you later. So that stuff's coming out. If it makes the speech-writing staff feel bad, well, they'll live."

There is a secondary reason for Harper's penchant for literal self-effacement. He wants to be damned sure which line in a speech will get quoted in the papers. So he repeats it in French and English, and to make sure that one line sounds interesting, he makes sure the rest of the speech doesn't.

Chrétien mostly left speeches to staff and had no strong opinion about how much personality his writers should make him seem to have. He would grind through the text like a millstone through oats, haul a well-worn cadenza off a mental shelf to get a belated rise out of the stultified audience ("Millions of people would give their shirts for our so-called problems") and call it a night. Mulroney and Martin were obsessive about reworking speech drafts to insert their own voice. Only Harper spends hours subtracting a voice from his speeches.

But then, Harper works hard to take himself out of many pictures. Reporters are banished from the doorstep of his cabinet meetings so he will not pause on his way out, as several of his predecessors did, to riff aimlessly on the events of the day while Julie van Dusen and Bob Fife toss questions. We are left with no video of Harper responding to assorted embarrassments or gloating over his foes' missteps or wishing the Habs well. Mostly we have to guess how he would respond. He doesn't comment after a visiting premier leaves Ottawa. Did they get along? Are they at daggers drawn? Who's to say?

In each of his two meetings with Aboriginal leaders since the 2011 election, his office left visitors to wonder, until very late in the planning, whether Harper would even attend after the opening ceremony. In the end he did but he barely spoke. Is he excited? Revolted? Bored? Who's to say?

Canadians know—actually know for a fact, from the evidence of his own testimony—less about Stephen Harper than about any other prime minister who has lasted as long as he has. This helps explain why he has lasted. He lies low because he wants to last.

The other day upon the stair, I met a man who was not there. He wasn't there again today, and while millions of voters wish that man would go away, he won't be there again tomorrow.

Formlessness makes Harper both harder for his detractors to hate (although never all that hard) and, paradoxically, easier for his admirers to like. Scholars of the storytelling craft tell us that when we know little about a protagonist it can actually be easier to identify with him. In his 1976 book *The Uses of Enchantment*, the psychologist Bruno Bettelheim examined the structure and enduring power of fairy tales. "The fairy tale . . . makes clear that it tells about everyman, people very much like us," Bettelheim wrote. In "Beauty and the Beast," you never learn much about Beauty. "The protagonists of fairy tales are referred to as 'a girl,' for instance, or 'the youngest brother' . . . fairies and witches, giants and godmothers remain equally unnamed, thus facilitating projections and identifications." If a stranger rides into town, we imagine he must be like us—that, in fact, he is us. If he is a blond stranger with a Flemish accent and henna tattoos, not so much.

When Harper first ran for prime minister in 2004, his name was so meaningless to Canadians that he sought to pour meaning into it with those issue-based television ads that ended with the oddly insistent "My name is Stephen Harper" tag. By 2006 his name had become a problem. His opponents had defined him, and he had been rather more successful at defining himself—as a jerk—than he wanted. So he kept his name out of his campaign advertising. Eventually he won the election, and then sought to reduce his presence in his own government. Some readers will recall that public servants have been told to refer systematically to the "Harper Government," but that didn't begin until he had been the prime minister for nearly five years. At first they were told to call it "Canada's New Government." Thus facilitating projections and identifications, Bettelheim would say.

I used to be surprised by e-mails from readers who, when they were not critical of Harper, were sure he was bold or compassionate or brilliant. On some days he has been all of those things. But on most days he is not, in public, much of anything. Observers looking for something to dislike get less fodder than they would if he were a loudmouth, although they manage with what's available. Observers looking for a hero draw the hero's chiselled features in the outline Harper leaves blank.

The point of this word craft and image manipulation is not to amuse a bored prime minister, or to help him cope with shyness, or to mess with the press gallery's head. It is to last. The point of everything he does is to last. The surest rebuttal Harper can offer to a half century of Liberal hegemony is not to race around doing things the next Liberal could undo. The surest rebuttal is to last and not be Liberal. "He always says, 'My models aren't Conservative prime ministers,'" one of his ministers told me. "'My models are successful prime ministers.'"

The most successful prime minister was William Lyon Mackenzie King, or at least the most durable. Flanagan, Harper's estranged former advisor, has called Harper "Mackenzie King without a ouija board." King held the job for a total of twenty-one years in three separate terms. But in a sense, that was not the end of him. When he was done, he handed the keys to Louis St. Laurent, who lost after eight years to Diefenbaker but was promptly avenged by Pearson and Trudeau and, after another pause, by Chrétien. This is what hegemony looks like.

King's style is taught in political science classes, never approvingly, as "muddling through." But if you muddle for twenty-one years you can get through a lot. King directed the wartime industrialization of the Canadian state and guided its transformation into the social postwar state. The Canada he left behind would have been unrecognizable to anyone in 1921, when he set to work. And when he finished, Canadians let his successors continue along his path. King was no saint, though he often sought to converse with saints. But he accomplished great change in the only lasting way it has ever been done in Canada: through endurance.

How many decisions does a prime minister make in a day? Sixty? A hundred? Almost none go reported. He doesn't even have to keep most of them secret: the rush of events ensures they won't be noticed and assayed by the gallery. As the 2011 election approached, Harper was approaching two thousand days in office. Imagine how different the outcome would have been if a different prime minister, with different assumptions, prejudices and instincts, had made those thousands of decisions.

Consider Insite, the Vancouver supervised-injection site for drug users. Harper granted temporary extensions to its licence until 2008, but then launched a campaign to get the place shut down. Finally, in 2011 the Supreme Court of Canada ruled that Insite must stay open. Since Harper was in power, Ken Dryden and Ujjal Dosanjh were not the Liberal ministers of health and public safety, and Insite, the pilot project, was not followed by injection sites in other provinces. Multiply that decision by thousands. Follow Harper with another Conservative prime minister who plays the long game—this is Harper's hope, not my prediction, for I offer none—and you start to get something that looks like Conservative hegemony.

As a student of successful prime ministers, Harper has certainly also contemplated those who failed. Some deserve little attention because they didn't understand politics or were robbed by fate: Joe Clark, John Turner, Kim Campbell, Paul Martin. In Harper's lifetime, this leaves Diefenbaker, Trudeau, Mulroney, Chrétien. Flanagan has also written that the largest majorities collapse under the weight of their own internal contradictions. That was Diefenbaker's burden, but because it has not been Harper's it needn't preoccupy us.

Are there lessons to learn from the others? Perhaps these two. Mulroney and Chrétien were destroyed by lieutenants who became rivals. Trudeau and Mulroney went off chasing dragons and exhausted the nation's patience.

By the time Lucien Bouchard and Paul Martin left cabinet and turned, in different ways, against the prime ministers who had made them stars, they had earned independent reputations as visionary leaders. They had built largely autonomous bases of power and influence within their respective parties. Bouchard's resignation from Mulroney's cabinet in 1990 consolidated the collapse of the Progressive Conservative coalition. He then built the Bloc Québécois from Mulroney's Quebec caucus and from the PC voter base in the province. The rise of the Bloc matched, and to some extent provoked, the Reform Party's expansion in the West. Defeat for the Progressive Conservatives followed in the next election. The party, as constituted, never really recovered.

Martin's resignation from Chrétien's cabinet in 2002—in his trademark style, Martin did not understand that he had quit until Chrétien swore in a new finance minister—turned the Liberal Party against itself. But only briefly. Martin had prepared well. Badly outnumbered, Chrétien manoeuvred with great skill, but his departure was coerced and his party badly damaged.

Harper has not permitted a Martin or a Bouchard to rise in his government. Nobody in his cabinet combines the two ingredients Bouchard and Martin had at the moment of their apostasies: an independent power base and antagonistic ambitions. David Emerson and Jim Prentice had no broad power base, so when they left they took nothing with them. John Baird and Jason Kenney might manage to hurt Harper in some Bizarro-universe revolt, but it is not easy to imagine them rebelling. Their political identity is indistinguishable from the Harper party's. During the 2000 election, Martin's associates were laying money bets all over Ottawa against a third Chrétien majority; in 2011, associates of Kenney and Baird were busy securing the first Harper majority. The biggest detonation Harper has suffered came early, before he won power, when Belinda Stronach left the Conservatives for the Liberals in 2005. Nobody went with her. He won the next election against her new friends. It is hard to imagine Peter MacKay, for instance, leaving to launch an outsider challenge to Harper, but even if he did, the scale of the thing could not match what Bouchard did to Mulroney. Of course there is ego in Harper's insistence that he remain top boss. But not only ego. A party that devours itself is fodder for its enemies; a party that resists the temptation of regicide can hope to replicate the King–St. Laurent–Pearson–Trudeau–Chrétien daisy chain.

Rivals are not the only enemy of longevity. So are projects. If the sponsorship scandal and Paul Martin's ambitions were enough to put paid to Jean Chrétien's career, the two other durable regimes of Harper's lifetime—Trudeau's and Mulroney's—were sapped in the end by the leaders' dogged pursuit of goals that bore little obvious relation to the preoccupations of most Canadians.

Amid global economic turmoil, Trudeau's three-year battle with René Lévesque's Parti Québécois after 1976 led to his defeat in the 1979 election, although the voters' hope that less Trudeau would mean less tension in the federation amounted to wishful thinking. On his return in 1980, Trudeau defeated Lévesque in the referendum and set off to repatriate the Constitution. After he succeeded, Trudeau often seemed bored with the routine stuff of government. His globe-trotting 1983–84 peace tour probably sealed many voters' perception that Trudeau would always find something to do besides routine public administration. Defeat for the Liberals soon followed.

For six interminable years, from 1987 to 1993, Mulroney devoted much of his time and some of his strongest cabinet ministers to building the Meech Lake consensus for constitutional reform, buttressing it against attack, and then managing the damage from its collapse. Then he did it all again with the Charlottetown Accord. Both attempts were complete failures. The respites he offered from more than half a decade of constitutional obsession were those noteworthy barrels of fun, continental free trade, the introduction of the GST and the Oka crisis.

Do not take this as a comprehensive attempt to weigh the value of Trudeau's contribution to public life, or Mulroney's. Both men accomplished much. Both lasted longer at 24 Sussex Drive than Harper has so far. It would have been odd if Trudeau had ignored Lévesque, or sought no resolution to constitutional negotiations that began before he became prime minister. It would have been odd if Mulroney had not sought a different solution to the same problems, given his Quebec roots and his competitive streak. But both prime ministers burned their parties out by setting aside the routine preoccupations of everyday political life for grander and more diffuse goals. Chrétien avoided that trap, for the most part, by meeting the premiers less frequently, seeking agreement whenever possible before each meeting, keeping the agenda relentlessly on routine economic and social files. And it worked like a charm: on the day Martin rose against him, the Liberals were still healthy in the polls.

Harper brings a temper and a vengeful streak to office, but he is also awesomely clear-eyed. Because he is temperamentally the most conservative Canadian prime minister of his lifetime, he will not ever run out of ideas for conservative things to do. So on any day he has a choice, he can do the big conservative thing that would be the end of his career, or he can do some of the small conservative things that won't. He is amazed that earlier leaders had a hard time choosing.

Of course Harper is often, and plausibly, dismissed as a mere fiddler and mucker-about because of the way he avoids grand battles. "His strong bias is towards arch-incrementalism," one of his advisors says. "He backs away from ideas which he feels may be controversial. And that creates a lot of frustration."

The former Chinese premier Zhou Enlai said in the early 1970s that it was "too early to tell" what the impact of the French Revolution had been. Assessing Harperism will take time too. He has often done his best to present the appearance of drift and indecision. It is worth noting that there are two groups who think he is making some kind of difference: partisans to his left and partisans on the right. Liberals and New Democrats are pretty sure Harper stands for something they don't like. Their antipathy is mirrored by stubborn support for Harper on the right. Brian Mulroney was, on the face of things, a bolder leader. But Mulroney suffered an exodus of millions of voters from his electoral base. Harper's smaller base has stayed solid and grown by hairs. A few newspaper columnists who proclaim their nonpartisanship—Dan Gardner in the *Ottawa Citizen*, Andrew Coyne in the *National Post*—are always eager to complain he is not sufficiently partisan. But conservatives are pretty sure he is a conservative.

———

The best explanation I have seen for Harper's management style comes not from Canada during his tenure at 24 Sussex Drive, but from the social science literature of a half century ago and a landmark paper written in 1959 by Charles Edward Lindblom, a professor of economics at Yale University. "The Science of 'Muddling Through'" was published in the journal *Public Administration Review* and quickly became a classic. I had always believed "muddling through" was a pejorative expression political scientists used to designate a lack of political courage. But Lindblom used the notion to subvert the mid-century conventional wisdom about how change happens, or should.

Lindblom's work challenged the whole concept of "rational planning," whereby public servants study problems and come up with the best solutions. To Lindblom the notion was fraught with pitfalls, beginning with the notion that anyone can agree on what the "best" solution would look like.

His paper begins by taking the rational-planning model seriously, the better to watch it collapse under the weight of its own absurdity. Lindblom invites his readers to imagine an administrator in charge of coming up with a government response to price inflation. One way to begin would be to list all the values he would try to address with his inflation policy—full employment, protecting business profits or individuals' savings, avoiding a stock market crash, and so on. Then the administrator would rank desirable values in order of importance. Next, make a list of all the possible outcomes any change in policy could achieve, and decide which outcomes would advance the largest number of the most desirable values. "This would of course require a prodigious inquiry into values held by members of society," Lindblom wrote, "and an equally prodigious set of calculations on how much of each value is equal to how much of each other value."

Only then would our administrator, presumably toiling in a cubicle a few feet from the person in charge of eliminating poverty, list all the possible mechanisms for achieving the outcome that could advance the desired values. These might range from the least interventionist—leaving all prices to the market—to the most interventionist, forcibly nationalizing the means of production. Plus every possible intermediate policy. Can't leave any possible mechanism out! We are rational plan-ners. We base our policy on evidence, not hunches!

Then the administrator would compare each policy mechanism against all the others, using commonly accepted models and theories, to predict its efficiency and effectiveness at producing the best outcome to promote the best values. All this with a nervous eye on the clock, because the task would need to be finished before the problem at issue fixed itself. And indeed, before all human life on Earth became extinct.

Then Lindblom proposes another administrator working in an entirely different manner. This one picks only one goal, based mostly on a best guess about what the best goal should be—in the case of inflation, say, to keep prices level. Our second administrator, if feeling especially ambitious, might throw in one or two secondary goals, such as full employment. Any other goals would be beyond the work of the day. "Were he pressed," Lindblom wrote, "he would quickly admit that he was ignoring many related values and many possible important conse-quences of his policies."

Step two for our more modest mandarin would be to "outline those relatively few policy alternatives" that came to mind and compare their likely outcomes. "In comparing his limited number of alternatives, most of them familiar from past controversies, he would not ordinarily find a body of theory precise enough to carry him through a comparison of their respective consequences," Lindblom writes. Instead, he would simply recall what worked in the past in similar circumstances. Time is short, the flesh is weak, and the concoction of a grand matrix for com-paring the advantages and costs of all possible decisions must always wait for another day, which never comes. Our second administrator simply picks something and tries it.

"Because practitioners of the second approach expect to achieve their goals only partially," Lindblom writes in a sentence that has haunted me since the first time I read it, "they would expect to repeat endlessly the sequence just described, as conditions and aspirations changed and as accuracy of prediction improved."

The fragment that leaps off the page for any student of Stephen Harper is, "expect to repeat endlessly." This is an ideal model for leaders who plan to be around for a while.

Having listed his two models for solving a policy problem, Lindblom dismisses the first. "For complex problems, the first of these two approaches is of course impossible," he writes. "It assumes intellectual capacities and sources of information that men simply do not possess, and it is even more absurd as an approach to policy when the time and money that can be allocated to a policy problem is limited, as is always the case." In fact, he points out that "public agencies are in effect usually instructed not to practice the first method." No administrator—no mid-level bureaucrat, no elected official—has ever been instructed to take infinite time and unlimited resources to exhaust an examination of all possible combinations of all possible solutions to a problem. It's always, "Have a paper on my desk by Tuesday."

And yet the public administration literature is full of rational-planning models. Quoting the head of the RAND Corporation's economics division, Lindblom says it might be possible to approximate a rational-planning solution to a traffic problem on the George Washington Bridge in New York. But the likelihood of listing, modelling and ranking the appropriate solutions to a major foreign-policy crisis—during the few hours or days the crisis might last—is close to zero. So, boldly for his time, Lindblom chooses to treat the more modest method, the only possible way of proceeding, as if it were desirable. He calls his muddling-through model more realistic than rational planning. He gives it a more palatable name, the "branch method," described as "continually building out from the current situation, step-by-step and by small degrees." The rational-planning model is the "root method," forever from the ground up.

To Lindblom the root method is so useless that it falls at the first hurdle. What is the end or goal a policy seeks to achieve? In practice, even that first question can rally no broadly accepted response. "On many critical objectives, citizens disagree, congressmen disagree, and public administrators disagree." This is the eternal problem with the officious technocrat who barges every now and then into politics, usually from the ranks of corporate management, the academy or the newspaper columns, and demands that "the best people" be gathered to crunch some problem and come up with "the right solution." Honest people genuinely disagree about who is best and what is right. Constrain cost or expand opportunity? Liberate business or rein in its excesses? Exhort or regulate? Create conditions so that a few may rise or so the many can worry less? Nobody agrees. This is why we have politics. Even if only one person makes the calls, he will not call similar problems in the same way every week. A value of paramount importance this week, in this context, may be less important next week in another.

There is, simply, no practical way to decide first what is important and then to select the method for achieving it. Acting is choosing. "Except roughly and vaguely, I know of no way to describe—or even to understand—what my relative evaluations are for, say, freedom and security, speed and accuracy in governmental decisions, or low taxes and better schools than to describe my preferences among specific policy choices that might be made between the alternatives in each of the pairs," Lindblom writes. You decide your values, and demonstrate them, with a succession of choices over time. This is Aristotle: character defined by habitual action. Or as Wynton Marsalis says, "What you do is what you will do."

But if all you do is toil away, how do you know you're doing the right thing? Simple: the "right thing" in the branch method is the policy that draws broad support. The administrator does not seek agreement on the end goal, merely on the next step. This "agreement on the policy itself . . . remains possible even when agreement on values is not," Lindblom writes.

This reasoning would be especially appealing to a government with a weak parliamentary minority, because it corresponds perfectly to the brutal reality of frequent confidence votes. The best policy for Harper was almost always the policy that allowed one of the opposition parties to support it. In the next chapter, we will watch Harper win a majority of seats in the 2011 election, but in fact he had a majority for every confidence motion he took to the Commons for the first five years he was prime minister. If the New Democrats had different reasons for, say, supporting a tax on income trusts than Harper did, he had the luxury of not caring. What mattered was their votes. More broadly, this helps explain how Harper can often command greater public-opinion support for some policies, like directly electing senators, than he enjoys for his government as such.

"In an important sense, therefore," Lindblom wrote, "it is not irrational for an administrator to defend a policy as good without being able to specify what it is good for."

To idealistic observers who are not comfortable with considering how the world actually works, muddling through is a horrible model. Lindblom's branch-method administrator selects from among policies that are pretty closely aligned with what is already being done. He ignores most of the possible outcomes of a decision. He relies on repetition to correct for both of these apparent shortcomings. If a policy works out poorly he stops doing it. If it works but is insufficient, he makes another incremental change that nudges outcomes further along a desirable path.

The "administrators" Lindblom was addressing were, for the most part, civil servants, but in a second paper published in 1979, twenty years after the first, he gives important hints about why politicians might embrace his method of successive limited comparisons, too. In "Still Muddling, Not Yet Through," Lindblom presents a more explicitly political case for his branch method: "It reduces the stakes in each political controversy, thus encouraging losers to bear their losses without disrupting the political system."

This is politics as boiling a frog: if you raise the temperature a degree at a time the frog won't notice. The big political upheavals in Canada have often come after leaders sought dramatic, system-wide change—the repatriation of the Constitution, the Meech and Charlottetown debacles. Suddenly potential losers self-identify, organize and put their hearts into the fight. Harper has never wanted any of that. He knows what happens when an opposition gets its act together, because he led an opposition that did that.

"Moreover," Lindblom adds, "incrementalism in politics is not, in principle, slow moving." Just as it's possible to advocate radical change forever without getting any. Quebec's sovereignty movement has held two secession referendums in forty-five years and gotten precisely nowhere. In contrast, "Incremental steps can be made quickly because they are only incremental. They do not rock the boat, and do not stir up the great antagonisms and paralyzing schisms as do proposals for more drastic change."

For this reason, "incremental politics is also a way of 'smuggling' changes into the political system." Lindblom mentions the rise of big bureaucracy, "a development that sneaked up on most citizens, who never debated the issues and who did not understand at the time that such a transformation was in process."

Of course, he adds, this may be a reason to object to incremental politics. But it "also suggests that a skilled reformer may learn paths of indirection and surprise, thus reaching objectives that would be successfully resisted were his program more fully revealed."

Nobody I have quizzed in Harper's circle has read Lindblom's papers, though they are classics of public administration literature. But that's fine. He did not write them as guidebooks. He wrote them to explain how public administrators often work even if they do not know they are following a model. And his explanation rings true for many of our most successful prime ministers, whether it's Mackenzie King or Chrétien or Harper. If you pick a fight, you might lose it. If you avoid fights, you can get more done than a half-alert observer would notice, you can fix errors before they become crises, and you live to do it all again tomorrow. This is not a much different lesson than the one Edmund Burke offered in his *Reflections on the Revolution in France*, when he wrote that it is risky to let each man depend on "his own private stock of reason, because we suspect that this stock in each man is small." Better for men to "avail themselves of the general bank and capital of nations and of ages." That's one book Harper did read.

There is one other lens through which we might regard Harper as we return to our chronological narrative. This one comes from his own staff.

In rough moments, whether it was in the overhaul of Harper's office before the 2006 election or during the perilous dip in the polls during the 2008 campaign, the Conservatives depended heavily on Doug Finley as a stabilizing influence. The wiley Scot came up in business, moving through cars, aeronautics and commercial horticulture—"real business," one of his associates said, "not politically connected fields such as law and consulting." There Finley learned that teamwork is more important than individual talent; that's the lesson he passed on repeatedly to the rest of Harper's entourage. "He would speak at length about the Spanish way of playing soccer and tell us how we could benefit from watching more games from La Liga."

I'm no soccer buff, so when I visited Finley, I asked him about Spanish soccer. He didn't chuckle when I asked him, and I reminded myself that real fans don't think their interests are cute. (I am the same way when you ask me about Haydn.)

"It's always goal-oriented," Finley said of the Spanish style that has emerged over decades. "It's very tight possession. Never give the ball away, because if you have the ball, they can't score a goal. And have the very best material that you can put on the field. The very best resources."

I read further about what the Spaniards sometimes call *tiqui-taca*, an onomatopoeia for the short-pass possession game. The parallels to Harper's game are obvious. Formal positions matter little; every player can attack or defend depending on circumstances. The goal is not to send the ball way down the field; it's to keep it close and deny others. There is a raging debate about whether *tiqui-taca* is an unlovely, unromantic way to play the game, but any criticism is muted by the amazing success Spanish teams have had in recent seasons. "If you watch the Spanish team, they can keep hold of the ball for twenty-five, thirty minutes," Finley told me. During that time, whatever the other team is doing, it is not scoring. "It might be boring to watch sometimes. But it sure works."

NINE
RISE UP,
SEA OF TROUBLES

The last speech Michael Ignatieff would ever deliver in the House of Commons lasted about fifteen minutes. The House met at ten a.m. on Friday, March 25, 2011. Peter Milliken, the long-suffering Liberal Speaker, read the assembled MPs his decision on a minor question of privilege and announced that the governor general had sent word of his royal assent to two bills. The morning's routine business thus disposed of, Milliken read the supply motion from Ignatieff that would be the subject of the day's debate:

"That the House agree with the finding of the Standing Committee on Procedure and House Affairs that the government is in contempt of Parliament, which is unprecedented in Canadian parliamentary history, and consequently, the House has lost confidence in the government."

Then Ignatieff rose to speak. He began with kind words for Milliken, who would at the end of the day finish his extraordinary tenure as the longest-serving Speaker in the history of the Canadian House of Commons. Then it was on to the business that would end Milliken's career, and those of not a few others. "I have to inform the House," Ignatieff said, "that the Official Opposition has lost confidence in the government."

The committee report with which Ignatieff wanted members to agree was "historic," he said. The previous October, the combined opposition majority on the Finance committee had requested estimates for a bunch of government programs—F-35 jets, corporate tax cuts, crime bills and the cost of hosting the G-20 summit. The government stalled, then offered only partial answers. The committee found the government in contempt. The committee's Conservative members dissented, calling the majority report "simply a piece of partisan gamesmanship." But it was the first time that a parliamentary committee has found the government in contempt. By endorsing that finding and voting the Harper government down, said Ignatieff, members would get "an opportunity . . . to confirm our commitment to parliamentary democracy and its fundamental principles."

Chief among those principles was the government's "obligation to provide members of this House with the information they need in order to hold the government accountable to the people of Canada." For four months, the opposition had asked Harper's government the cost of its budget plans. It had asked the true cost of "fighter jets, prisons and corporate tax breaks." To no avail. Well, it was time for democracy to put its foot down. "We have had enough. If this vote results in an election, the Canadian people will have the opportunity to replace an arrogant government with one that respects democracy."

After Ignatieff's statement, members of other parties had a chance to ask him questions. Harold Albrecht, the government member for Kitchener-Conestoga, asked whether this whole thing wasn't just a put-up job by an "opposition coalition" that had cooked the committee report from the outset in a bid to have the government's hide. No, Ignatieff said, this was the very thundering voice of democracy roaring for justice. The next question, from the B.C. New Democrat Nathan Cullen, revealed an analysis more closely approximating Ignatieff's own.

"A government is being found in contempt, which has never happened before," Cullen marvelled. "There have been bad governments, lying governments, and contemptuous governments in this country before, but the present government has achieved this low bar of ethics and morality. How is it we find ourselves in this position and what must we all do collectively to never allow this to happen again?"

"What has to be done," Ignatieff said in reply, "to put things right and have democracy respected? The motion moved by the Liberal Party of Canada, the Official Opposition, has to be supported and adopted. That is what."

The next question came from one of Ignatieff's own caucus colleagues, the Vancouver Liberal Joyce Murray. She wanted to make sure this business about democracy would not become too abstract for people to understand. "Would the Leader of the Official Opposition tell us how the government's abuses of power and contempt of Parliament affect the very character of Canada? How do they affect the daily lives of people in their homes and communities in Canada?"

Ignatieff was ready to answer. "Many Canadians enjoy the very special privilege of rich and lucky countries, of not having to think and worry about their democracy," he said. "They do not look up from the more important things they have to do in their lives, such as getting the kids to hockey practice and to school, doing their jobs, being with their neighbours and friends."

Here, Ignatieff was engaged in fairly advanced mimicry. He had seen the strange creatures across the centre aisle of the Commons spend much of their time in the root cellar of Maslow's hierarchy of needs, going on and on about security of employment and family and property. Ignatieff had written seventeen books from a cubbyhole in Maslow's penthouse, tracing the heady contours of morality and spontaneity, charity, conflict and problem solving. But he had to admit this business about hockey and neighbours had well served his opponents. He was not loath to try to learn from them. Yes, yes, he allowed, it's important to get the kids to hockey practice.

"However, in the deep background of their lives, there must always be a confidence that their democracy works and that it works for them," he said. "That is the crux of our democratic system: that on behalf of the woman taking her son or daughter to hockey practice, on behalf of the man going to work in the mill, they can count on us in the House of Commons to ask the questions that those citizens need to know in order to hold our government accountable. When that government fails in this most elementary task of democratic freedom, it is the duty of the members of the House to bring the government down."

Stephen Harper dismissed his beleaguered but hopeful Liberal colleagues as plotters and vandals, then spent the day claiming to be the only shield Canadians could trust as they hurried from the mill to hockey practice. Finally Ignatieff's motion came to a vote and the Conservatives proved, for once, unable to scare the tide out of rolling in. By 165 votes to 145, the motion passed. Harper announced he'd be off to visit the governor general soon. Ignatieff left the rapidly emptying Commons with a handful of his MPs for a microphone in the lobby and awaited the reporters' questions.

His first problem was that none of the reporters he faced was asking about the quality of the democracy he was protecting. They wouldn't stop questioning him about coalitions. They wanted to know whether he would conspire with the other opposition parties to take power from Stephen Harper after an election, just as Stéphane Dion had tried to do in 2008. Ignatieff was trying to explain that if he had his wish, there wouldn't even be any other opposition parties. All he wanted was a fair fight between his Liberals and Stephen Harper's Conservatives. His attempts to make this argument were not going well.

"Let me make it more clear: if you vote for the NDP, if you vote for the Greens, if you vote for the Bloc, you'll get more of this," he said, tilting his head back toward the Commons chamber with its implied stink of Harperism. "And Canadians are saying, 'Enough.' I can't be clearer than that."

Tonda MacCharles, who writes for the *Toronto Star*, cut in. "No, you're not clear at all. You're not clear at all, sir, actually. Do you believe that a coalition is a legitimate parliamentary option that you will pursue?" Go talk to the governor general if you want to debate "abstract constitutional principles," Ignatieff said.

Ignatieff was intent on avoiding abstract principles. At one point earlier in the week he had delivered a scrum almost as miserable as this one. "Folks," he had said then, in response to the same question—because it really wasn't hard to predict that the question would come up, was it?—"in the election that's coming up, there's a blue door." He held out his right hand, palm forward, miming a door. "You go through that door, you get jets, you get jails, you get corporate tax cuts. You go through the red door"—left hand, palm forward—"you get compassion, you get fiscal responsibility, and you get a government relentlessly focused on the real priorities of Canadian families."

Between then and now he must have decided red-door blue-door was not an image that helped his case. What he hadn't done was find an answer that did help. Terry Milewski from the CBC phrased the question more bluntly than anyone. "Surely this coalition monkey is going to stay on your back every day of the campaign," the veteran broadcaster scolded him. "Because people will assume that if you don't rule it out, that's because you've got something to hide."

Ignatieff's forehead went shiny as he started to perspire. "You're buying the Conservative line here. There's nothing to hide. I am saying as clearly as I can to the Canadian people, looking them straight in the eye"—here he focused his gaze into the TV camera directly in front of him—"if you want to replace the Harper government, you've got to vote Liberal. It can't be clearer than that."

With that, Ignatieff wheeled ninety degrees and fled to the safety of a nearby corridor, his MPs marching briskly in his wake. The beginning of the election was still a day away. The Liberal leader was already fighting ghosts. He couldn't get a clear shot at Harper; the press kept playing game theory with him.

A week later a senior Liberal campaign strategist sat in a leather chair in a Toronto office tower and looked back on that scrum as the first sign of trouble in the Liberal campaign. "I thought it was a terrible day," the strategist said. "I thought he didn't answer the question right on the coalition thing—a total Ottawa issue which I hadn't heard a single person outside of Ottawa talk about. But anyway, I understand why it is what it is. But I thought he looked bad; he looked evasive answering the question. He was sweaty. I don't think he was dressed properly.

"Other than that, I thought it was a terrific day." The Liberal paused to consider whether he had laid on the sarcasm so thickly that his meaning might be obscured. He decided clarity would be best: "I thought it was just a shitty day."

Still, a bad start needn't count for much. Five weeks of campaigning lay ahead. By voting day on May 2, almost nobody would be thinking about Ignatieff's post-confidence-vote scrum. And everything else about this campaign was breaking the way Ignatieff wanted. The moment, hard on the heels of a lacklustre Conservative budget, was the one the Liberals had identified for months as their preferred election kickoff date. Ignatieff had the best staff, the best equipment, the most up-to-date software, the most motivated troops any Liberal leader had brought to a fight in at least a decade. He had spent the previous summer rehearsing for this ordeal with weeks of touring. He couldn't be readier. In the end none of it would help him.

The very fact of the election was a decision in which Ignatieff was a bit player. The election happened because the Conservatives and New Democrats didn't understand each other.

A few hours before his budget speech on March 23, Jim Flaherty told a news conference he had made specific concessions to obtain NDP support. It should have been easy to calculate what that support would cost, since Layton had given Harper a list. At Harper's invitation, Layton had met with the prime minister in the Langevin Block five weeks before budget day. Layton named the measures he wanted to see in a budget. These included restoring the EcoEnergy home retrofit program, increasing the Guaranteed Income Supplement, bolstering the Canada Pension Plan and hiring more doctors and nurses. Both leaders' offices said later it was a cordial chat.

Harper decided Layton would settle for a little less than half a loaf. The budget included $400 million for energy retrofits but only for a limited time. It enriched the Guaranteed Income Supplement, but less than Layton had hoped. There was nothing on the other demands.

Harper's calculation was that Layton would be looking for an excuse to avoid an election. He was recovering from hip surgery and cancer treatment. He walked with a cane. He was notably cagey about the details of his medical condition. All the polls showed weak support for the NDP. Surely Layton would take what Harper offered as cover for a tactical retreat.

"The PM didn't want an election," a Conservative war room operative said later. "That's not spin, that's a reality. I know that for a fact because I was in the budget lock-up so I got briefed on the budget before the journalists got briefed on it. And so we all saw the budget, and our reaction was, 'Wow, maybe this guy really does want to win the confidence vote,' you know? 'Not only are there no poison pills. There are genuine attempts to reach out.'"

Sometimes you guess wrong. The finance department had officials in the opposition lock-up, held so members of non-government parties can familiarize themselves with the details of the budget in the hours before it becomes public. What they reported via cell phone to Harper's political staffers was surprising. As he read the budget, Layton became visibly agitated. He sighed theatrically, held his head in his hands, grimaced. Word quickly spread among the Conservatives that they appeared to have miscalculated.

Minutes after Flaherty's budget speech, Layton confirmed that hunch in his remarks to reporters. "Mr. Harper had an opportunity to address the needs of hard-working middle-class Canadians and families, and he missed that opportunity," he said. "He just doesn't get it. New Democrats will not support the budget as presented." From that moment, the outcome of Friday's confidence vote was a foregone conclusion.

The Conservatives would spend the entire campaign saying it was their budget that had triggered the election. "Our messaging was always: we were defeated on the budget," the Conservative war room staffer said. "You know, we kind of elide that distinction as to the specific vote on which we were defeated."

"Elide" was one way to put it. Ignatieff was right: Harper's government had been found in contempt of Parliament, not only the first Canadian government to meet that fate, but the first in the Commonwealth. But Harper didn't want this campaign to be a debate about his democratic bona fides. He wanted to go to the voters as a man who had simply been taking care of the nation's economic business and wanted nothing better than to be sent back to his task. The only obstacle to that happy conclusion, he would argue, was the scheming opposition parties.

It would be handy if Ignatieff had spent the campaign's first day talking about coalitions instead of government ethics. Fortunately for Harper, Ignatieff's need to recover from his flop-sweat scrum had ensured he would oblige.

On Saturday morning, shortly before Ignatieff appeared for his campaign launch news conference, reporters received an e-mailed copy of a statement from the Liberal leader. "Let's be clear about the rules," it said. "Whoever leads the party that wins the most seats on election day should be called on to form the government." That was clear enough, but it was not the end of it. "If that is the Liberal party, then I will be required to rapidly seek the confidence of the newly elected Parliament. If our government cannot win the support of the House, then Mr. Harper will be called on to form a government and face the same challenge."

This had the advantage of being technically correct while proposing a path of events that had no recent precedent. In a parliamentary system, every important vote a government faces is a test of the members' confidence in the government. Each of Harper's six budgets since 2006, for instance, had faced a series of votes that put the confidence of the Commons in play. But Ignatieff was describing an immediate, explicit confidence test of a minority government as the first order of business after an election—certainly if the Liberals won the most seats, and by implication, perhaps if the Conservatives did too. This would actually be something new. Harper had faced no explicit first-order-of-business confidence test after the 2006 election. Neither had Joe Clark after the 1979 election. Defeat came later, after much ordinary business had been transacted by governments whose legitimacy was not questioned by their opponents.

Guy Giorno had left as Harper's chief of staff at the end of 2010. Now he was the Conservatives' campaign chairman. Giorno had been famously taciturn at the PMO, never speaking to reporters about anything the government did. Now he spent his days sending out a surprising number of messages on Twitter. "Ignatieff statement pretty clear he will try to form government even if Harper wins most seats," Giorno tweeted as soon as the Liberal leader's statement was out. Actually it was really hard to tell, but Ignatieff's business about "rapidly seeking confidence" suggested it was at least possible.

As Harper arrived at Rideau Hall, he had been prime minister for five years and two months. Since his last trip here to dissolve a Parliament, in 2008, he had passed Alexander Mackenzie and Lester Pearson in longevity. During the five-week campaign he would outlast R.B. Bennett to become Canada's tenth-longest-serving prime minister. To do more he would need another election victory, and by his own measure this time it would need to be a majority. Reporters at Rideau Hall asked Harper whether a coalition challenge to a Conservative plurality was in fact Ignatieff's plan. You bet it is, Harper said. But reporters wanted to ask him about something else too: a letter Harper, Layton and Gilles Duceppe had sent to the governor general of the day, Adrienne Clarkson, in 2004 after Paul Martin's Liberal majority had been reduced to a minority.

"Excellency," the letter had read in part. "You could be asked by the Prime Minister to dissolve the 38th Parliament at any time should the House of Commons fail to support some part of the government's program." If that happened, "this should give you cause, as constitutional practice has determined, to consult the opposition leaders and consider all of your options before exercising your constitutional authority."

This was rather transparently the prelude to a coalition play, no? Not at all, Harper said. Neither had he intended to form a coalition nor had he ever formed one. That led Duceppe and Layton to dispute their co-signatory's version of events. "Harper lied to the people, he agreed with the coalition," the Bloc leader tweeted.

For the next three days, every national leader had to face questions about whether they would form a coalition government after the May 2 election. Harper, meanwhile, was asked continually whether he had plotted to form one in 2004.

This was one of many instances when the reporters who thought they were being toughest on Harper were in fact helping him along. Questions about coalitions were fine with him. Even if they were questions about coalitions in which he might have participated. "The PM has, according to our focus groups, so much source credibility on coalitions—by which I mean Canadians just don't believe he's going to form a coalition. They just don't believe it," the Conservative war room staffer said. "Regardless of what was happening in 2004, they just don't believe it. And so our view was that by keeping that in the news, by keeping the word 'coalitions' in the news, it was probably still a net positive, even though guys like Terry Milewski and so on were focusing on our coalition, not Ignatieff's coalition."

As a result, the reporters weren't focusing on the Speaker's contempt finding and Parliament's contempt vote. "To the extent that Ignatieff wanted at least the first week of the election to be dominated by coverage of contempt, he failed miserably," the Conservative staffer said.

While Harper was visiting the governor general, the Conservatives released their first two campaign ads. One was a stark and characteristically simplistic attempt to frame the "ballot question," the idea that Conservatives hoped would be in voters' minds when they were walking into a voting booth. The ad began with an image of an election ballot unfolding to reveal the words of a question. (That'd be your ballot question right there.) "What's this election all about?" a soothing female voice asked. "It starts with leadership. Stephen Harper has led our country through a global recession with a steady, determined hand . . . why would we risk changing course?"

Like many of the Conservatives' favourites, the second ad in this campaign-opening volley would have seemed, to any self-made connoisseur of the political advertiser's art, almost unfathomably dumb. "Fact," said a male voice in a tone of unmistakable disdain. In case anyone had missed that, a single word appeared on the screen: "FACT." "This election, a vote for the Liberals is a vote for Michael Ignatieff," the voice said. Words on the screen reinforced this information: "A VOTE FOR THE LIBERALS IS A VOTE FOR MICHAEL IGNATIEFF." The ad cut to black-and-white footage of Ignatieff (identified in block letters as MICHAEL IGNATIEFF) saying, "Nobody speaks for the Liberal Party of Canada but me."

Um, what the hell? As usual, there was a point to all this. "The one thing the internal polling is showing is that across the country, 'Stephen Harper vs. Michael Ignatieff' is more advantageous to us than 'candidate vs. candidate,'" the Conservative war room staffer explained. "That is to say, if you do [Fabian] Manning," a Newfoundland Conservative candidate, "against whoever he's running against, Manning's margin is smaller than 'Stephen Harper vs. Michael Ignatieff' in Newfoundland. By which I mean that [Harper]'s the guy who wins us. He's the only reason that we're talking about winning a majority."

Hence the "somewhat imbecilic" Ignatieff's-a-Liberal ad, this staffer said. "That summarizes our appeal. It is, 'You may even consider yourself a Liberal, but if you vote Liberal you're voting for that guy.' And if Canadians are thinking that, that does more to move votes in our corner than any other question."

The Conservative then mentioned a Léger poll that ran in newspapers of the *Sun* chain at the start of the campaign. It asked which leader Canadians wanted to have a beer with, which one they wanted as a neighbour, and so on. "About the same number of Canadians said they would want their daughter to marry Elizabeth May as would want their daughter to marry Michael Ignatieff." In both cases the number of polled Canadians in question was about 7 percent.

The Conservative strategist didn't mention the most significant numbers in the Léger poll. Ignatieff was down at the bottom with Liz May, but look who led. The leader most likely to look like marrying material for respondents' daughters was Jack Layton. Their preferred neighbour was Layton. Their favourite hockey coach for their kids was Layton. Respondents wanted to have a beer with Layton and would rather have him as their parent. They did score Harper over Layton as the best-dressed leader, but as for the rest, it was a clean sweep. "Jack Layton is the nice guy. The good guy. The buddy," Léger vice-president Christian Bourque said.

What he wasn't, for now, was the guy voters were flocking to see. "Did you hear about Jack last night?" Peter Donolo asked reporters as Michael Ignatieff's tour buses rolled down Spadina Avenue in Toronto. "Regina. Birthplace of the NDP. Seventy people in the room." Donolo shook his head in an approximation of sympathy.

Few reporters within earshot of Donolo's voice had heard, and none of them had been present. Reporters who were stuck on the NDP bus were the ones who had drawn the short straw. Most of the veterans from the TV networks and the big print outlets were travelling with Harper or Ignatieff. The emerging story by the end of the campaign's first week was the contrast in the two leaders' styles.

Harper had an event every morning at a secluded location in front of a hand-picked crowd. He would re-announce part of his budget and take five questions from reporters. Never six. Every afternoon, somewhere else, he'd attend an invitation-only rally where he would stare at a teleprompter screen and read a tale of woe. He had been hard at work, the tale scrolling across the screen said, when a bunch of losers had ejected him from his workplace. He told a crowd west of Montreal that it was great to be in Quebec. "But this is not where I should be. All members of Parliament should be in Ottawa working on the economy. We should be working to protect our economic advantage."

"Yes, Canada is doing relatively well," he said in St. John's. "But a sea of troubles is lapping at our shores." And in this uncertain world, Canada itself was facing more uncertainty. "There won't be a Conservative minority government after this election," he told the St. John's crowd. "There will either be Mr. Ignatieff, put in power by the NDP and the Bloc Québécois, or there will be what Canada needs—a strong, stable, majority Conservative government."

Majority or chaos. It was the frame Harper had sought for this election since the polls had spiked in his favour during the 2008 coalition crisis. He had warned the Liberals a hundred times that he would come at them in just this way and still they had no rebuttal ready. But Harper took care to describe his half of the choice in as soothing a manner as possible. "It's not just any majority," one of his cabinet ministers said later, "it's a majority in a box. A strong, stable, national majority." Stability was key. A vote for the Conservatives was portrayed as a vote against monkey business. Harper had begun rolling out new policy, such as an income-splitting scheme to reduce couples' tax burden. But he would introduce these policies only after the deficit was eliminated, a few years down the road.

Ignatieff had great fun mocking Harper's time-delayed promises. "He's not going to deliver it until rainwater turns to beer!" But the Conservatives calculated that "later" was precisely when voters felt like seeing governments spend their money.

The strategy was a refinement of the plan that had won Harper re-election, but not a majority, in 2008. Then, too, he had run as an agent of comfort against radicals. The nature of the radicalism had changed. In 2008, it had been Dion's Green Shift, which Harper depicted as mad science in the policy lab. In 2011, Ignatieff was not offering any plan as bold. But the three-year-old bungled coalition experiment allowed Harper to depict his opponents—not just Ignatieff, but the lot of them—as a procedural risk. You cannot be sure of a Harper government, he was saying, unless you make sure to vote for Harper Conservatives.

Meanwhile, he took care to eliminate a potential irritant, just as he had done in each previous election. In 2000, conservatives had lost because their movement was split into two parties; by 2004 Harper had united the parties. In 2004, they had lost because a few yahoos had said ridiculous things; by 2006 Harper had imposed rigorous message discipline. In 2006, it was too easy to doubt he loved his country; in the 2008 campaign, he ran around hugging farmers and pulling the Canadian Shield out of his back pocket.

In 2008, his own big mouth had handed his opponents an excellent buying opportunity. So in 2011, he would keep it shut as much as he could without making his reticence a story. There would be no chatty-Cathy fake breakfasts with the scribes this campaign. And, as I've already mentioned, there would be precisely five questions a day at news conferences. Not six, five. Four from the travelling press, one from a local reporter.

This advice came from Jenni Byrne. She was Harper's campaign manager in this election, a more direct operational role than Giorno's as campaign chair. She believed that when Harper lost control of his message it usually happened in one of two ways. Sometimes the boss became "Angry Stephen," getting way too hot for his own good. Sometimes he became "Professor Stephen," wandering off into theoretical discussions that left him saying something much more interesting than what he meant to say. Interesting clips turned up on the television news. They obliterated message discipline. The longer Harper talked, the more likely Angry Stephen and Professor Stephen were to show up. According to lore around the Conservative war room, Harper's 2008 mention of "excellent buying opportunities" amid global banking turmoil came in response to a seventh question. So now he stopped at five.

But you could ask Ignatieff whatever you liked. The Liberal leader did have a few choreographed message events. At one, on March 29 at Sheridan College in Oakville, Ontario, he gave a detailed presentation of his plan to make university tuition more affordable. It was a neater package, more modest and better presented, than Dion's equivalent event three years earlier. But it was at the evening rallies that Ignatieff really blossomed. When he turned a couple of the rallies into town-hall events where anyone could ask him about anything, he was hooked.

He had rehearsed the town-hall format throughout his 2010 tours under that catchy name, "Open Mike." Unfortunately, openness came with a risk. Or rather, a certainty: each time Ignatieff took a dozen questions on as many topics, it was impossible to know which clip would show up on the evening news. The freewheeling energy of the events was lost on most voters, who saw none of it. But Ignatieff's improvisational skill was intoxicating to everyone on the Liberal bus. Here again, the Liberals had a problem they didn't even notice. Ignatieff had most of his best thinkers travelling with him, including Donolo. Harper had most of his campaign brass—Byrne, Giorno, Muttart, Nigel Wright—on the ground. The leader's tour is still the most important part of a national campaign, but it's not the whole campaign. That nuance got lost around the open mike.

When the travelling Liberal campaign staff collapsed at the hotel each night and turned on the TV, they were bemused by what they saw. None of the Open Mike energy was making it onto the news. The travelling reporters, relaxing down in the hotel bar, were telling one another that this was a fresh, energized Michael Ignatieff. But on the first Thursday night CBC-TV "At Issue" panel of the campaign, the pundits, who like almost everyone else in Canada were not travelling with the Liberal leader, said not a word about Open Mike. To them there was no such thing.

Ignatieff had a chance to improve his campaign's focus on April 3, two weeks into the campaign, with the release in Ottawa of the Liberal party's electoral platform. This event played to several strengths of the current Liberal team. Ignatieff spoke off the cuff, and well. The event was webcast on the Internet (the party said nearly ten thousand people watched), so it felt modern. The platform's themes and the event's tone were consistent with discussions during Ignatieff's April 2010 thinkers' conference in Montreal, so for once the Liberals looked like a party with consistent ideas and some follow-through.

The centrepiece of the platform was a "Family Pack," designed to pitch the Liberals as a party of modest, pragmatic activism. Five inter-related policies: $1 billion for tuition assistance; $400 million to improve the Guaranteed Income Supplement; $400 million for a green home-renovation tax credit; $1 billion in benefits for people who stay home to care for family members; and $500 million a year for new child care spaces.

The platform was an effort to re-establish the party as a champion of working families. To the extent that it offered the Liberals as an answer to ordinary people's real-life preoccupations, it helped position Ignatieff as an alternative to what he called Harper's obsession with "jets, jails and corporate tax cuts." If the Liberals had stayed steadily on that theme since December they would have been in better shape now. But if they could at least stay steadily on that theme through April, all would not be lost.

They could not stay steadily on that theme, or any theme. On the very day Ignatieff released his platform, the Canadian Press revealed that Bruce Carson had been convicted of fraud five times before he became a senior advisor in Harper's PMO. That was three more than the number of convictions Harper claimed to know about before he hired Carson anyway. Given a choice between discussing home retrofit tax credits and Bruce Carson's criminal record, Ignatieff much preferred the latter.

Meanwhile, the crowd control around Harper's campaign events started to backfire. A steady trickle of headlines revealed that ordinary Canadians were being turned away from Harper events. In one case, a young woman was apparently rejected because the RCMP had found a picture on her Facebook page that showed her standing with Ignatieff. Ignatieff started devoting the first several minutes of his town-hall events to welcoming all visitors from any party. "It's called democracy," he would say. In Toronto, Liberal adman Bob Richardson produced an online-only ad on a day's notice: shots of a computer screen as somebody inspected, and then rejected, some innocent's Facebook page. The "Hey Stephen Harper, Stop Creeping Me on Facebook" ad passed 100,000 views on YouTube within days.

Privately, these attacks drew mixed reactions from bemused Conservatives. After a few days of the ejections-from-rallies stories, Harper's staff decided to be contrite. Giorno and Byrne found most of the complaints from the travelling press to be self-serving and not worth worrying about. But ordinary people were a different matter. "When Terry Milewski is asking, 'Why aren't you letting me ask another question?' we kind of like laugh at it," the Conservative war room staffer said. "When Terry Milewski's asking, 'Why are you kicking people out of your rallies?' we're like, 'This is not good. This needs to be fixed.'" After three days, Harper apologized for the excesses of his event organizers.

But as was so often the case, the Conservatives believed the only damage they could suffer was of their own making and, once they found they were doing that sort of damage, they adjusted to stop. Attacks from the Liberals were not much of a problem, precisely because they came from Liberals.

"Ethics is not a real wedge for the Liberal Party," a senior Conservative strategist said. "For an issue to be a wedge, you have to be on one side, the other guys have to be on the other, and the voters have to actually believe that you are on one side and the other guys are on the other." Liberals couldn't ever see this, but accountability and ethics were a lousy wedge for them. "I know [the sponsorship scandal] isn't top of mind for most people right now, but the Liberal brand has not exactly been reinvented on this front. People think that they're a bunch of scoundrels and we're a bunch of scoundrels."

Monday morning, April 11, was the eve of the English-language leaders' debate. The Liberal war room did what it did best, leaking a disruptor designed to throw the Conservatives off guard. The Canadian Press newswire moved what would, in any normal month, have been a blockbuster story. "The Harper government misinformed Parliament to win approval for a $50-million G8 fund that lavished money on dubious projects in a Conservative riding, the auditor general has concluded. And she suggests the process by which the funding was approved may have been illegal."

"The initial CP story was terrible for us because it accused us of illegality and contempt of Parliament. Contempt of Parliament is bad, illegality is terrible," the Conservative war room staffer said later. So the Conservatives found a later version of Sheila Fraser's audit; it reached conclusions similar to those in the draft the Liberals had handed to CP, but in more decorous language. "That turned it into a process story as to who was the leaker. Competing drafts. That's the sort of tactic of which Jenni Byrne would likely approve, because she knows how to make a quick decision. And she knows that sometimes when you're losing, muddying the waters is considered a win."

Voters watching the spectacle of two political parties duelling to define the extent of government misfeasance might have wished they had more of a choice. As it happened, the NDP had just started running an ad called "You Have a Choice." At two minutes long, the ad was too long to place in commercial television ad time. It became the opening show at a number of NDP rallies and it helped fill those late-night free-time slots for election advertising that almost nobody is awake to watch. The ad's total audience probably numbered in the thousands, so it cannot have produced the shift in attitude toward the NDP that made this campaign historic. But it can help us understand the reasons behind that shift.

The ad was all text, no faces, no voices. For the first half, the background was Tory blue or Liberal red and the music was ominous. Blocks of text spelled out the message. "For too long in Ottawa, scandals and political games have gotten in the way of getting anything done," the text said. A little later: "And now other leaders are telling you that you have no choice. That you have to vote for more of the same." Who could this be about? The screen helpfully displayed a blue door and a red door, just as Ignatieff had described them. "Doesn't sound right, does it?"

The tone of the music changed—to celestial trumpets. "They've been telling JACK LAYTON the same thing for over EIGHT YEARS," the text read. "Jack Layton has proven them wrong." The blue background switched to orange. The doom music became peppy acoustic guitar, Layton's preferred instrument for serenading trapped reporters on the NDP campaign plane. "Fighting for our families. Our veterans. Our seniors." Here the content of the pitch changed, from hope to accomplishment. "New Democrats sit first or second in 104 ridings across Canada . . . ridings where only New Democrats defeat Conservatives." In the remaining forty-five seconds, the words "You can choose" appeared five times.

You can choose. It was the message Layton had pushed in four campaigns since 2004, while the Liberals gave voters three new leaders. In 2004 Layton had nearly doubled the NDP's share of the popular vote, to 15.68 percent, and the party grew in the House from thirteen seats to nineteen. In 2008 he nudged his score up to 18 percent of the vote and thirty-seven seats. Each gain was a disappointment because Layton always hoped for so much more. But it was still a gain.

Preparing Layton for the debate was Brian Topp's job. Most of the time Topp worked for the show-business union ACTRA in Toronto. He'd spent many years as former NDP premier Roy Romanow's chief of staff in Saskatchewan. In 2006 and 2008 he was effectively Layton's campaign manager, but this time Topp stood back while party director Brad Lavigne and Layton's chief of staff, Anne McGrath, ran most of the campaign.

For the debates, Topp did what he often does first: he called Romanow for a reminder about how they used to do things in Saskatchewan. Romanow said long discussions of the strategic goals helped him before a debate. Layton had prepared for the 2004, 2006 and 2008 debates by rehearsing scripted answers, but it just made him stiff and nervous. Topp asked whether Layton was prepared to wing it a bit more. You bet, Layton said.

"The format this year had changed," Topp said later. "There would be a videotaped question from an ordinary Canadian, and then a direct exchange between two leaders, and a free-form exchange among all four. So we needed two sets of Lego blocks here. First, a substantive answer. We owed that person who had asked the question a substantive answer. And then in the plenary, saying some key things that brought out the differences with other leaders."

In 2008 Layton had ignored everyone in the studio except Harper, inadvertently giving Dion room to shine. This year he would diversify his portfolio of targets. "In many ways, we had business with three of the other leaders." If an NDP breakthrough in Quebec could be blocked, Duceppe would do the blocking. Ignatieff was betting everything on his ability to stop the NDP outside Quebec. "The Liberal campaign was predicated on breaking our vote," Topp said. "And, also, part of our vote is parked with the Liberals." So Layton needed to look more credible, as a repository for non-Conservative votes, than Ignatieff. And he needed to look competitive with Harper as a potential prime minister.

Because Harper's tight campaign-event security had provoked Ignatieff into returning to one of his preferred personas, that of a champion of democracy, Layton's team knew Ignatieff would play up his credentials as a great democrat at the debates. "How," Topp said, "do you bomb that bridge?" The newspapers provided one handy option, because they had been carrying stories about Ignatieff's lousy attendance record for votes in Parliament. His absences were easy to explain. He had spent months learning how to do a leader's tour, and he couldn't be in two places at once. Still, "That seemed to me to be a vivid way to make our point," Topp said. "Mr. Ignatieff talks a lot about democracy, but he's got lead boots."

Harper's debate preparation was almost completely different from Layton's. Like any sane man, Harper hated rehearsing for debates. He is a hard man to contradict. In earlier elections his campaign team had not put much effort into trying. Instead they delivered the candidate to Michael Coates, the Hill+Knowlton Canada boss, who spent a few days going over briefing books and general strategy with the leader. Rehearsal attempts had been half-hearted at best. But in 2008 that time-honoured process had produced a stiff, subdued and weirdly smiling Stephen Harper who had let Stéphane Dion walk all over him.

So this time Harper's regular campaign team hung on to him for debate preparation. "The PM, to his credit, bought in 100 percent," one of them said. One detail of the preparation: Harper would look into the camera for every answer, even when the others were trying to get his attention with a personal criticism. "The goal was to try and recast or reframe it so that rather than looking like we were the ones under attack, there would be a pivot away from the others, into the camera, to use the opportunity to drive the ballot question with the viewers at home," one of his advisors said. "Number one, don't make a mistake. Number two, try and strategically minimize the others by making a more direct connection with the viewer at home."

The campaign's best guess was that this would annoy Ignatieff especially. "We'd watched a lot of footage," another Harper advisor said. "It got Ignatieff angry if you didn't engage with him."

So for once Harper had rehearsed his lines and Layton had learned to relax. Both had prepared little tricks to get Ignatieff's goat. And with all that in mind they all filed into the Government Conference Centre for the first debate.

As planned, Harper spent the first debate physically pivoting away from whoever was accusing him of something and staring into the camera. "That's simply not true," he said again and again, before telling the home audience a tale of modest, responsible government that had little to do with whatever the other guy had just shouted at him.

For his part, Ignatieff spent most of the night turned toward Harper.

"You waste public money," he said in one typical exchange. "That's the issue. And that's why the auditor general's report is saying, not just that you wasted money, but you didn't tell Parliament the truth about it." No matter what Ignatieff said, Harper turned away from him. And each time it made Ignatieff steam a little more.

One of the surprises Ignatieff's staff had to deal with when he moved back to Canada was that this veteran of Harvard and the BBC was a lousy debater. His skin was thin. He had an acute tendency to over-personalize the questions at hand. Once, during the 2006 Liberal leadership debates, Bob Rae made an offhand, not unkind remark about Ignatieff's mother. Ignatieff wandered way off topic to defend his family's honour, horrifying his young entourage. When he became Liberal leader in early 2009, they had actually scheduled rehearsal time to improve his game. Dwight Duncan, the Ontario finance minister, would show up for these rehearsals and pretend to be Stephen Harper. He would go up one side of Ignatieff and down the other. Gradually it became harder and harder to get Ignatieff to make time for the sessions. Eventually they stopped. Unfortunately, now there was an election on and Ignatieff couldn't ignore these debates because they made him feel bad.

In the English debate, Duceppe was off to one end. The luck of the draw put Layton between Ignatieff and Harper so they had to shout past him to get at each other. Layton was able to strike a more conversational tone. He set about making the populist pitch that had been the basis for Ignatieff's "jets, jails and corporate tax cuts" attack. On the tax cuts: "You did get it through," he said to Harper, "with the support of Mr. Ignatieff, who now, by the way, pretends to oppose the things that he voted for."

Then Layton made a more general point. "I'm asking myself, because I remember a Stephen Harper once upon a time who came here to change Ottawa. Was going to stick up for the little guy. But you've become what you used to oppose."

And, when his one-on-one with Ignatieff came, Layton bombed the democracy bridge. He talked about Ignatieff's lousy attendance record for Commons votes. Ignatieff's smile slowly curdled. "You know, most Canadians, if they don't show up for work, they don't get a promotion," Layton said.

After the debate the Angus Reid polling group ran a series of focus groups using an Internet-based response tool called ReactionPlus. For years pollsters have sat audiences down and made them watch debates with a dial to record whether they like what they're seeing or not. Angus Reid measured their responses on ten different axes to indicate whether they were "curious," "engaged," "confused," "happy" and so on.

For the most part, the focus groups did not need the happy button. "The primary reaction of Canadians to the English debate was annoyance," Angus Reid reported later. "Certain feelings, such as engagement, excitement, happiness and even interest, barely registered." But the level of annoyance was not a monotone. It grew markedly when the leaders attacked each other. And it declined when leaders discussed their concrete policy proposals, especially if those proposals were about the economy, health care or education.

Canadians were sick to tears of watching Harper and Ignatieff go at each other. "The level of interest and happiness definitely soars," the ReactionPlus report read, "when attacks are avoided and the party leaders express their policy ideas in a clear and concrete fashion." And despite his shots at Harper for losing sight of the little guy and at Ignatieff for losing sight of Parliament, respondents felt Layton had been the most constructive of the leaders.

The next night, the leaders debated in French. Angus Reid ran a similar set of multi-dimensional focus groups. "Respondents clearly reacted more strongly to some leaders and themes than to others," the firm reported later. "Prime Minister Harper elicited strongly negative reactions, no matter what he was talking about. Duceppe and Layton inspire more interest and happy sentiments, whereas Ignatieff provokes a decidedly mixed reaction." Here again, Angus Reid found that attacking and interrupting were a bad idea. The audience, they reported, was in a much better mood "when leaders outline concrete policies or talk about working collaboratively more."

Taken together, the Angus Reid focus groups showed that voters were done with leaders who spent all their time attacking one another. They were almost pleading for leaders to work together. Stephen Harper was simply not going to do that. For two years he had said the alternative to a Conservative majority was anarchy. It was a marvellous, polarizing argument: less than half of the electorate thought a Harper majority would be preferable, in all circumstances, to an opposition coalition. But less than half the electorate was all he needed anyway.

Most of the rest of the population, however, thought a coalition was a pretty good idea. In a polarized landscape, most Canadians who were not planning to vote Conservative were eager to get Harper out of 24 Sussex Drive. It made them more likely to be fond of any mechanism for achieving that end. Coalitions are about working together and overcoming differences. But what did those voters see when they looked at the alternatives to Harper? They saw Ignatieff, who offered them a red door and a blue door, as if they were idiots. They saw Duceppe, whose separatist party destroyed the legitimacy of coalitions even when it wanted to support one. And then, as if for the first time, they saw Jack Layton, whose message seemed simple, respectful and empowering: you have a choice.

Profoundly missing the point, the Liberals saw that their leader had failed to catch on with voters in the debates and promptly released their most negative ad of the campaign. "Where would Harper's cuts leave your family's health? The stakes are too high," the new Liberal ad said, as a cardiogram line on the screen flatlined. It was hard to imagine a generic tool less suited to the particular circumstance. Ignatieff had not asked a single question about health care in Question Period in 2011. But Liberals always used medicare scare ads when they were losing. It was a revered tradition in the party. Meanwhile the Liberals were not using precious ad time to explain how they would govern. The most important event of the campaign, the English-language debate, had come and gone, and with it Ignatieff's hope of changing the dynamic. Now he had to try something new. His problem was that he had been trying something new every day or so. Now he needed to try something new and a little crazy. He was the right man for the job.

———

On Friday, April 15, Ignatieff was doing another town hall, in a hotel ballroom in Sudbury. "While I was on the bus this afternoon I found myself thinking about a wonderful singer called Bruce Springsteen," he said. "Does everybody like Bruce Springsteen? I like Bruce Springsteen." He told the crowd about "a wonderful song called 'The Rising.' And in that song there's a wonderful refrain: 'Rise up.'" In fact, that refrain is actually in "My City of Ruins," another song from the album *The Rising*, but it's a common error. "And I began thinking about it today. Because we're in a funny place in this election campaign right now."

Ignatieff was hunched, his tall body curving gently around the microphone he held in both hands.

"We've got a prime minister who shut down Parliament twice and Canadians kind of shrugged," he said, quietly. "We've got a prime minister who's found in contempt of Parliament. It's never happened before in the history of our country and people say, kind of, 'So what?' We got a prime minister who tried to shut down the long-form census and people thought, that's crazy, but kind of, 'So what?' And then we have a prime minister who just went out and smeared a member of his own caucus, tried to destroy her public reputation, and people say, kind of, 'So what?'"

There was more in this vein. Nobody travelling with the Liberal leader had planned or expected any of this. "And I kept hearing that refrain from Bruce Springsteen—Rise up. Rise up. Rise up, Canada!" He nearly shouted this. The crowd began to clap, but Ignatieff kept going. "Why do we have to put up with this? Rise up! Rise up! . . . Rise up! This goes beyond partisan politics! This goes beyond the Liberal Party! This is about our country! This is about our democracy! Rise up! Rise up!" Many members of the crowd plainly had taken a moment to decide how to respond to all this energy, but by now almost all of them were on their feet.

Later, on the flight to Regina, the campaign videographer showed the footage of the sermon to Peter Donolo. The video guy then took his computer to the front of the plane where Ignatieff sat. The campaign crew made two decisions: First, get that Sudbury footage up on YouTube post-haste. Second, get more of the off-the-cuff Ignatieff in front of Canadians. This idea came from Patrice Ryan, one of the leader's Quebec advisors, a son of Claude Ryan, the former Quebec provincial Liberal leader. Right there on the flight to Regina they decided to buy a half-hour of TV time eight days hence, on Easter Sunday, to show Michael Ignatieff to Canadians once again.

That weekend, the "rise up" video appeared on YouTube, with Ignatieff's sermon accompanied by quiet inspirational music. Guy Giorno and Jason Lietaer, the Conservatives' war room communications director, watched it in the office they shared at the party's sprawling campaign headquarters in an industrial park outside Ottawa. Giorno's and Lietaer's reaction would not have pleased the Liberals. They briefly wondered whether the video was some kind of cruel hoax against the Liberals. But no, it couldn't be: that really was Ignatieff saying that stuff, after all. They did consider the possibility that this was the ad that would finally turn the nation against them. Naah. They started sharing the footage as widely as possible. "With any luck," Lietaer wrote on Twitter, "this will go viral."

Giorno and Lietaer were persuaded that the spectacle of Ignatieff urging crowds to rebellion could look good only to Liberal partisans. "You've got Stephen Harper on the one hand saying times are dangerous and we need a stable government," our Conservative war room source said later. "And then you got a guy yelling at people to rise up?"

Recall the lesson of the Angus Reid real-time focus groups: "The level of annoyance grew markedly when the leaders attacked each other." Here was Michael Ignatieff travelling the country staging a re-enactment of those moments.

The same weekend, another party leader gave another speech that wound up sounding better to him than to a lot of voters. The Parti Québécois was holding its national convention in Montreal. Pauline Marois, the party's leader, won a resounding 93.08 percent endorsement from delegates in a confidence vote on April 16 as she prepared for a campaign against the Liberal premier, Jean Charest. Gilles Duceppe was a guest speaker at the convention.

When Bloc support is strong, the party's leaders have tended to present it as the federal voice of all Quebecers, sovereignist and federalist alike. When it sags a little, as it was doing now, Bloc leaders like to remind sovereignist voters of their duty to support the movement's Ottawa operation. "My friends, I say this often," Duceppe told the convention. "Before being Péquistes and Bloquistes, we are all sovereigntists. We are going to finish the campaign side-by-side. More united than ever. We have only one task to accomplish. Elect the maximum number of sovereigntists in Ottawa and then we go to the next phase: electing a PQ government."

In fact, he had not been campaigning on a promise to make his party a cog in a great separatist scheme. This was something of a rebranding exercise. "A strong Bloc in Ottawa. A PQ in power in Quebec. And everything becomes possible again." That last sentence echoed the "yes" camp's slogan during the 1995 referendum, which had split the province against itself. The crowd in the room loved it, as the crowd in the room had loved Ignatieff's "rise up" speech. Partisans always love the partisan stuff. The people outside, who have had quite enough of feuds and quarrels, were less enamoured. The day before Duceppe spoke, the daily Nanos tracking poll put the Bloc at 38.7 percent support in Quebec. Within a week they would fall to 30.3 percent, losing one-fifth of that support. From there the collapse would only accelerate.

As voters looked around for a respite from the campaign's dominant discourse, they found a man who had been putting things a little differently for most of the time he had been in federal politics. "It's whether we elect parliamentarians to bicker or build that will be the defining issue of our time," Jack Layton had said in January 2003, at the Toronto convention where he became NDP leader. "And we say, let's build."

Now it was more than eight years later. When the reward for all the building began to accumulate, it was in Quebec. There are reasons for that. The NDP's attempt to reach out to Quebec francophones was as old as the party itself.

Since the 1930s, the party's predecessor, the Co-operative Commonwealth Federation, had support only among Quebec's anglophone Montrealers. Francophones saw it as a creature of English Canada. The archbishop of Montreal warned Roman Catholics not to support this socialist menace. So, at the NDP's founding convention in 1961, organizers were so happy to see a few francophone nationalists show up that they basically let them write the party's constitutional policy. The results included very Quebec-friendly language on "co-operative federalism, equality of rights for the French and English languages, the right of a province to opt out of joint federal-provincial programs within provincial jurisdiction without financial penalty, and the recognition of French Canada as a nation," Michael Oliver and Charles Taylor wrote in a 1991 book, *Our Canada*. The party's first president, associate president and vice-president were Quebec francophones.

But from the beginning the NDP was squeezed between extremes: the rising separatist movement and Pierre Trudeau's hardline federalism. In the 1968 election Tommy Douglas's formidable Quebec lieutenant, Robert Cliche, lost narrowly to Eric Kierans, a former provincial health minister running for the federal Liberals. The party had no more momentum in Quebec until 1984, when Trudeau retired, Brian Mulroney swept Quebec, and the Liberals were reduced to forty seats Canada-wide. Ed Broadbent saw a chance to mow the Liberals' lawn. He visited Quebec constantly. In the Commons, he and Lorne Nystrom and a few others asked questions in French as often as they could. In 1988, the party won its highest-ever share of the popular vote in Quebec, 14.4 percent. That didn't translate into a single elected NDP MP from Quebec. Then Broadbent retired and the party was nearly swept away in the 1993 election.

Layton didn't run for his party's leadership as the candidate of a Quebec rapprochement. If anything, his target market was Toronto. But he had been born in Hudson on Montreal's West Island, so he had some roots in Quebec. He had inherited a half century of NDP effort in Quebec. Unlike the recent succession of Liberal leaders, he was playing a long game, so he was content to keep the NDP's Quebec effort going. In 2004, Layton nearly tripled the NDP's vote share in Quebec—to 4.6 percent. By 2008, it was at 12.2, almost back to where Ed Broadbent had brought the party twenty years earlier. It was a cruelly limited return on political investment.

But even before that modest result, the basis for longer-term Quebec growth had come along in the person of Thomas Mulcair. After he won the Outremont by-election in 2007 and held it in the 2008 general election, Mulcair became, with Vancouver's Libby Davies, one of Layton's two deputy leaders. So Quebec was genuinely familiar territory for the NDP by the time Layton arrived for a rally at the Olympia Theatre, an ornate vaudeville house in Duceppe's riding of Laurier–Sainte-Marie, on April 23. When the crowd finally filed in—maybe two thousand people in Duceppe's own riding—Layton delivered a version of his stump speech with one addition. "My friends," he said, "I am ready to be your prime minister. And I fully understand what that means."

· While the NDP's growth in Quebec was little short of spectacular, it was soon impressive everywhere else. Everywhere except Ontario. By the morning of April 25, according to the daily Nanos tracking polls, NDP support there was four points lower than in the Atlantic region, seven points lower than in the Prairies, ten points lower than in British Columbia, thirteen points lower than in Quebec. This was looking less like a Quebec-led NDP wave than like a national wave from which Ontarians were opting out. Ontario was the only region of the country where NDP support was no higher than on the day of the English-language debate.

That was what Nanos said in the morning. EKOS that afternoon told a different story. Frank Graves, the chairman of the rival polling firm, released the astonishing results of his own weekend survey. EKOS found the NDP finally picking up momentum in Ontario, while they raced ahead in Quebec. Now Layton's party was only five points behind the Conservatives nationally—and four points ahead of Ignatieff's Liberals.

"These results, if they were to hold, would produce a profound transformation in the Canadian political firmament, tantamount and arguably more far-reaching than the Reform explosion in 1993," Graves wrote. He projected as many as a hundred seats for the NDP—and a combined Liberal–NDP seat count that would easily top the Conservatives. Harper had spent the campaign telling voters what that would mean: Jack Layton as prime minister.

Ignatieff soldiered on, sometimes sticking with the modest, constructive policy-wonk stuff that informed his "family pack" platform. At one point, he promised to convene a first ministers' meeting on health care within sixty days of becoming prime minister. He had to keep acting as if such a thing could ever happen. But the Liberals knew Layton was becoming a serious threat. They responded with one of their curiously Byzantine TV ads. This one featured a traffic light flashing NDP orange while circus music played. The ad criticized Layton for being a "career politician" and his candidates for being "ridiculously inexperienced." Finally the orange light turned red. "Not so fast, Jack."

The Conservatives paid Layton the compliment of a clear, hard-hitting ad about the 2008 coalition. It reminded everyone of a detail in Brian Topp's own book about that period: that Layton had begun discussing a coalition with Duceppe "before our votes were even counted."

Harper was facing a growing number of questions about the polls from a travelling press corps that seemed to think questions about polls are hard to answer. In fact his campaign was increasingly confident that all the movement in public opinion was among people who had not been considering voting Conservative in the first place. When the Conservatives finally hit trouble, once again it was at their own hand.

On April 27, every *Sun* paper in the country carried an article signed by Pierre Karl Péladeau, the company CEO. Sun Media had launched an upstart cable TV news and commentary network during the campaign's second week. The company VP in charge was Kory Teneycke, Harper's former communications director. Sun News clearly had Ignatieff on the brain. One of its first "scoops" had been a laughable account by reporter Brian Lilley asserting that Ignatieff had been a major planner of the Iraq war. The evidence was his presence at a 2002 conference in Washington. As Glen McGregor, a reporter for the rival *Ottawa Citizen*, pointed out within hours of Lilley's report, Amnesty International and Human Rights Watch attended the conference too. So if Ignatieff planned the war, so did they.

But what Péladeau now revealed went much further than torquing a story. "Three weeks ago, our vice-president for Sun News, Kory Teneycke, was contacted by the former deputy chief of staff to Prime Minister Harper, Patrick Muttart. He claimed to be in possession of a report prepared by a 'U.S. source,' outlining the activities and where-abouts of Liberal Leader Michael Ignatieff in the weeks and months leading to the American invasion of Iraq in 2003."This was clearly the basis for Lilley's story. But Muttart's shady source had offered more than attendance at a conference: "Muttart also provided a compelling electronic image of a man very closely resembling Michael Ignatieff in American military fatigues, brandishing a rifle in a picture purported to have been taken in Kuwait in December 2002."

This would be—well, it would be something if it were true.Teneycke, Péladeau wrote, "was properly skeptical and due diligence was con-ducted." In dramatic terms, Péladeau said that after putting "a lot of pres-sure" on Muttart, Teneycke got a better copy of the photo and it turned out to be bunk. "But it is the ultimate source of this material that is pro-foundly troubling to me, my colleagues and, I think, should be of concern to all Canadians. It is my belief that this planted information was intended to first and foremost seriously damage Michael Ignatieff's campaign, but in the process to damage the integrity and credibility of Sun Media and, more pointedly, that of our new television operation, Sun News. If any proof is needed to dispel the false yet still prevalent notion that Sun Media and the Sun News Network are the official organs of the Conservative Party of Canada, I offer this unfortunate episode as Exhibit A."

As proof of his network's independence, this was incomplete. Sun News had in fact run everything Muttart had given them except the bogus photo. And while they may not feel like the official organs of the Conservative Party, four days after they published Péladeau's *nostra* not entirely *culpa*, every Sun paper in the country (outside Toronto, where there was a wrestling match to cover) would carry Harper's photo on Page One with the words, "HE'S OUR MAN."

Still, on the morning Péladeau's op-ed ran, members of the Conservative campaign team were told that Muttart, the architect of Harper's 2006 victory and of everything the party had done to Stéphane Dion and Michael Ignatieff for four years, had been dumped from the campaign. It was a classic Harper move. One person on his team was indispensable: the guy in the ads. Everyone else would be cut loose if they became a liability. The harsh treatment of Muttart, a soft-spoken and likeable man to whom the Conservatives owed so much, made many in the Conservative campaign angry. They grumbled briefly and went back to work for Harper. Just as he knew they would.

Perhaps the most effective weapon remaining to the Conservatives was Jason Kenney. The immigration minister had been key to the Conservatives' outreach to immigrants and ethnic minority groups for years. But in the 2006 and 2008 elections he had stayed in Ottawa to oversee war room communications. This time Kenney spent almost the entire campaign on the road, and almost all of that around Toronto and Vancouver, where the biggest gains in ethnic vote could be logged.

"I just didn't think me sitting around Ottawa, working with a bunch of twenty-five-year-olds at the tactics meeting, was a great use of my time," Kenney said. Now he was doing half a dozen events a day. "I did an editorial board meeting with *Sing Tao* Toronto. The editor said, 'You're getting more coverage in our papers than the three leaders. And you're now getting to the point of overexposure.' I think that week I had three separate Chinese media conferences alone doing policy announcements."

Kenney was already known as the "minister for curry in a hurry" because of his prominence at ethnic community events. But "I'm learning a lot on this campaign," he said. "I'm kind of finding new frontiers here. Like Punjabi talk radio. Huge! People talk for days about what was said on the radio show a few days ago. They've got huge advertisers, cutthroat competition."

The Conservatives were banking heavily on what Kenney once called "very ethnic" ridings for their seat gains. "I can tell you that in the polling we've done in Cantonese and Mandarin households that we are in the range of two-thirds of the decided vote," he said. "I think what we've seen in this election is the initial erosion of the Liberal base amongst new Canadians going to complete erosion. And I think a huge amount of that has gone in our direction."

On Friday night, April 29, with only three days until the election, Sun News journalists announced on Twitter that they were about to break into regular programming. The story was a kind of blockbuster. In 1996, the network's single anonymous former police source said, Jack Layton had been found naked in a massage parlour at which illegal activities had been going on. The story was served up in high Sun TV fashion, with Layton described as the "suspected John."

The campaign put out an immediate statement from Olivia Chow, Layton's wife, an incumbent NDP MP, calling the story "nothing more than a smear campaign." Layton scrummed in British Columbia. "Absolutely nothing wrong was done. There's no wrongdoing here and yet the smears start," he said Friday night. "This is why a lot of people get turned off politics and don't even want to get involved."

That the story was popping up on a network whose affiliated newspapers were about to call Harper "OUR MAN" made some observers wonder whether the Conservatives might be the story's source. Then and forever after, Conservatives swore it wasn't so. "I know the oppo we have on Layton," the war room staffer said, using the term for potentially damaging opposition research. "That's not the oppo we have. And Jack Layton's not our enemy in Toronto. He's our friend in Toronto. We want him to go up in Toronto."

The Conservatives were playing two big games, to some extent contradictory, in different parts of the country. Their best hope for keeping their majority was for the New Democrats and Liberals to split the anti-Conservative vote in Ontario. Their second-best hope was to drive down the NDP vote in British Columbia. To that end, the Conservatives uncorked the largest ad buy of the campaign during the last five days before the Elections Canada ad blackout came into effect at midnight on Saturday, April 30. Almost the largest ad buy any party would make in this campaign.

Unlike most campaign ads, these didn't appear on the party's website or on YouTube. The Conservatives never announced they were running them. In British Columbia, the ads carried a straight anti-Layton message using the two most potent arguments the Conservatives had. They accused Layton of wanting to impose a gas tax through his carbon cap-and-trade scheme, and of scheming with the Bloc separatists to form a coalition. In Ontario, the ads didn't even mention Layton. They featured a mix of the Conservatives' patriotic and anti-Ignatieff messages. They began with Harper standing tall while Canadian flags flapped and inspirational music played. Then they faded to the old TV footage of Ignatieff telling an American audience that the United States was "your country as much as it is mine."

The Ontario ads were designed to send Liberal votes in two directions, either to Harper if voters could stomach that option, or to the NDP if that option was more palatable. In the closing days of the campaign, the Conservatives were, in a real sense, campaigning for Jack Layton in Ontario without admitting it. Harper's five questions a day were now almost entirely about how he would react if he fell short of a majority. In the Conservative war room, staffers chipped in a few bucks for the traditional betting pool. The bulk of the betting action put the Conservatives between 151 and 165 seats. They would need 155 for a majority.

In the end, Stephen Harper's party won 167 seats and 39.62 percent of the popular vote. The players in the Conservative war room betting pool had guessed low. Harper walked back out onto the stage of the Telus Convention Centre in Calgary, as he had done now on three previous election nights. This was almost becoming routine. Not quite. Laureen, always happy on these nights, was weeping openly. Her husband had won power twice before. Now he had won time.

"What a great night!" Harper said. *"Quelle belle soirée!"* A pause to bask in the applause. "Friends, I have to say it: 'A strong, stable, national, majority Conservative government.'"

He thanked the voters of Calgary Southwest for returning him—and "for giving me the honour of following in the footsteps of Preston Manning," a bit of family detail that has been true since Harper first ran in this riding in 2002, but which he had not mentioned in front of a national audience before this night. He spoke of his love for his children, Ben and Rachel, and for Laureen. He thanked the voters, who "chose hope, unity of purpose and a strong Canada."

As is always the case in victory speeches, there was a measure of claptrap in this one. Six voters in ten had not voted for his party. So much for unity of purpose. Those who voted against the Conservatives were so desperate for a sturdy alternative that more than a million of them had abandoned the Liberals and Bloc for a bicyclists' party led by a former city councillor with a bum hip. They too had voted for a strong Canada. They disagreed with Harper, in almost every particular, over what would make Canada strong.

Every election comes down to a choice between "change" and "more of the same." But in a parliamentary system we get to have both. Those Canadians who wanted stability had it. Only seven incumbent

Conservatives were defeated in this election, compared with eighty-two incumbents from other parties. The Conservative vote had grown again, by about 600,000 votes, but most of the voters who supported one of Harper's candidates were doing so for the fourth time. Harper vexed his detractors as few prime ministers ever had, but he satisfied his supporters. He was becoming what he had hoped conservatism could become in this country: a habit.

Those voters who rejected Harper's brand of stability showed their preference for risk by taking a big one. For twenty years, the largest (or, in 2000, second-largest) segment of Quebec's voting population had chosen to abstain from real engagement in federal politics by supporting the Bloc. On May 2, 2011, they tried something different. Layton became the first anglophone leader of a national party to win in Quebec when a party led by a francophone was also on offer. Fifty-seven percent of his caucus now came from Quebec. But 64 percent of the NDP's popular vote came from outside Quebec. Layton had MPs from eight provinces. Even in Saskatchewan, where a trick of the electoral system locked him out, his party won nearly a third of the vote. He was a truly national opposition leader, facing a truly national prime minister. In a sense it was not wrong of Harper to say the voters "chose hope." They simply disagreed about what constituted hope.

"Because Canadians chose hope, we can now begin to come together again," Harper said on election night. "For our part, we are intensely aware that we are, and we must be, the government of all Canadians, including those who did not vote for us." What on earth could that mean? "All those lessons of the past few years—holding to our principles, but also of listening, of caring, of adapting—those lessons that have come with a minority government, we must continue to practise as a majority government."

Within weeks Harper would use his majority to pass the budget that had precipitated this election. That budget listed, but gave no detail on, more than $2 billion in cuts to government spending. Fully two years later, the Parliamentary Budget Officer would still be in court trying to decipher those cuts to public services for Canadians paid with Canadians' tax dollars. The two drafts of Sheila Fraser's G-8 audit that leaked during the campaign were not the final draft. Soon a final draft would be public. The daily grind would continue. But it was not grinding Stephen Harper down. On his fourth try, he had won his biggest victory. Layton had secured a historic breakthrough for his own party. Then there was Ignatieff.

In 1984, in *The Needs of Strangers*, Ignatieff had written, with the innocence of a man who does not anticipate the tests life exacts, about what motivated him. "If you ask me what my needs are," he wrote, "I will tell you that I need the chance to understand and be understood, to love and be loved, to forgive and be forgiven, and the chance to create something which will outlast my life, and the chance to belong to a society whose purposes and commitments I share."

Ignatieff had held up well as the first election returns came in. But when the results arrived in his own riding, Etobicoke-Lakeshore, and showed that he had lost to a Conservative management consultant named Bernard Trottier, Ignatieff's whole body shook. Under him, the Liberals had won the lowest share of the popular vote in the party's history. Now this personal humiliation. The next day he would announce his resignation from his party's leadership.

TEN

CAN'T STOP WON'T STOP

On June 3, 2011, everybody in Ottawa with a fancy title and a dry-cleaning budget crowded into the Senate to hear the new governor general, David Johnston, read the Speech from the Throne. There is a protocol to these things. The GG gets the first page or so to wax poetic about what a wonderful country this is. Then he reads several pages of drearier stuff provided by the PMO, vaguely sketching government priorities for the coming parliamentary session. Once you know the routine, it is fairly easy to spot the joint between the vice-regal prose and the business of government.

"Each of us can answer the call to service in our own way and, together, continue this bold experiment that we call Canada," Johnston read, and it really was Johnston speaking. "Canadians have expressed their desire for a strong, stable national government in this new Parliament," he said next, transforming into a ventriloquist's puppet. Truly the constitutional monarchy is a wondrous thing.

What was not part of the script was the grim-faced and pigtailed twenty-one-year-old woman who strode to the middle of the Senate's red-carpeted centre aisle and held up a red cardboard stop sign with the words STOP HARPER! carefully written on it in white. Brigette DePape, a University of Ottawa graduate who had been working in the Senate as a page, was promptly hustled out of the Red Chamber by security, but she had a news release ready for distribution to the press gallery. "Harper's agenda is disastrous for this country and for my generation," she had written. "We have to stop him from wasting billions on fighter jets, military bases, and corporate tax cuts while cutting social programs and destroying the climate."

DePape's career as a part-time defender of the nation's honour was launched. Unfortunately, if she really had wanted to STOP HARPER, her timing was lousy. His party had, as a matter of some public notoriety, just won a majority of seats in the less elegant green-carpeted House of Commons down the hall. It had been hard enough to STOP HARPER when his elected opponents had him and his colleagues outnumbered. As a matter of simple arithmetic, it would now be impossible. "Those who now see the NDP as the wave of the future, inevitably seizing the commanding heights of the nation's polity, should look again," Conrad Black wrote from his Florida prison cell for the *National Post*. "Harper is safer than Chrétien was in the days of four sizable opposition parties."

Indeed, as Chantal Hébert wrote in the *Star*, an NDP opposition leader "may in fact wield even less influence than most of those who have held the same position in past majority Parliaments." That's because all the unelected networks of power that had vexed Harper his whole adult life—Senate, courts and bureaucracy—had been built and staffed by Liberals. Harper was slowly changing each of those organizations with new appointments, transforming them from Liberal-appointed bastions to Conservative-appointed bastions. At no point in between had they ever been NDP-appointed bastions.

What could possibly stop this man from imposing his will on the people of Canada? Perhaps only a strong sense of what had got him this far. In Calgary the morning after his election victory he held a news conference. A reporter asked Harper how he would reassure people who had feared a Conservative majority. He had been expecting the question. "One of the things I've learned is that surprises are not generally well received by the public," he replied. It was a clear reference to the aftermath of the 2008 election, when he had sprung the party-financing changes without having campaigned for them. He had paid dearly for that, and learned a lesson. "So, we intend to move forward with what Canadians understand about us, and I think with what they are more and more comfortable with."

Maintaining the public's trust was essential. "It's what every government needs to realize. You know it well when you're a minority government," he said. "You face a sense of hanging every day. But even as a majority you have to, on an ongoing basis, keep the trust of the population. And that's what we will be committed to doing—not only where we won but in areas where we didn't win. Trying to gain more trust."

He meant it as he said it, and the argument was the fruit of long reflection. His opponents had always claimed that the more power Canadians gave Harper, the further he would stray from Canadian values. He had grown the Conservative vote by proving the prediction wrong—not to the people who had never voted Conservative and would never consider it, of course, not to them; but to a broad-enough coalition of other voters.

Now with a majority, he needed to be more of an incrementalist, not less, because the likelihood of any grand plan being read as proof of some hidden agenda was higher than ever before. He would recall Parliament to pass exactly the same budget he had failed to pass in March, confirming his campaign argument that all he had ever intended to do was to proceed with the nation's business, unhindered by confidence votes and forced elections. In the months ahead, Harper would make ostentatious peace offerings to parts of the country where Conservatives had done poorly. At the beginning of September 2011, in the most visible example, he would travel to Quebec's Assemblée nationale to give the province $2.2 billion. Successive Quebec governments had argued for fourteen years that Ottawa owed the province that much after Quebec harmonized its provincial sales tax with the Goods and Services Tax. The federal finance department had always rejected the claim, since Quebec's harmonization had been incomplete and its losses had been smaller than those of other provinces that had more consistently aligned their sales-tax systems with Ottawa's. Harper ignored the argument and offered compensation; even after Quebec returned half as many Conservative MPs in 2011 as it had in 2008, he followed through.

But at the same post-victory news conference in which he laid out an agenda that sounded as though it would be modest on most days and generous on some, he revealed another enduring characteristic: a suspicion that when other parties disagreed with his own, it was because they didn't like his party's geographic and emotional heartland. Now that the election returns were in, he said, "I think Western Canada can breathe a lot easier. There were a lot of policies being floated by the other parties—whether it's on west coast transportation or the energy sector—that simply did not reflect the needs and concerns of this part of the country." He didn't specify. In Calgary he hardly needed to. The opposition parties had united to support an NDP motion calling for a ban on tanker ships off the British Columbia coast. Ignatieff and Layton had both advocated cap-and-trade schemes to limit carbon emissions. As recently as 2009, Harper's ministers had once advocated the same thing, but those days were forgotten now, at least by Harper. "I actually agreed during the campaign that the economic policies of our opponents were actually quite dangerous for the country as a whole. Obviously some specific policies seem to be almost targeted to do damage in Western Canada. I think it's a great thing that those policies won't be coming to fruition in the West."

Taken together, Harper's statements the morning after the 2011 election foreshadowed much of his third mandate, the most consequential to date. He would advance steadily and, as far as possible, with no sudden moves. But his instincts, including a deep suspicion of anyone who challenged the resource-producing base of Alberta power, would often get in the way.

Two weeks after the election, Harper named a new cabinet much like the old one. John Baird replaced the defeated Lawrence Cannon as foreign minister. Tony Clement moved from Industry to Treasury Board, where he would have a substantial say in spending cuts. The new-old cabinet was "fundamentally about stability and continuity," Harper said.

At the beginning of June, Parliament met, watched bemused as Brigette DePape was hustled out of the Throne Speech, passed the familiar budget, and sat for a little longer than expected when the NDP filibustered back-to-work legislation for striking Canada Post workers. The Conservatives were amazed that Layton would hold up Parliament, for more than fifty hours non-stop, over something as unfashionable as union rights. But Layton had learned from Harper: as the NDP continued to work toward the centre, he wanted to make sure his party's traditional base did not feel left out. As a bonus, the NDP caucus, with dozens of rookie MPs, had the opportunity to camp out for a few days in the opposition lobbies and bond. Finally the legislation passed, the postal lockout ended, and everyone went home for the summer.

Two unusual things happened. On the Conservative side, for the first time anyone could remember, everyone took a vacation. Cabinet ministers scattered to the winds. The PMO staff went home to their families. "From 2004 on, we were never sure whether we'd be in an election from one month to the next," one member of the government said. "That went on for years. The PM would schedule meetings over the Christmas holidays, just to make sure nobody let their guard down. Suddenly we were in, and we were safe for a while. It was time for a break." Hard thinking about the deeper meaning of this mandate could wait. By autumn, two cabinet ministers, Peter MacKay and James Moore, were engaged to be married. Not to each other.

The summer's other surprise was bigger. Jack Layton died. It was almost that sudden. Everyone knew he'd been ill. But he had been such a force on the campaign trail, despite the cane he used after hip surgery. The election had been such a triumph. And then it was over so quickly. On June 15 he'd invited the news cameras to Stornoway, where a National Capital Commission guy in chinos and a blue polo shirt handed him the keys to the place. "History," Layton said for the cameras. Two weeks later he and his wife, Olivia Chow, threw a garden party for reporters. There were nice crab sandwiches. On July 3, after the House rose for the summer, he and Chow rode a rickshaw in Toronto's Pride parade. He used to walk the length of the parade route, but those days were gone.

Then, on July 25, he gave that news conference, gaunt and hoarse under the TV lights, announcing he would step aside from the leadership to fight "a new form of cancer." On August 22 he was dead. So much in politics is contrived drama and fake emotion. Then something like this happens.

Harper and Layton had chatted on the floor of the House during the postal-worker filibuster. "I don't mind telling you that I could see at that point that he was a much sicker man than he had been before the election," Harper told reporters the day after Layton died. "But even at that moment, with the big personal challenge he had in front of him and with the big political battle we had going on between us, he was just still full of optimism and goodwill. And that's what I will remember."

Two days before he died, Layton huddled with his family and close associates to write a public farewell letter. "Canada is a great country, one of the hopes of the world," he wrote. "We can be a better one . . . because we finally have a party system at the national level where there are real choices; where your vote matters; where working for change can actually bring about change." The letter ended with an exhortation that would become famous. "So let us be loving, hopeful and optimistic. And we'll change the world."

It's possible to overstate the significance of the contrast between the tone of Layton's farewell letter and the tone Harper tried to set as he settled at last into the luxury of confidence in power. The comparison was hardly fair, for one thing. Layton was leaving the cares of the world, cares that would still be with Harper for years to come. But Harper would struggle, through the summer and well beyond, to find a discourse that matched his government's new situation.

Once the shock and genuine grief caused by Layton's death began to fade, the strangeness of Harper's position would begin to sink in. Duceppe and Ignatieff had lost their seats in the election. Now Layton was dead. Of the leaders who had shown up for the televised debates in April, only Harper still led his party. Leaderless and outnumbered even in the aggregate, his foes could do him no harm. But the situation was less novel than it appeared, and less safe. Except during the near coup of December 2008, his foes had never come close to harming him as much as he could harm himself. Given more of the playing field than he had ever enjoyed before, Harper would soon increase his rate of goal scoring. Some of the loveliest shots would be on his own net.

From the outset, simply finding an appropriate tone was a challenge. "Friends, remember we are not here to do politics," he said in July at a Conservative Calgary Stampede breakfast. "Sure, we do politics. But that's the instrument—it's not the music. Our party is called to a great purpose. Our mission is to preserve and promote the future of our great nation and its people in a time of extraordinary, global change." New forces were rising in the world, he said. "Some we will be pleased to work with. Some we must resist." In a way he was echoing his Civitas speech, more than a decade earlier, in which he had argued that conservatism had been the West's staunchest defender against evil and decadence for centuries.

But then came this odd bit, which he'd first uttered a few weeks earlier in Ottawa. "In a few short years, we will celebrate the 150th anniversary of our united country. If, in fifty more years, we wish our descendants to celebrate Canada's 200th anniversary, then we must be all we can be in the world today, and we must shoulder a bigger load, in a world that will require it of us."

What was with the "if"? Why was a freshly re-elected prime minister calling the country's long-term survival into question? It's possible he meant nothing at all; after I wrote about that line on my blog, Harper stopped using it in his speeches. But at a minimum it suggested Harper was not immune to a common fallacy among the country's national leaders: the tendency to believe the country will fall apart if not handled properly—that is, by the person worrying about the falling apart. In 2010 the Conservatives had, properly, mocked Ignatieff for framing just about every issue as a national-unity issue. Now Harper was ringing the same bells. Sometimes it seems the best guarantee of the nation's survival is the hope that someone will protect it from the careful attention of its leaders.

As the September return of Parliament approached, Harper made a key change to his PMO staff and, as it turned out, kicked off a season of missteps. His latest communications director, Dimitri Soudas, had been with Harper in various capacities since his opposition days in the Canadian Alliance. When Soudas left to move to Toronto, Harper reached out to a near stranger as a replacement: Angelo Persichilli, sixty-three, an amiable veteran Toronto journalist for both English- and Italian-language publications. Persichilli's appointment came straight from the Department of Seemed Like a Good Idea at the Time. His biggest selling point was a stint at Omni TV, a multilingual station serving several of Canada's ethnic communities.

Encouraged by Jason Kenney, Harper's PMO had become increasingly preoccupied with ethnic media. Omni, and the formidable Chinese-language television chain Fairchild, and Punjabi talk radio, and the daily *Sing Tao* and *Ming Pao* newspapers were included in daily media-monitoring reports prepared for the government by public servants. The ethnic news organizations' numbers were robust, and their audiences didn't get much news from other sources. *Star* readers also read the *Globe* or the *Post*, listened to the CBC or to satellite radio, maybe checked out some blogs they liked. *Ming Pao* readers read *Ming Pao*. If they liked what they read about the Harper government, increasingly they voted Conservative. The vote was not monolithic—Liberals and New Democrats still competed for votes among assorted ethnic communities—but the Conservatives were patient and attentive.

In an analysis in *Policy Options* magazine, Harper's former advisor Tom Flanagan had described the increasing prominence of ethnic voters in the Conservative coalition. "In the Greater Toronto Area, once the Liberal equivalent of the Tory Fortress Alberta, the Conservatives won 30 of 45 seats" in the 2011 election, Flanagan wrote, "including many in areas such as Brampton that are heavily ethnic." That was the key to Harper's majority, because the Conservatives actually lost seats outside Ontario. In fact, Flanagan wrote, "The Conservatives would still have a majority in 2011 even if they had won no seats at all in Quebec."

Flanagan's thesis was provocative and intriguing. A decade earlier, he and Harper had argued that a new Conservative coalition must appeal to "three sisters": Prairie Reform conservatism; the Toryism of Ontario and the Atlantic provinces; and a nationalist *bleu* conservatism in Quebec. Harper had done better at producing that alliance in a shorter time than either of them had expected. But with hindsight, Flanagan was starting to believe it was possible to switch the Quebec sister for a new and more faithful coalition partner.

"Francophone nationalists always present a problem, even when they can be brought to offer support to the Conservatives," he wrote. "They tend to have an instrumental orientation toward the federal government, seeing it primarily as a source of benefits for Quebec. This raises resistance among other Conservatives, who fear they will have to pay for these benefits to Quebec." And really, why bother? "By comparison, the support of ethnic voters in Toronto and other metropolitan areas seems more likely to be stable, precisely because the Conservatives have attracted those ethnic voters who were already most like themselves in terms of demographics and politics."

So this was the strategy Persichilli represented. Unfortunately, he made it too obvious. Harper's new spokesman was impeccably bilingual: English and Italian. He spoke no French. And he was only the first of a succession of high-level appointments that seemed to ignore the concerns of francophones inside Quebec and across Canada. On October 17, Harper appointed two new justices to the Supreme Court, both from Ontario. One, Michael Moldaver, spoke no French. At the end of October the government announced that Michael Ferguson would replace the redoubtable Sheila Fraser as auditor general. But even though the job description for the post stipulated that proficiency in English and French was a requirement, Ferguson spoke no French. Taken together, the three appointments seemed like a calculated snub. "Le bilinguisme? So What?" was the headline in *Le Devoir*. Harper might as well have kept the $2.2-billion payment to Charest's government for tax harmonization for all the goodwill that remained in Quebec after the trio of appointments.

Did it matter? Flanagan said Harper didn't need Quebec. But another veteran Harper advisor disagreed in an interview with me. "Quebec is still seventy-five, soon to be seventy-eight, seats. And lots of things can go wrong elsewhere [in future elections]. So don't think you can construct a secure majority and forget Quebec." But beyond the numbers, this person said, "no prime minister ever lets the allure of Quebec and national reconciliation and national-unity issues get far from their mind. Even a redneck, recovering libertarian from Calgary. Nobody gets that far in Canadian politics without the allure of Quebec being a constant presence."

Despite these moves, Harper continued, in other ways, to show un-requited interest in Quebec. He appointed André Bachand, a former Progressive Conservative MP who had left politics in 2004 declaring that Harper had "the charisma of a picnic table," as a senior Quebec advisor in the PMO. Harper visited Quebec for public events at least once a month. They were written into his schedule—rendezvous he never missed—but the regular visits went unnoticed by reporters and did nothing to help the Conservatives' poll standings in Quebec. The notion that Harper had not written Quebec off had its own disquieting corollary. He seemed to be trying, but trying was doing him little good. He kept undermining his own efforts with countervailing slights. He kept losing the tune.

Harper's efforts with the conservative "sister" he knew best, Western Reform populism, went better. Here he knew the tune as well as if the Beatles had written it. At the end of September 2011, Rob Nicholson, the justice minister, tabled Bill C-10, which bundled together nine tough-on-crime measures the Conservatives had not yet managed to pass before the bills had died on the order paper, victims of assorted previous elections and prorogations. These included mandatory minimum jail terms for drug- and sex-related offences, longer sentences, delay or elimination of pardon eligibility, and more. Tough-on-crime measures were a perennial for this government, and while criminologists worried that such changes would end hope of rehabilitation and produce a hardened criminal under-class, the stance was popular with voters.

Passing this latest bill had been an election commitment for the Conservatives. Their next three moves were also designed to reward the party's voter base. On October 18, Gerry Ritz, the agriculture minister, introduced a bill to end the Canadian Wheat Board monopoly. A week later Vic Toews, the minister of public safety, introduced a bill to end the national long-gun registry. In the 1990s, when Reform was the dominant party in Western Canada, you used to be able to find a bumper sticker on Alberta cars with a great big "NO" on it. Beside the big word were little words explaining what the driver was against:

- Kyoto
- Wheat Board
- Gun Registry

On December 11, Harper completed the bumper-sticker trifecta. "We are invoking Canada's legal right to formally withdraw from Kyoto," Peter Kent, Harper's latest environment minister, told reporters in the foyer outside the House of Commons. "This decision formalizes what we've said since 2006: that we will not implement the Kyoto Protocol." In combination with the measures on the Wheat Board and the long-gun registry, abandoning Kyoto durably marked Harper as a man who would at least sometimes deliver the kind of government Albertans, in particular, had longed for: laissez-faire, less interventionist, willing to scrap programs that had seemed designed in Ottawa to penalize the rural and resource-producing regions of the country for doing what came naturally. "As long as Mr. Harper's in charge," Kevin Libin wrote in the *National Post*, "the Conservatives will continue to be animated by the alienated spirit of the West, ever suspicious of the potential excesses of federal power." (In the years ahead the Conservatives would sometimes seem to be on the ropes, their popularity finally in danger of running out. Harper's opponents could be certain that whenever an election came, Conservatives would remind every riding in the Prairie West that it was Harper who had finally buried the bumper-sticker Liberal demons of the 1990s—and only Harper who could ensure those demons would not rise again.)

The decision to get out of Kyoto was deeply embarrassing to Canadians who cared about government taking a role in controlling greenhouse gas emissions. But it came as no surprise. From the accord's first days, the Liberals had been more eager to advertise their fondness for the notion of a global pact to reduce carbon emissions than to do anything to meet the onerous target Jean Chrétien had volunteered to meet. Since his election Harper had continued to do nearly nothing to reduce carbon emissions, while accusing the Liberals of the past for doing less and the Liberals across the aisle for wanting to do more. In 2007 the government's own National Round Table on the Environment and the Economy had predicted that the Conservatives' policies on carbon emissions would "leave Canada in non-compliance" with Kyoto. And 2007, when John Baird was the environment minister and the Conservatives were shielding themselves against Stéphane Dion, was the high-water mark of Harper's pretend enthusiasm for the environment. Since then, Dion had lost and gone away, Barack Obama had proven easy to distract from environmental issues, and economic uncertainty had pushed the environment far down on the list of Canadians' preoccupations. Affecting a blasé attitude toward greenhouse gas emissions seemed a cost-free position to Harper. And then the bill came due.

————

"I support the State Department's announcement today regarding the need to seek additional information about the Keystone XL Pipeline proposal," Barack Obama said in a White House news release on November 10, 2011. "We should take the time to ensure that all questions are properly addressed and all the potential impacts are properly understood."

Keystone XL was a peculiar beast. A $5-billion project, the pipeline was designed to carry oil released from the northern Alberta oil sands its full 1,179-mile length, from Hardisty, Alberta, to Steele City, Nebraska, in the American heartland. A second component of the Keystone pipeline network would complete the line all the way to the Gulf Coast. Once completed, the network would move 830,000 barrels of oil-sands oil into the U.S. energy grid every day, a figure that represented about half of U.S. oil imports from the Middle East. That's a lot.

TransCanada, the pipeline's proponent, announced the project in 2008, before Obama was elected president. In October 2010, Obama's secretary of state, Hillary Clinton, said the administration was "inclined" to approve Keystone. This was about the same time the U.S. environmentalist lobby was starting to focus on Keystone for precisely one reason: it needed the administration's approval. Essentially it needed Barack Obama's approval. In the highly decentralized U.S. congressional and regulatory system, there weren't a lot of things the president could control directly, but Keystone XL was one of them. If Obama approved it, the pipeline from Canada would be built. If he refused, it would not.

This rare concentration of authority in the president's office made it worth environmentalists' effort to concentrate a lot of energy on swaying the Keystone decision. The protests intensified. In August 2011, Daryl Hannah, who once played a mermaid in a Ron Howard movie, was arrested in front of the White House for protesting against Keystone. "President Obama's decision on this enormous fossil fuel project will not be a quiet deal with oil industry lobbyists," she wrote in a *Huffington Post* article the same day. "It will be witnessed by millions of voters." In September, nine Nobel peace prize winners, including Desmond Tutu and the Dalai Lama, sent Obama a letter urging him to back off on Keystone.

So Obama did. The delay meant a final decision would come only after the 2012 presidential election. "While we are disappointed with the delay, we remain hopeful the project will be decided on its merits and eventually approved," Harper's spokesman Andrew MacDougall told reporters. (Less than two months after Harper had appointed him as his communications director, Angelo Persichilli was already rarely speaking to reporters. He would resign from the PMO the following spring, pleading inability to keep up with Ottawa workloads.)

MacDougall's comment understated the boss's mood. Harper wasn't disappointed, he was furious. Three days after Obama announced the delay, Harper flew to Hawaii for the Asia-Pacific Economic Cooperation summit, where he chatted with the president at an outdoor picnic table under a beach umbrella. Reporters watching the exchange wrote that the two men looked relaxed and laughed more than once. "The leaders discussed the recent announcement regarding the presidential permit process for the Keystone XL pipeline application," a White House press release said later.

Whatever Obama told Harper, by the time the prime minister got back to Ottawa, he had concluded the United States must no longer be Canada's only important energy export market. The conversation in Hawaii had happened on a Sunday. On Tuesday, at a meeting of cabinet's Priorities and Planning committee in Ottawa, Harper handed out orders to a half-dozen ministers. "It was awesome," someone who was there said later. Energy exports were the government's new top strategic priority, Harper said. Asia was now the most important region to target as an export market, China the most important country. Enbridge's Northern Gateway pipeline to the seaport at Kitimat, B.C.—the most important petroleum export project after Keystone— must get built. Environmental assessment for that project and dozens of others must be streamlined. Reconciliation with Aboriginal groups that could block those pipelines must be fast-tracked. Environmental groups that tried to slow the process down were opponents of Canadian prosperity and must be treated as such.

Some of the decisions Harper announced at that Tuesday morning cabinet committee meeting had roots deeper than annoyance at Keystone's being temporarily thwarted by Obama. Mark Carney, the Bank of Canada governor, had been badgering Harper for months over the global distribution of Canadian trade and investment. Canada was over-invested in the United States and Europe, where there was barely any economic growth at best and looming catastrophe at worst, and under-invested in Asia. Sure, China might be a bubble about to burst. But nobody could be sure, and the cost of staying away from China and missing a continued boom would be higher than the cost of getting in just as a boom ended. Similarly, two of Jim Flaherty's previous budgets had included language about speeding up environmental assessments of resource development projects. In a lot of ways, the angry orders Harper barked to his ministers after the Keystone delay weren't out of character. But they kicked off a long arc of activity, lasting until the spring of 2012, that he would come to regret.

———

Less than two weeks after that cabinet meeting, Harper was in Vancouver for the Grey Cup game. He sat for an interview with a local television station and chatted happily about his love of football. Then he was asked about Enbridge Inc.'s Northern Gateway project. Environmental hearings would soon begin on the project, which aimed to run twin pipelines from Bruderheim, north of Edmonton, across British Columbia to the sea terminal at Kitimat, to put oil-sands bitumen onto Asia-bound tanker ships. Harper's mood darkened.

"I think we'll see significant American interests trying to line up against the Northern Gateway project, precisely because it's not in the interests of the United States. It's in the interests of Canada," he said. "They'll funnel money through environmental groups and others in order to try to slow it down. But, as I say, we'll make sure that the best interests of Canada are protected."

With that statement, he had just accused the Canadian environmental movement of being a front for U.S. energy interests. There was, depending how far you cared to stretch it, some truth in that notion. Certainly, Canadian environmentalist organizations had been getting money from abroad. As Gary Mason had written in the *Globe and Mail* that September: "In 2006, for instance, the Rockefeller Brothers Fund of New York paid a couple of Canadian environmental groups a total of $200,000 to 'prevent the development of a tanker port and pipeline that would endanger the Great Bear Rainforest.' The Brainerd Foundation of Washington State gave money to the B.C.-based Dogwood Initiative to 'help grow public opposition to counter the Enbridge pipeline construction.'"

So, were the Brainerd Foundation and the Rockefeller Brothers Fund fronts for ExxonMobil, kneecapping Enbridge to keep Canada on top? That was where credulity came in for some stretching. The Brainerd Foundation was endowed with nothing more nefarious than software money—for desktop publishing, to be specific. And while it's true that the Rockefeller family got rich in oil, that happened before Alberta joined Confederation. The Rockefeller Foundation, founded in 1913, helped create the Johns Hopkins School of Public Health and (in another of the foundation's periodic fits of cross-border meddling) the Montreal Neurological Institute. Tying these activities into a global theory of U.S. oil-industry hegemony would take some doing, but by the end of 2011 Harper was in a mood to try.

His mood was, in general, expansive. Lisa LaFlamme from CTV sat him down in December and asked how he liked having a parliamentary majority. "I want to make sure that we use it," he said. "You know, I've seen too many majority governments—the bureaucracy talks them into going to sleep for three years, and then they all of a sudden realize they're close to an election." For a prime minister usually intent on under-promising, this was cheeky. The majority governments he had seen in his life included Trudeau's, Mulroney's and Chrétien's. Harper was implicitly dismissing them as nappers. What on earth did he have in mind to top them?

What, indeed. Harper's other big year-end interview was with the Chinese-language Fairchild chain of stations. "What can we do to make some major transformations so we can bring more capital into this country?" he asked himself. He promised "major reforms" in "a whole range of areas" to "secure the sustainability of our key programs . . . for a generation to come." He called Obama's indecision on Keystone "a wake-up call . . . that we've simply got to broaden our markets."

———

By now Harper was evolving a two-track strategy. One track led to these as-yet-undefined "major transformations" in the economy. The other consisted of badmouthing opponents of resource development. Each track was receiving roughly equal attention from the Langevin Block minions. On January 9, an open letter was released over the signature of Joe Oliver, the natural resources minister. Oliver, an investment banker who had knocked off the veteran Liberal Joe Volpe in the Toronto riding of Eglinton-Lawrence to join the rookie Conservative class of 2011, had made barely a peep until now. Suddenly he experienced a major transformation of his own, revealing fangs.

"We must expand our trade with the fast growing Asian economies," Oliver wrote. "Unfortunately, there are environmental and other radical groups that would seek to block this opportunity to diversify our trade. Their goal is to stop any major project no matter what the cost to Canadian families in lost jobs and economic growth." These groups wanted to "hijack our regulatory system" in the service of a "radical political agenda" so they could "kill good projects." Using "funding from foreign special-interest groups," they "attract jet-setting celebrities with some of the largest carbon footprints in the world to lecture Canadians not to develop our natural resources." And if all their other tactics didn't work, the radical groups would twirl their moustaches and "take a quintessential American approach: sue everyone." Repairing this state of affairs, the minister wrote, "is an urgent matter of Canada's national interest."

When Oliver's letter appeared, I assumed he was the front for a piece of writing concocted by Harper's staff, if not by Harper himself. Conservatives later told me it did in fact contain Oliver's own writing as well as that of PMO worker bees, and that it reflected Oliver's preferred mode of operation, which was full-tilt, head down and roaring like a bull elk in full rut. In any case, Harper surely knew about the letter and approved it. Two days after the letter's release, Harper welcomed the Chinese ambassador, Zhang Junsai, to his office to announce that he would visit China in February. Oliver's language about jet-set celebrities with their fancy lawsuits and their ripped jeans was so eye-catching it might lead a reader to overlook the significance of the letter's last line. Governments do not lightly identify something as an urgent matter in the national interest. In less blessed lands, that kind of freighted language sometimes precedes a declaration of war.

———

Oliver's letter had two effects, one surely intended, the other perhaps accidental. It demonstrated that nothing was more important for the government than speeding the approval process for natural-resources projects, even if it meant rolling right over any group that tried to slow those projects down. And it implied that, if Harper did not succeed in getting that oil to market quickly, he would have failed to safeguard the national interest according to a yardstick of his own choosing.

It quickly became apparent that Oliver's salvo was only part of an effort that extended across government and even outside. On January 2 a new website was launched called ourdecision.ca. "Countless . . . foreigners from Europe to South America and a long list of foreign-funded lobbyists," it said, were "hiring front groups to swamp the hearings to block the Northern Gateway pipeline project." The site included a "donate" button so right-thinking Canadians could help "ban foreigners and their local puppets from appearing before the pipeline review panel."

Ourdecision.ca was built and maintained by Go NewClear Productions, a small ad firm run by a quiet young man named Hamish Marshall, who used to work in a junior capacity in Harper's PMO. Go NewClear ran websites for several Conservative MPs. Its own website proclaimed the firm was "experienced in the development of both conventional and unconventional online weaponry" to "blow away your competition." Its ads had aired "in both Canada and Australia," and it had deployed its "expertise on social networking in Russia and Iran."

Marshall's wife was Kathryn Marshall, a law student and former political staffer who was working as a spokesperson for Ethical Oil, an organization launched in defence of an argument: that whatever the flaws of northern Alberta's oil industry, the region was a bastion of democracy and environmental responsibility compared with petro-states such as Iran and Venezuela. Hamish Marshall ran the Ethical Oil website along with Our Decision and the others. The idea of "ethical oil" began life as a book of the same name by Ezra Levant, the Calgary lawyer and former Reform political staffer who would go on to host a nightly program on Sun News Channel. Levant's cheeky argument—that the oil sands had nothing to apologize for and should instead inspire Canadian pride—quickly found sympathetic ears in Harper's government. Four months after the book was published in September 2010, Harper's environment minister, Peter Kent, started using the term "ethical oil" to describe Canada's petroleum exports.

But Ethical Oil might have been nothing more than a book if Levant hadn't won the National Business Book Award just days after Harper won the 2011 election. The award was bestowed by a jury that included CBC News chief correspondent Peter Mansbridge, and it came with a $20,000 prize. That money caught the eye of Alykhan Velshi, a Toronto-born lawyer in his twenties who was coming off four years as a spokesperson for Immigration Minister Jason Kenney and two months as a strategist in the Conservatives' election war room. Velshi believed he'd had enough of government, though not of politics. He told Levant that, in return for the $20,000 prize money, he would launch an Ethical Oil blog that would form the basis for a political movement.

Since the beginning of 2012, thanks to donations from individuals and organizations that Ethical Oil, because it's not a charity, has never been required by law to divulge, the organization has run radio and newspaper ad campaigns and spawned the Our Decision sub-campaign. As for Velshi, he had handed day-to-day operation of the organization off to Kathryn Marshall because he was back in government—in Harper's PMO as director of planning, a rough equivalent to the job Patrick Muttart had in the government's early days.

None of the above describes a conspiracy. It was more like a community of interest and style, a network of like-minded friends and associates extending through the government and beyond, defined by a few ideas: that Canada's resource wealth was a source of its prosperity; that the environmental movement, to the extent it opposed the exploitation of the oil sands, had declared itself an enemy of Canada; and that there was no need to be genteel in fighting back. And if there was something triumphalist and a bit over-the-top about it all, well, it was the times.

Harper had a lot of justification for feeling that the resource-producing West was rising in Canada and could not be flouted. In October 2011, his minister for democratic reform, Tim Uppal, had revealed plans for an expanded House of Commons to reflect regions of growing population. Ontario would get fifteen more seats, Alberta and British Columbia six each, Quebec three. That last number, decided by Harper himself, was a fig leaf designed to cover a substantial net shift of political clout to the West.

By some estimates, the Conservatives should expect to win twenty-four of those thirty new seats if the distribution of votes among parties in 2015 resembles that in 2011. That shift in political power followed a shift in populations: in February 2012 Statistics Canada released figures showing that, between 2006 and 2011, the five slowest-growing provincial populations had been those of Quebec and the Atlantic provinces. The fastest population growth had been in Alberta, British Columbia and Saskatchewan. The populations, in turn, were following money. Some estimates put the total value of Canada's natural resource reserves at $1.16 trillion, and of that, the value of the bitumen in the oil sands alone accounted for nearly half: $460 billion.

And if the Yankees were dumb enough to turn up their pointy Harvard noses at that kind of bounty, well, you know what? To hell with them. Over the ocean was a new Eldorado, a land where business was business and goods found a buyer. In 2008 Harper had skipped the opening ceremonies of the Beijing Olympics. He had put up with no end of grief from Grits who lectured him on letting the world pass him buy. Michael Ignatieff had used Harper's failure to visit India and China to chide him on his inability to grasp the greatness of great nations, until Harper had finally thrown up his hands and visited China just to get there before Ignatieff could. But that 2009 trip was nearly a guerrilla mission—just Harper and Laureen and six others.

But at some point Harper realized it made less and less sense for him to hold China's Communist ideology and human rights record against it; the country's economic growth had become the kind of phenomenon you'd have to be blind to miss. Canadian pork exports to China had tripled in one year, from 2010 to 2011. Lumber exports doubled in 2010, then doubled again in 2011 to $1.5 billion. Chinese investment in Canada had in turn tripled between 2008 and 2010, to $14.1 billion. Harper's central bank governor was telling him China was the future. The oil patch was telling him to get over his China aversion. Chinese communities in British Columbia and Ontario were key growth markets for the Conservative vote, and while their relationship with the Beijing regime was sometimes complicated, none of those voters wanted Harper to shun China. And now Barack Obama was letting Daryl Hannah tell him how to run oil imports. So Harper landed in Beijing on February 7, 2012, with Laureen, Joe Oliver, thirty business executives, two dozen members of Canada's Chinese community, and a full contingent of scribes from the press gallery.

During several days of visits in three cities, Harper presided over mass signings of business agreements, business round tables, and a steady stream of photo ops. He peered at a Giant panda bear cub sitting on Laureen's lap in Chongqing while camera shutters clicked madly, before announcing that two of the bamboo-munching superstars would soon take up residence at Canadian zoos. "He has come at an important moment when both sides feel an increasing need to bring bilateral ties to a new level," the semi-official *China Daily* wrote in a warm editorial.

But when Harper returned to Canada, evidence began to accumulate that the world does not change just because a prime minister decides he has come up with an agenda.

In a speech to the Calgary Chamber of Commerce on March 1, Shawn Atleo, the soft-spoken grand chief of the Assembly of First Nations, reminded everyone that it was a bad idea to take Canada's Aboriginal populations for granted. "The pattern of unilateral application of business practices and of laws and regulation in our territories is a practice that has to stop," he said.

In June the message would be echoed by Jim Prentice, Harper's former environment minister. "The absence of private and public sector leadership," Prentice wrote in the *Vancouver Sun*, is "a serious impediment" to getting Alberta bitumen to market. And where did most of the blame lie? Prentice was not coy. "The constitutional obligation to consult with first nations is not a corporate obligation. It is the federal government's responsibility." Same with "the obligation to define an ocean management regime for terminals and shipping on the west coast. . . . It is the federal government's responsibility."

Atleo and Prentice were pleading for a simple recognition that varying points of view were legitimate and that some measure of agreement among diverse interests was not merely a nice idea, it was a prerequisite for getting anything done. "These issues cannot be resolved by regulatory fiat," Prentice wrote. "They require negotiation. The real risk is not regulatory rejection but regulatory approval, undermined by subsequent legal challenges and the absence of 'social license' to operate." Translation: Enbridge might get the pipeline approved by a process jiggered to suit Harper's idea of fair play. But frustrated citizens could still bury it under a mountain of lawsuits.

Now if there is a lesson Stephen Harper would not normally be expected to forget, it's the value of moderation. He had built the body of a winner around his radical's heart by feasting, for a decade, on a strict diet of half loaves. He had reached out to Joe Clark in his first weeks as Canadian Alliance leader and did not give up, his associates say, until many months after the 2006 election victory, despite his personal low regard for Clark and the way Clark always took pains to make it clear that the sentiment was mutual. He had made peace with Quebec nationalists and still maintained the courtship of Quebec long after it had stopped paying electoral dividends. He had taken over the operation of regional development agencies he used to mock, blocked foreign investment he had urged earlier governments to welcome, embraced official bilingualism and, with Barack Obama, bailed out General Motors.

And if any man in Canada knew that the Ezra Levant playbook of derision and polarization is of limited use to anyone who actually wants to win something, it should have been Harper. When he returned to lead the Alliance in 2002 after five years away from Parliament, Harper needed a seat to represent in Parliament. Preston Manning's old Calgary Southwest riding looked pretty good. Unfortunately, as Flanagan wrote in his book *Harper's Team*, Levant had already wrapped up the Alliance nomination there before Manning's resignation as an MP took effect. Soon Levant "was putting up billboards and running radio and TV ads slagging Joe Clark as 'Kyoto Joe,'" Flanagan wrote. "We grew increasingly concerned. . . . Polls suggested that Ezra's takeover of Calgary Southwest, far from securing the riding as an Alliance bastion, had put it up for grabs to the PCs and Liberals." It took a lot of pressure from a lot of people to get Levant to step aside. In the end, the weeks of spectacle had a predictable effect: Harper was elected with 71.7 percent of the vote, a "minimally satisfactory" result given that no Liberal or Progressive Conservative had run against him.

But something made Harper decide to spend the fall and winter of 2011–12 aligning his analysis and rhetoric with those of Levant's favourite advocacy organization. More likely a bunch of somethings:

Pride: he had built the Conservative Party and grown it, through four elections, to a majority that must have felt like vindication.

Embarrassment: only six months after that election, he had begun to provoke questions about whether he actually had anything in particular he wanted to do with that historic mandate.

Anger: Barack Obama, of all people, had delayed a pipeline, the sort of policy decision Harper had viewed as "almost designed to do damage to Western Canada" when the NDP and Liberals had proposed that sort of thing. (Recall that Harper receives much of his U.S. news from Fox, which is almost never inclined to give the president much benefit of the doubt.)

And finally, perhaps, fatigue: He had been so nice to everyone for so long. Sure, he had called Stéphane Dion a terrorist sympathizer, questioned Michael Ignatieff's loyalty to Canada, fired the nuclear safety lady for worrying about nuclear safety, and stacked the Rights and Democracy board with clowns from a Shriner circus, but by and large he had put the long game ahead of the instinct to scratch whatever itched. But come on, after a while a lion's got to roar. The Obama snub had made the noise burst forth from the back of Harper's throat.

But in making oil-sands oil a big issue and declaring his willingness to fight a big fight, Harper had made precisely the same mistake he had privately claimed Mulroney had made with Meech and free trade. He had led with his chin. He had told his opponents what to oppose. He had forced people who would not normally have expressed any position to get off the fence. One of those people was the premier of British Columbia. By midsummer 2012 Christy Clark had announced a set of financial and environmental conditions for accepting Northern Gateway that made the pipeline unlikely ever to get built. And no wonder: an Abacus poll in late August showed that British Columbians strongly opposed Gateway, just as Albertans strongly supported it. The notion of a shift in power or clout to "the West" is coherent only if the West is. On pipelines, Abacus found the residents of the two largest Western provinces "more divided than ever before."

Much later, a senior Harper advisor admitted there had been "a lot of overreach" in the approach to pipeline politics at the end of 2011 and the beginning of 2012. "We knew that these hearings were going to take place and that they would be ugly," the advisor said, referring to

Enbridge's Gateway hearings. "We knew environmentalists were going to take over. We needed a message that would help pre-but—rebut them prematurely—before they happened." Tying the environmental movement to foreign funding, as Joe Oliver's open letter had done, "seemed like a logical argument that we could make" but "with the benefit of hindsight it was a bad move." Why? "It is a problem when the PM is seen as vindictive. This is not something we seek to cultivate. And I would say the attack on environmentalists, to the extent that we feel it was unwise, was unwise because it shows that we're vindictive towards our political opponents, we have a sort of take-no-prisoners approach."

The government began throttling its rhetoric. The budget Flaherty tabled on March 29, 2012, was a much more low-key document than the broadsides from Oliver. "The reforms we present today are substantial, responsible, and necessary," Flaherty said. "We will maintain our consistent, pragmatic, and responsible approach to the economy." The word "transformation" did not appear in the budget document. This was no accident. "Some of the stuff that's been out there about 'major transformations' may have been a bit off," a Flaherty advisor told me in the hours before the minister tabled the budget.

But the softening was, in large measure, only rhetorical. Flaherty's 2012 budget was one of the most intensely political he had ever delivered; the most striking language was buried at the end of chapter 4, "Sustainable Social Programs and a Secure Retirement." A PMO staffer was on hand at the budget lockdown to point out the juicy passages. "Recently, concerns have been raised that some charities may not be respecting the rules regarding political activities," the budget document said. "There have also been calls for greater public transparency related to the political activities of charities, including the extent to which they may be funded by foreign sources." The budget announced government plans to impose a legal requirement that charities disclose their foreign funding for political activities.

There was more. When John Baird was environment minister and the Conservatives were running their green shield play, Baird had announced the appointment of David McLaughlin as president of the National Round Table on the Environment and the Economy. McLaughlin had been Kim Campbell's chief of staff during her heady summer stint as prime minister in 1993. He would "give excellent leadership to the Round Table," Baird had said in 2007. Now, it turned out McLaughlin had also provided its last leadership. The budget shut down the NRTEE. "A mature and expanded community of environmental policy stakeholders" would advise the government, the budget announced. Like who? Like the environmental NGOs the budget now threatened with audits.

At least the government offered an explanation for the NRTEE closure. Not so for the First Nations Statistical Institute, which was essentially Statistics Canada, ahem, for Aboriginal populations. A chart in Annex 1 showed the FNSI would have its budget cut by $5 million in 2013–14. I asked a Treasury Board guy at the budget lock-up how much the institute's current budget was. He looked in the Estimates. "Five million dollars," he said. Buh-bye.

Near the beginning of this book, I chronicled the opposition's coordinated effort to block the nomination of Calgary oilman Gwyn Morgan as head of a Public Appointments Commission. Harper promptly said he would not propose another nominee, and that "of course" he could only proceed with the review committee after he won a majority. Now he had his majority. The budget shut down the appointments commission secretariat. Why was the government doing the opposite of what Harper had said it would do in 2006? "The Government has significantly strengthened the rigour and accessibility of the public appointments system over the past five years," the budget said with an admirably straight face.

Finally, the budget hinted at further changes to the balance between the environment and business considerations. It would be autumn before the significance of those hints became clear. That's when Flaherty tabled his second budget implementation bill of the year, a 457-page behemoth that included amendments to the Indian Act, the Fisheries Act, the Canadian Environmental Assessment Act and the Navigable Waters Protection Act. That last change gives some of the flavour of the bill, because it changed the act's name to the Navigation Protection Act. The law was originally designed to protect water against boats. Now it would protect boats against water.

Within weeks of the tabling of the Budget Implementation Act, a small group of Aboriginal women launched a series of protests that would spread across the country before Christmas. Dubbed "Idle No More," the protests would last for weeks and serve as vivid notice of the strife Jim Prentice had described when he warned against "the absence of 'social license.'" Harper had vowed to be busier than any majority prime minister in his lifetime. Within months of making that promise, he was indeed very busy, because he was dealing with a crisis in Canada–U.S. relations, a crisis in Aboriginal relations, a divided West, and blocked paths west and south for oil-sands bitumen. At the end of April 2012, Tom Mulcair became leader of the NDP opposition. The strange interlude during which Harper faced no real opposition had come to an end. And not a moment too soon. He had spent months slapping himself silly.

ELEVEN

SELF-UNMADE MAN?

In September 2012, the Information Commissioner, Suzanne Legault, released an unusually optimistic report to Parliament. "We also saw, for the first time in 10 years, a reversal of the declining performance of federal institutions in their fulfillment of their obligations under the Access to Information Act," she wrote. The decline in open government that began under Jean Chrétien and had continued through Paul Martin's brief tenure and on throughout Stephen Harper's years had now been partly compensated by a modest improvement. And although "this improvement was only slight," and the access to information system remained "fragile," Legault thought it was "nonetheless noteworthy."

Five months later she announced that the thaw in the Harper government's information freeze was already over. "We are at a record low in terms of timeliness," she told CBC Radio. "Requests for extensions [by departments] are at a record high." The Department of National Defence, in one case, had asked for a 1,110-day extension. Stephen Harper was continuing to put as much space as he could between what he was doing and what he was willing to let Canadians know about it.

Still, diligent reporters in Ottawa and elsewhere kept nagging. In most cases delays eventually came to an end. And so it came to light, one morning in April 2012, that Bev Oda was finicky about hotels.

Canadian Press reporter Jennifer Ditchburn had requested Oda's expense account for a June 2011 trip to London to attend a conference on immunization. Because Bill Gates and other high-flying types were on hand for the meeting, the venue was the lovely Grange St. Paul's hotel. Oda took one look at the dump and told her staff she needed to decamp to something more suited to her tastes. Off she went in her chauffeured luxury car to the Savoy, where rooms were more than double the rate at the Grange and where, cementing her fate, the minister from a resolutely Tim Hortons–branded government slaked her thirst—the night before discussing policies for alleviating the consequences of grinding poverty—with a yummy $16 glass of room-service orange juice.

The government's immediate response to the ensuing five-alarm shitstorm was to see how much money it would take to make the story go away. Justin Broekema, Oda's press spokesperson, said the minister had "personally paid the portion of the expenses in question." It took only a few hours' pushing for this line of defence to collapse: Oda's staff admitted, upon reflection, that she had paid, not a few days after the conference in 2011, but in a panic when the story was about to splatter across the Internet in 2012. The next line of defence was a rare show of contrition from a member of this government in the House of Commons, where Oda apologized "unreservedly" for her poor judgment.

Of course she had apologized only when caught, not because her conscience held her to a high standard. Opposition MPs roared: Where was Oda's pink slip? Commentators joined the chorus, including some with impeccable conservative credentials. "Whatever one thinks of the

Harper government, it's pretty hard to see why Bev Oda remains a cabinet minister," wrote *Toronto Sun* co-founder Peter Worthington. Worthington did pause to note that Oda's background before politics was in media: TVOntario first, then City-TV, then Global, and finally at CTV. "Perhaps all that time working for rich TV outlets conditioned her to spend her employers' money without accountability," he wrote. "Maybe such habits were hard to break." At any rate, Oda had little to show for her time in government except for providing "a horrid example to the rest of the country of politicians feeding at the trough, then saying 'sorry' when they're caught."

Two days after her apology, Oda's office said she had repaid "all incremental costs . . . including the car service in London." She just gave and gave. But . . . when had she paid for that car? Minutes before the release came out. So, like, two days after she first apologized for the extravagance. Three days after she had paid the difference between the Grange rooms and the Savoy.

In the Commons, Harper proclaimed his support for Oda. Perhaps not as robustly as on the many previous occasions when he had needed to do the same. "The minister has apologized and has taken appropriate measures," he said wearily in Question Period. This was after she had repaid the hotel bill but before she repaid the car bill. But his public show of support masked a private decision. The pink slip everyone was clamouring for was on its way, and would arrive rather more rapidly than the access-to-information memos that had made it necessary. On July 4, Oda announced she was retiring from politics. Julian Fantino, the former head of Ontario's provincial police and a relative newcomer to Ottawa, would replace her. Andrew MacDougall, Harper's latest communications director, tweeted a categorical announcement: "There will be no other cabinet shuffles. *Il n'y aura aucun autre remaniement ministériel.*"

———

At the time, Oda's tale seemed anecdotal, the story of a Conservative who had forgotten—apparently from the outset, for she had a long history of getting into trouble for salty expense bills—that her party's appeal was supposed to be populist, not plutocratic. But the government's response to the mess became characteristic. It foreshadowed Harper's response to later, bigger trouble. And it came during a week of nasty news of various sorts that would characterize much of Harper's star-crossed majority mandate.

The indiscretion that kicked off Oda-gate was simple human nature. Bev Oda liked her creature comforts was all. It was perhaps worth noting, as Worthington had, that she developed her lifestyle habits in the field of broadcasting at a time when quasi-monopoly broadcast licences and copious ad revenues meant nobody was looking too closely at expense accounts.

The next step, despite the government's best efforts to stem the flow of information, was that the story broke in public. As soon as it became clear the news was going to get out, a two-track response kicked in. First, minimize the problem. This could include an acknowledgement that, while there may once have been a problem, it was already fixed. In other situations the government would insist that, whatever the nature of today's unpleasantness, it was nothing compared with the mess the Liberals made; messes they would make again, too, if Canadians recklessly restored them or their ilk (wary glance at the NDP benches) to power.

Even while minimizing the problem, Harper, or his political machine, would also seek to make the problem go away. Often the erasure would be attempted through the judicious application of money. Oda had spent too much taxpayer money too sloppily? Then, she would be made to pay it back, and if the problem kept growing, she would be made to pay again.

Even the delay between the damage control and the ejection of the offending team player was characteristic of the Harper damage-control style. Like many political leaders, Harper was rarely eager to let anyone go, because each time he did, the opposition parties ignored the victory and simply started clamouring for the next sacrifice. But more than once Harper had marked a Conservative for demotion or dismissal even while defending the person in public. He had backed Gordon O'Connor, Helena Guergis and, of course, Oda herself for a long time before removing them.

No part of this pattern was unique to Harper. But he was ruthless in damage control, as in much else, because he was convinced that an unscheduled bit of trouble, a careless remark or an unexpected move could threaten his hold on power. Such things had given him serious trouble before. He lost the 2004 election because a few of his candidates said things that didn't square with his attempts to present a moderate face for the Conservatives. He had nearly blown an easy win in 2008 because he had let overconfidence lull him into discussing excellent buying opportunities. When his opponents or the press gallery called him ruthless, he could hardly believe what he was hearing. If he had not been ruthless, he would never have survived this long. Usually he believed that, if anything, he was too soft.

He had displayed many of his damage-control techniques during an odd episode in 2006, little noticed at the time but significant in hindsight— after Nigel Wright's payment to Senator Mike Duffy came to light. In the early days of the campaign for the 2006 election, an Ottawa lawyer named Alan Riddell stepped aside as the Conservatives' nominated candidate in the Ottawa South riding. The party wanted to run Alan Cutler, a public servant who had blown the whistle on the Liberal sponsorship scandal, in the riding. In addition, Riddell had run for the Conservatives in 2004 and lost after the *Ottawa Sun* ran an embarrassing story about a prank Riddell had played in his student days. After he lost, the *Sun* retracted its story, but the damage was done. So Riddell dropped out, the party thanked him for his efforts, and Cutler became the candidate.

Then a CBC reporter asked Riddell why he had pulled out of the race so late. Riddell replied that the party had made it easy by agreeing to cover his campaign expenses. He put the cost at about $50,000. Reporters following Harper on the campaign trail promptly asked him about the deal with Riddell. "In fact there is no agreement and he hasn't been paid anything," Harper said. When asked again later that day—it was the end of 2005 and Harper was still an underdog scrumming twice a day—he repeated himself: "The party does not have an agreement to pay Mr. Riddell these expenses, and Mr. Riddell has not been paid anything to date."

Unfortunately for Harper's version of events, there was an e-mail trail, which somebody on Riddell's campaign promptly leaked to reporters. Riddell wound up suing the party for his expenses, and on January 11, 2007, Judge Denis Power of Ontario Superior Court ruled "that Alan M. Riddell and the Conservative Party of Canada entered into a binding agreement on November 25, 2005." He could hardly reach any other conclusion. Among the pieces of evidence produced in court was a November 25 e-mail from Mike Donison, the Conservatives' former director general, to Riddell's lawyer. The e-mail read, in part: "There is now a binding agreement between Mr. Riddell and the Conservative Party of Canada."

Donison and Don Plett, the party's former president, testified that Riddell had cancelled the agreement by speaking about it to reporters. What they couldn't do was produce any written evidence of such a confidentiality clause. How much did Harper know about the deal? Apparently a fair bit. In testimony at trial, Plett said he and other party officials had met with Riddell on November 21. "We assure[d] Mr. Riddell that we were representatives there representing, among others, the Prime Minister, at that time the Leader of the Opposition," Plett testified. "Ian Brodie made it quite clear that's who he was representing when he came. We discussed some financial compensation, paying Alan Riddell's nomination expenses." The evidence also included an earlier e-mail from Donison to Ray Novak, Harper's closest advisor and future chief of staff, informing him of the status of negotiations. ("He truly is an idiot," Donison writes in that e-mail, referring to Riddell.) So it was clear there was a "binding agreement." It was clear Harper was in the loop. And it was clear that, even after his party's private business became public, Harper preferred to claim there was no such business. This story is worth repeating because it demonstrates again two of Harper's work habits: a preoccupation with confidentiality and a willingness to use money to make a problem go away.

———

So in 2012, when word of Oda's spending habits got out and the attempts to use her money to make the problem go away didn't work, the resulting lousy headlines put Harper in a vile mood. Oda wasn't even his only problem. He had come to realize he was being seriously pressed, for the first time he could remember, by an effective opposition leader. Thomas Mulcair had spent a dozen years in Quebec's National Assembly, most of them in opposition, before he jumped to federal politics. The second-largest province's legislature has its quirks but it's a serious place. Debate is intense. The stakes are always high, because the fate of at least one nation is in play, depending on how you count these things. Quebec politicians learn how to parse opponents' words, and expect their own will be examined as closely. In that pressure cooker, Mulcair had spent years honing a low-key, persistent line of attack.

"They're very good at defining their adversaries," Mulcair had said after his first Question Period in late March. "We're going to start to define them." He had a little lectern on his desk, from which he would read a simple question in a steady voice. Other New Democrats soon followed suit. The level of histrionics plummeted, at least on the opposition side of the House. There was strategy in this. The Conservatives had long preferred the NDP to the Liberals because they feared the Liberals, the party's strong brand, its long record of winning. They figured New Democrats should be easy to beat: to Conservatives, the party simply looked crazy. The Conservative Party greeted Mulcair's arrival in Jack Layton's old job at first not with attack ads against Mulcair, but with a website designed to portray the NDP caucus as a pack of loons. You could click on any member of Mulcair's shadow cabinet and a pop-up window would explain what an extremist flake he or she was. Toronto MP Andrew Cash, who used to sing in a rock band, "supports Occupy Toronto's plans to replace Canada's economic system with radical alternatives," the website said. Quebec's Charmaine Borg "apparently thinks the tax relief offered by our government is a mistake." Sudbury's Glenn Thibeault "cannot be counted on to stand up for his constituents in the face of radical special interests."

But in Question Period the New Democrats were so nice and low-key. It was plainly getting under Harper's skin. A couple of days into the Oda mess, Mulcair asked Harper the kind of flat, uninflected question that was his specialty. "Will he," he asked of Harper, "keep our troops in Afghanistan past 2014? Yes, or no?"

Harper had had just about enough of this . . . this . . . this using Question Period for questions. "Unlike the NDP we are not going to ideologically have a position regardless of circumstances," he said. "The leader of the NDP, in 1939, did not even want to support war against Hitler."

It was not Harper's best line. The current leader of the NDP was born in 1954. The NDP itself was born in 1961. J.S. Woodsworth's pacifism had basically cost him the leadership of the Co-operative Commonwealth Federation in 1939 because his caucus backed the war despite his wishes. "Okay, CCF, same difference," Harper grumbled. "Parties do change their names from time to time."

"I guess we can start talking about Reform Party policies," Mulcair replied.

It was turning into a lousy week.

A few different things were going on here. Harper's minister for helping the world's poor was paying as much for orange juice as the median Afghan earned in two weeks. The crazy opposition kept refusing to act crazy; their stubborn sanity was driving Harper crazy. To top it all off, Harper faced mounting trouble from a most unfamiliar quarter: the Conservative MPs sitting around and behind him.

Stephen Woodworth was the cheerful Conservative MP for Kitchener Centre, a lifelong resident of that Ontario city who had first been elected in 2008. He had a motion before the House calling for a special committee of Parliament to study section 223(1) of the Criminal Code, which defines when a human being becomes a human being for the purpose of criminal law. The answer: "when it has completely pro-ceeded, in a living state, from the body of its mother." Woodworth was pretty clearly picking a fight over the notion that a child is not a human being before it is born. Which was almost the same as saying he wanted Parliament to examine the ethics of abortion.

But Harper had said a hundred times that he didn't want to reopen the abortion debate. "As long as I'm prime minister," he'd said, "we are not reopening the abortion debate." For him the question was nearly life-or-death for the Conservatives: every other party campaigned, every time, on accusations that the Conservatives would take away a woman's right to choose. Harper was damned if he would ever give them a chance to claim they were right. Social conservatives would have to be content with the government's tax benefits for parents, or its tough-on-crime policy, or its strong support for Israel's Likud govern-ment. There were plenty of side doors into social conservatism. Harper kept the front door barred tight. So Woodworth was careful not to say his motion was about abortion. "Don't accept any law that says some human beings are not human beings!" he'd said when he tabled it in February. "It does not matter what result you're trying to achieve with such a misrepresentation or whose philosophy supports such a misrepresentation. History is littered with disastrous examples of laws which pretended some people were not human beings to achieve some desired result or suit someone's philosophy."

Private members' motions are among the lowest priorities in the Commons. Few survive for long; most of the rest pop up at random intervals over months or years, debated for an hour in spring and another in autumn. By the luck of things, Woodworth's motion came up for debate on Thursday, April 26, the fourth day of the week that had seen Bev Oda on every front page and Harper calling the NDP a bastion of support for Hitler. Harper had had plenty of trouble this week without letting his God squad hand the salivating opposition a stick to beat the party with at the next election. He sent his chief government whip, Gordon O'Connor, to shut this Woodworth sideshow down but good.

"The ultimate intention of this motion is to restrict abortions in Canada at some fetal development stage," O'Connor said in the House during debate, stripping away Woodworth's fig leaf. "I cannot understand why those who are adamantly opposed to abortion want to impose their beliefs on others by way of the Criminal Code. There is no law that says that a woman must have an abortion. No one is forcing those who oppose abortion to have one." Not only had Harper stated repeatedly that he would oppose any attempt to regulate abortion, O'Connor continued, but "society has moved on and I do not believe this proposal should proceed."

This was the clearest possible message to anti-abortion Conservatives. They were flat out of luck with this prime minister. MPs who wanted to do anything that had even a whiff of pro-life sentiment to it could abandon any hope of getting it past Harper. They had been waiting for a majority. Now he had sent his chief caucus enforcer to tell them they could wait a lot longer than that. Until the hell in which many of them sincerely believed froze over, say.

"In the beginning when you're the new prime minister and everybody is just anxious to get into cabinet . . . you can bully your backbench," a member of Harper's government told me at about the time O'Connor blocked Woodworth's motion. "And now of course, six and a half years in, the backbench is starting to rise up."

In a minority, fresh after the 2006 election, Conservatives were willing to be flexible on ideology because they just wanted to survive in government. After the 2008 election and the coalition near-death experience, Conservatives were willing to be flexible on ideology because they just wanted to survive in government. But now they had a majority—had had one for nearly a year—and Harper's big oil-to-China play looked like it was going bust, and his caucus members were getting mighty antsy.

If the external situation had enforced discipline until now, a powerful internal incentive to maintain ranks had been Harper's own performance at the weekly Wednesday morning meeting of the Conservative caucus in the Reading Room of Parliament's Centre Block. There might be a lot of people in Canada who felt that Stephen Harper didn't listen to them, but Conservative MPs and senators had been given a weekly chance to feel that they had Harper's ear.

"The structure of our national caucus meeting," the government member told me, "is: we get in the room at 9:30, call to order, sing 'O Canada,' there's a run-down of the agenda and the first person to speak is the prime minister. He talks about what's in the news. Where he's been over the past week. Gives his assessment of things. Gives kudos to MPs: those who have done good things, those who have done unique things that people don't know about but maybe you should. He also strokes egos of people who need their egos stroked." After a few other reports from senior caucus officers, there are questions from the floor.

MPs and senators line up at two microphones. "Probably in a given caucus meeting, twenty or twenty-five MPs will go to the mikes and they'll talk about everything. From John Weston saying, 'Oh, don't forget, everybody, we gotta get exercise,' to somebody coming to the microphone and saying, 'We really need to do something about the amount of debt that the CMHC has,' to some substantive questions.

"Sometimes people just come to the microphone and rail. And he always pays attention. He always looks people in the eye. He's always taking notes. He doesn't engage right away. He lets people come to the microphone and vent and speak and vent and speak. That usually lasts a good solid half an hour. And then at the end he comments on everything that's been said. He cherry-picks: he doesn't comment on every comment. I don't know that he's thought about it to this extent, but he for sure picks his battles. Over the sweep of our government, there's certain issues that frequently get raised at the microphone that he just doesn't touch. Official languages or some sensitive subject, abortion or what have you, he just doesn't touch."

There is something extraordinarily intimate about these meetings, because often the only person in the room who isn't an elected MP or an appointed senator is Harper's chief of staff. Ian Brodie in the early days, Guy Giorno later, Nigel Wright after that. Sometimes the director of communications would also be in the room. But nobody else. Just the happy few, the band of brothers and sisters. One constant throughout Harper's time as a party leader, from 2002 right through to 2013, was the admiration—genuine, as far as I can tell, from dozens of conversations with members of the Conservative caucus—for Harper's confident dominance of the weekly caucus meeting.

The election of a majority in 2011 could have given ordinary Conservative members good reason to become even more marginalized: there were forty-two more Conservative MPs after the 2011 election than there had been after the 2006 election, and Harper didn't need all of their votes to stay in power. That would tend to make some backbenchers lonely and moody, even a little chippy in public. So would the fact that, the longer Harper was prime minister, the greater the number of Conservative MPs who met the six-year qualifying term for their MP pensions. "Once you qualify for the pension, all of a sudden you get a little more cocky about things," the government member said. One final ingredient in a potential cocktail of alienation: after enough years in government, an ordinary MP starts to realize he will never get into cabinet no matter how clean he keeps his nose.

So, some time before the 2011 election, Harper set up caucus advisory committees for every minister. A minister who wanted to propose a bill on any subject or who wanted the government to take a position on an opposition Private Member's Bill had to get the approval of his caucus advisory committee. Each committee met once a month, chaired by the minister's parliamentary secretary. A minister bringing an MC—a Memo to Cabinet proposing a new bill—to the cabinet's Priorities and Planning or Ops committee had to include mention that the bill had been endorsed by his caucus advisory committee. No committee support, no dice. Harper was not shy about sending ministers back to get caucus support they hadn't bothered to get. Bernard Valcourt, the Mulroney-era veteran who was back in cabinet after twenty years, was floored by the clout Harper had granted ordinary MPs. In the old days, Valcourt told colleagues, Mulroney would simply tell caucus what the proper government had decided on their behalf.

That was the good news, as far as empowering the caucus went. The bad news was that a caucus advisory committee was still barely a half a dozen MPs out of a caucus of 166 MPs and 50 senators. By the nature of things it couldn't be fully representative, so a minister could still get blindsided by reactions from part of the country to something his committee thought would be fine. It still left the great majority of the caucus unconsulted on any given question. Finally, it was simply a veto mechanism—a way to stop things from happening instead of making things happen. Harper had promised major transformations. His own caucus wondered what those might be. And the only formal new tool they had was to block, not to build. "The role of the caucus, of reaching out to the caucus—there is a growing gap there in our party right now," the government member said. "And that's why you're seeing Private Members' Bills on abortion, like Stephen Woodworth's and a few other people's. Idle hands—with pensions, and the assumption that they're going to get re-elected. Deadly combo."

———

It was a curious moment for Harper, and indeed for the entire Canadian conservative movement. They had spent a decade in opposition, divided against one another. Under Harper they had found a measure of unity, then growing confidence, and now, at last, a majority. And it was starting to be no fun at all.

Harper's attempt to come up with a sweeping agenda for change was sputtering. Making deals with China wasn't easier than making deals in the United States. The courts were picking off some of the Conservatives' most cherished objectives. In October 2011 the Supreme Court had thrown out the Harper government's attempt to shut down Vancouver's Insite supervised-injection site for narcotic drug users. Two months later Jim Flaherty's project for a national securities regulator that would simplify Canadian money markets was also blocked by the top court. In a series of lower-court decisions through 2012 and 2013, judges simply ignored the minimum sentences set by new federal legislation, using words such as "outrageous," "cruel" and "intolerable" to describe them. But there remained one element of Harper's agenda that he could still implement.

At the beginning of 2001, in the bitter aftermath of the disjointed conservative movement's third straight defeat by Jean Chrétien's Liberals,

Harper, Tom Flanagan and four others had sent the so-called Firewall Letter to Alberta premier Ralph Klein. Recall what that letter's sentence on firewalls actually said: "It is imperative to take the initiative, to build firewalls around Alberta, to limit the extent to which an aggressive and hostile federal government can encroach upon legitimate provincial jurisdiction."

But there are ways and ways to limit an aggressive federal government's encroachments. You can build a firewall against Ottawa—or you can declaw the federal government. As we saw in chapter 3, Harper set out early to do the latter. The GST cut substantially reduced the federal government's revenues by an annually recurring $12 billion or so, according to Université Laval economist Stephen Gordon. The decision to continue Paul Martin's health-care transfer agreement with the provinces, which ran through 2014, ensured that a growing stream of money was leaving Ottawa. Martin had made those transfers heavily conditional on the provinces cooperating closely with the federal government and one another, reporting results regularly, and jumping through other accountability hoops. Harper cut all those threads. By Harper's third term in office, the health transfers had been free windfalls for the provinces for years.

Next came the Canada First Defence Strategy, announced in 2008 as a plan to increase defence spending from $18 billion in 2008/09 to more than $30 billion in 2027/28. By 2010, as Harper began to rein in stimulus spending and get deficits under control, he trimmed future defence allocations substantially. His early enthusiasm for a heavily militarized Canada had taken a bit of a beating in the sands of Afghanistan. But the general goal of increasing military budgets remained, and every dollar earmarked for armies was one that could not be used to encroach on provincial jurisdictions.

Jails were yet another boom industry under the Conservatives. According to a 2011 report from Correctional Services Canada, the cost of the federal penitentiaries system was on track to grow from $1.6 billion in 2005/06 to $3.1 billion in 2013/14.

Harper sent Jim Flaherty to Victoria for a meeting with provincial finance ministers a week before Christmas 2011, to lock in the next step in this long-term strategy. Everyone knew Martin's ten-year agreement on health funding would wrap up in 2014. At some point, what would surely be arduous negotiations over the structure of the transfers after 2014 would have to begin. If previous haggling over transfer payments was any indication, the negotiations could take many months, open up rifts among governments, and generally be a headache for everyone concerned.

Harper decided to skip all that.

The provincial finance ministers in Victoria had expected only to receive a general update on the economy from Flaherty. But the finance minister arrived at a working lunch with his provincial counterparts to tell them the negotiations were already over, quite literally before they could begin. He handed out copies of a funding formula to them all. Graham Steele, Nova Scotia's finance minister, asked Flaherty what the process would be from now on, according to one news report. There's no process, Flaherty replied. Here's your funding formula. Good luck with it.

Well, they howled about that for months in the provincial capitals. No negotiation. No offer and counter-offer. It wasn't even a take-it-or-leave-it proposal; it was just, "Here it comes." And what was most galling of all was that Flaherty's plan called for growth in federal transfers to the provinces to decline once the Martin deal ran out.

Flaherty's offer was this: The 6 percent annual increase in the Canada Health Transfer and 3 percent annual increase in the Canada Social Transfer, mandated in the Martin deal, would continue for three more years, until the 2016/17 fiscal year. But after that, until at least 2024, increases in the CHT would be tied to economic growth, while the CST would continue at 3 percent. In a period of ordinary growth, that translated into maybe 4 or 5 percent growth in the total transfer envelope per year. In no case would annual transfer growth fall below 3 percent before 2024.

The contrast of this approach with the history of federal transfers was striking. As the Mulroney and Chrétien governments wrestled with deficits, the cash component of federal transfers for health and social programs was cut in every single year from 1988 to 1995. Chrétien had returned to transfer growth in 1997, Martin had locked the growth in, and Harper was ensuring it would continue through 2024, by far the longest period of growth in federal transfers to the provinces in the period after the Second World War.

The contrast with Harper's plans for other federal spending, net of transfers, was perhaps even more striking. While health transfers would continue growing, total federal spending was projected to decline. There wasn't a cabinet minister or federal department in Ottawa who could look forward to the steadily growing fiscal pie Flaherty had given to the provinces. What's more, the transfers were blank cheques. Martin and Chrétien had convened all those Ottawa first ministers' meetings on health care because they were demanding a lot in return for their money: public accountability, new national programs, a shared health information network and more. Harper and Flaherty made no such demand. There was not a syllable in Flaherty's papers about provincial health reforms in return for federal money. If the provinces wanted to spend the new money on Frisbees, Harper and Flaherty would not stop them.

What was the net effect of all these changes? When the Conservatives were elected in 2006, total federal government revenues amounted to about 16.2 percent of Canada's GDP. That was low-ish by recent historical standards, thanks largely to the substantial income-tax cuts Chrétien implemented to win the 2000 election. Harper cut taxes again, to under 14.5 percent of GDP, where, as I write this in mid-2013, they are projected to remain until 2018. This is the lowest federal revenue as a fraction of the total economy in Stephen Harper's lifetime. Spending has had a more dramatic time of it, because Harper and Flaherty injected billions in infrastructure stimulus after the 2008–09 recession. But they were diligent about winding that spending down after 2010. So from a peak of 14.5 percent of GDP in 2009/10, total program spending is projected to fall to 12.5 percent in 2017/18. It has been this low only once before in Harper's lifetime, again when Chrétien cut spending to afford the 2000 tax cuts.

But that's total spending, and it includes three main envelopes: transfers to persons, such as employment insurance and elderly benefits; transfers to other levels of government, for health care, welfare and the like; and direct program expenses, which means everything Ottawa runs itself. The three streams aren't projected to evolve the same way through this decade. Transfers to persons and to provinces are projected to hold steady as a fraction of GDP. Direct federal spending is declining.

What's been cut? What will be cut next? Harper has resisted all calls for a list of cuts. Each of Flaherty's last three budgets has actually provided fewer details than its predecessor. Kevin Page, the first parliamentary budget officer, spent the last year of his five-year term in court trying to force federal departments to account for their cuts. He received only limited cooperation. But it is possible to produce a partial list. Since 2010, the Harper government has shut down the National Council of Welfare, the National Round Table on the Environment and the Economy, the First Nations Statistical Institute, the National Council of Visible Minorities, Rights and Democracy, and the Health Council of Canada. The end of the mandatory long-form census did not mean an end to cuts at Statistics Canada; in 2012 the agency cut thirty-four other programs, including the Survey of Income and Labour Dynamics, and the National Population Health Survey.

In theory, fiscal conservatives don't like spending money they don't have. But there is also pedagogical power in an empty purse. The string of budget deficits after 2009 actually gave Harper political cover to keep making cuts because it gave him a target to reach—the elimination of the deficit by 2015—which depended on constraining the growth of government. Over Harper's lifetime, surpluses have been the best predictor of increased government spending; deficits, especially after 1988, a pretty good predictor of restraint. Every time Paul Martin finished the year with a surplus, he or Jean Chrétien or Chrétien's man Eddie Goldenberg would come up with some way to spend it. Typically, it was a way that drove Harper and the other authors of the firewall letter crazy. Take away the surpluses and you take away the temptation.

If Harper did reach his goal of a balanced budget, give or take a few billion dollars, by 2015, he stood to turn the next election into a referendum on still more cuts to activist government. In the first week of the 2011 campaign he had promised two policies that were designed to kick in only once the budget was balanced. (At this writing they still haven't.) Income splitting would allow a higher-earning taxpayer to transfer part of his salary to a spouse for tax purposes, reducing the couple's combined tax bill. Applying the policy across all the couples who would take it up would cost $2.5 billion a year to Ottawa in foregone revenue. The second proposal, to double contribution limits to tax-free savings accounts (TFSA), would cost even more. Economist Kevin Milligan estimated a "revenue cost" of $6.6 billion a year once the TFSA increase was fully phased in.

An opposition leader running against Harper—Tom Mulcair, Justin Trudeau, whoever it might be—would find himself arguing against that $9.1 billion in highly visible, revenue-reducing new benefits, and in favour of whatever tax increases he would need to pay for his own proposals. The constant claim from just about every Conservative MP through the winter of 2013 that Mulcair wanted to impose a "job-killing $21-billion carbon tax" was only a hint of what would come in a general election campaign.

Harper has already won on a straight choice between his style of government and his opponents' more ambitious plans in 2008 and 2011. (In 2006 the choice was more confused and less clear, because the Liberal corruption scandals meant voters faced a choice about much more than the role of government.) But it cannot be emphasized often enough that Harper's goal is not merely to win; it's to win on his own terms. He and his associates set those terms in the 2001 firewall letter: "to limit the extent to which an aggressive and hostile federal government can encroach upon legitimate provincial jurisdiction." His goal is to hobble not just his own government, but any federal government of any party stripe that will come after it.

Harper had spent close to a decade starving the beast. He had sought at every turn to delegitimize the very notion of a larger, more activist government. He must have felt a moment of triumph reading Justin Trudeau's comments in *La Presse* on April 11, 2013, mere days before the young Montreal MP became the new Liberal leader. "I don't want to increase Canadians' taxes," Trudeau said. "Canada has lots of money at the federal level but I find we spend it poorly." In fact the federal government had less revenue as a share of the economy than it had ever had at any point during Pierre Trudeau's time in office. "It seems to me the middle class has suffered enough," the younger Trudeau said. "So I'm not interested."

Trudeau would not have phrased it this way, but he was talking the talk of Conservative hegemony. Harper had sought, by degrees and over nearly a decade, to change perceptions about the proper role of the federal government, and this tax-freezing, oil-export-supporting, Chinese-investment-boosting young matinee-idol scion of the family that once represented everything Harper wanted to fight was now singing Harper's tune, even as he rose in the polls in a way that made even some Conservatives wonder whether Trudeau represented a real challenge to Conservative power.

Harper retained advantages that, in the first flush of Trudeaumania II, were easy to forget. Thirty new seats in 2015 (or whenever) would be created, disproportionately, in parts of the country where the

Conservatives had won most recent elections. Harper would be the only party leader in 2015 who already had fought a national campaign. Campaigning is a complex skill; party leaders often need to get one botched campaign out of their system before running a winning one, as Harper had done in 2004. But all of that would come later. Meanwhile, in any fight, there's "who wins" and then there's "on what terms." Harper, much more than any of his opponents, had set the terms.

But the longer Stephen Harper was prime minister, the further he drifted from his best habits and the deeper he sank into his worst. As 2013 progressed, even his own close associates were starting to worry about him.

"His focus, in terms of the legacy he's trying to create, is very much on identifying what he sees as the long-term challenges and opportunities for the country," one advisor said. "Yet his strong bias is towards arch-incrementalism. He backs away from ideas which he feels may be controversial. And that creates a lot of frustration."

A former insider, now looking on from the private sector, said: "This government's a lot older than its years in office would indicate. Every political office becomes less political over time. And this one is not an exception. There are a couple of people around with some campaign experience, but it's a couple." Brodie, who helped set the tone for the government's first years, had helped run Harper's leadership campaigns in 2002 and 2004, as well as the election campaigns of 2004 and 2006. Giorno got into Harper's PMO by understanding, and publicly advocating, Harper's political mission. Wright, who had taken over at the beginning of 2011 and was largely on the sidelines during the 2011 election, was a different kind of talent chosen for different reasons. Wright's experience was in high finance, his personality gentle, his principal connections with Toronto's business community, a world as foreign to Harper as Venus. Conservatives admired Wright because he had succeeded in the real world—at a young age, he became a managing director of Onex Corp., the huge and diversified private-equity investment firm whose chairman was Gerry Schwartz—and because he lived the sort of ascetic life Harper prized, rising early to run long distances, working late hours and weekends. Under Wright there weren't a lot of personality clashes in the PMO. What some Conservatives were slower to notice was that Harper made fewer surprising moves while Wright ran the shop, fewer grand gestures. These were signs of the "less political office" some veterans of earlier Harper PMOs grumbled about. Brodie and Giorno were always preoccupied with the next campaign because they never knew when it would come. They ran tightly disciplined, highly partisan organizations. Wright's shop was nicer, but it also seemed to be less decisive—and far, far more risk-averse. Indeed, by 2013, the government was sinking into unmistakable doldrums. The former insider characterized its style as "fence-sitting and micro-managing."

After snubbing China and then embracing it, Harper had heard an earful from his own MPs, including in Alberta, about their constituents' discomfort with the $15-billion takeover of the Canadian oil and gas company Nexen Inc. by China's state-owned CNOOC. He finally announced a policy that would make such takeovers less likely in the future, but the whole business plainly turned him off his earlier fascination with China. Ministerial visits to the middle kingdom slowed to a trickle. The country vanished from his speeches.

Negotiations toward an ambitious trade deal with Europe dragged on interminably. In February 2013, Karel de Gucht, the former Belgian foreign minister who served as the European trade commissioner, landed in Ottawa to wrap up negotiations with Canada's trade minister Ed Fast. But de Gucht quickly realized Fast had no serious mandate to negotiate. He returned to Brussels in a huff, telling his associates there was no point discussing serious matters with anyone but Harper. And Harper wasn't talking.

Barack Obama was taking longer to make a decision on Keystone than anyone could have imagined, and Harper seemed to have no lever to influence his U.S. counterpart. Northern Gateway was going nowhere. On any file you could care to name, Harper had no provincial ally, no foreign leader with whom he was identified, no great project on the go. In politics, it is always best to keep moving. Harper had stayed one step ahead of his opponents when he won control of the Canadian Alliance, merged it with the Progressive Conservatives, reached out to Atlantic and Ontario Tories and Quebec nationalists. He had found unlikely allies such as David Emerson, taken astonishing gambles like the Québécois nation resolution. Now he seemed stalled, and trouble was not long coming. And as had happened just about every time before, the most serious threats to his hold on power came not from outside the Conservative tent, but from within.

———

At the end of 2012 another Conservative backbencher, Mark Warawa from Langley, B.C., had tabled another motion that seemed to be a clever way to pick at the abortion issue. Warawa's motion would have the House of Commons "condemn discrimination against females occurring through sex-selective pregnancy termination." Warawa had a snappy term for such sex-selective abortions, "gendercide." By March 2013, he was tired of seeing his motion blocked in his attempts to bring it to a vote, and he wanted to speak in the Commons about it.

Fifteen minutes a day were set aside before Question Period for members to talk about what they wanted—well, theoretically. In fact each party's whip had a list of approved statement-makers, and among the Conservatives, each designated speaker also had a scripted statement to make. Warawa was kept off the list. Harper wanted none of his MPs saying anything about abortion in the Commons. Warawa was having none of it, and rose after Question Period to complain that his privileges as an MP had been infringed by his own party. More than half a dozen Conservatives rose, in the days that followed, to agree with him. Some were ardent pro-lifers like Warawa, but others simply wanted to be able to speak for themselves. It was a crack in iron Conservative caucus discipline. Harper's advisors were badly divided over how to handle it. If they increased back-benchers' freedom, it might embolden them to press further demands. If they cracked down, it might create martyrs. Either way, it was a public sign of fraying solidarity.

That kind of chink in the armour was manageable if nothing else went wrong. But that's not what happened. On November 21, 2012, a Senate committee had ordered an internal investigation into Senator Patrick Brazeau's housing allowance. In theory, Brazeau represented a community in Maniwaki, Quebec, but he had hardly ever been seen at his listed residence there. Meanwhile, he was billing the Senate for a housing allowance for his Ottawa residence, which seemed to be the only one he ever actually used.

Two weeks after the inquiry into Brazeau's issue began, the *Ottawa Citizen* reported that Mike Duffy was billing $33,413 in living expenses for his Ottawa home. It was a remarkably similar situation. Duffy was supposed to represent Prince Edward Island. He was not often spotted there. To inquiries from the *Citizen*'s reporter, Glen McGregor, Duffy replied with an e-mail: "I have done nothing wrong, and am frankly tired of your B.S."

Similar questions soon arose over the residency claims of two other senators, Mac Harb and Pam Wallin. Harb, at least, was a Liberal. Brazeau, Duffy and Wallin had all been among the first batch of Senate appointments Harper made in the wake of the 2008 coalition crisis. For two years after his appointment, Duffy had been a fundraising star

for the party, travelling across the country and appearing in personal-
ized videos sent to big fundraisers to encourage them to keep digging
into their pockets.

At one point Duffy tried to get express approval for his PEI provincial
health card. The province's Liberal government promptly leaked his
efforts to reporters. Finally, on February 22, Duffy walked into the CBC
studio in Charlottetown and announced that he would pay back the
housing money he had claimed. Not because he actually needed to, you
know. "The Senate rules on housing allowances aren't clear, and the
forms are confusing," he said in a statement. "I filled out the Senate
forms in good faith and believed I was in compliance with the rules.
Now it turns out I may have been mistaken."

At the end of March, Duffy repaid the Senate more than $90,000 and
at the end of April the Senate publicly acknowledged as much, and by
mid-May the Conservatives were holding Duffy up—no mean feat—as
the sort of fellow more senators should emulate. "He showed the kind
of leadership we would like to see from Liberal senator Mac Harb,"
Peter Van Loan told the Commons.

And there it all might have ended if Duffy hadn't started e-mailing
around town to brag about his exploits. On May 14 Bob Fife, CTV's
Ottawa bureau chief, led the national news with an astonishing revelation: Nigel Wright had worked out a deal with Duffy to help him repay
the money. Duffy had a long-standing habit of sending out late-night
e-mails to lists of people who might, he thought, be interested in his
latest business. When he was a journalist it was charming, or harmless.
Now that he was a senator, it was reckless. Duffy had hinted at the deal
in a February 20 e-mail to somebody, or several somebodies, one of
whom forwarded it to Bob Fife. This was two days before Duffy walked
into the Charlottetown CBC studio. In this e-mail, Duffy described "a
scenario" he had reached with Wright. The next morning, as reporters
started pressing the PMO for more detail, Fife went back on the air to

reveal that the scenario was pretty simple: Wright had written Duffy a personal cheque for the more than $90,000 Duffy owed.

What followed was a kind of slow-motion grotesque. Faced with the news that Wright, a manicured Bay Street swell with millions of dollars to his name, had reached into his capacious back pocket to bail out a double-dipping TV celebrity turned senator, the PMO's first response was to claim that this was all model behaviour. "The Government believes that taxpayers should not be on the hook for improper expense claims made by Senators," a PMO statement said. "Mr. Duffy agreed to repay the expenses because it was the right thing to do. However, Mr. Duffy was unable to make a timely repayment. Mr. Wright therefore wrote a cheque from his personal account for the full amount owing so that Mr. Duffy could repay the outstanding amount." Because who wouldn't be a mensch at a time like that?

"Mr. Duffy has reimbursed taxpayers for his impugned claims," the statement concluded, with breathtaking cheek. "Mr. Harb and Mr. Brazeau should pay taxpayers back immediately." In effect, the office of the prime minister of Canada was chiding Harb and Brazeau for failing to secure sugar daddies as generous as Wright. In a long career of reading bullshit from politicians, I have never seen anything quite as arrogantly contemptuous of its intended audience, the Canadian people.

It took four more days for Wright to hand in his resignation. In the days that followed, various Conservative cabinet ministers and MPs would say in Harper's defence that he had accepted Wright's resignation immediately. But Wright had not tendered his resignation immediately, and Harper had attempted days of amateurish stonewalling before Wright finally did give up his job.

———

As the last days of the wretched spring 2013 session of Parliament limped toward the summer break, what was most striking about the Duffy business was that it was so familiar. It was like a Hollywood sequel to the business with Alan Riddell in 2006 and Bev Oda in 2012, and as with most Hollywood sequels it mostly featured the same people in the same situations saying the same things. There was the long denial that anything untoward had happened. There was the preliminary attempt, once the mess became public, to deny it was a mess. And above all, there was the instinct to chase the problem away with money. The only wrinkle with Wright and Duffy was that it was Wright's own money, not (as far as could immediately be ascertained by reporters facing the customary PMO stonewall) the taxpayers' or the Conservative Party's. Some observers were amazed that Wright would toss off a cheque to make a problem as risible as Mike Duffy go away. But surely Wright was only a keen student of the Harper manner. Harper's goal, since long before Nigel Wright came on the scene, was political survival. Any serious obstacle to that survival had to be eliminated as a matter of the highest priority. Duffy needed money, Wright had money, and as soon as Wright's money was applied to Duffy, the problem would—or so it seemed possible, at first, to hope—disappear. Wright's cheque was an ultimate expression of loyalty, not to Duffy, of course, but to Stephen Harper. Loyalty was all Harper had ever asked. All he had ever demanded.

But no man can forever demand loyalty if he cannot repay it in some decent coin, whether it be in companionship, gold or another treasure. Harper had given Canadian conservatives so much: unity after years of division, then a taste of power, then great accomplishment. He had given them something many had never believed they would see: a prime minister who thought and talked like them, and who won because of that, not despite it.

What could he give them next? Would it be enough to repay their continued loyalty? Surely there must be something. But if Harper knew what the next chapter of his extraordinary career might look like, he showed no sign of it.

IT'S A BIG COUNTRY

I have never forgotten something Jean Chrétien said during his last week in politics.

It was December 2003. Chrétien had flown to Abuja, Nigeria, and then to Paris for an extended valedictory visit with France's president, Jacques Chirac. On his way home, in his Canadian Forces Challenger jet flying west over the Atlantic, he took questions from journalists. After a while he left the impromptu scrum, turned around and headed toward the front of the plane where reporters could not follow. One of the scribes called out a final question: "What's a good politician?"

Chrétien answered over his shoulder without missing a beat: "The one who wins."

In eighteen years in Ottawa I have wound up covering two winners, Jean Chrétien and Stephen Harper, plus some other people. For a city that is forever falling in love with the Next Big Thing, Ottawa has never been very good at understanding actual winners.

For years while Chrétien was prime minister, conventional wisdom in the capital was impatient for Paul Martin to push the old buffoon out of the way. As for Harper, until 2011 his victories were tenuous enough that you could always find someone at an Empire Club lunch table willing to lean forward and explain why Harper's inexplicable lucky streak was about to run out. *Oh, he won, but he won't last. Oh, he may win again but he won't get a majority. Oh, his trick bag is emptying fast, the ads are backfiring, the people are on to him, and soon his own party will turn on him. And let me tell you, it couldn't happen to a nicer guy.*

In Christina McCall's great social history of the Trudeau Liberals in the 1970s, *Grits*, there is an unmistakable current of longing for the return of John Turner, then in exile from Trudeau's Liberal Party. That one of the household gods of Canadian political journalism could look at Trudeau and wish for Turner is a stark demonstration of the penchant among Canadian political reporters for staring gift horses in the mouth.

Eventually, after enough predictions of a swift demise prove wrong, the very fact of winning, and enduring, is held against a winner. Chrétien's smiling face found its way onto the cover of Jeffrey Simpson's book *The Friendly Dictatorship*, with a South American junta leader's uniform pasted clumsily beneath it. Of Harper, Frances Russell wrote in the *Winnipeg Free Press* in April 2013: "The Conservatives under Stephen Harper are running an effective dictatorship. They believe they are quite within their rights to muzzle Parliament, gag civil servants, use taxpayer money for blatant political self-promotion, stand accused of trying to subvert a federal election and hand over much of Canada's magnificent natural heritage to the multinational oil and gas lobby." In lines like Russell's there is much that is true about Harper, and much that is true about both him and others.

But Chrétien's brief career-closing salute to "the one who wins" is worth contemplating because it makes an obvious point. In a democracy you can get a lot more done by winning an election than by not winning it. History is written by the victors. All Harper's opponents ever had to do was beat him. If they don't like his policies, they need to beat him and implement other policies. If they don't like the way he won a parliamentary majority with a minority of the popular vote, they are welcome to reform the electoral system—after they beat him under the system in place.

Beating Harper was absolutely Stéphane Dion's goal when he became the Liberal leader in 2006. Dion's motivation was to save the planet, a goal he cherished with perfect sincerity. But he lost the 2008 election. Incredibly, he managed to rally the other opposition leaders against Harper again, weeks later—and he lost again. Now, on most days the only time Dion ever mentions Kyoto, in public at least, is when he's calling his dog. Harper endures, so Harper governs, so Harper gets his turn to read in the papers about what a lousy son-of-a-bitch he is. It's one of the perks of office.

I am not sure he is done winning yet. Then again, he might be. The omens and portents look worse for Harper than they have in years. His lousy 2012 turned into a nightmarish first half of 2013. Thomas Mulcair is the most competent opposition leader he has faced; Justin Trudeau makes Liberals feel good about being Liberal. Maybe one or the other of the opposition leaders will finally be luckier than Harper. Maybe the next time, Mulcair and Trudeau won't divide the anti-Conservative vote between their parties and leave Harper to win on yet another electoral-split decision. Maybe the Liberals won't fade in the stretch, as Liberals often do. Maybe Mulcair won't be whipsawed between the political culture of Quebec, where most of his MPs live, and that of the rest of the country, where most NDP voters do.

Harper has rarely faced sure victory and he doesn't now. But, say there is an election on the date supposedly "fixed" by law, October 19, 2015, and that Stephen Harper is still the Conservative party leader on that day—even if he loses that election, he will still have been prime minister for nearly a decade. He will have outlasted three more of his predecessors in the longevity stakes: Louis St. Laurent, Robert Borden and Brian Mulroney. Only Chrétien, Laurier, Trudeau, Macdonald and King will have held the job for longer.

To what purpose? What has he accomplished? It is in the nature of Harper's project that he would have less to show for his time in office than some of his predecessors. They saw themselves as builders; he is a skeptic and, to use the gentlest available word, an editor. He has always wanted a federal government that meddled less in health care, less in executive federalism, less in municipal affairs, and to some extent less in the world than Liberals have done. He has zigzagged wildly while pursuing those goals, but always in the hope of lasting long enough to pursue them further. He cut taxes so his government and any that succeeded his could not be tempted by ambition. Then he tipped the accounts into the red, to win Michael Ignatieff's approval after the coalition crisis, before realizing he liked the steady pressure to cut that only a deficit can provide. He is the first prime minister in the history of the country who has wanted to leave behind a government that is doing substantially less than when he arrived. That may be the simplest way to explain why he is so polarizing—why he excites so many voters and infuriates so many more.

Because he is polarizing, he provokes both his admirers and his detractors into extravagant claims. He is tearing down the beautiful Canadian house, the detractors lament. He's the only bulwark against the return of a corrupt regime, his supporters warn. Neither position is particularly democratic. Each assumes there is only one proper way to govern. In functioning democracies there are usually at least two, and it is not too early for Canada to become a functioning democracy.

Here, too, I will probably upset some readers by associating Stephen Harper with any *increase* in Canadian democracy. Harper is no model parliamentarian. He has always been about doing as much as he can get away with, and explaining himself only later, or not at all, or disingenuously at best. But how much of that is new? Very few elected leaders in Western democracies govern in a sagacious effort to find a Solomonic balance of available views. They take their ball and run as far down the field as they can, spewing boundless contempt on their foes. Just look at Tony Blair at the 1999 Labour Conference. "Today's Tory party: the party of fox hunting, Pinochet and hereditary peers," he chided. "The uneatable, the unspeakable and the unelectable."

The process is often unlovely. I hope I have helped explain here a lot of what has made the Harper years divisive and disillusioning for admirers of open, thoughtful debate. But voters always get to judge the result, and what Harper does has been broadly approved, for close to a decade, by millions of voters who had despaired of ever seeing someone like them in power. The country cannot stay healthy for long if it systematically shuts out those millions of voters, concentrated between suburban Ontario and the rural British Columbia interior. Harper has given those voters a voice. The country has held up pretty well. It's a big country.

The result hardly looks like whatever dream of a conservative utopia a thirty-year-old Stephen Harper might once have cherished. More than a decade ago Chrétien's introduction of same-sex marriage legislation helped spur social conservatives to find common cause with economic conservatives. But all these years later, same-sex couples are still getting married, and that will never change. Paul Martin warned us, through two elections, about Harper's secret agenda on abortion, but it turned out to be odder than even Martin supposed: Harper has fought some of his toughest political battles, not to restrict abortion rights, but to defend them against the anti-abortion MPs in his own caucus. His policy on official languages is not easily distinguished from Pierre Trudeau's, and Chrétien would heartily approve of his frosty relations with two successive U.S. presidents—Obama, of course, but also Bush.

Even where Harper tries his best to change Canada's political culture— instituting a harshly punitive vision of criminal justice, for example— the culture pushes back, in the form of courts that Harper has taken conspicuous care *not* to stack with political conservatives. So criminal justice in Canada remains an active dialogue between Harper's laws and Trudeau's Charter.

Throw in the fights Harper has declined to pick. The thirty-year-old would have been amused to hear he would wind up as a fierce defender of supply management, the baroque system of market protection designed by Liberals to coddle agriculture in Quebec and Ontario. Harper helped Barack Obama briefly nationalize General Motors. He is the politician who had Parliament declare Quebec—sorry, "the Québécois"—a nation.

It should be the business of an author to make the grandest possible claims for his subject. If I'm writing about Harper, it must be because Harper is the damnedest thing you ever did see. But I'm stuck with the evidence of my eyes, which is that Canada, nearly eight years into the Harper era, still looks a lot like Canada. Its weaknesses remain: the timid pulse of its entrepreneurial spirit, its citizens' chronic incuriosity about the world, a cultural tendency toward reticence that made its democratic debates insufficiently robust before and leaves them barely breathing now.

But its strengths persist. A strong suspicion that governments should not indefinitely spend more than they raise in revenue. A hardy tolerance for cultural difference. A strong optimistic streak. Persistent faith that the marriage of French and English cultural traditions continues to be more of a strong point than a hassle—though Lord knows it has been plenty of that.

A big country is the sum of all its political currents, an often chaotic conversation stretching across generations. Stephen Harper has brought to that conversation millions of Canadians who believed they had been shut out before. In so doing he has put many others, who had grown to assume their voices would be the ones that mattered, through an extended ordeal. It's been healthy for all of them, empowering in one case, humbling in another. One day Harper's opponents will grow tired of losing and figure out how to win. Harper's successors, strengthened by his example, will continue his project. The result will be the same as always: Canada, glorious, a little dented, and free.

ACKNOWLEDGEMENTS

In 2002 I made a deal to write a book for Anne Collins, then chickened out. That made her the first publisher to think I had a book in me, and I've felt since then that I owed her one. She made the entire process as painless and sometimes pleasant as it could be, and her confidence came in handy when I couldn't find my own.

Jackie Kaiser was my agent for that long-lost un-book and for two successful book projects since then. I never venture into the wilds of Toronto publishing without her, and I'm always grateful for her wisdom and support.

Much of this book, especially the chapters on the 2008 and 2011 elections, is based on reporting and writing I did for *Maclean's* magazine. I'm forever grateful to Anthony Wilson-Smith for giving me a home there a decade ago and to Ken Whyte for encouraging me to think big at every step of a long professional collaboration that has come to define my career. I am especially grateful to Mark Stevenson and Anne-Marie Owens for giving me the time, during a hectic period in the magazine's history, to do this book. I am proud to have the company of many other authors at *Maclean's*, which has become the kind of place where just about everyone thinks about ways to give good stories the length and depth they need. My extended absences from the Ottawa bureau put pressure on John Geddes, Aaron Wherry, Susan Allan, Jason Kirby, Michael Petrou and Nick Taylor-Vaisey. They all accepted without complaint. I'm looking forward to pulling my weight again.

My sources, most of whom spoke anonymously, were generous with their time and their insight. One reason for Stephen Harper's success is that he doesn't run a chatty shop. I suspect he would have been relieved to see how out of practice some of his current and former staffers were, as they tried to dish with a reporter. To everyone who shared their insight, to the limit of their comfort zone and sometimes a little further, I'm thankful. Harper could have tried to fight this project and made my life harder; he didn't. Nigel Wright, who politely declined to speak to me, put the word out in the PMO that others should be less reticent, and thus helped me immensely.

One night, as I wondered how I was going to get this thing done, I put out an open call on Twitter for research help. Many answered the call. I decided Melissa Bourgeois was a serious customer; her interview transcription, research memos, secondary-source reading and other assistance proved my hunch was correct and improved my work at every stage.

In figuring out this book's format and pacing I drew inspiration from two musicians, Randy Weston and Hector Berlioz, and two authors, John Steinbeck and Jean-François Lisée. Strange but true.

I have been a pain in the ass to a bunch of friends for two years, and if that continues I am now officially out of excuses. Thanks for their patience to Tabatha Southey, Lorne and Joan Samson, Eugene Haslam and Kari Howard, Sean McAdam and Carrie Wallace, Howard Singleton, Kady O'Malley, Andrew Potter, Scott Gilmore and Catherine McKenna, Joanne Chianello, Graham Fraser and Barbara Uteck.

Everything good I have ever done springs from the love and support of my parents, Allen and Eleanor Wells. My final thanks go to the woman who is first in my heart. Lisa Samson appears in the prologue of this book as Lisa McAdam. She managed to keep her curiosity in check while I wrote all this without showing her any of it. I'm so happy that now I get to share this book, and the rest of my life, with Lisa and Katie and Thomas.

Any errors of fact or judgment are, of course, mine alone.

INDEX

NDP in 2011 election, 325–26
negative, during elections, 15, 70
response to negative, 250–51
Afghanistan
Canada's military involvement
in, 276–77
commission on abuse of prison-
ers in, 260–66, 267
and defence spending, 391
Harper and prisoner issue,
260–66, 267
Harper policy, 276–77
Akin, David, 168
Albrecht, Harold, 308
Alcock, Reg, 17
Ambrose, Rona, 106, 107, 108, 113
Anderson, Rick, 112
Angus, David, 94
Apps, Alfred "Alf", 85, 235, 250, 252
Arbour, Louise, 249
Ashworth, Gordon, 279
Assembly of First Nations, 370
Atleo, Shawn, 370
Atomic Energy of Canada Limited,
121–22, 125
Auger, Michel C., 175

Bachand, André, 357
backbench concerns, 385–90,
399–400
Bain, Sarah, 182

Baird, John
appointed environment minister,
106
appointed foreign minister, 351
and coalition issue, 214
environmental views and policy,
107–9, 111, 113, 114, 115,
167, 359, 374
Harper opinion of, 113
political background, 109–10
support for Harper, 110, 295
Barriault, Ronald, 124
Beltrame, Julian, 201, 202
Bernier, Maxime, 72, 129–31, 135,
274
Bettelheim, Bruno, 291–92
Bezan, James, 163
BigCityLib, 153
Binns, Pat, 6, 9
Black, Conrad, 348
Blackburn, Jean-Pierre, 94
Blair, Tony, 60, 241, 243, 409
Blakeney, Allan, 204
Blanchfield, Mike, 35
Bloc Québécois
and 2006 election, 14
and 2008 election, 150, 169,
204–5
and 2009 budget, 239
and 2011 election, 334–35
and Bernier scandal, 130

control of information, 33–39

as conversationalist, 284–85

criticism of Green Shift, 133, 135

criticisms of, 408

cuts by, 168–69, 394–95

damage-control techniques, 380–81, 383

and deficits, 275

and democracy, 408–9

desire for majority government, 319–20

desire for Senate reform, 234

as dictator, 406

eating habits, 285

as economic manager, 134, 253, 278

and the economy, 170, 174–75

election 2008 debates, 170–77, 328

election 2011 debates, 327–31

energy policy, 361–63, 364, 365

and environmental issues, 108–9, 115, 125

and the ethnic vote, 162–63, . 355–56

federal-provincial relations, 76–78, 80–81, 82–84

feelings for Canada, 67–68

Firewall Letter, 79, 80

first cabinet meeting, 24

and fiscal imbalance, 76–78

Five Priorities, 22–23

fixed-date elections, 140–42

former prime ministers as models, 292–94

goals for Canada, 10

grudges of, 286–87

hands-on approach of, 8–9, 282–83

impact of, 297

on importance of family, 146

influences on, 44, 45–53, 63–65, 92–96, 111, 398

infrastructure stimulus, 393

interest in the environment, 93

invisibility of, 291–92

isolation of, 399

on Layton, 352

as leader of Canadian Alliance, 54–55

legacy creation, 397

longevity as prime minister, 315–16

and loyalty, 111–12, 403

and majority government, 348–50, 353, 363–64, 371–72

management style, 297–304

and mandate letters, 23–24

and media, 11, 40–41, 73, 155–56, 281–82, 284, 285,

Paul Wells is the political editor of *Maclean's* magazine. His previous book, *Right Side Up: The Fall of Paul Martin and the Rise of Stephen Harper's New Conservatism,* was a national bestseller and his blog, Inkless Wells, is a must-read among Canadians who follow politics. He has worked for the *National Post* and *The Gazette* in Montreal, and has written for *L'actualité, La Presse, Time* and the *Literary Review of Canada.* He lives in Ottawa.